The Complete Book of

Questions

and Answers

The Complete Book of

Questions

and Answers

McGraw-Hill Children's Publishing

Columbus, Ohio

This edition published in 2002 by American Education Publishing
an imprint of McGraw-Hill Children's Publishing

Send all enquiries to:
McGraw-Hill Children's Publishing
8787 Orion Place
Columbus, OH 43240-4027

Copyright © 2001 Octopus Publishing Group Ltd.

Printed in 2002

ISBN 1-56189-107-X
UPC 7-19531-90001-6

Children's Publishing

Editorial Director: Paula Borton
Art Director: Clare Sleven
Project Management: Mark Darling
Editor: Belinda Gallagher
Assistant Editor: Helen Parker
Copy Editor: Jane Walker
Design: Gardner Quainton
Additional Design: Phil Kay, Cathy May
Artwork Commissioning: Lynne French, Suzanne Grant, Natasha Smith
Picture Research: Janice Bracken, Lesley Cartlidge, Kate Miles , Liberty Newton
Indexer and Proofreader: Lynn Bresler
Color Reproduction: DPI Colour

3 4 5 6 7 8 9 10 TOP 07 06 05 04 03 02

The McGraw·Hill Companies

CONTENTS

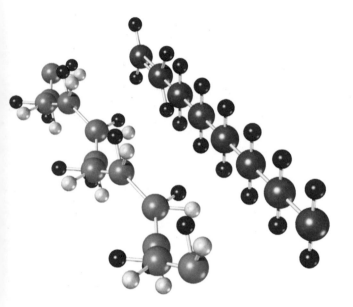

INTRODUCTION

Who? What? Why? Where? When? This fascinating book gives you the answers even before you've thought of the questions!

How fast does light travel? You'll find the answer in the Science section. What was the Berlin Wall? Look it up in History, and find out why it was built. Which flying reptile had a wingspan of more than 16 yards? Read about it in Prehistoric Life, and marvel that such an animal ever existed. Are humans the most successful animals on Earth? No, we are not, but look up *rats* in the Index and you'll find out why.

The material in this book is conveniently divided into simple topics to make it easy to browse through. Answers to problems relating to the world around us, history, science, and many other topics are conveniently grouped, so it is simple to find your way around.

You can go straight to a particular subject by using the Index at the back of the book. Like any reference

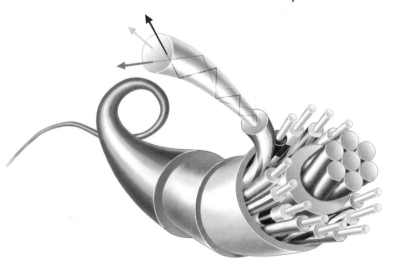

book, there are some technical terms that you might need to understand, so there is a convenient Glossary at the end of the book explaining the key words and phrases used in each section.

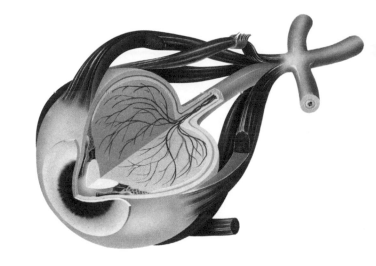

The pages are laid out clearly, and a wide range of pictures is used to give more information or to clarify points that are hard to describe using words. You will find photographs and illustrations, together with diagrams, that show how complicated processes work. All of these visual features have captions that provide even more information, and important parts of diagrams are clearly labeled.

On many pages you will find a box or panel featuring an especially interesting piece of information. Did you know that a close relative of the elephant once lived in the snow and ice of Siberia? Or that you have a clock built into every cell of your body? Check the Fact Boxes and Did You Know? panels as you look through this book, and you'll pick up lots of fascinating bits of information.

Earth and
Space

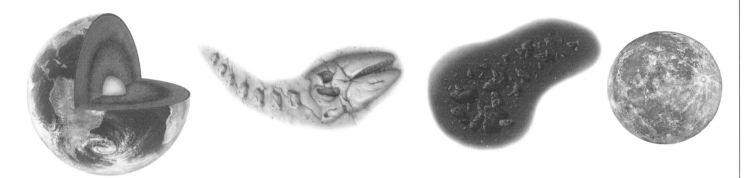

Huge though it is, our world is tiny in astronomical terms, just one of the many billions of planets that are believed to exist throughout the universe. Until recently, there was no proof that there were any other planets outside our own solar system, but now satellite technology has shown that there are planets close to several nearby stars, and almost certainly, planets orbiting most of the countless other stars in the vast expanse of our universe.

The structure of the solar system governs our life, because it is the means by which we measure time and experience the changing seasons. The movement of the Earth and the moon control day and night, together with the ocean tides. These nearby events are well understood, but the distant parts of the universe are still a mystery, debated by scientists and mathematicians. Strange signals from space are received by radio telescopes, light is sucked into black holes, and time itself might be distorted by high-speed space travel.

Back on Earth, things are better understood. We can see and experience the forces that change the shape of our world and can use them to generate power by wind, waves, and even by radioactivity. We understand the seasons, and this tells us when to plant crops. We are also beginning to understand how catastrophes like earthquakes, volcanic eruptions, droughts, and floods occur, and can take measures to reduce their effects. The activities of mankind have shaped our world and have sometimes been the cause of these catastrophes.

The Universe

What was the big bang?

The big bang is the most popular theory about the creation of the universe. According to this theory, the whole universe was created in a split second in one huge explosion. All matter was squeezed together into a tiny, super-hot, dense ball that was smaller than an atom. The ball gradually expanded as it cooled, then exploded, releasing energy and matter in all directions. We cannot see the big bang because it would have happened billions of years ago. But we can see that the universe is growing steadily bigger. All the galaxies are speeding away from each other as the universe expands.

What is the universe made of?

The universe is made up almost entirely of hydrogen and helium. These are the two lightest elements. All the rest of the matter in the universe is very rare. Elements such as silicon, carbon, and others are concentrated into clouds, stars, and planets. The universe is held together by four invisible forces. Gravity and electromagnetism are the two familiar forces. The other two kinds are strong and weak nuclear forces. These operate only inside the incredibly tiny nucleus of atoms, holding the tiny particles together.

How old is the universe?

It is possible to calculate the approximate age of the universe by looking at how fast distant galaxies are moving away from us. However, it is not possible for us to make this calculation accurately. Scientists have estimated that the universe is between 13,000 and 18,000 million years old.

◄ All of the matter in the universe is flying out at an enormous speed from the central point where the big bang took place.

The super supernova

Sometimes a star appears in the sky quite suddenly. This happens when there are a pair of stars rotating together. These are called binaries, and there is usually one large star called a red giant orbiting with a smaller, hotter star. The nova takes place when gas is drawn from the red giant into the smaller star, where the heat causes a massive explosion and emits huge amounts of light. A supernova takes place when a star collapses as it begins to burn out, then suddenly explodes, producing a huge amount of light energy, and leaving behind a tiny core of neutrons, which is the heaviest substance in the universe. A pinhead-sized mass of neutrons weighs many thousands of tons.

▲ Stars are born as huge masses of interstellar gas condense, eventually becoming so large that their own gravity forces the molecules together and begins the fission reaction that will power the young star for millions of years.

▼ A nebula is a huge mass of gas and solid material that appears to be solid. However, it is mostly composed of dust and gas slowly condensing into stars.

Alien life

No one has yet shown that life exists on other planets. However, since there are billions of stars, some with planets, it seems unlikely that Earth is the only place with the right conditions for life. Astronomers use radio telescopes to search for messages from other civilizations. In 1963, they thought they had found the first traces of intelligent extraterrestrial life when regular pulses of radio waves were detected. In fact, they had found strange distant galaxies called quasars.

? What is the Milky Way?

The Milky Way is a huge mass of gas and stars that can be clearly seen as a band of light across the night sky.

The Earth, and everything else in the solar system, is part of the Milky Way. It is known as our galaxy. It is so huge that light takes nearly 100,000 years to travel from one side to another. Where stars are packed closely together, the Milky Way is bright, but huge clouds of gas and dust block the light from the other parts of the galaxy. These clouds prevent astronomers from observing the whole Milky Way.

? How does gravity work?

The force of gravity is the attraction between every piece of matter, even the smallest particles. The more matter there is in something, and the closer its particles are packed together, the stronger the attraction. Stars are large and very dense bodies, and so they have a strong field of gravity. It is our sun's force of gravity that holds the planets in their orbits. The Earth's gravity keeps the moon in its orbit. Small bodies such as the moon have a very weak gravity. This explains why astronauts on the moon's surface were able to jump up high with very little effort.

? What is a star?

Stars are huge balls of burning gas that are scattered throughout the universe. They burn for millions of years, giving off both light and heat. Stars produce energy by a process called nuclear fusion. The coolest stars are red and dim, while the hottest stars give off blue-white light. The temperatures on the surface range from 112,000°F for cooler stars to over 1,280,000°F for the hottest stars.

A new star is born when gas and dust are drawn together by gravity, forming a huge clump. It heats up until nuclear fusion begins, and the new star appears.

? How big are stars?

Our own sun is quite a small star, even though it measures 864,761 miles across, which is 109 times more than the Earth's diameter. If the sun were the size of a football, the Earth would be less than one tenth of one inch across. Some stars are known as supergiants. The star Antares, for example, is 700 times bigger than the sun. There is a star in the constellation of Auriga that may be 1,863 million miles in diameter, or 4,000 times bigger than our sun. The neutron star that remains after the explosion of a supernova may be only 12 miles in diameter, but of enormous mass. If it weighs more than two or three times that of our sun, it begins to collapse into a black hole.

? How does a star die?

Stars die when they eventually use up all their fuel and burn out, but this process takes many millions of years.

Towards the end of its life, a star starts to run out of hydrogen to power its nuclear fusion. It starts to cool, becoming a red giant. The red giant swells, and the pressure at its center becomes so great that the star begins to absorb energy instead of emitting it. In a matter of seconds, the star collapses, then explodes into a supernova. This is a huge explosion of light and energy that can be seen right across the galaxy.

▾ **Our sun is part of the Milky Way, a huge disc-shaped collection of billions of stars and interstellar debris. Most of these stars cannot be seen with the naked eye, but their combined light produces a huge milky-looking path across the night sky.**

What is a black hole?

A black hole is an area in space where the force of gravity is so strong that even light cannot escape from it. Black holes are created when a burned-out star collapses. Eventually it shrinks into a tiny sphere of material. The gravity of this material is so powerful that it pulls in everything around it. Even light itself is sucked into the black hole. Nothing that goes into a black hole ever comes out. We cannot see black holes. We can sometimes identify them from the radio waves given off as a star is drawn into a black hole.

◄ Some black holes could be entrances to 'wormholes.' These are tunnels that may act as shortcuts through space and time.

How far away are stars?

The nearest star to the Earth is our own sun, which is 94 million miles away. After the sun, the closest stars are Proxima Centauri and Barnard's Star. The farthest stars in our galaxy are 80,000 light-years away. Other galaxies, each one containing millions of stars, are much more distant.

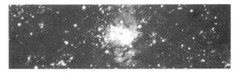

▲ Light is distorted as it passes through the atmosphere, making stars twinkle.

Why do stars twinkle?

Most stars burn steadily, and if we could see them from space they would not be twinkling at all. As the light from a star passes through the Earth's atmosphere, it is bent by changes in the air temperature. This makes the light appear to flicker. Because of this effect, astronomical observatories are situated on mountaintops. Higher up, the air is thinner and is less likely to cause this twinkling effect.

Neutron stars

When massive stars explode violently, they can become supernovas. If the core survives, it may become a neutron star. The rapid collapse of the outer part of the star leads to temperatures of over 30, 000 million°F and leaves the core with an average diameter of just 12 miles. However, the star still has a mass of up to three times that of our sun making it incredibly dense. One teaspoonful of neutron star weighs over three billion tons!

❓ Which planet is closest to the sun?

Mercury is the closest planet to the sun. The temperature on the side of the planet facing the sun is as high as 806°F. The shaded side of Mercury, which faces away from the sun is bitterly cold at -356°F.

Mercury has almost no atmosphere, because it has been burned off by the sun. The planet consists of bare rock, pitted and scarred by the impact of meteorites. It has extremely steep cliffs that are hundreds of miles long. These were formed when the planet cooled from its original molten (liquid) state millions of years ago.

❓ What are the inner planets?

The four planets that are nearest the sun are called the inner planets. In order from the sun, they are Mercury, Venus, Earth, and Mars. The inner planets are different from the outer planets, which are farther away from the sun, because they are made of rock. The outer planets are mostly composed of gas. Each of the inner planets has an atmosphere. However, apart from the Earth's atmosphere, the atmospheres of the inner planets are very thin and would be poisonous to humans.

Crash, bang!

In 1994, the most spectacular event ever seen by human eye in the solar system happened — a newly discovered comet struck the planet Jupiter. The comet had been shattered by Jupiter's gravity in 1992, and the fragments were now in orbit around the planet. Between July 16 and 23, 1994 Jupiter was struck by a string of fragments with an average diameter of 1/2 to 1 mile. The impact of the largest fragment was about 600 times more powerful than all the world's nuclear weapons.

Saturn

Uranus

▾ The four inner planets are quite small, and orbit closely to the sun. All are solid and rocky, and have an atmosphere.

Mercury

Venus

Mars

Earth

Jupiter

▲ The outer planets are composed mostly of frozen gases, so although they are very large, they are comparatively light.

❓ What are sunspots?

Groups of black blotches appear on the surface of the sun every 11 years. These blotches are called sunspots. They are areas that are about 1,800°F cooler than the rest of the sun's surface. Sunspots are caused by changes in the sun's magnetic field. When they appear, sunspots cause radiation that often interferes with the radio and television signals on the Earth. Some groups of sunspots can be as much as ten times the size of the Earth.

🔹 Could we live on Venus?

Science fiction writers thought that life might exist beneath the thick clouds covering Venus. We now know that conditions there are too extreme for life as we know it. Robot spacecraft have landed on Venus and studied its atmosphere, which is mostly poisonous carbon dioxide and sulphuric acid. We cannot see the planet's surface through its thick atmosphere, but enough sunlight gets through to raise the surface temperature to 860°F. This atmosphere reflects sunlight, making Venus very bright when viewed from Earth.

Pluto

Neptune

The Red Planet

Mars is covered by a stony desert that contains lots of iron oxide, making it appear a rusty-red color. At one time, Mars had an atmosphere containing oxygen, and it had valleys through which water may have flowed. Now the water and oxygen are locked up in the rusty iron deposits, and the planet has hardly any atmosphere.

Mars has small polar icecaps that grow larger during the Martian winter. These probably contain water and frozen carbon dioxide. It is possible that there is enough water in these icecaps to support a human space mission to Mars.

🔹 Where is the largest known canyon?

On Mars! There is no running water to wear away the rocky landscape on Mars, so huge valleys can survive for millions of years. A system of enormous canyons called the Valles Marineris (Mariner Valleys) was discovered by the space probe Mariner 9. It is more than 2,000 miles long, and four times as deep as the Grand Canyon in the U.S.A. Scientists think that these valleys were caused by erosion (wearing away). During storms, the gritty Martian dust is blasted by winds reaching up to 280 mph, wearing away the softer rock.

🔹 What are the rings of Saturn?

Shining rings of billions of tiny chips of ice, rock, and dust surround Saturn. The rings reflect light strongly and can be clearly seen through a telescope from the Earth. It was first thought that Saturn had three wide rings, but it is now known that the rings are actually made of thousands of narrow ringlets. The rings are only about 100 yards thick, but they extend into space for 47,000 miles. The material in the rings was probably captured by Saturn's gravity when the solar system was forming, or it might be the remains of a moon that has broken up. Recently, space probes discovered that some of the rings are braided, or twisted, but so far there is no explanation for this strange effect.

🔹 Which are the outer planets?

Uranus, Neptune, and Pluto are the outer planets. They are so far away that they were discovered only when powerful telescopes were developed. Pluto, the smallest and most remote of the planets, is on the edge of deep space. It was only discovered in 1930, as a result of mathematical calculations to find out why Neptune's orbit was being disturbed by an unknown body. Pluto has an oval orbit that occasionally takes it inside the orbit of Neptune. As recently as 1978, scientists found that Pluto, which is only 1,418 miles across, has an even smaller companion planet, or moon, called Charon.

🔹 What makes Neptune blue?

Neptune is covered with a blue ocean of liquid methane gas. It is a very cold place – at the farthest part of its orbit, it is 2,500 million miles from the sun. Its surface temperature drops to -346°F. Neptune is made of hydrogen, helium, and methane, and probably has a rocky core. It takes an amazing 164.8 years to travel just once around the sun.

Neptune was first identified in 1846 when astronomers found that an unidentified planet was disturbing the orbit of Uranus. Neptune has huge storms, and one of these, the Great Dark Spot, was larger than the Earth.

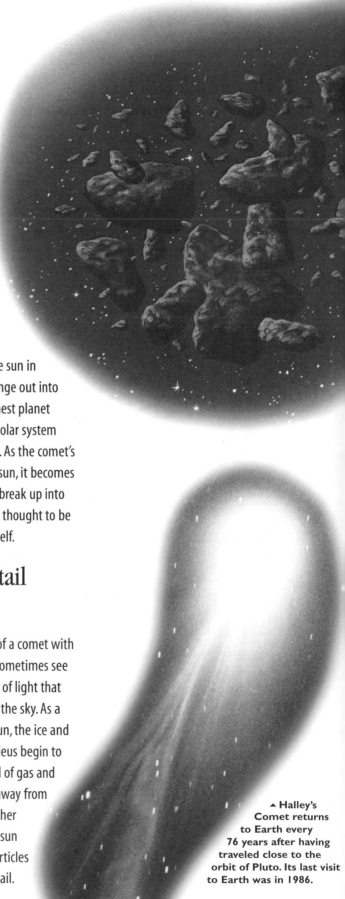

Do other planets have moons?

Apart from the Earth, most of the other planets have moons, although these are usually quite small. Saturn has the most moons – it has at least 18. Some of these are very strange. Enceladus has a smooth surface covered with shiny beads of ice that make it shine and glitter. Iapetus is black on one side and white on the other.

Jupiter has 16 moons, four of which are very large. One of Jupiter's moons is larger than Mercury and the other three are larger than our moon. Charon, which orbits Pluto, is either a large moon or a small companion planet.

What are shooting stars?

Shooting stars, or meteors, are streaks of light that cross the night sky, although they can only be seen for one or two seconds. They are caused when a solid piece of rock, called a meteoroid, plunges through the Earth's atmosphere, burning up due to air friction. When the rock enters the atmosphere, it is known as a meteor. If, as rarely happens, a small fragment reaches the Earth, it is called a meteorite.

The Earth regularly passes through clouds of meteors orbiting the sun. The best known cloud, called the Perseids, reappears each year on August 12–13, sometimes producing spectacular meteor showers. There is also a regular meteor shower in December called the Geminids.

What is a comet?

Comets are often described as 'dirty snowballs.' The solid center, or nucleus, of a comet consists mostly of ice mixed with sooty material. The nucleus is quite small, and is usually only a few miles across.

Comets travel around the sun in an elongated orbit. They plunge out into deep space beyond the farthest planet before diving back into the solar system and passing close to the sun. As the comet's nucleus comes closer to the sun, it becomes smaller and may eventually break up into small fragments. Comets are thought to be as old as the solar system itself.

What is the tail of a comet?

You cannot see the nucleus of a comet with the naked eye, but you can sometimes see its tail. It appears as a smear of light that moves very gradually across the sky. As a comet moves closer to the sun, the ice and other frozen gases in its nucleus begin to boil off, producing a long tail of gas and dust. The tail always points away from the sun because light and other forms of radiation from the sun push against the minute particles that are present within the tail.

▲ Halley's Comet returns to Earth every 76 years after having traveled close to the orbit of Pluto. Its last visit to Earth was in 1986.

◄ The asteroid belt lies between the orbits of Mars and Jupiter. It is thought that this may be the shattered remains of a planet destroyed by Jupiter's enormous gravity.

▲ There are over 100,000 asteroids in orbit around the sun. Some measure less than 1 mile across, while the largest is 623 miles.

⁇ What is an asteroid?

Asteroids are small rocky or icy bodies that orbit the sun. They are sometimes called minor planets. Most asteroids are found in an orbit between Mars and Jupiter, and more than 7,000 of them have been identified.

Asteroids are smaller than any of the planets, and only a few have a diameter of over 19 miles. The term asteroid is usually applied to objects larger than 1 mile in diameter. One asteroid, called Ida, has a tiny moon of its own; this is the smallest known satellite in the solar system. Asteroids were probably formed at the same time as the planets.

⁇ What happens when a meteorite hits the ground?

When a large meteorite hits the ground, it can produce a crater. Meteorite craters are rare on the Earth, because the atmosphere slows the meteorite and also usually burns it up. Many ancient meteorite craters have been worn away by water and weather over thousands of years.

On planets and moons with no atmosphere, huge numbers of meteorites strike with enormous power. Our own moon is estimated to have 30,000 billion meteorite craters measuring 1 yard or more in diameter. Some of the large geographical features on the moon and other planets and moons throughout the solar system are probably the result of strikes by large meteors hitting their surfaces.

⁇ What are meteorites made of?

Meteorites are made of rock or metal. They enter the Earth's atmosphere at speeds of at least 7 miles per second, which makes them glow brightly. Several thousand meteorites enter the Earth's atmosphere every year, but very few of them reach the ground. The largest known meteorite was made of iron and weighed 73 tons. It probably fell to the Earth in prehistoric times in what is now Namibia, southwest Africa.

In general, it is hard to find meteorites. Recently, researchers have been locating them on the ice sheets in the Arctic and the Antarctic, where they are easier to find.

⁇ Why is Europa especially interesting?

Europa is one of Jupiter's moons. In 1979, the Voyager spacecraft passed by Europa and found that it had a very smooth surface covered with ice. It has very few craters, which has led astronomers to suspect that there may be liquid water beneath the surface. In theory, there might even be a form of primitive life hidden beneath the ice, where water remains as a liquid.

Space bombardment

Many asteroids have struck the Earth already, and many scientists believe that such an impact resulted in the extinction of the dinosaurs about 65 million years ago. At that time, an asteroid or huge meteorite about 6 miles in diameter struck the Yucatan region of Mexico. It gouged out a huge crater and hurled so much dust into the Earth's atmosphere that the world's climate changed drastically, causing the death of the dinosaurs.

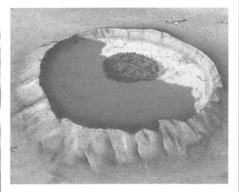

▲ This impact crater at Wolf Creek in Australia was caused by a huge meteorite or small asteroid. The amount of energy the impact released would have been equivalent to hundreds of nuclear weapons.

? What is the Moon?

The Moon is the Earth's only satellite, and it has been orbiting our planet for at least 4,000 million years. It is a rocky sphere about 1,140 miles in diameter, which is about one-quarter the size of the Earth.

Scientists believe that the Moon formed when another planet about the size of Mars collided with the Earth. The collision splashed a huge mass of molten (liquid) rock into space. This molten rock quickly formed into a sphere, and the Moon rapidly cooled into its solid form. The Moon's surface is heavily pitted by collisions with debris such as asteroids.

? Why does the Moon seem to change shape each month?

The appearance of the Moon alters, depending on the position of the Sun in relation to the Moon. The Sun lights up only one side of the Moon. As the Moon orbits the Earth, we see this lit-up area from different angles. When the Sun is almost behind the Earth, it lights up the whole of the Moon; this is called a Full Moon. When the Sun is off to one side, part of the Moon is in deep shadow and all we can see is a thin slice, or crescent, of the Moon's lit surface.

? What is a lunar eclipse?

The Earth casts a long shadow into space, and when this shadow passes over the Moon it causes an eclipse.

A lunar eclipse can only happen during a full Moon, when the Sun is directly behind the Earth. It happens only occasionally, because the orbit of the Moon is slightly tilted and so the shadow usually misses it. Lunar eclipses can last for over one hour, but they do not completely black out the shadowed part of the Moon. Some sunlight always filters through, making the shadow look a reddish-brown color.

? Why does the Moon shine?

The Moon is by far the brightest object in the night sky, but it has no light of its own. Moonlight is simply the reflected light of the Sun. Parts of the Moon that are not in sunlight are invisible against the deep blackness of space. Although the Moon appears bright and silvery, only a small proportion of the light that falls on it from the Sun is reflected back towards us. This is because the Moon's surface is grey and rocky, and does not reflect light well.

? What is a lunar month?

For thousands of years people have used the Moon to measure the passing of time and the seasons. The Moon revolves around its own axis every 29 1/2 days, which is also the time it takes to complete one orbit around the Earth. This period of time is known as a lunar month. Our calendar has been devised to follow this astronomical pattern fairly closely. It has to be adjusted slightly to round up the number of days in each month to a more convenient figure. The sidereal month, of 27.32 days, measures the time it takes for the stars to return to an identical position in the sky.

Wobbling Moon

We always see the same side of the moon as it rotates around the Earth. However, it wobbles slightly as it orbits the Earth, giving us a glimpse of some of the features around the edges of its hidden side. Because of this wobble, we can actually see about 59 percent of the moon's surface from the Earth.

❓ How far away is the moon?

The distance of the moon away from the Earth was settled once and for all after the Apollo astronauts left a small reflector on the moon's surface. Lasers were directed at this reflector, and the time taken for the laser light to reach the moon and be reflected back again was measured. As light has a constant speed, this enabled the exact distance of the moon from the Earth to be calculated. This distance is 238,606 miles, though it varies slightly because the moon does not have a perfectly circular orbit.

Dead planet!

Living things need air and water to stay alive, and neither of these is available on the moon. The atmosphere of the moon is a higher vacuum than can be created in most scientific laboratories. The moon also suffers extreme temperature swings between the lunar day and night. Lunar conditions have been recreated in laboratories on the Earth, but no form of terrestrial life has been able to survive them. There is some water on the moon's surface in the form of frost that can be found in shadowed craters near the moon's poles.

❓ What is the moon made of?

The moon is a rocky satellite, and is made of similar material to the Earth. It has an outer layer, or mantle, of rock, and a core that is probably made up mostly of iron. Unlike the Earth's liquid mantle, the interior of the moon is cool and solid. There is little or no volcanic activity on the moon. However, while it was cooling early in its life, floods or streams of lava ran out across the moon's surface.

❓ What does the surface of the moon look like?

The moon's surface is covered with a thick layer of gravel-like rock and dust. This material was created by the impact of millions of meteorites. The moon also has mountain ranges, many of which are the remains of impact craters and volcanoes that were active when the moon was still hot. There are some huge valleys called rilles, which can be hundreds of miles in length and look like river-beds. However, scientists do not yet fully understand their origins.

▲ The astronaut's space suit is a highly complex life support system. As well as supplying air it must insulate him from changes in temperature, and also allow him to move around in the vacuum of space.

❓ What's on the far side of the moon?

The far side of the moon was a mystery until 1959, when a Soviet space probe took the first photographs of it.

The actual appearance of the far side was something of a disappointment, because it had far fewer craters and other physical features than the familiar side that always faces the Earth.

? Who was the first man into space?

Yuri Gagarin was the first man to orbit the Earth. On April 12, 1961 the Soviet Union launched him into space, carried by a converted intercontinental ballistic missile. He only made a single orbit of the Earth and landed safely by parachute.

? What is the space shuttle?

The space shuttle is the first re-usable spacecraft. It was developed to provide a re-usable, and therefore cheaper, vehicle for launching satellites and for other work in space. The shuttle is a bulky delta-winged aircraft with powerful rocket motors. At launch, two solid-fuel booster rockets are strapped to its sides, and a giant fuel tank is fixed to its belly. The rockets and fuel tank fall away after launch, and the rockets are recovered and re-used. In orbit, the shuttle's cargo bay opens to release satellites or allow the crew to work in space. The shuttle lands on a runway like a conventional aircraft.

◄ **At takeoff, the space shuttle weighs 2,200 tons. It burns almost all of its fuel in the first few minutes after launch, then continues to coast into its orbit 186 miles above the surface of Earth.**

? What do space satellites do?

Space satellites have revolutionized communications, making possible everyday developments such as mobile phones and television. Communications satellites receive signals beamed at them from the Earth, and send them on to other places. They transmit television and telephone signals around the world, even to remote areas. They are also used for defense communications, including checking on the movement of military forces. Satellites can survey the Earth's surface, predict weather changes, and track hurricanes. They can also help to examine resources such as crops, forests, and even minerals. Navigation satellites enable people on land or at sea to work out their exact map position, to within a few yards.

Rocket power!

All space flight depends on the use of rockets that burn huge amounts of fuel. They burn high-energy fuel in a chamber that directs the burning gases through a nozzle. As the gases stream out through the nozzle, they provide the thrust to push the rocket up into space.
Some rockets are powered by burning kerosene or liquid hydrogen with liquid oxygen, but this requires very careful handling. Other rockets burn solid fuel in a controlled explosion.

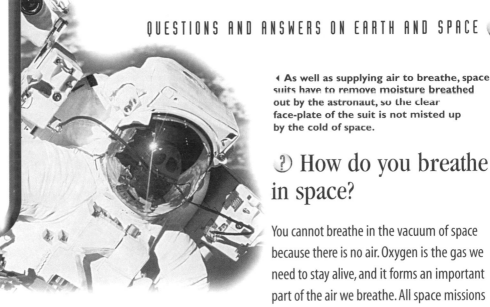

One giant leap!

The Apollo project was the United States' plan to get humans on the Moon during the 1960s. It used the world's most powerful rocket, Saturn V, to launch the three-man Apollo spacecraft. While orbiting the Moon, the Apollo craft would separate into two parts. The landing module carried two astronauts down onto the Moon's surface, while the main part remained in orbit with the third astronaut.

◄ As well as supplying air to breathe, space suits have to remove moisture breathed out by the astronaut, so the clear face-plate of the suit is not misted up by the cold of space.

How do you breathe in space?

You cannot breathe in the vacuum of space because there is no air. Oxygen is the gas we need to stay alive, and it forms an important part of the air we breathe. All space missions have to carry their own air supply. Pure oxygen was used on the earliest space flights, but after a tragic fire it was realized that pure oxygen was too dangerous. Spacecraft and space stations now carry supplies of air instead. When astronauts go on a "space walk" they wear a space suit that provides them with air at the correct pressure, while still allowing them to move freely.

How far do space probes travel?

Space probes are small packages of instruments that are launched from the Earth to explore planets. They may also travel deeper into space. Probes do not have their own rocket power, apart from tiny thrusters for steering. Probes have landed small instrument capsules on Mars and Venus; these sent back pictures and information. Some probes use the gravity of other planets to extend their voyage. They pass close by a planet, using its gravity to swing around it and be hurled off towards another planet. Using this technique, the Voyager 2 probe was able to visit Jupiter, Saturn, Uranus and Neptune.

How do satellites stay up?

The speed with which a satellite is launched helps to keep it in orbit. To stay up above the Earth, a satellite must be launched at a speed of about 5 miles per second. If the orbit is less than 124 miles above the Earth, faint traces of air will gradually slow the satellite so it loses height and eventually crashes to the ground. Satellites that are much higher can stay up indefinitely. Some satellites are placed in a geostationary orbit. This means that their speed exactly matches that of the Earth's rotation, and they seem to stay above a fixed point on the ground.

Has any spacecraft ever left the Solar System?

Pioneer 10 is the first man-made object to leave the Solar System. This probe was launched towards Jupiter in 1972 and by 1983 it had reached deep space. Pioneer 10 carried messages about life on Earth to be read by any extraterrestrial travellers who might meet the probe.

What is a space station?

Space stations allow the crew to work in space for long periods in conditions of zero gravity. While conditions in space capsules and the space shuttle are cramped, space stations are more suitable for longer stays in space. Rockets or the space shuttle bring supplies of air and food to the space station, and often a new crew. Space stations are usually made up of several modules that are sent into orbit, one at a time, and assembled in space. Some space stations, such as the Russian Mir, stayed up for many years, and their crews remained in space for months at a time.

▲ Space stations are constructed from modules small enough to be carried by rockets or the space shuttle, which are assembled once in orbit.

? What is inside the Earth?

The Earth is not solid rock all the way through. It has an inner core of solid rock, which is mostly iron. The temperature here is probably around 8,000°F. Beyond the inner core is a layer of liquid rock, called the outer core, which extends about halfway to the surface. Beyond this is a thick layer of rock called the mantle, which is partly molten and runny. The thinnest layer, or crust, is on the Earth's surface, floating on the red-hot liquid mantle. The crust is about 4 miles thick under the oceans, but 19 to 25 miles thick beneath the land.

▼ The Earth's crust is the thinnest of the layers. It floats on the semi-liquid mantle beneath. The inner core is probably made of solid iron.

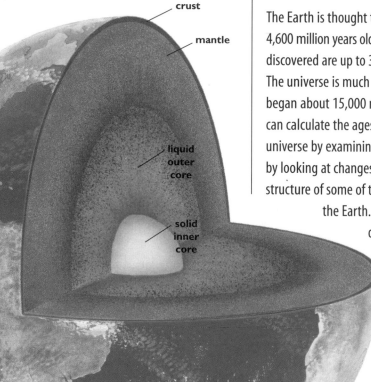

crust

mantle

liquid outer core

solid inner core

? Why is the Earth like a magnet?

The Earth acts as if it is a huge magnet. When the solid rocky core moves inside the liquid rock above it, it creates a magnetic field with a north pole and a south pole. This field surrounds the Earth and extends right out into space. The Earth's magnetic field is changing constantly. This means that the magnetic north pole is not always the same as the geographic, or true, North Pole that you find on a map, although it wanders about in the same region. Millions of years ago, the north magnetic pole lay in what is now the Sahara desert.

? How old is our Earth?

The Earth is thought to be about 4,600 million years old. The oldest rocks so far discovered are up to 3,800 million years old. The universe is much older, and probably began about 15,000 million years ago. We can calculate the ages of the Earth and the universe by examining meteorites, and also by looking at changes in the atomic structure of some of the elements found on the Earth. Radioactive elements decay at a steady rate, and these changes can indicate the age of the Earth and other planets, as well as the age of the stars.

? What is the Earth made of?

The Earth is made up of elements. These are the simplest possible substances, which are composed of one kind of atom. Elements cannot normally be broken down into other substances, except under the special conditions that you might find inside the hot core of a star. A total of 92 different elements are found in nature. Other elements can be made in laboratories, but they have only a very short life.

Minerals, which make up the solid surface of the Earth, consist mostly of combinations of elements. The minerals gold, diamond, and graphite are examples of single elements, while most others contain several elements.

? What are crystals?

Crystals are solid substances that are naturally formed into regular geometric, angular shapes. All crystals can be classified into seven systems. Sometimes a crystal is formed when water evaporates and substances dissolved in the water gradually grow into a crystal. Other crystals are formed under great pressure. Diamond crystals are made when carbon dissolves in molten rock deep down below the Earth's surface. The diamond crystallizes out and is later uncovered on the surface either by volcanic action or by erosion of the Earth's crust. Other valuable gems are formed in a similar way, and most of them contain compounds of aluminum.

Make it crystal clear!

It is easy to grow your own crystals. Take a glass jar containing hot water, and stir into it either table salt or sugar. Keep adding more salt or sugar and stirring until no more will dissolve. Now let the solution cool, place a lid on loosely and put the jar away for a while. As the water gradually evaporates, crystals will begin to form. The longer you leave the jar, the larger the crystals will grow.

You can experiment with other substances too. Baking soda will also produce crystals, as will most solid substances that dissolve to form a clear solution.

What is the equator?

The equator is an imaginary line drawn around the outside of the Earth. It lies midway between the North Pole and the South Pole, at the Earth's broadest point.

The equator was invented by map-makers because it makes a convenient point from which to measure distances, together with the geographic North Pole and South Pole. On a map, the equator is positioned at 0 degrees of latitude. It divides the Earth into two halves, which we call the north and south hemispheres.

▼ The Earth has five oceans. These are the Pacific, Atlantic, Indian, Arctic, and Antarctic. In addition, there are several substantial seas such as the Mediterranean and Black.

What are metals?

Metals are one of the major groups of elements. Most of them are shiny and hard. Mercury is the only metal that is a liquid at normal temperatures. Most metals can be bent and stretched, and they can be mixed to make alloys.

Metals are usually found with other elements in the form of compounds. Bauxite is an ore, or mixture of substances, that contains aluminum, the most common metal. It makes up about eight percent of the Earth's crust. Osmium is the heaviest metal, and is twice as heavy as lead. Lithium is the lightest metal. It is half the weight of the same volume of water, so it floats in water.

How much of the Earth is covered by water?

More than two-thirds of the Earth's surface is covered by seas and oceans. About 72 percent of the Earth's surface is water. This water is either in the oceans, locked away as ice at the poles, or held as water vapor in the atmosphere. All of the Earth's water is known as the hydrosphere.

▲ Seen from space, the Earth looks like a perfect ball, covered with blue seas and wisps of cloud. However, it is not round, but is flattened at the poles.

Why is the Earth round?

Gravity pulled the Earth and the other planets into a sphere when they were being formed. The Earth is not truly round, but is slightly flattened, making it bulge out at the equator. This effect is due to the speed with which the Earth spins, causing the equator to try to fly out from the axis of the spinning Earth. It is rather like a heavy object whirling around on the end of a piece of string. The shape of some of the other planets is distorted in the same way.

? Why do we have day and night?

As the Earth spins on its axis, the sun always shines on one side, giving us daylight. It is night on the shaded side. As the Earth continues to turn, the shaded side moves into the sun's light, and the sunlit side turns away from the light. It takes 24 hours for the Earth to make one complete turn on its axis, and our clocks are based on this principle.

In the 1940s, people discovered that the Earth speeds up and slows down a little as it spins, although the reason for these changes is not fully understood. We have now developed atomic clocks that can measure time exactly.

? Why do we have seasons?

We have seasons because the Earth is tilted on its axis. As the Earth moves around the sun, the hemisphere tilted towards the sun receives more sunlight, and this is summer time. The days are longer and the weather is warm because of the extra sunlight. The hemisphere tilted away from the sun receives less sunshine, has shorter days, and is cooler – it is winter time. The area near the equator is always exposed to the sun's rays, so it is warm all the year round. This means that there is little difference between the seasons.

? Why do we have colored sunsets?

Colored sunsets happen when light is scattered by dust and water particles in the air as the sun sets. At sunset, the light passes through a much greater thickness of air, because it strikes the atmosphere at a shallow angle. The farther the light has to pass through the air, the more likely it is to be scattered by the dust particles, causing the red coloration.

? Why does the sun rise in the east?

The direction of the Earth's rotation means that the sun appears to rise in the east and set in the west. If you imagine that you are standing at the North Pole and looking down on the Earth, it would rotate anti-clockwise. In other words, the Earth rotates towards the east, so the sun first becomes visible from that direction.

? What is the Earth's axis?

The Earth's axis is an imaginary line through the geographic center of the Earth, about which it spins. You can think of the axis as being like a stick pushed through the middle of an orange. The axis is tilted at an angle of 23.5° from the vertical, in relation to the sun. We still do not know the reason for this tilt.

Jet lag

Jet lag is a feeling of confusion that often occurs when people travel long distances by fast jet plane. Modern aircraft travel very fast and may cross several time zones in a short time during a long flight. When you land in a different time zone, your brain is still adjusted to the zone you have just left. It can take a couple of days for your brain to adjust.

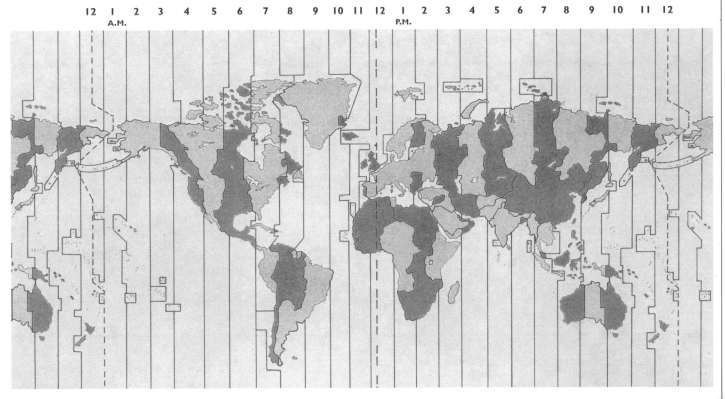

Explore the time zones!

The chart above shows the difference in times around the world. These are all measured against 12:00 noon, Greenwich Mean Time (the time in Britain):

Amsterdam, The Netherlands	1:00 P.M.
Athens, Greece	2:00 P.M.
Auckland, New Zealand	12:00 A.M.
Bangkok, Thailand	7:00 P.M.
Cairo, Egypt	2:00 P.M.
Delhi, India	5:30 P.M.
Hong Kong, China	8:00 P.M.
Jamaica, West Indies	7:00 A.M.
Los Angeles, U.S.A.	4:00 A.M.
Moscow, Russia	3:00 P.M.
New York, U.S.A.	7:00 A.M.
Paris, France	1:00 P.M.
Rio de Janeiro, Brazil	9:00 A.M.
Sydney, Australia	10:00 P.M.
Tokyo, Japan	9:00 P.M.
Toronto, Canada	7:00 A.M.
Washington D.C., U.S.A.	7:00 A.M.

? Why are times different in other countries?

Clocks in other countries need to be adjusted so that it gets light and dark at approximately the same time everywhere. Without this adjustment, people might find that dawn was at 10 o'clock in the evening, for example.

In 1884, time zones were set up around the world, measured from Greenwich in London, England. Every time zone east or west of Greenwich has noon at a different time. Each zone is either one hour ahead or behind of its neighboring zone — it is one hour earlier to the west of each zone, and one hour later to the east.

? What are the northern lights?

The northern lights are streaks and sheets of pale, flickering, colored lights that are sometimes seen in the night sky in far northern regions. Their proper name is the aurora borealis. The same effect also occurs in the far south, where it is known as the aurora australis.

Auroras take place between 60 and 620 miles above the Earth's surface. They are caused by electrically charged particles from the sun. These particles strike the Earth's atmosphere and release energy in the form of light. Auroras are most common when there are many sunspots, which increase the amount of energy released by the sun.

⍰ Why is the sea salty?

A mixture of salty substances is washed out of rocks by rivers and deposited in the sea. When rain falls on the land, it gradually dissolves minerals. The dissolved salts slowly enter rivers and stream, and are carried down into the sea. This process is happening all the time, and so the oceans and seas gradually become more salty.

⍰ What is the Gulf Stream?

The Gulf Stream is an ocean current that controls the climate and weather of the whole of Europe. The current starts in the Gulf of Mexico, carrying warm water across the Atlantic Ocean and traveling northeast until it reaches the European coast. Water evaporates from the surface of the Gulf Stream causing rainfall in western Europe.

⍰ What causes waves?

A combination of wind and the shape of the seabed causes waves. Wind blows the surface layers of the sea, gradually forming a rolling movement of waves. As these waves near the coast, the seabed interrupts their rolling movement, and they mount up and break onto the beach. On beaches with a shallow slope, the waves pile up to a great height before breaking, causing surf. Out in the open sea, the waves may be very far apart, but they are closer together as they reach the shore. The highest wave ever recorded, during a hurricane in 1933, was 37 yards high.

▾ **Waves created by tropical storms form huge swells, which are rounded waves capable of traveling for thousands of kilometres, gradually diminishing as they lose their energy and the distance between the waves increases. They get closer together as they near land and the water become shallower. Waves usually break when the water depth becomes 1.3 times the height of the waves. When storms take place close to shore, waves of enormous height are produced.**

⍰ What causes the tides?

Tides are caused by the gravity of the moon. As the Earth spins, the water in the oceans is 'pulled' toward the moon slightly, making a bulge. There is a corresponding bulge on the other side of the Earth. Wherever the bulges are positioned, it is high tide. In between, the water is shallower, and so it is low tide. High tides occur every 25 hours, because at the same time that the Earth is spinning on its axis, the moon is traveling around the Earth once every $27\frac{1}{2}$ days. This means that high tide is about one hour later every day.

⍰ What is the continental shelf?

The shallow underwater plateaus of land surrounding the continents form the continental shelf. They slope gently down to a depth of about 197 yards, after which they slope more sharply towards the deep ocean. The continental shelf can extend out from the coast for long distances, or it may be narrow, for example, off the coast of Chile where the Andes Mountains plunge down into the Pacific Ocean with hardly any shelf. Usually the shelves are wider off low-lying regions. The continental shelf is a valuable resource, as most fish are found here. Also, there are plans to mine some of the minerals on the seabed in these shallow waters.

Whirling to destruction

For centuries sailors have been in terror of being sucked into a whirlpool that would swallow them and their ships. Whirlpools happen when opposing currents meet, causing the water to spin around very rapidly. Huge whirlpools in the sea are usually caused by powerful tides. The most famous is the Maelstrom, which appears between two islands off the coast of Norway. At times, this whirlpool is strong enough to destroy small ships. Another dangerous whirlpool is Charybdis in the Mediterranean, which was a hazard to the ancient Greek and Roman sailors. The ancient Greeks believed that a monster caused this whirlpool.

▲ The Maelstrom is a powerful and treacherous tidal race in the channel between the Lofoten islands off the north coast of Norway. Currents often reach a speed of 7 mph, making it dangerous for small ships. It often causes huge whirlpools, which were made famous by the writings of Jules Verne and Edgar Alan Poe.

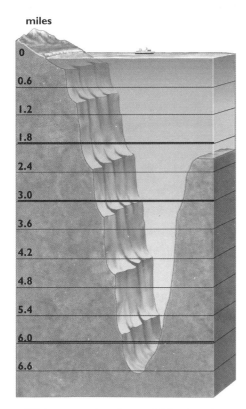

miles

▲ With an amazing depth of 6.8 miles the Marianas Trench could easily swallow the whole of Mount Everest, which has a height of only 5.5 miles.

How deep are the oceans?

The depth of the oceans varies widely, but the deepest part found so far is called the Marianas Trench. This trench is a deep cut in the bed of the Pacific Ocean, and its depth is as much as 6.8 miles. Even at this enormous depth, signs of marine life have been seen in the trench. In 1960, Dr. Jacques Piccard and Lt. Donald Walsh reached a depth of 6.7 miles in a U.S. Navy vessel, Trieste. The Pacific Ocean is home to nine of the ten deepest sea trenches. The exception is the Puerto Rico trench in the western Atlantic Ocean, which has a maximum depth of 5.7 miles.

Why did sailors fear the Sargasso Sea?

Sailors feared that the Sargasso Sea was haunted by sea monsters and filled with seaweed that would entangle their ships and prevent their escape. The Sargasso Sea is a patch of ocean in the North Atlantic, about 1,980 miles west of the Canary Islands. The ocean currents in this area are very slow, although they are surrounded by fast-moving currents. This means that any seaweed floating in the Sargasso Sea will not be carried away. Patches of floating weed can be as large as 33 yards in diameter. Despite the legends, they are never thick enough to entangle a ship.

Which is the world's longest river?

The Nile in Africa and the Amazon in South America are the world's longest rivers. The Nile is 4,412 miles long, and the Amazon is 4,000 miles long. It is difficult to give an exact length because these huge rivers split into tiny tributaries near their sources, and some of these dry up or change course.

The Amazon is by far the largest river because it carries more water than the Nile, Mississippi, and the Yangtze put together. The Amazon is 87 miles wide at its mouth, and up to 100 yards deep in places.

How does a river begin?

Most of the rainwater that falls on the land returns to the sea by way of rivers. Rainwater first soaks into the ground, but once the ground is saturated, the excess water begins to run off in small streams. More water comes from melting ice and snow. Small streams gradually merge and become bigger, until they eventually form a river. The tiny streams that are the source of a river often begin in damp areas such as swamps or bogs, or may flow out of a pond or lake. Usually they are in hills or mountains where the rainfall is heaviest.

▶ The character of a river changes along its course. The rushing stream near its source slows as it reaches flatter ground, and as it nears the sea, the river becomes wider and the flow is more sluggish.

What is a delta?

As a river reaches the sea, its flow becomes slower, forming an area known as a delta. As the water slows, the tiny particles of silt carried by the current settle to the bottom, forming mud banks. These make the river-bed shallower, so the water spreads out to form a wide estuary. In large rivers like the Danube, islands form among these exposed mud banks, and the river water trickles through a maze of small waterways. This region, which is rich in plants and other wildlife, forms the river's delta.

Uphill flow!

Water always flows down a river, but occasionally the flow is reversed. This happens only in very large rivers, when very high tides overcome the normal river currents. In narrow parts of the river valley, the water begins to pile up, and eventually a wave called a tidal bore passes back up the river, sometimes for a great distance. This happens in the Amazon in South America, where there is a bore as high as 5 yards.

source

mountain stream

slow flowing river

meander

estuary

What is a spring?

Many types of rock contain tiny holes like a sponge, in which rainwater collects. The water gradually sinks down and eventually flows out lower down. Water stored in such porous rocks sometimes bubbles to the surface in springs. They are usually found near the foot of hills. Spring water is often used for drinking because as it passes through rock, any harmful substances or germs are filtered out. On more level ground, spring water is found by digging a well to reach the underground water. Small outflows of water can lead to the formation of isolated bogs or marshes.

How are limestone caves formed?

Water can actually dissolve certain types of rock, eventually forming underground streams and caves.

Carbon dioxide in the air dissolves in rainwater to form a very weak acid, which can slowly dissolve soft limestone rock. Over thousands of years, water seeping into cracks in limestone rock dissolves so much that the cracks become holes. Slowly the holes grow even larger and form caves. These may be many miles in length and very deep. Sometimes the roofs of huge caves collapse, forming narrow valleys or gorges.

▶ **The world's highest waterfall, Angel Falls, tumbles from the flat top of a hill, hardly touching the cliff face. It was discovered in 1935 by an American pilot, Jimmy Angel. It remained undiscovered for so long due to dense rainforest and its remote location.**

Can water wear away solid rock?

Water itself cannot wear away rock, but tiny particles of grit carried in the water can eventually wear away the hardest rocks. It is this continuous wearing process that cuts valleys through mountains and hills. The faster the water flows, the more the grit it carries wears away at the rock. You can see the same process in action along the coast. There, rocks are worn away by the action of sand dashed against them by the waves.

Which is the world's highest waterfall?

The Angel Falls in Venezuela, South America, fall 2,894 feet in a single drop. Much more water flows over Victoria Falls in southern Africa and Niagara Falls on the U.S.-Canadian border, but these falls are not as high. Waterfalls occur when a river flows over hard rock lying over softer rock. The hard rock forms a 'lip' for the waterfall, and the water wears away the softer rock below, forming a step that gradually becomes deeper.

Mountains

? How are mountains formed?

There are three main ways in which mountains can be formed. Volcanoes form mountains when lava from deep inside the Earth cools and hardens on the surface. Other mountains are formed when layers of rock are forced up into folds, or when rocks fracture to cause faults, allowing slabs of rock to be raised up. These movements are caused by the very gradual shifting of the land areas, which sets up stresses in the Earth's crust.

? Which are the oldest mountains?

Low, smooth mountain ranges are the oldest. The most recently formed mountains are usually jagged and steep, because their rocks have not been worn away and smoothed by erosion. Over millions of years, the rocks wear away and the shape of the mountains becomes more rounded.

Eventually, they may wear away completely. When measured in geological time, most of the world's mountains are still relatively young.

On top of the world

After many years Mount Everest was finally surmounted on May 29, 1953, when a Nepalese guide, Tenzing Norgay, and a New Zealander, Edmund Hillary, reached the highest point on the Earth's surface. Since then, many people have climbed Everest, and all the world's major peaks have been conquered. It is now possible to map mountains from the air so that mountaineering routes can be carefully worked out in advance. Also, equipment has improved so that sheer rock faces can be readily climbed. Altitude sickness and avalanches of ice and snow are now the main hazards faced by climbers.

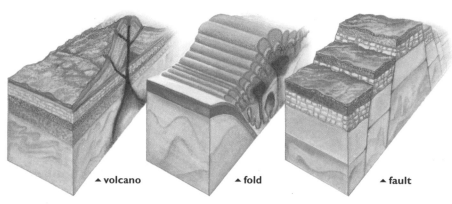

▲ volcano   ▲ fold   ▲ fault

▲ Sediments are deposited in the seas and form layers, which eventually turn into rock. Movement of the Earth's crust can force these layers up into folds, and stresses in the crust lead to cracks. This may cause whole areas of crust to subside or be forced up into mountain chains.

? Which are the highest mountains in the world?

The world's highest mountains are in the Himalaya-Karakoram range to the north of India. The Andes Mountains in South America cover a larger area but are not so high. The Himalayas contain 79 peaks that are over 4 miles high. The highest of these is

Mount Everest, which is 5.5 miles high. At these altitudes, mountains are always covered in snow and ice, and there is little oxygen to breathe. Although Mount Everest is the tallest mountain when measured from sea level, Mauna Kea in Hawaii is actually the tallest if measured from its base. It reaches over 3 miles below the surface of the Pacific Ocean. From its base to its peak, Mauna Kea is 6.2 miles high.

? Are climbers able to breathe at high altitudes?

The higher you climb, the thinner the air becomes, until there is not enough oxygen to support life. On the highest mountains, there is just about enough oxygen for life to survive for a short time. Extremely fit mountaineers have managed to climb to the top of Mount Everest without the use of oxygen cylinders.

Our bodies can adapt slowly to a lack of oxygen, which is why expeditions to the Himalayas and other high ranges camp at progressively higher levels to get used to the thinner air. People living at high altitudes in the Andes and the Himalayas develop enlarged chests and changes in their lungs to help them breathe.

? What is chalk?

Chalk is formed from the skeletons of millions and millions of tiny animals called foraminifera. It is a sedimentary rock that formed millions of years ago beneath shallow seas. Chalk is used in the manufacture of rubber goods and paint.

? Why do clouds form near mountains?

Clouds form when damp air is forced upwards to pass over a mountain range. Air is forced up the face of the mountain because it is unable to go around it. There is usually a high wind on the top of the mountain. As it rises, the air becomes cooler, and the moisture in the air condenses to form water droplets, resulting in the formation of clouds. This explains why there is often high rainfall and snow in mountainous regions.

▼ As winds laden with water vapor are blown towards mountains, they are forced to rise, and the temperature drops. The water condenses into clouds at these higher altitudes. This is why mountain peaks are often seen to be surrounded by layers of cloud.

? What is a rockslide?

Rock is broken away from the mountainside by the effects of freezing. Rainwater enters cracks in the rock, and as it freezes, it expands and opens the crack wider. As the thaw begins, the pieces of rock splinter and separate from the bedrock. Loose rock builds up continuously on a mountainside, but usually only small pieces slide down. This loose, broken rock is called scree. A rockslide takes place when the mass of broken pieces of rock slides down the side of a mountain. This usually happens in very wet weather, when rain lubricates the rock and allows it to slide freely down the mountainside mixed with a torrent of mud.

? How can rocks be folded up?

Most rocks are too brittle to be reshaped, but folding is common in sedimentary rocks. Movements in the Earth's crust force flexible sedimentary rocks into folds. These folds are sometimes so large that the rock lays back on itself in layers. Geologists may find that the layers of rock are actually upside down, with the youngest rocks on top.

▲ Rockslides are common where deforestation has taken place and there are no longer any tree roots to stabilize the loose material.

? What is a mountain range?

A group of mountains is called a range. Nearly all large mountains are grouped in ranges. Single high peaks are usually old volcanoes. Mount Kilimanjaro in Tanzania is the highest mountain in Africa. It is a single peak and is an extinct volcano. These isolated peaks always look much higher than mountains in ranges, because they are not surrounded by the usual lower foothills that disguise a mountain's true height.

❓ What is a volcano?

Volcanoes are openings in the Earth's crust through which molten lava, red hot rocks, steam, and fumes pour out. We usually think of a volcano as a smoking mountain that erupts explosively, but most volcanoes are simply cracks in the crust through which lava flows continuously.

The more familiar kind of volcano has a single central pipe though which lava reaches the surface, building up into a cone as it cools. The cone consists of layers of lava and volcanic ash. There is usually a crater at the center. Most active volcanoes smoke and spit out occasional pieces of lava. Dramatic eruptions are rare.

❓ What is lava?

Lava is molten rock that reaches the Earth's surface. Its temperature may be as high as 2,100°F. Lava may be as runny as water or so thick that it scarcely moves at all. The liquid type of lava that flows from Hawaiian volcanoes runs downhill in sheets and streams, traveling very fast. Sometimes the surface of these streams cools and hardens, and the liquid lava continues to flow underneath, eventually producing lava tubes when it cools. The thicker type of lava inches its way down the side of a volcano like a very slow avalanche, carrying with it anything in its path, as well as red hot lava.

❓ What happened to Pompeii and Herculaneum?

Two busy Roman towns were completely buried in lava and ash by an eruption of Mount Vesuvius in A.D. 79.

A burning rain of ash, lava, and volcanic debris covered Pompeii to a depth of more than 3 yards. Nearby Herculaneum was buried under about 20 yards of ash. Many people were overcome while trying to escape the eruption. In Pompeii, cavities were found in the ash where bodies had lain and then rotted away. The two towns preserved everyday Roman life, and they are still being excavated.

❓ How fast do volcanoes grow?

Unlike most geological happenings, the growth of a volcano can be very rapid. In 1943, a farmer in Mexico noticed smoke coming from a crack in the ground in his cornfield. Lava began to ooze out, and six days later it had piled up into a volcanic cone 164 yards high. By the end of the year, the cone had grown to 492 yards. The eruption finally stopped in 1952, when the volcano Paricutín had reached a height of 3072 yards (1.7 miles) above sea level. The volcano had buried two whole villages.

▶ **Masses of dust and rocks hurled out from an active volcano fall back and cause a volcanic cone to develop. Lava may escape from the crater in the center or find its way out through vents in the side of the volcano. The flowing lava solidifies as it cools in the air.**

gas and ashes

main vent

secondary vent

lava

layers of ash and lava

Volcanic bombs

A major volcanic eruption can hurl boulders high into the air. These boulders, called volcanic bombs, can be very large. Most of the material thrown out of the erupting volcano is ash, which forms a huge cloud. Steam and sulphurous gases are also released, and these can be very dangerous to bystanders. Pumice is a kind of foamed rock that is often thrown out during an eruption. It is full of tiny holes, making it very light. It is formed when gases in molten rock are boiled off, creating a foam that solidifies as it cools.

⸮ Why do geysers spout hot water?

When water seeps through the ground and reaches magma, hot rock, or volcanic gases, it boils violently. This produces steam that can shoot the water out of cracks, causing a geyser. Geysers can be very spectacular, and some shoot water as high as 500 yards into the air, although most are much less powerful. Sometimes they erupt at regular intervals, but most erupt only occasionally.

▸ **Boiling water is blasted out of the ground by a geyser. When the hot water emerges, it forms a hot spring. These can be very useful, and in several countries the hot water is used for heating purposes.**

⸮ What is the Ring of Fire?

All around the rim of the Pacific Ocean is a circle of places of volcanic activity known as the Ring of Fire. The Ring of Fire is caused by shifts in the giant plates that make up the Earth's crust. The Pacific plate is gradually disappearing under the surrounding continental plates, and volcanic activity marks the points where this movement is taking place. Frequent earthquakes accompany the volcanic action in the countries surrounding the Pacific. Ocean trenches and underwater volcanoes also form around the Ring of Fire.

▾ **The edges of the Pacific plate are surrounded by volcanic activity, earthquakes, and hot springs, caused as the crust shifts and hot lava rises near the surface. There is even a volcano in the cold wastes of the Antarctic.**

⸮ What happened when Krakatoa erupted?

The eruption of Krakatoa, in Indonesia, in 1883 was the biggest explosion in recorded history. Krakatoa was a small island between Java and Sumatra, on which there was a small cluster of volcanoes that were not dangerously active. On May 20, 1883, one of the cones erupted violently, and three months later the whole island blew up. The explosion could be heard in Australia, 2,170 miles away, and a cloud of ash rose 50 miles into the air. For two and a half days the island was in total darkness because of the amount of dust in the air.

? Who studies the weather?

People called meteorologists study the world's weather and the changes in the atmosphere that produce our weather. They observe and analyze the weather, and try to understand the processes that lead to changing weather conditions. The study of weather is known as meteorology.

? Why does rain fall?

Water evaporates from the Earth's surface, condenses into water droplets and falls back down to the ground as rain. Heat from the sun causes water to evaporate from the land, from rivers and lakes, and from the sea. The water vapor rises with the warm air and eventually reaches high altitudes where it cools and condenses into water droplets, forming clouds. The droplets grow larger until they are too heavy to stay in the cloud, and they fall as rain. Rain usually falls from the largest and darkest clouds, which contain the most water vapor.

? What is a monsoon?

A monsoon is a season of very heavy rain falling in tropical countries. They are most common near the Equator, when seasonal winds spring up, carrying moist air in from the sea. Important crops such as rice depend entirely on the monsoon to provide the right growing conditions. If the monsoon rains fail, famine commonly follows.

? What is smog?

Smog is a serious form of air pollution that can cause breathing problems. The term smog was first used to describe a type of air pollution in London, when smoke from coal fires combined with fog to produce dense yellow clouds that sometimes persisted for days. The term now describes the hazy fog that is caused mainly by vehicle exhausts and smoke from factories. It builds up when there is little air movement, and can occur when a layer of warm air traps cooler air near the ground, preventing the smog from being blown away. Cities in bowls or sheltered valleys are particularly vulnerable to this condition.

▼ All the water on Earth is constantly being recycled in a process known as the water cycle.

? What causes mist and fog?

Tiny water droplets condensing from moist air cause both mist and fog. They can occur at ground level. The air can only hold a limited amount of water vapor. If the air suddenly cools, its capacity to hold water is reduced, resulting in mist or fog. When fog occurs, visibility can be affected. Mist is less dense. It commonly occurs on calm, clear nights when heat rises, forming a thin layer of mist close to the ground.

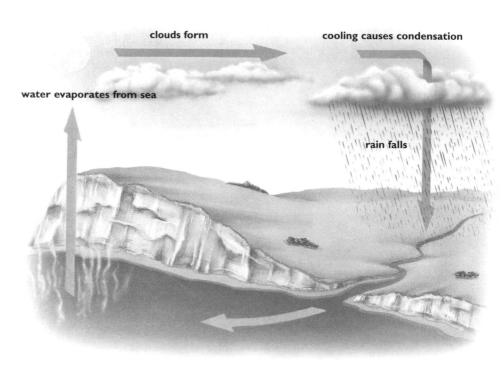

clouds form

cooling causes condensation

water evaporates from sea

rain falls

How are hailstones formed?

Hail is produced when particles of ice bounce up and down inside a cloud. In cold temperatures, water droplets inside a cloud will freeze into small pellets of ice. As these begin to fall, they may meet warm air rising, which carries them back up into the cloud. There they cool once more, and the process is repeated. As more and more water freezes onto their surface, the ice pellets gradually grow in size. Eventually they become so heavy that they fall to the ground as hailstones. Some hailstones are as big as a clenched fist and can do serious damage to buildings and livestock.

Thunderbolts

A lightning strike discharges about 100 million volts of electricity, and heats the air in its path to more than 59,000°F. The lightning strike travels at 186,171 miles per second, which is almost the speed of light. A strike between a cloud and the ground may be 9 miles long, and a strike between clouds can be over 87 miles long.

Ball lightning is a small fiery ball that occasionally appears during thunderstorms. There is no accepted scientific explanation for it.

How can forecasters predict the weather?

Meteorologists use a wide range of instruments and techniques to help them track changes in the weather and to predict future weather conditions. Weather forecasters have used simple instruments, such as thermometers, rain gauges, barometers, and wind gauges, for many years, but the advent of satellite photography has transformed weather forecasting. Weather satellites can track the movements of clouds and show the positions of high and low pressure areas and weather fronts. Radar measures the size, speed, and direction of storms, so accurate warnings of severe weather can be given. With the use of computers, increasingly accurate forecasting is now possible.

What are 'highs' and 'lows?'

Air pressure varies across different parts of the Earth's surface, and this difference causes winds. Air moves from an area of high pressure, or an anticyclone, to an area of low pressure, or a depression. Depressions are usually associated with worsening weather conditions and rain. These changes in air pressure can be measured by an instrument called a barometer. In a mercury barometer, the air pressure pushes down on the mercury, which is forced up the barometer to give an accurate reading.

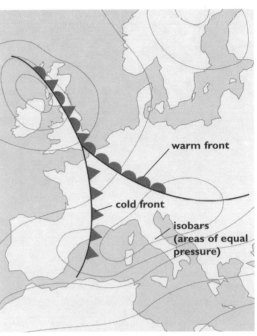

▲ A weather front is the boundary between two masses of air at different temperatures and pressures.

Why do we get thunder and lightning?

Lightning is a huge spark of electricity that is produced in a cloud. Thunder is the loud noise made by the lightning as it rips through the air.

During thunderstorms, enormous electrical charges build up inside a cloud. Eventually, the charges seem to flow down to the ground when lightning strikes. In fact, the electrical charges flow up from the ground and down from the cloud at the same time. The tremendous heat generated by the lightning causes the explosive noise of thunder. Lightning frequently strikes in the same place repeatedly, and along the same path through the air. It can also strike between two clouds.

Mountains such as the Rockies in North America have a typical alpine climate, because of their height. They are very cold in winter, and the summers are brief.

? Where is the world's driest place?

The world's driest place is the Atacama desert in Chile. It is a narrow strip between the Andes and the Pacific, where the first rain for 400 years fell in 1971. Like other hot deserts, the Atacama lies in a region where air pressure is constantly high, with little air movement or cloud. Rainfall is very low in other deserts. Near Cairo, Egypt, annual rainfall averages about 1 inch each year, while in Bahrain, on the edge of the Arabian desert, there is as much as 3 inches of rainfall. The rain may come in a single heavy storm, and some years there is no rainfall at all.

? How much of the world is covered by desert?

About one-third of the world's land surface is covered by desert. Deserts are found wherever there is too little water to allow much plant life to grow. This lack of vegetation leaves large areas of soil exposed. The largest desert in the world is the Sahara in Africa. It has an area of about 3.5 million square miles.

? Are there cold deserts?

Antarctica is the biggest cold desert in the world. All of its water is locked up in ice and snow, so nothing can grow. The Gobi desert in Mongolia and western China is also very cold in the winter, when temperatures drop below freezing. However, it is hot in the summer.

? What is a mirage?

Mirages form in hot deserts, where the air is so hot it bends and distorts light rays. The shimmering images that a mirage produces have often tricked travellers in deserts. People think that they can see a town or oasis on the horizon, but in reality there is none.

? Where are the most extreme temperatures found?

Libya and the Antarctic have recorded the most extreme temperatures. The hottest shade temperature was in Libya in 1922, when the temperature in the Sahara desert reached 136° F. Temperatures nearly as high as this were recorded in Death Valley in the U.S.A. in 1913. The coldest ever recorded temperature was in Antarctica in 1983, when Russian scientists measured a temperature low of -128.6° F.

Salt deserts form when shallow seas and lakes dry up, leaving a deposit of smooth salt in which almost no animals can live or plants grow.

The tropical rainforest is the richest habitat in the world, containing hundreds of thousands of plant species and many animals not found elsewhere. These vulnerable regions are rapidly being cleared for farmland.

The desert process

Deserts were once green and fertile areas, until a climate change altered them permanently. Just a small reduction in rainfall causes plants to die off. Without plant roots to bind and nourish the soil, the land gradually becomes barren. Soon the animals move away, and only desert remains. Very few deserts are completely barren, and plants and animals have evolved to live in the driest conditions, conserving their body water so they do not need to rely on rainfall.

? What is permafrost?

Permafrost is a layer of ice and frozen soil that never thaws. It lies beneath nearly one-quarter of the Earth's surface, throughout Alaska, Canada, and Russia. Sometimes the soil in these places is frozen to a depth of up to 1,640 miles. The surface layers may melt enough in summer for plants to grow, but the soil beneath is permanently frozen.

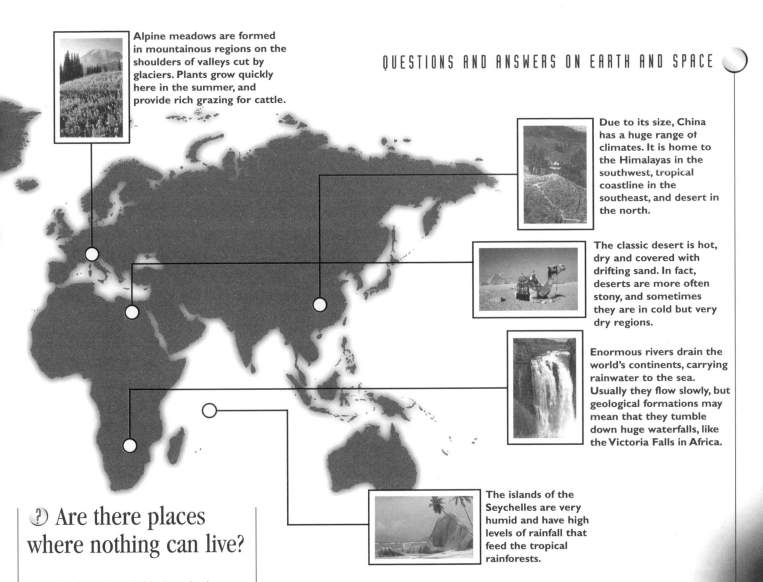

Alpine meadows are formed in mountainous regions on the shoulders of valleys cut by glaciers. Plants grow quickly here in the summer, and provide rich grazing for cattle.

Due to its size, China has a huge range of climates. It is home to the Himalayas in the southwest, tropical coastline in the southeast, and desert in the north.

The classic desert is hot, dry and covered with drifting sand. In fact, deserts are more often stony, and sometimes they are in cold but very dry regions.

Enormous rivers drain the world's continents, carrying rainwater to the sea. Usually they flow slowly, but geological formations may mean that they tumble down huge waterfalls, like the Victoria Falls in Africa.

The islands of the Seychelles are very humid and have high levels of rainfall that feed the tropical rainforests.

❓ Are there places where nothing can live?

Hot volcanic lava is probably the only place on the Earth's surface where there is no life at all. Living things have evolved to survive in the harshest environments. Tiny bacteria can be found everywhere on the Earth, even buried in thick ice at the poles or in the very deepest parts of the ocean.

❓ Can sand dunes move?

Sand dunes can move slowly, causing deserts to spread over more fertile land. Continuous winds blow the sand to form crescent-shaped dunes. Sand from the top of the dune is blown farther away, and it gradually collects to form a new dune.

▲ There are three factors that influence the climate of an area; latitude and the amount of solar radiation it receives, the amount of land and sea, and the altitude.

❓ How can people live in extreme climates?

Over millions of years, the human body has altered to suit the climate of the regions we inhabit. In general, the hotter the region, the darker the skin of its inhabitants. Also, many people from Asia have a fold of skin in their eyelid to protect them from strong sunlight. People living in hot climates do not need a fat layer to keep warm, so they are usually slim. The Inuits of the Arctic, however, are mostly shorter and stockier to help conserve heat.

❓ Which are the wettest places on the Earth?

Tropical rainforests are among the wettest places in the world. In general, most rainfall occurs on the sides of hills and mountains. The wettest place of all is Cherrapunji, in Assam, India. It faces the full force of the monsoon winds that sweep in from the Indian Ocean in July. Their warm, damp air rises in the Himalayan foothills, causing torrential rain. Mount Wai-'ale-'ale in Hawaii has the most wet days each year. It rains on 350 days on average, and the annual rainfall is the highest recorded anywhere.

What causes floods?

Flooding occurs when water cannot drain away fast enough in the rivers. In areas of non-porous rock, water runs off the land very quickly, and streams and rivers soon overflow. Flooding also happens when winter snows thaw in spring. Huge floods cover parts of Siberia every spring, when snow melts while the rivers are still iced up. Low-lying coastal lands are vulnerable to flooding, especially when gales and high tides cause water to flow inland. Low-lying Bangladesh is particularly vulnerable to this kind of flooding. In addition, melting snow in the Himalayan mountains adds huge amounts of water to Bangladesh's rivers, increasing the flood risk.

Where were the worst floods?

Some of the most terrible floods known were in China along the Hwang-he, or Yellow River. The river burst its banks in 1931, killing more than 3.5 million people. For centuries, dykes have been built to prevent flooding, but these burst when the water flow is too great. Huge dams and sluice gates have been installed to reduce the risk of flooding.

▲ Flooding usually occurs when rivers burst their banks after heavy rainfall.

▲ Low-lying cities such as Venice are at constant risk of flooding at high tides.

Which world cities are at risk from flooding?

Many of the world's cities are low lying and threatened by flooding. Bangkok, in Thailand, and Venice, in Italy, are typical old cities built by water because they relied on shipping. Both cities are built on mud and are gradually sinking, increasing the risk of flooding. Sea levels around the world are predicted to rise during this century, with the possibility of devastating flooding in places. Many cities in the Netherlands are below or at sea level. They are always in danger of flooding, although elaborate defenses help to protect them.

What are tornadoes?

Tornadoes are violent destructive whirlwinds whose force is concentrated into a much smaller area than that of a hurricane. They are very common in the central United States, where they cause enormous damage. Tornadoes travel across the land at high speed, and the roaring noise they make can be heard 25 miles away. A tornado happens when huge masses of clouds moving in different directions meet. The air begins to spin in a spiral, and a funnel of twisting air reaches out towards the ground. The low pressure in the funnel sucks up soil, dust and anything else it touches – even cattle.

The eye of the storm

What would you see inside the center of a hurricane? If you stood in this area, called the eye of the hurricane, you would be in for a surprise. After the violent winds and torrential rain pass over, the wind suddenly drops. A wall of dark churning clouds, hundreds of yards high, surrounds you. There are light breezes and the sun shines brightly. But you don't have long to enjoy this peaceful sunny weather, because as the hurricane continues its destructive path, it carries the eye with it. You will soon be enveloped in the storm once again.

❓ How big are hurricanes?

Hurricanes can measure between 200 and 300 miles across. They travel at speeds of 10 to 15 mph, growing larger and stronger as they move. Usually they travel west, then swing east as they reach cooler regions, before gradually dying out. Repeated hurricanes occur during the storm season, and there may be as many as 15 in a single year. In the U.S.A., the National Weather Service tracks hurricanes coming out of the Caribbean and the Gulf of Mexico. It forecasts the time when they will reach land and the strength of the accompanying wind.

◂ Tornadoes are a regular meteorological event in the south central states of the U.S.A. They cause huge damage in a narrow strip as they pass over the land.

❓ How are hurricanes formed?

Hurricanes are powerful tropical storms that can cause serious damage. They form near the equator, where warm, moist air rises, drawing in cooler air below. The air moves in a spiral, eventually forming a whirling mass. Rising warm air continues to cool and drop down in the center of the spiral to repeat the process. The winds inside a hurricane travel at speeds up to 124 mph. Hurricanes form in the Atlantic Ocean, passing over the West Indies and the southern United States. Similar storms in the Pacific Ocean are called typhoons. In the Indian Ocean, they are called cyclones.

▴ Enormous hurricanes sweep across the tropical oceans and over the land, causing flooding and devastation.

❓ What is a tsunami?

Tsunamis are tidal waves that are often caused by an undersea earthquake. Usually there is some warning of a tsunami because scientists can detect the seismic waves caused by the earthquake. The tsunami rushes along at up to 600 mph, building into a wall of water 30 yards high as it approaches land. Tsunamis are most common in earthquake zones, particularly around Japan.

Another form of tsunami is called a storm surge, in which giant waves are whipped up by a storm. In 1970, a storm surge and cyclone hit Bangladesh, killing 266,000 people. It returned again in 1985, killing another 10,000 people.

❓ How fast can the wind blow?

The fastest wind speed ever recorded was measured on a mountaintop in New Hampshire, U.S.A. It reached 371 mph. However, the wind inside a tornado probably blows much faster.
Wind speed is measured according to the Beaufort scale, which was invented in 1805 by a British admiral. On this scale, the strength of the wind is measured by a series of numbers from 0 to 12. Wind speed 0 means that the air is calm; wind speed 9 is a gale strong enough to damage houses. A wind of 12 on the Beaufort scale means a hurricane of over 70 mph.

Ice and Snow

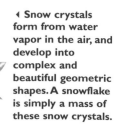

Why does snow fall?

Snow forms when water vapor inside a cloud freezes into tiny crystals. The water vapor usually crystallizes around a tiny dust particle called a nucleus, and the snow crystal continues to grow. Crystals of snow clump together to form snowflakes, which fall from the clouds. As many as 100 snow crystals group together to form a 1-inch snowflake. Snow crystals are very beautiful in form. They are flat and six-sided and can grow in the shape of elaborate stars.

▼ Glaciers have shaped most of the world's highest mountains, carving out huge valleys. The lakes that are characteristic of mountainous areas are formed from flooded glacial valleys that become dammed by debris as the glacier melts.

What is the snow line?

The snow line marks out the area above which a mountain is permanently covered with snow. Because it gets colder as you move higher up, the snow will never thaw on a high mountain. However, the snow line moves higher up during the summer when some of the snow melts. The snow line is close to ground level in cold regions, but it is very high near the equator where the air is much warmer.

Is there such a thing as red snow?

Red snow is found in many parts of the world, when tiny plants grow over the snow and ice. Microscopic algae growing on the surface of snow and ice can give it a red color. This rare event happens when the weather warms up slightly, and the algae that have been dormant throughout the cold period suddenly start to grow again.

What are glaciers?

Glaciers are large masses of ice that form on land and move slowly under their own weight. They are found in cold mountainous places or polar regions. Some glaciers are huge continuous sheets of ice, such as those covering Antarctica and Greenland. But most are rivers of ice that move slowly through valleys until they melt and become rivers. Such glaciers are common in the Himalayas, Alps, and Rocky Mountains. Because of its enormous weight, a glacier scrapes off large amounts of rock and debris, wearing away the valley floor and sides until it carves out a deep 'U-shaped' valley. Glaciers formed the deep fjords that line the coast of Norway.

glacier

debris carried by glacier

deposited debris

Frozen

Glaciers and ice sheets sometimes give up their secrets centuries later. Thawing ice has revealed the bodies of people who fell into crevasses hundreds of years ago. The ice has preserved their clothes and their internal organs. Even more astonishing are the bodies of mammoths found occasionally in the permafrost under Alaska and Siberia. Scientists are trying to extract their DNA so they can study these extinct beasts in minute detail.

How big are icebergs?

Some icebergs are bigger than an entire country. The biggest iceberg ever recorded was larger than Belgium, with an area of 12,090 square miles. These giant icebergs break away from the polar ice sheets when the rise and fall of the tide cracks the ice.

▾ For centuries, icebergs have been feared as a hazard to shipping, culminating in the famous sinking of the *Titanic*. Now meteorological aircraft and space satellites plot the path of drifting icebergs so ships can be warned of their presence.

How does frost break up rocks?

Frost can shatter rocks, making it one of the most important causes of erosion in cold regions. Water seeps into small cracks in rocks and freezes at night, when frost appears. As water freezes, it expands slightly, opening up cracks in the rock until parts of it flake away. This process continues until large masses of rock are broken up. It is the cause of the piles of shattered rock, or scree, that are commonly found at the foot of mountains. You can see the same process at work when a clay flowerpot left in the garden in winter begins to flake and crack.

Why do icebergs float?

Ice floats because it is lighter than water. Most objects shrink when they get cold, but when water freezes it expands slightly. In this way, ice becomes lighter than water. It is only slightly lighter however, and so nine-tenths of a floating iceberg lie under the water.

Where does most snow fall?

Snow can fall wherever the weather is very cold, and it falls throughout the year in the Arctic and Antarctic.

Most snow falls in temperate climates during the winter, especially in the Alps in Italy and Switzerland and in the Rocky Mountains in the U.S.A. In fact, almost every mountain range is associated with heavy snowfalls. Snow can even fall on the equator on mountains more than 3 miles high, where the air is very cold.

How thick is the ice at the South Pole?

The thickest ice at the South Pole is 5,251 yards deep — that's ten times the height of a tall skyscraper. The ice covers a huge area of 5.5 million square miles, which is bigger than the whole of Europe. However, the land area under the ice is much smaller because the ice sheet extends out over the sea. Antarctica contains 90 percent of all the ice on the Earth. Scientists have calculated that should all this ice melt sea levels would rise by 66 yards, causing worldwide flooding.

Fossils

What are fossils?

Fossils are the traces of ancient animals and plants found buried in rock. Sometimes a fossil retains the shape and structure of the hard parts of an animal, such as fossilized dinosaur bones. These are not the original bones, because minerals have replaced them over millions of years, but they have the same shape. Other fossils are just the impression of an animal or plant, created when the plant or animal was buried in mud that has gradually solidified into rock. Even footprints of animals such as dinosaurs have been preserved.

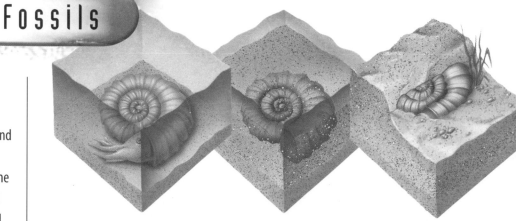

▲ When an organism dies, the soft parts rot away.

▲ The hard shell is covered with a layer of silt.

▲ A hard mineral fossil is gradually formed.

How old are fossils?

Ancient history has been divided up into eras, which are periods of time identified by the fossilized forms of life from that period. The oldest era, called the Palaeozoic, contains fossils ranging from many primitive life forms up to some of the earliest land-dwelling animals. During this era, fish, amphibians, and early reptiles appeared. The Mesozoic era was the age of giant reptiles, when dinosaurs walked the Earth. The Cenozoic era, in which we still live, is the age of mammals and birds. All fossils can be placed in these eras, which are subdivided further into smaller periods.

▸ **The characteristic fossils found in different periods measure geological time. Most primitive organisms lived in the Palaeozoic Period, dinosaurs predominated in the Mesozoic Period, and modern life forms such as mammals and birds developed and thrived in the Cenozoic Period.**

How are fossils formed?

Fossils result from the death of an animal millions of years ago. The soft parts rot quickly, and the bones or shell are scattered by scavenging animals. Some of these remains are buried in mud or sand. If they are not disturbed, more mud is deposited until the remains are deeply buried. Under great pressure from deposits above, the mud eventually compacts into sedimentary rock.

The fossil of a complete animal is a very rare find. Unless the animal fell into mud or was buried, its remains would have been eaten by other animals. This is the reason why fossils of small parts of an animal are much more common.

Period		Era
QUATERNARY		CENOZOIC 65 million years ago–present
PLIOCENE		
MIOCENE		
OLIGOCENE		
PALAEOCENE AND EOCENE		
CRETACEOUS		MESOZOIC 240–65 million years ago
JURASSIC		
TRIASSIC		
PERMIAN		PALAEOZOIC 590–240 million years ago
CARBONIFEROUS		
DEVONIAN		
SILURIAN		
ORDOVICIAN		
CAMBRIAN		

? What are trilobites?

Trilobites are common fossils of extinct arthropods (animals with jointed legs). These creatures first appeared in the Cambrian period 540 million years ago, and they died out 245 million years ago. They have no modern relatives. Trilobites were flattish creatures with many legs, and looked rather like a sowbug. They were marine creatures that survived for millions of years. No one knows why they became extinct.

▸ **Trilobites were once among the most abundant animals on Earth. They lived only in the sea, and survived for millions of years, evolving into some strangely shaped forms before they suddenly became extinct.**

? Why did prehistoric animals become extinct?

There are many opinions about why extinctions occurred. Many people believe that it was the result of asteroids or meteorites striking the Earth. There is evidence of ancient impacts caused by asteroids or meteorites, and some of these seem to coincide with the disappearance of some prehistoric animals. One such event was the impact that formed the Gulf of Mexico. Some scientists believe this event led to the extinction of the dinosaurs.

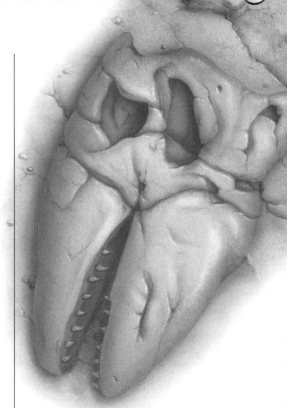

▲ **Fossils provide us with fascinating information about prehistoric life.**

? What are "living fossils"?

Many animals and plants living today remain almost unchanged after millions of years. Most of these survivors are small sea creatures, such as shellfish and worms. Coelacanths, however, are primitive fish that were thought to be the ancestors of reptiles.

? What is coal?

Coal is formed from the remains of plants that died and were buried millions of years ago. Gradually the weight of sedimentary rock crushed the plants. Hot rock around these deposits created changes that left only carbon, which we now dig out as coal.

? What are ammonites?

An ammonite is a very common fossil. It looks like a shellfish but the fossil is actually the shell of an extinct relative of the octopus and squid. The ammonite's shell is coiled in a flat spiral, and can be almost 2 yards in diameter. Ammonites lived for many millions of years, but like other extinct animals they disappeared quite suddenly.

The fossil hunters

Fossils used to be found accidentally by people working in mines or quarries. Sometimes they became exposed by erosion, and could be seen sticking out of cliff faces. Geologists are now able to identify those rock formations likely to contain fossils. More and more fossils are being found by properly organized expeditions.

Large numbers of new types of fossil are now being found in Mongolia and China. There, fossil hunters have unearthed what are probably the ancestors of modern birds.

❓ What is global warming?

Since the late 1800s, the temperature of the Earth's surface has risen, and it is predicted that this increase will continue. This phenomenon, known as global warming, is thought to result from human activities. By burning wood and fossil fuels such as coal, we have increased the amount of carbon dioxide in the atmosphere by 25 percent. At the same time, the average temperature of the world's surface has increased by about 2.6 °F. It seems likely that there is a connection between this temperature increase and increased levels of greenhouse gases, such as carbon dioxide.

❓ What causes air pollution?

Air pollution is mostly a result of human activity. The exhaust from motor vehicles is one of the main pollutants. It contains greenhouse gases that are thought to contribute to global warming. Exhaust gases also contain substances such as sulphur and nitrogen oxides that can damage the lungs. Recently, vast clouds of choking smoke have appeared over parts of Asia. The smoke comes from the rainforest fires that clear land for farming.

❓ What is acid rain?

Rain containing dissolved acids falls to the ground, damaging trees, crops, and other wildlife, as well as harming water supplies. Acid rain is caused by air pollutants such as nitric and sulphuric acids, which are released by burning coal, oil, or petrol. Damage due to acid rain has destroyed huge areas of trees in North America, Europe, and parts of Asia, and has had serious effects on forestry. Attempts are being made to limit the damage by removing nitrogen and sulphur from fuels before they are burned, and by reducing emissions from factories.

▾ **Huge amounts of air pollution are produced as industries develop. In many countries, industrial pollution is now controlled, but it still causes huge damage to health and the environment in many developing countries.**

❓ What was the Chernobyl disaster?

In 1986, an explosion in a nuclear power station in the Ukraine was the worst ever nuclear accident. Large amounts of radioactive material were released into the atmosphere, and many people died. Large areas of the Ukraine and neighboring Belarus were contaminated, and there has been a huge increase in the number of cancers and abnormal births in the region. The radioactive fallout was carried by the wind right across Europe into Sweden and the UK. It is still too dangerous to live in the area around Chernobyl because of the continuing high levels of radioactivity.

❓ Can we push back the sea?

The action of the waves continually erodes beaches and cliffs, so sea walls are often constructed to protect them. It is very expensive to control the action of the sea in this way. Much of the Netherlands originally lay under the North Sea. For centuries, the Dutch have built enormous dykes (banks) to hold the water back. They have also reclaimed land from the sea, increasing the size of their country by almost one-third.

Hole in one

In the 1970s, scientists discovered a gap in the protective ozone layer around the Earth. Ozone, a form of oxygen, filters out more than 90 percent of the sun's damaging ultraviolet rays. So, when a gap in the ozone layer was found over Antarctica, scientists were very concerned. Increased ultraviolet radiation can cause skin cancer. The hole in the ozone layer has been blamed on our use of chemicals called chlorofluorocarbons (CFCs). They were widely used in refrigerators, freezers, and aerosol cans. Although the use of CFCs is now heavily restricted, it may take years before the ozone layer repairs itself.

CFCs trap heat, adding to the effects of global warming.

Heat from the sun hits the Earth.

◄ Most human activities produce some form of pollution, and the hole in the ozone layer is thought to have been caused by refrigerant gases released into the atmosphere. This may contribute to global warming.

? What is irrigation

Irrigation is a method of supplying water to crops artificially. It was used in ancient Egypt, and possibly even earlier. Water is pumped out of rivers or wells and fed into channels or canals that carry it for long distances. Modern irrigation systems are usually very extensive.

Elaborate irrigation was used centuries ago in some parts of the world. Native Americans cut long canals along the foot of the Andes to irrigate their crops, which they grew on artificial terraces. Even today, many Asian hillsides are covered with flooded terraces where rice is grown. The terraces are irrigated by complicated canal systems.

? What are the effects of deforestation?

Many areas of tropical rainforest are burned to provide farmland, but the effects of this deforestation can be disastrous. After the forest is burned, new fertile ground is exposed. But after one or two years, this new land is exhausted. The clearing process is repeated, eventually destroying the forest and its wildlife. The bare ground becomes eroded because there is little vegetation to slow the run-off of rainwater. The water strips away the topsoil, dumping it into rivers. The end-result is useless, infertile land that is prone to flash floods. Also, the smoke from burning forests contributes to global air pollution.

? Can rivers run backwards?

In the former Soviet Union, the direction of several rivers was diverted or even reversed to provide water for irrigation. Some of the rivers running into the Aral Sea were diverted northwards in a huge water management project to irrigate land north of the region. In some cases, the direction of their flow was reversed. The result was that the Aral Sea began to dry up because no more river water flowed into it.

? How do dams affect the environment?

Most dams are built to meet people's growing demand for water, but sometimes dams cause unforeseen environmental damage. Dams are usually built across valley entrances, creating enormous reservoirs of water. Some are built to provide water for hydroelectric power stations while others control the flow of rivers that are liable to flood. Unfortunately, the best places to build dams are usually in the most picturesque parts of the countryside.

The Aswan High Dam was built to control the flow of the River Nile. However, it has prevented the river's annual flooding, which covered agricultural land with silt.

▲ **Deforestation can have an unforeseen outcome on the ecology of a region, and its effects may be irreversible.**

❓ What was the Earth like when it was formed?

The Earth had probably existed for around 3,000 million years before the first signs of life appeared. As it cooled after forming from a ball of hot gases, the Earth would have been a relatively smooth sphere. It was covered with shallow seas that contained a mixture of dissolved chemicals, and was surrounded by an atmosphere of mixed gases. The atmosphere was full of swirling clouds of vapor, which probably caused huge electrical storms.

❓ When did life first appear?

The first signs of life are thought to have appeared about 3,000 million years ago. Some rocks from this time contain substances that are characteristic of life, although fossils appear from much later. Scientists believe that primitive life forms altered the original poisonous composition of the atmosphere, eventually releasing the oxygen that we need to survive. The seas were probably once filled with a mixture of chemicals from which life may have developed. It is more likely, however, that life first appeared in areas such as those around undersea vents. These first forms of life would have been bacteria and microscopic blue-green algae.

❓ What is an ice age?

Ice ages were periods when large parts of the Earth's surface were covered by sheets of ice. Each ice age has lasted about 100,000 years, with gaps between of up to 20,000 years when the weather was warmer and the ice melted. The last ice age ended about 12,000 years ago. Ice ages appear in groups in geological time, each lasting for 20 to 50 million years. The oldest known glacial periods were as long as 2.3 billion years ago. A minor ice age began in the 1500s and lasted for 300 years, during which glaciers were more widespread than at any time for thousands of years.

▸ **The primeval Earth was a violent place. Its poisonous atmosphere was bombarded by meteors and filled with fumes from erupting volcanoes. This mass of seething chemicals gave rise to primitive life. It was the presence of these life forms that began the changes to the atmosphere that eventually produced the Earth we know.**

Gigantic waterfall!

More than five million years ago, the Mediterranean Sea was a dry basin. Then, movements in the Earth's crust opened up the Straits of Gibraltar between the land masses of Europe and Africa. The waters of the Atlantic Ocean poured through the gap, flooding the basin. The result was the creation of a gigantic waterfall, at least 2,500 feet high, which let through so much water that the whole of the Mediterranean filled up in a few years.

Poisonous air

The Earth's original atmosphere was very poisonous. It contained almost no oxygen. It consisted of gases such as hydrogen, helium, methane and ammonia, as well as carbon dioxide. It would have been impossible to breathe in such an atmosphere. Lightning and the sun's radiation caused chemical reactions in these gases, producing some of the substances characteristic of life, and this may have triggered the development of the first primitive life forms.

▲ Floodwater rapidly washes away fertile soil, and erosion can cause the loss of much fertile land.

How has the Earth been reshaped?

Erosion is one of the most powerful ways in which the Earth's surface has been altered. Moving ice and flowing water wear away the surface of rocks and cut out valleys, as well as wearing down the peaks of mountains. Along the coast, tides and wave action wear away exposed cliffs, and currents carry away sand and mud to be deposited elsewhere. The tides and windblown sand polish and wear away rocks and pebbles.

Why did the world's climate change?

The appearance of living things changed the Earth's atmosphere, providing the conditions for climate change. The first living things were plantlike creatures. They used the sun's energy to change carbon dioxide and water into sugars, which they used for food, and oxygen, which they released into the atmosphere. Some of this oxygen turned into ozone, forming the layer that now protects us from the sun's ultraviolet radiation.

What effect did the ice age have on the world and its animals?

During an ice age, the enormous weight of the ice sheet presses the underlying rocks down, while those around the edges rise to form hills and valleys. The constant scouring action of glaciers shapes the Earth's surface, wearing away complete mountain ranges. In an ice age, animals are forced to migrate to warmer areas. The ones that cannot adapt, for example mammoths and the woolly rhinoceroses, become extinct. The ice sheets on Greenland and in the Antarctic are the remains of the most recent ice age.

How do we know that the climate has changed?

In more recent times, geologists and palaeontologists have been able to make more accurate measurements of the age of ancient rocks. Trees produce a new 'ring' every year, and these can be measured and counted. The width of the ring shows how well the tree grew in any year, reflecting climatic conditions at that time. The rings of even partly fossilized trees buried in bogs can be measured, and these measurements provide accurate records of climate changes over the past 750,000 years. By measuring the radioactivity of once living material, scientists can make accurate measurements up to 40,000 years ago.

▲ Mammoths lived in cool climates, and as the glaciers and cold weather advanced, they moved farther south. Their remains are found in huge numbers in the tundra of Alaska and Siberia.

How was oil formed?

Most scientists think that oil was formed from the remains of tiny plants and animals that inhabited the seas millions of years ago. When these creatures died, their remains were buried in layers of rock. Substances in their bodies gradually altered to form oil. Other scientists disagree and believe that oil formed from carbon-containing materials that were trapped inside the rock when the Earth was formed. Oil is found in rocks buried beneath all of the continents, and beneath the shallow parts of the oceans. More than half of the world's known oil resources are in the Middle East.

? What are tectonic plates?

The Earth's crust is made up of about 30 huge plates that float on the semi–liquid mantle surrounding the Earth's core. There are currents and movements in the mantle, so these plates move very slowly in relation to each other – about 4 inches per year on average. The floor of the Pacific Ocean is one enormous plate. Some of the plates carrying continents also carry parts of the ocean floor. The thickness of the plates varies from 5 miles to 125 miles.

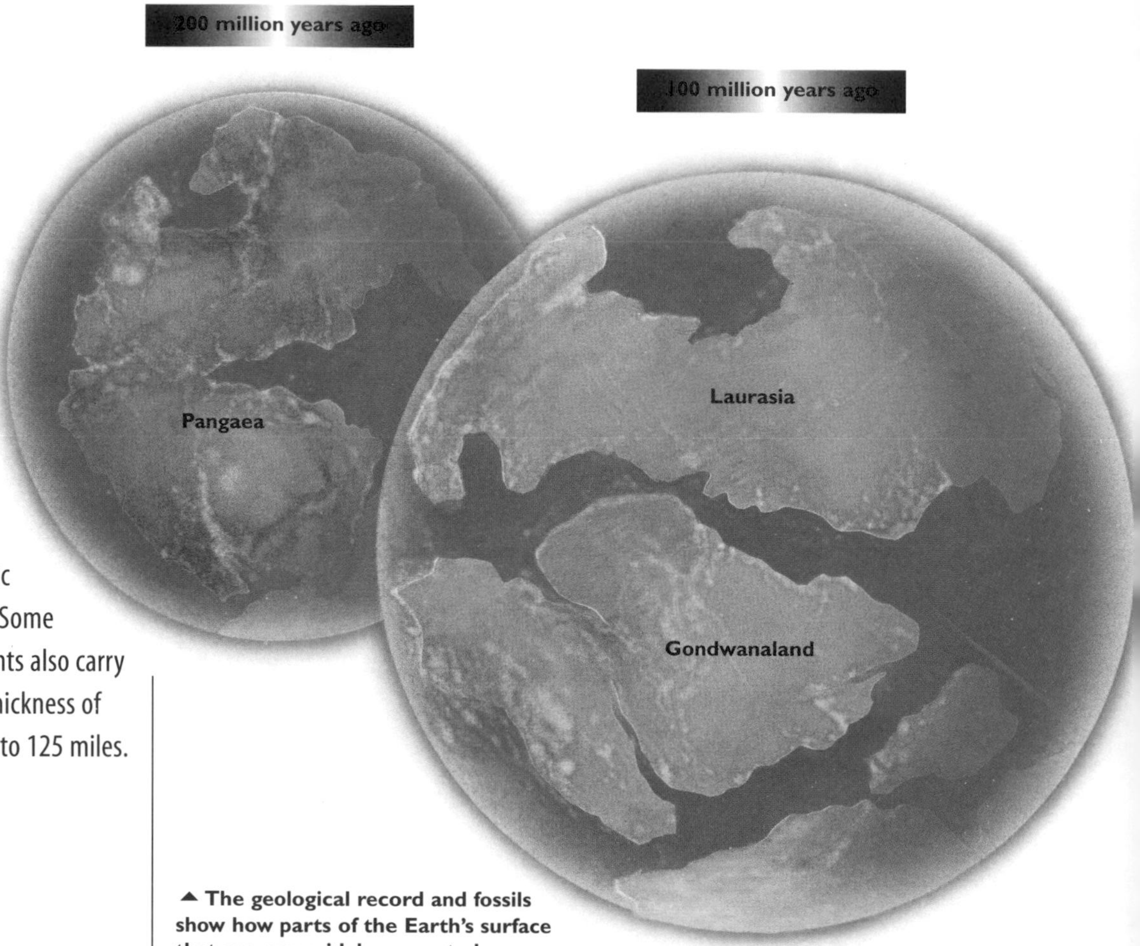

? What causes earthquakes?

Earthquakes are evidence of movement of the tectonic plates that carry the continents. Most of the areas where earthquakes take place are along the edges of plates. Friction holds the plate edges together for a while, but continuing movement means that huge stresses build up. The tension is suddenly released when the plates shift sharply, but this causes an earthquake. There are other causes of earthquakes, but they all involve sudden movement of the crust along a fault or crack. The energy released in an earthquake is enormous – as much as 10,000 times the power released by the world's first atomic bomb.

200 million years ago

100 million years ago

Pangaea

Laurasia

Gondwanaland

▲ The geological record and fossils show how parts of the Earth's surface that are now widely separated were once locked together in a super-continent. The theory of continental drift explains why animals such as marsupials, for instance, live in both South America and Australia.

? What is continental drift?

The continents are able to drift about because they are carried on the tectonic plates that make up the Earth's crust. This moving process is incredibly slow, but it has been going on for hundreds of millions of years. In this way, the process of continental drift is constantly reshaping the Earth's surface.

Dam destruction!

Both mining and tunneling operations are known to have caused earthquakes in areas that are already under tension due to movements in the Earth's crust. The most important artificial cause of earthquakes is the construction of dams. These can hold back enormous amounts of water. The weight of this water has caused earthquakes near the High Aswan Dam in Egypt and the Hoover Dam in the U.S.A. Fortunately, these were not serious.

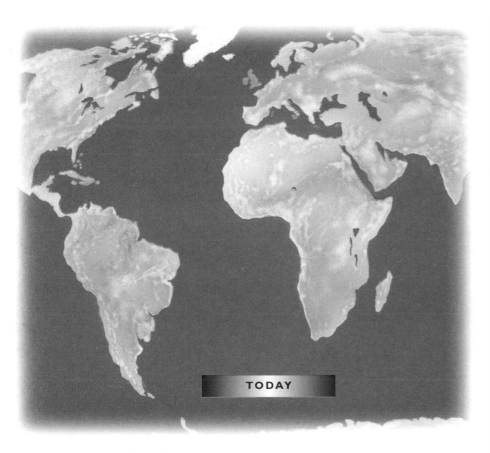

TODAY

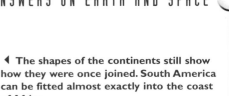

◀ **The shapes of the continents still show how they were once joined. South America can be fitted almost exactly into the coast of Africa.**

❓ Can animals predict an earthquake?

There is a lot of evidence that mammals and birds are able to detect the onset of an earthquake, but no one knows how they do this. For centuries, observers have said that animals seem to give advance warning of earthquakes by changes in their behavior. It has been suggested that they may be able to hear the faint creaking and groaning noise of the crust as it stretches. Or they may be able to smell gases released along the fault line as tension builds up.

❓ How is the strength of an earthquake measured?

The strength and location of earthquakes are measured by an instrument called a seismograph, which can detect ground movements. Sometimes the movements from an earthquake can be detected thousands of miles away. The Richter scale measures their strength. An earthquake measuring two on the Richter scale is very slight and would probably not be detected, but one measuring more than seven will destroy buildings.

The most severe earthquake ever recorded, in Chile, measured 9.5 on the Richter scale. In 1811 and 1812, the U.S.A.s most powerful earthquakes changed the course of the Mississippi River.

❓ What is the San Andreas Fault?

The San Andreas Fault is a long crack in the Earth's crust that extends 600 miles through California, in the U.S.A. It runs along the edges of the tectonic plates carrying the Pacific Ocean and North America. These plates have shifted about 180 miles over the past 15 million years. They continue to move about 2 inches each year, building up enormous stresses in the crust. Along the fault line, the ground bulges, cracks open up, and roads and railways develop a noticeable kink. The San Andreas Fault is carefully monitored, because it is expected to slip at any time.

❓ What happened in the great San Francisco earthquake?

The last time the San Andreas Fault slipped, it caused the worst disaster in San Francisco's history. The earthquake happened in April 1906. It devastated the city by damaging buildings and causing uncontrollable fires, which raged for several days. At least 3,000 people were killed, and 250,000 people lost their homes. People fear that this disaster may be repeated, because reconstruction of the city has taken place across the San Andreas Fault. However, scientists constantly monitor the area for signs of earthquake activity.

⑦ Who were the earliest explorers?

About 50,000 years ago, the first explorers sailed from Southeast Asia to colonize Australia and New Guinea, which were joined together at that time. Later, people crossed from Siberia into Alaska, passing over a land bridge that has since disappeared. By 10,000 years ago, people had migrated to all parts of North and South America.

Around 3,000 years ago, people from Southeast Asia began to explore the Pacific. They sailed in double canoes, navigating by the position of the stars, and eventually settled all of the Pacific islands.

⑦ When was the first voyage around the world?

In 1519, a small fleet of ships left Spain led by a Portuguese sailor called Ferdinand Magellan. Three years later, his ship returned alone after sailing all round the world. Like most of his sailors, Magellan himself did not return, having been killed during the voyage.

⑦ Who found America by mistake?

In 1492 Christopher Columbus set out to find a new route to India and the Far East, in order to open up trading links for Spain. He arrived at the Bahamas, off the American coast, where he mistakenly called the native people "Indian".

⑦ Who first explored the South Seas?

Although other explorers had briefly passed through the region, Captain James Cook, a British explorer, was the first person to explore thoroughly the South Pacific region, including Australia and New Zealand.

He sailed there between 1768 and 1779, and soon realized that another great continent lay farther to the south. This was Antarctica, but Cook never set foot there. He was eventually murdered by local people when he visited Hawaii.

⑦ Who never noticed Australia?

In 1642, a Dutch navigator called Abel Tasman reached New Zealand and Tasmania, an island south of Australia. During this journey Tasman sailed all the way round Australia without realizing that it was there. He did not think that New Zealand was worthy of further investigation.

⑦ Who was Ibn Battuta?

The Arab explorer Ibn Battuta spent 30 years travelling around Asia and Africa during the 1300s. He visited Persia (now Iran), India, Russia, Mongolia, China, Egypt and the West African country of Mali.

⑦ Did the Vikings reach America?

Recent archaeological studies have shown that legends about Viking colonies in America were true.

In AD1000 a Viking called Leif Ericsson reached Labrador, in North America. He then travelled southwards until he came to warmer lands. He started a small colony that survived for a while before being driven out by Native Americans.

⑦ Who found a land route from Europe to China?

The first famous European traveler was Marco Polo, a Venetian merchant who travelled to China in the 13th century. He met the Chinese emperor, Kublai Khan, and travelled widely throughout China. On his return Polo wrote a book called Description of the World, in which he gave detailed information about China and the other countries in which he had traveled.

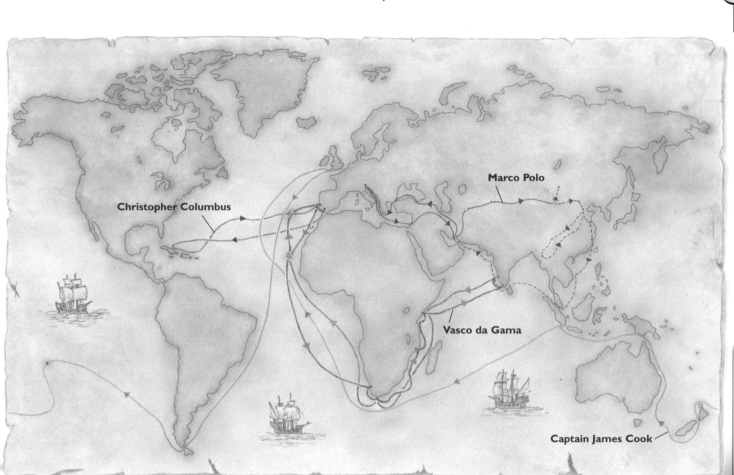

▲ Marco Polo began his voyage to China in 1271. He reached his destination, but parts of his journey (shown with a dotted line) are in doubt.

▲ Christopher Columbus discovered Cuba and Haiti in 1492. Despite making three further voyages, he never actually reached what is now the United States.

▲ In 1497 Vasco da Gama set out to find a sea route to India by sailing around the southern tip of Africa.

▲ Captain James Cook made three voyages to the South Seas. During his first voyage he discovered Australia.

❔ What is the "orange peel" effect?

It is not possible to draw the curved surface of the globe accurately on a flat sheet of paper. This problem puzzled mapmakers for many years. In 1569, Gerardus Mercator showed how to convert the rounded shape of the world into a cylindrical shape, which could be unrolled to make a flat map. However, this can distort the size of countries in the far north and south. Dividing the Earth into "orange peel" segments gives a truer image of the size of countries.

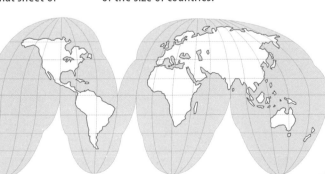

❔ Who made the first maps?

The earliest known maps were made in Babylon on clay tablets, as long ago as 2300BC. Some Egyptian drawings and paintings found in tombs are almost as old. The Greek mathematician Ptolemy (AD90–168) produced an enormous eight-volume guide to geography and map-making called The Guide to Geography. It was followed carefully by map-makers for almost 1,000 years.

Science

When you switch on a light, you set in motion a chain of events that is seldom considered. Do you know why the filament in a light bulb glows? How does electricity reach your home, and where does it come from? Science is behind almost every object or process we use in daily life.

Everyday technology has been developed by scientists who discovered the basic principles that govern the world around us. By trial and error, people learned how to smelt iron; fathomed out how water wheels could be used to provide power; and realized how a whole range of simple technologies could be put into practice. Now the basic principles of science allow technology to be planned and put into use to suit our needs. For example, no one could have made a computer by mistake. It was necessary to decide what was needed and then to design the circuitry that allowed the device to be built.

Science is a way of understanding our world and the universe, and taking advantage of its available resources in a logical manner. Just think how much we rely on science every day. When we travel by air in a plane built from millions of parts, we trust that all of them will work properly. In the same way, people expect their cars to start on a cold, wet morning; their CD players to reproduce perfect music; and immensely complicated computer games to work so well that you can imagine you are actually part of the action. None of these things are possible without science and the development of technology, which is constantly progressing.

? Can we see atoms?

Atoms are the smallest pieces of matter. They are the tiniest particles into which a substance can be divided without changing into something else. Atoms actually consist almost entirely of open space, in which tiny particles orbit the central particle, or nucleus. The particles travel so fast that they seem to be solid.

Atoms are so tiny that the smallest particle visible to the naked eye would contain about one million billion atoms. Despite their tiny size, atoms can be seen individually under very powerful electron microscopes.

? Is an atom the smallest type of particle?

There are many smaller particles, and more are being discovered. These very small particles are known as subatomic particles. The electron revolving around the atom, and the neutron and the proton that make up the nucleus, are all subatomic particles.

Another type of subatomic particle is the positron. It is the same as an electron but with a positive electrical charge. If a positron collides with an electron they are both destroyed and form a shower of even smaller particles. Even neutrons and protons are thought to consist of even smaller particles, called quarks. Photons, gluons, and bosons are other forms of subatomic particles, and there may be as many as 100 different types altogether.

? What is at the center of an atom?

The center of an atom is its nucleus, which has shells of electrons hurtling around it. The nucleus consists of protons, which are electrically charged particles, and neutrons, which have no electrical charge at all. The nuclei of similar atoms usually contain the same numbers of electrons and protons, but sometimes the number of neutrons varies. These atoms with different numbers of neutrons are known as isotopes.

? How much space is in an atom?

Atoms consist almost entirely of empty space, because almost all their mass is concentrated into the nucleus. If an atom were enlarged to the size of a football, its nucleus would still be too small for you to see it with the naked eye.

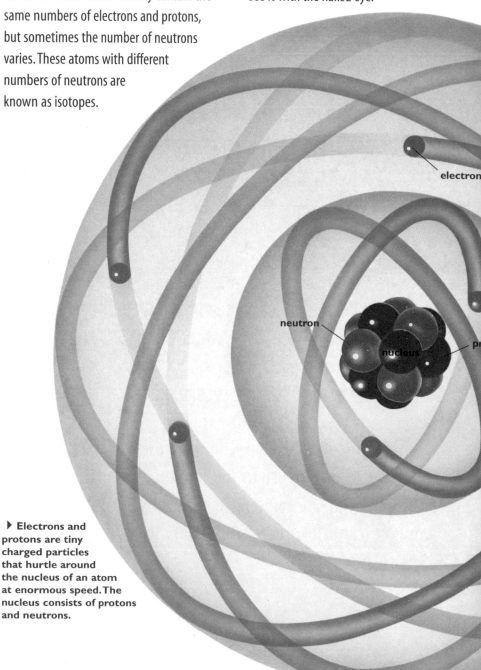

▶ Electrons and protons are tiny charged particles that hurtle around the nucleus of an atom at enormous speed. The nucleus consists of protons and neutrons.

electron

neutron

nucleus

pro

What are electrons?

Electrons are the very tiny particles that travel around the nucleus of an atom at incredibly high speed. They carry a negative electrical charge.

The circling electrons are arranged in different layers, called shells. If there are many electrons circling around the atom, and the outer shell is full, the atom will not react with other substances. If the outer shell is not full, the atom can gain or lose its electrons as it reacts chemically with other atoms around it.

electron orbit

Hooked up

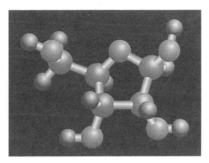

Atoms become linked to other atoms by electrical bonds, which work rather like chemical hooks. Some atoms only carry one of these hooks, while others have many. Atoms with many hooks can build up with other atoms into complicated molecules or chemical compounds.

What is 'Quantum mechanics?'

Quantum mechanics helps us to understand how energy is used or released by atoms. Negatively charged electrons circle about the positively charged nucleus of the atom. They stay in the same orbit, until this is disturbed, and each orbit has its own level of energy. If more energy is added when the atom is heated or when light shines on it, the electron jumps out to another orbit, absorbing the extra energy. Then when it drops back again to its original orbit, it releases this energy as heat or light. This tiny packet of energy is called a quantum. Heisenberg's Uncertainty Principle states that it is not possible to measure exactly where a subatomic particle is and how fast it is moving because any attempt to measure it will disturb the particle and change its characteristics.

What are molecules?

The smallest part of a substance that can exist on its own is a molecule. This consists of anything between two and several thousand atoms, which are linked together by chemical bonds. Sometimes the molecule consists of identical atoms, and it is called an element. When a group of different types of atoms is connected together in this way, it forms a compound.

The way in which the atoms become linked depends on the types of chemical bonds. This, in turn, determines the shape of the molecule and its chemical properties.

Who discovered the structure of the atom?

Niels Bohr, a Danish physicist, was awarded the Nobel Prize in 1922 for his discovery of the structure of the atom. He went on to help develop the atomic bomb in 1943.

What is antimatter?

Antimatter is like normal matter, but it is made up of particles that are exactly the opposite to those making up ordinary matter. A normal electron, for example, has a negative charge, but in anti-matter, the corresponding particle has a positive charge. Antimatter was first proposed in 1930, and it is now possible to make it in tiny amounts, using a machine called a particle accelerator. When antimatter and normal matter make contact, huge amounts of energy are released.

▼ The periodic table groups together elements with similar properties. It is arranged in order of increasing atomic number. This number depends upon the numbers of electrons and protons present in the element. From their position on the table, it is possible to predict the properties of an element or of a new compound made by combining two elements.

GROUPS OF ELEMENTS

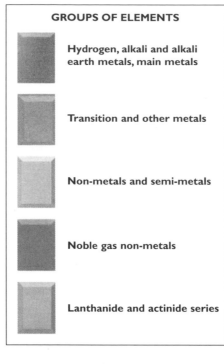

Hydrogen, alkali and alkali earth metals, main metals

Transition and other metals

Non-metals and semi-metals

Noble gas non-metals

Lanthanide and actinide series

⟨?⟩ What is the periodic table?

The periodic table is a list of all the elements, arranged in such a way that elements with similar properties are grouped together. Each element in the table is given a number, called an atomic number, which indicates the number of protons the atom has. (A single atom has the same number of protons as electrons.) Elements with the same number of electrons in their outer shells are grouped together in the table.

H hydrogen 1																	B boron 5
Li lithium 3	Be beryllium 4																
Na sodium 11	Mg magnesium 12																Al aluminium 13
K potassium 19	Ca calcium 20	Sc scandium 21	Ti titanium 22	V vanadium 23	Cr chromium 24	Mn manganese 25	Fe iron 26	Co cobalt 27	Ni nickel 28	Cu copper 29	Zn zinc 30	Ga gallium 31
Rb rubidium 37	Sr strontium 38	Y yttrium 39	Zr zirconium 40	Nb niobium 41	Mo molybdenum 42	Tc technetium 43	Ru ruthenium 44	Rh rhodium 45	Pd palladium 46	Ag silver 47	Cd cadmium 48	In indium 49
Cs caesium 55	Ba barium 56	Lu lutetium 71	Hf hafnium 72	Ta tantalum 73	W tungsten 74	Re rhenium 75	Os osmium 76	Ir iridium 77	Pt platinum 78	Au gold 79	Hg mercury 80	Ti thalium 81
Fr francium 87	Ra radium 88	Lr lawrencium 103	Rf rutherfordium 104	Db dubnium 105	Sg seaborgium 106	Bh bohrium 107	Hs hassium 108	Mt meitnerium 109	Uun ununnilium 110	Uuu unununium 111	Uub ununbium 112
		La lanthanum 57	Ce cerium 58	Pr praseodymium 59	Nd neodymium 60	Pm promethium 61	Sm samarium 62	Eu europium 63	Gd gadolinium 64	Tb terbium 65	Dy dysprosium 66	Ho holmium 67
		Ac actinium 89	Th thorium 90	Pa protactinium 91	U uranium 92	Np neptunium 93	Pu plutonium 94	Am americium 95	Cm curium 96	Bk berkelium 97	Cf californium 98	Es einsteinium 99

? How many different elements are there?

There are 92 elements that exist naturally, but it has been possible for scientists to create many more in the laboratory. These artificial elements are radioactive and they quickly decay or lose their radioactivity. Some exist for only a few seconds or less.

				He helium 2
C carbon 6	N nitrogen 7	O oxygen 8	F fluorine 9	Ne neon 10
Si silicon 14	P phosphorus 15	S sulphur 16	Cl chlorine 17	Ar argon 18
Ge germanium 32	As arsenic 33	Se selenium 34	Br bromine 35	Kr krypton 36
Sn tin 50	Sb antimony 51	Te tellurium 52	I iodine 53	Xe xenon 54
Pb lead 82	Bi bismuth 83	Po polonium 84	At astatine 85	Rn radon 86

Er erbium 68	Tm thulium 69	Yb ytterbium 70
Fm fermium 100	Md mendelevium 101	No nobelium 102

? Which are the lightest and heaviest elements?

Hydrogen is the lightest and simplest element, and its atomic number is 1. Uranium is the heaviest and its atomic number is 92 — indicating that it has 92 protons in each atom.

? What is radioactivity?

Radioactivity is a form of energy given off by some types of atoms with a high atomic number, such as uranium, radium, and plutonium. Some forms of radiation consist of protons and neutrons bound together, while other forms consist of electrons or other particles called positrons. As radiation is emitted, the loss of particles from the original atoms changes their properties to those of another atom with a lower atomic number.

? How is it possible to make new elements?

New elements are created by bombarding other elements with radiation in an atomic reactor. Scientists have made 16 artificial elements by bombarding uranium and other radioactive elements.

▲ Many pure elements occur in different forms. Carbon can be a black powder like soot, but it can also be crystals, like the hard grey graphite used in pencil 'leads,' or glassy crystals of diamonds.

? What are organic compounds?

Organic compounds always contain the element carbon. Carbon compounds often have a very complicated structure, and they are responsible for most of the chemical reactions that sustain life. Carbon is found in some very large molecules, such as those in proteins and plastics. It has proved relatively easy to manufacture many of these substances artificially.

? How does radiation change substances?

Radioactivity can contain large amounts of energy, which causes damage to matter, including living cells. These forms of radioactivity can knock electrons out of the atoms of a substance to produce ions, which have different properties.

? What are gases?

Matter exists in three states: solid, liquid, and gas. The molecules in all matter are in constant motion, and in a gas they are held together so loosely that they can move freely. Gas molecules move about rapidly and at random. This means that a gas will expand to fill any space it occupies. The molecules in a gas press against anything that restrains them, causing pressure. As a gas is heated, the molecules move further apart and move about more rapidly. If it is restricted in a container, the pressure will increase. If any gas is cooled sufficiently, it will condense into a liquid. This is why some of the outer planets of the solar system are composed of liquid methane and hydrogen.

? What are metals?

Almost 80 percent of all elements are metals. They can be distinguished from other elements because when cut, they reflect light and appear shiny. Metals also conduct heat and electricity. Most metals are malleable, which means that they can be beaten or molded into different shapes.

Most metals react with oxygen in the air, or with other kinds of elements, to form compounds. They are rarely found in the natural metallic state. However, gold is an exception because it does not react easily with other elements and is often found in its natural state as grains or nuggets. Mixtures of metals are called alloys.

? What is glass?

Glass forms when melted solid materials are cooled quickly, so that they do not produce crystals. There are many types of glass, but the transparent glass that is most familiar to us is a very useful material. It is resistant to most corrosive substances, and it is a very good electrical insulator and heat insulator. Glass is stronger than most metals, but because it is brittle, it shatters easily.

The most common forms of glass are made from a melted mixture of silica (sand), sodium oxide, and calcium oxide. Lead crystal is a form of glass in which the calcium oxide is replaced by lead oxide. The most heat-resistant glass can be made from pure silica.

Quicksilver

Mercury is the only metal that is a liquid at ordinary room temperatures. It is a bright, shiny color and flows rapidly when poured out of a container (this is why it used to be called 'quicksilver'). Mercury does not stick to glass, so it is used in thermometers to indicate the temperature.

Mercury compounds are often brightly colored and were once widely used in colored paints. However, mercury is an extremely poisonous substance and its use is now strictly controlled. Some other uses of mercury are in the manufacture of batteries and in medicine. Dentists still use a mixture of mercury and silver, in the form of amalgam, to fill cavities in teeth.

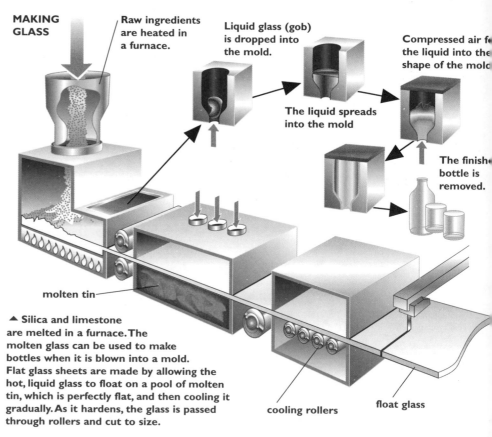

MAKING GLASS

Raw ingredients are heated in a furnace.

Liquid glass (gob) is dropped into the mold.

Compressed air f[...] the liquid into the shape of the mol[...]

The liquid spreads into the mold

The finish[...] bottle is removed.

molten tin

▲ Silica and limestone are melted in a furnace. The molten glass can be used to make bottles when it is blown into a mold. Flat glass sheets are made by allowing the hot, liquid glass to float on a pool of molten tin, which is perfectly flat, and then cooling it gradually. As it hardens, the glass is passed through rollers and cut to size.

cooling rollers

float glass

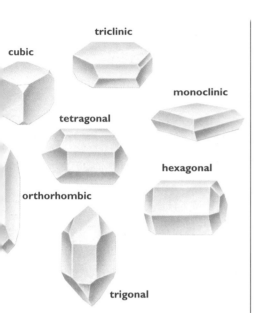

cubic

triclinic

monoclinic

tetragonal

hexagonal

orthorhombic

trigonal

▲ Crystals form from dissolved substances or when molten substances cool slowly. They form into regular geometric shapes, and the shape and color can be used to identify a substance.

How are crystals formed?

Crystals are solid substances that have their atoms arranged in regular patterns. Most naturally occurring substances form crystals under the right conditions, although they are not always apparent. Crystals form into regular geometric shapes, and crystals of the same substance or mixture of substances will always have the same regular appearance.

Crystals are formed from solutions or melted materials. As the solutions evaporate or the melted materials cool, their atoms are forced closer together, producing a crystal. This crystal gradually grows as the process continues. Some crystals grow into complicated and beautiful shapes, which are often brightly colored.

What happens when a chemical substance dissolves?

When sugar is stirred into water, it dissolves and forms a solution. This means that the solid sugar molecules have split apart and become distributed equally throughout the water, so that no particles can be seen. The warmer the water, the more sugar can be dissolved into the solution. There are some molecules that do not behave in this way. Fats and oils, for example, will not dissolve in water — they can be seen floating on it — although they will dissolve in some other types of liquid.

Solutions are not always liquids. Brass is a yellowish metal that is actually a solid solution containing copper and tin.

What is burning?

When a substance burns, there is a very rapid chemical reaction with oxygen in the air. This reaction generates heat and light, producing a flame. There are other forms of burning, too. Some metals burn in corrosive gases, for example. Explosions are a form of burning in which the reaction takes place extremely rapidly, releasing very large amounts of heat.

▶ Excess natural gas from oil wells and refineries is often burned off because it cannot economically be saved or used.

Can metals float in water?

Some very light metals such as lithium and calcium can float in water. They also react with the oxygen in water, releasing hydrogen. The similar (but heavier) metals, such as sodium and potassium, generate so much heat when they are dropped into water that the hydrogen they release burns on the water's surface.

What are plastics?

Plastics are synthetically produced materials that are capable of being molded and made into useful shapes such as bottles and flat sheets. They usually soften under heat and pressure so they can be forced into a mold. Some types of plastic are set into a hard solid form by the application of heat, causing a chemical reaction between the component substances.

Most plastics are light in weight, are good electrical insulators, and are tough enough to have many domestic and industrial uses.

? What happens when a liquid boils?

When a liquid is heated at a certain point, it begins to change to a gas, or vapor. This happens because at high temperatures the molecules in the liquid move faster, until they escape into the air. Light molecules escape more easily than heavy molecules, which means that heavy, thick liquids only boil at very high temperatures.

The boiling point of a liquid depends on the air pressure. The pressure becomes lower at altitude, so high up on a mountain slope, water boils at a much lower temperature than normal. Water boils at 212°F at sea level, but at only 162°F at an altitude of 10,000 feet.

? Why does my breath 'steam' in cold weather?

When water boils, the steam it produces is not visible while the water remains at boiling point. As the steam cools, it forms tiny droplets of water, making it look cloudy. This is called water vapor, which is what you see when your breath 'steams' in very cold weather. Explorers in the Arctic and Antarctic find that water vapor condenses and freezes to form ice around their nostrils and mouths.

▼ A geyser is a spectacular natural phenomenon, caused when underground water is boiled by volcanic activity and the expanding steam shoots a jet of water into the air.

? What is evaporation?

Evaporation happens when a liquid or a solid changes to a gas. It is a process similar to boiling, because it involves the molecules of a liquid passing into the air. The process of evaporation is much slower when the air above the liquid is already full of molecules of vapor. For example, water will evaporate only very slowly on a warm, damp day when the air is already saturated with water vapor.

As a liquid evaporates, it loses heat energy, making it cooler. This is the principle on which refrigerators and air conditioners work. Evaporation of water from the seas and land produces water vapor in the form of clouds, which eventually drop water back onto the Earth's surface as rain.

? What happens when iron rusts?

The reddish powdery rust that forms on unprotected iron and steel is the result of a process called oxidation. It takes place when the metal reacts with oxygen from the air and water. Both air and water are needed for rusting to take place. This form of rusting eats into the metal until it collapses into scales and dust of iron oxide.

When aluminium is cut, it oxidizes very quickly, but the newly formed layer of aluminium oxide prevents exposure of the metal to more oxygen. The aluminium oxide stops the process of oxidation, so the metal remains bright and shiny.

⁇ What are acids?

Acids are a group of chemicals with very similar properties. They all have a very sour taste and are capable of burning the skin, although some are much more powerful than others. Many metals will dissolve when they come into contact with acids. This is because acids can release hydrogen ions when they are dissolved in water. Strong acids such as hydrochloric, sulphuric, and nitric acids release many hydrogen ions, so they react very fiercely with many substances. Acetic acid, which is an ingredient of vinegar, releases only a limited number of ions and is not a strong acid. This is the reason why it can be used safely in our food.

▼ Bee stings are acidic. An acid is neutralized by an alkali. To reduce the painful effects of a bee sting, soap, which is alkaline, should be applied.

Burning up

Like acids, alkalis are powerful chemicals that can attack human skin. They are in some ways the opposite of acids, because when the two substances are mixed together in the right proportions they cancel each other out, becoming neutral (neither acid nor alkaline).

Alkalis are chemical compounds that contain one of a number of metals grouped together in the periodic table, such as sodium and potassium. When these substances react with water, they form hydroxides such as sodium hydroxide (caustic soda). These are powerful substances that react with many other chemicals. They can burn skin very badly because they attack fats and other substances found in the human body. Soap is made by mixing these alkalis with fat or oil.

⁇ How can we identify acids and alkalis?

Dyes, called indicators, show very quickly if a substance dissolved in water is acid or alkaline. One of these dyes is litmus. If a piece of paper saturated with litmus is dipped into a solution, it immediately turns red if the solution is acid. If the solution is alkaline, the litmus turns blue.

A similar dye is present in some red vegetables such as red cabbage and beetroot, and this dye changes color in the same way during cooking. If your tap water is hard (alkaline, because it contains dissolved lime), the vegetables will be colored a deep purplish-blue. Red cabbage and beetroot are often pickled in vinegar, as the acid in vinegar gives them an attractive deep red coloration.

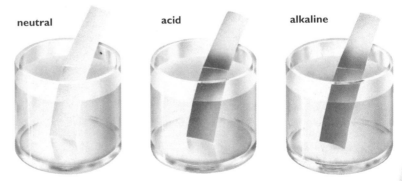

neutral   acid   alkaline

▲ Litmus paper is a quick way to test a liquid to see if it is acid or alkaline. The absorbent paper turns red in the presence of an acid and blue in an alkaline solution.

? What is light?

Light is a form of electromagnetic energy. It is produced by electrons that have gained extra energy from another source. This energy can be given off as heat or light. Light travels in waves of energy that consist of very tiny particles called photons. Atoms emit (give off) photons when heated to a high temperature. The extreme heat causes the atoms to collide with each other, and the extra energy is given off as light. The amount of energy released determines the colour of the light. The hotter an object, the more high-energy blue light is produced. As the object cools, the lower energy produces red light. When metal is heated to white hot, it gradually becomes red as it cools.

? How fast does light travel?

The speed of light is the fastest speed known – light travels through the vacuum of space at 186,000 miles per second. Nothing else can travel at this speed, and the theory of relativity, conceived by Albert Einstein, says that nothing can even approach this speed. This means that travel to the stars will not be possible, because it would take hundreds of years to reach them.

▶ Albert Einstein was one of the world's greatest scientists. His theories explained the basic properties of matter and the Universe, and made possible the development of nuclear power. His equations also showed that nothing can exceed the speed of light.

? Where does the Earth's energy come from?

There is a basic law of physics that says that energy is never created or destroyed; it is simply transferred from one place to another, or from one form of energy to another. So all the energy that exists today has been around since the formation of the Universe.

The Earth's energy comes from heat trapped inside the Earth when it was originally formed, or from energy radiated out from the Sun. We cannot make energy, but we can extract it from coal, oil, fast-flowing rivers, nuclear fuel and various other sources. Even the wind can supply us with a source of energy.

On the move

For centuries people have tried to cheat the laws of physics by inventing perpetual motion machines. These are machines that would run forever without any power, or would produce their own energy. Both types of machine are impossible. All machines need power to overcome friction and all the other forces that cause machinery to slow down. A law of physics says that energy cannot be created, so any machine that runs continuously must obtain its energy from somewhere else.

? How do we measure temperature?

Temperature is a measurement of the amount of heat that is stored in an object. It is measured against a scale in either degrees Celsius (°C) or degrees Fahrenheit (°F) on a thermometer. The Fahrenheit scale starts at the freezing point of water (32°F) and measures the boiling point of water at 212°F. The center of the Sun probably reaches an incredible temperature of 300 million°F.

The absolute minimum temperature possible is -459°F, or absolute zero, where it is so cold that molecules and atoms stop moving altogether. More ordinary temperatures are measured using thermometers that contain a liquid such as mercury or colored alcohol. Other thermometers use electronic sensors or the expansion of a metal coil to turn an indicating needle.

What are microwaves?

Microwaves are a form of radiation. They can pass through things that would block ordinary radio waves, such as rain and fog. Microwaves can also be focused and sent in a narrow beam, making them very useful for transmitting radio messages over long distances. Microwaves are widely used to transmit television signals to and from orbiting satellites in space, and they are also the basis on which modern mobile telephones work.

In radar, a beam of microwave energy scans the target area and bounces back signals, producing a picture of the object. Microwaves penetrate the food in a microwave oven, causing the molecules to move about very rapidly. This rapid movement generates the heat that cooks the food.

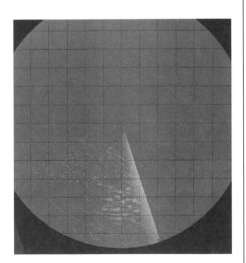

▲ Radar uses microwave radiation to detect distant objects. The microwaves usually scan in a circle, and the echoes sent back produce an image on a screen. This can be used for navigation or other purposes.

What is infrared energy?

Infrared radiation, or heat, is a form of electromagnetic energy that is not visible to our eyes. The wavelength of infrared radiation is greater than that of visible light, but much shorter than the wavelength of microwaves. All forms of heat are based on infrared radiation. Infrared photography allows objects to be seen in the dark. It uses cameras that are sensitive to infrared radiation, and so they can detect warm objects in the dark.

Why do rainbows form?

Rainbows are formed when sunlight falling on raindrops is split into the different colors of the spectrum (range) of light. Sunlight is really a mixture of all the colors of the spectrum: red, orange, yellow, green, blue, indigo, and violet, but our eyes always see them as ordinary white light.

When a beam of light passes at an angle through a curved transparent surface, such as a raindrop, the beam is bent when it emerges. The different colors of light are bent by different amounts, so the white light is split into the colors of the spectrum. This effect can also be seen when light passes through a piece of glass cut at different angles, such as a prism.

▼ Although it might seem that gravity carries food and drink down our throats, astronauts are able to eat and drink perfectly well in zero gravity. This is because it is muscular contractions of the gullet that actually transport food and drink to the stomach.

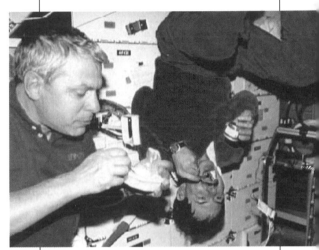

Why don't people fall off the Earth?

Gravity is the force that holds us on the Earth. It is also the force that keeps the Earth from flying off into space as it orbits the sun. The larger the mass of any object, the more it attracts other objects with the force of its gravity. The sun's gravity helps to pull the Earth's oceans, causing tides. Astronauts in space experience zero gravity, because they orbit the Earth so quickly that the effects of gravity are neutralized. The moon is much smaller than the Earth, and so it produces less gravity. Astronauts on the moon weighed only one-sixth of their normal weight on the Earth, even though their body mass remained the same.

◄ As light is split by water droplets into a rainbow, colors are always produced in the same sequence: red, orange, yellow, green, blue, indigo, and violet. Ultraviolet and infrared are also produced, but are not visible to the human eye.

▲ A huge electrical charge can be built up in certain weather conditions, and this leads to thunderstorms when a bolt of lightning leaps between the earth and a cloud. The air is heated to a tremendous temperature, causing the explosive noise of thunder as it expands suddenly.

? What is electricity?

Electricity powers our lights, heating, electronic appliances such as computers and television, and a host of other essential services that we take for granted. However, electricity has much more important aspects because it is a fundamental feature of all matter. Electricity is the force that holds together the molecules and atoms of all substances.

The type of electricity that is most familiar to us is electrical current. This is the flow of electrical charges through a substance called a conductor, such as a metal wire. This flow happens because some of the negatively charged electrons circling the nuclei of the conductor's atoms are held loosely. The electrons can move from one atom to the next, producing an electrical current.

? What is an insulator?

Some materials do not have the loosely attached electrons that are needed to conduct electricity — these substances are called insulators. Rubber, most plastics, ceramics, and glass are examples of good insulators. They do not allow the passage of electrical current, and so they are used to cover electrical wiring or to prevent electrical current leaking away. The more free electrons that are present in a conductor, the better it will be at conducting electrical current. Metals and many liquids are very good conductors of electricity, and some gases conduct electricity when they are very hot.

? How is electricity made?

Energy cannot be created. An electrical generator is simply a means of converting mechanical energy into electrical energy. In its simplest form, a generator spins coils of wire in a magnetic field, causing the flow of electrical current in the conducting wire. The power to spin the generator comes from other forms of energy. This energy might be stored energy in fossil fuels such as coal or oil, hydroelectric power from dams, wind power from turning huge windmills, or nuclear power produced by the radioactive decay of elements. In all these cases, one form of energy is simply converted into electrical energy.

▲ Concerns about pollution resulting from the production of electrical power have led to the development of wind farms. Huge windmills situated on exposed and windy areas drive dynamos to produce electricity.

How do batteries work?

Batteries produce electricity by means of chemical action. A battery contains two different conductors, or electrodes. Usually, one of these is the metal case of the battery. The electrodes are separated by a conducting liquid or paste, called the electrolyte. The substances in the battery react chemically with each other to produce an electrical current. As a result of chemical activity, a positive charge builds up at one electrode, and this can flow through a conductor such as a wire to the other (negative) electrode. Eventually the chemical energy runs out and the battery becomes exhausted.

▼ A battery consists of a central positive electrode and a metal outer case that acts as the negative electrode. The space between the two is filled with a conducting paste or liquid.

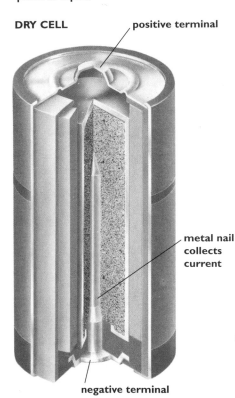

DRY CELL

positive terminal

metal nail collects current

negative terminal

▶ In an electric light bulb, a current is passed through a very thin filament of metal that has a high resistance to the flow of electricity. The filament becomes white-hot and produces light. The bulb contains an inert gas so the filament will not burn.

How does electricity produce heat and light?

A good conductor such as copper has only very low electrical resistance. It does not get very hot when electricity flows though it, making copper suitable for household wiring.

Other metals such as iron and nickel have much greater resistance to the passage of electricity, so they become hot. A very thin wire has more resistance than a thick one, and a long wire has more resistance than a short wire. In an electric fire, coils of thin, high-resistance wire glow and produce heat when an electrical current passes though them.

In a light bulb, coils of an extremely thin conductor ensure that heat cannot be radiated away quickly enough and some of the energy is converted to light.

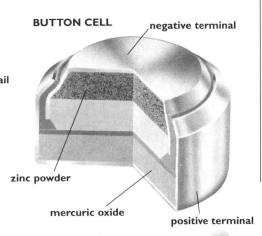

BUTTON CELL

negative terminal

zinc powder

mercuric oxide

positive terminal

What is alternating current?

Electrical currents normally flow in one direction through an electrical conductor. This kind of electricity, which is produced by batteries for example, is called direct current. When the electrical current is made to reverse its direction rapidly, it is known as alternating current. This kind of electrical current is used in domestic wiring, and it usually switches direction and back again about 50 to 60 times per second. This is the cause of the hum that you can sometimes hear near electrical equipment such as fluorescent lights.

What is a superconductor?

When electrons flow through a conductor they collide with atoms, and electrical energy is gradually lost in the form of heat. This process is called electrical resistance. However, when some substances become very cold, all electrical resistance is lost and the current flows freely without loss of energy. These substances are called superconductors. Their use allows some devices to work faster and more efficiently than ever before. Because of the difficulty in keeping superconductors cold, their use is limited. In the future, superconductors may be used to make efficient computers.

❓ What is magnetism?

Electrical currents are able to influence other electrical currents, and this force is called magnetism. Permanent magnets are materials in which this magnetic effect occurs because of the natural movement of electrons. Magnetism can also be caused by the flow of an electrical current through wires. The magnetic force of a magnet can repel (push) or attract (pull) another magnet or magnetic material.

❓ What is a magnetic field?

The area around a magnet where its magnetic force can be detected is called the magnetic field. You can see how this works if you lay a piece of paper over a magnet and sprinkle iron filings on it. The filings immediately arrange themselves in curved lines. You can see how these lines of magnetic force align themselves between the two poles, or ends, of the magnet.

❓ Why do some metals stick to magnets?

An ordinary magnet has two poles, which are usually referred to as the north pole and south pole. Similar (like) poles repel each other, while unlike poles attract each other. You can easily see this happening if you hold two magnets close together. The north pole of one magnet will stick firmly to the south pole of the other magnet, while any two similar poles will be forced apart.

❓ Which substances are magnetic?

Iron, steel, and nickel are magnetic substances, that is, they can be attracted by another magnet. Once these materials are in a magnetic field, they act as magnets themselves because the electrons in their atoms become aligned along the magnetic lines of force. This means that you can pick up a whole string of paperclips attached to a single magnet. Once the first paperclip is separated from the magnet, the whole string will collapse because the paperclips are only temporarily magnetized.

❓ Is the Earth a magnet?

The Earth is actually a huge magnet, with a magnetic north and a magnetic south pole. These poles are not quite the same as the true geographical poles, and they wander about slightly. There is geological evidence that the magnetic north and south poles sometimes switch their positions completely. The reasons for the Earth's magnetism are not really understood, but it is thought to be due to the movement of electrical charges around the Earth's core, which is probably mostly made up of iron.

The Earth's magnetic field extends out into space. The sun and the other planets in the solar system also have magnetic fields. Some distant stars are known to have exceptionally powerful magnetic fields.

❓ How does a compass work?

The magnetized needle of a compass tries to align itself towards the Earth's field of magnetic force. The magnetized needle balances on a pointed pin or floats on oil to allow it to rotate freely and to reduce friction. A compass needs to be used with care, because if it is near any object that can distort the Earth's magnetic field it will give a false reading. A nearby object made of iron or steel, or any source of electrical power, will cause the compass needle to swing wildly.

▼ The core of the Earth functions like a huge magnet. Lines of force run from the north to the south magnetic poles, and a compass can detect these. The magnetic poles are close to the true poles, but move slightly each year.

Magnetic motors

One of the most important uses of magnets is electric motors, which are used to power machines ranging from small toys to enormous railway engines. Video and audio tape recorders also depend on magnetism. Their tapes contain tiny metal particles that are magnetized by the recording heads. When played back, another part of the head decodes the magnetic patterns. The hard drive and floppy disks in a computer work in a similar way.

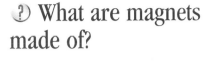

? What are magnets made of?

Permanent magnets are usually made from mixtures of iron, cobalt, and nickel, but others contain far more complicated mixtures of metals. Magnetite is a natural magnetic substance, which used to be called lodestone. It is a material that contains iron, and it was originally used to make the first primitive compasses.

? What is an electromagnet?

Electromagnets only produce magnetism when an electrical current passes through them. They usually consist of a metal core made of iron or a similar material, around which are wrapped many coils of thin insulated wire. The metal core becomes magnetized when an electric current passes through the wire coil, but the effect disappears when the current is shut off. Very powerful electromagnets can be created by using many coils and strong electrical currents.

? How can a train float in the air?

Some experimental trains have been made to float a few centimeters above the ground by using a system of electromagnetic coils embedded in the track. Electromagnetic force can also be made to propel these trains. They have no wheels, so there is very little friction to waste energy. This magnetic propulsion system, which is completely silent, is called magnetic levitation.

? How do animals make use of magnetic forces?

Many animals migrate for very long distances, but they arrive back at their birthplace in order to breed. This behavior has puzzled scientists for many years, but they have now found that many of these creatures contain tiny particles of magnetite in special organs, allowing them to orientate themselves accurately.

Magnetic navigation alone is not enough to account for the amazing ability of these animals to find their way over vast distances. It is thought that they also use other navigation aids, such as the position of the sun, to help them.

◀ Many animals, such as the albatross, are able to travel enormous distances in order to arrive at a particular destination. Their accurate navigation is helped by the presence of tiny magnetic particles in special organs, acting like a compass.

What are radio waves?

Radio waves form part of the electromagnetic spectrum. They are not part of the visible spectrum of light, and they have even longer wavelengths than infrared radiation. Radio waves with the longest wavelengths are bounced off a layer high up in the Earth's atmosphere, called the ionosphere. In this way, radio messages can be bounced for very long distances. Radio waves with shorter wavelengths penetrate the Earth's atmosphere completely and can be used to communicate with spacecraft.

How does radio communication work?

Radio signals are transmitted using a carrier wave. A radio transmitter changes, or modulates, this radio wave in order to convey information. In AM radio, the height of the carrier wave is altered according to the sound picked up by a microphone. In FM radio, the frequency, or distance between the peaks in the radio wave, is changed. The radio receiver picks up these signals and amplifies and decodes them. If the signal is weak, AM radio sounds crackly. It is now being replaced by FM radio, which gives much clearer reception.

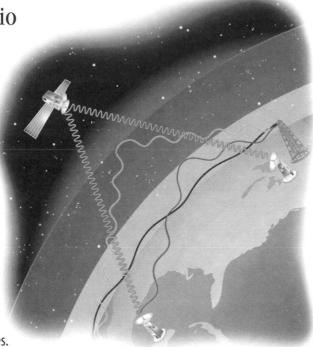

◀ Radio waves do not always travel around the curvature of the Earth. Radio transmissions can be beamed up to an orbiting satellite, which can then transmit them back to a very wide area beneath them or to other satellites broadcasting to different areas of the Earth's surface.

What is a printed circuit?

Any modern electrical device requires a huge number of connections to join together all the small components needed for it to work effectively. At one time these connections were made by wires that had to be soldered together. The wires have now been replaced by the printed circuit, which is effectively a picture of the wiring that works just as well.

A thin sheet of copper is attached to a special board made of insulating material. An image of the electrical circuit is then printed photographically onto the copper sheet. Chemicals are used to dissolve most of the copper, leaving behind a thin film of metal bands, to which all the necessary components can be attached. This process can be carried out automatically.

What does 'electronics' mean?

Electronics depends on electricity. It uses changes in the voltage of an electrical current to convey messages or signals, usually in a coded form. The use of electronics is responsible for many activities that we now take for granted, such as radio and television, computers and calculators.

Semi-miniature marvels!

Transistors are called solid-state devices, because their signals flow through a solid material, instead of through a vacuum (as used to happen with radio valves). Transistors and other solid-state devices are made of substances called semiconductors. These substances can be made to change their electrical properties when a current is applied to them.

Semiconductors may be insulators, which conduct electricity when a current is applied to a part of the transistor. In this way, transistors can be used as switches. The invention of transistors allowed electronic devices to be made much smaller than previously. Transistors consume little power and do not produce a lot of heat.

? What are silicon chips?

A silicon chip is a tiny wafer of silicon (a semiconductor) on which a complete electronic device can be produced. An image is produced photographically and etched onto the chip, but it differs from a printed circuit in some important ways. The chip is often microscopically small and contains huge amounts of 'wiring.' More importantly, part of the process allows other devices to be produced in the manufacturing process, such as tiny resistors and capacitors. So a silicon chip, or integrated circuit, which measures just a few millimeters across, is a complete electronic device.

▲ Printed circuits are complex electrical circuits that are literally photographed on to a layer of insulating material. This makes them light, compact and inexpensive.

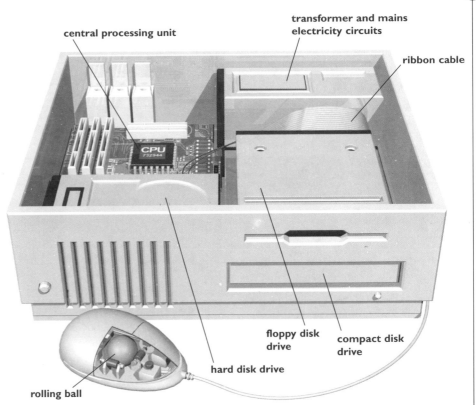

central processing unit

transformer and mains electricity circuits

ribbon cable

floppy disk drive

compact disk drive

hard disk drive

rolling ball

▲ Inside the outer case of a computer is mostly empty space. The heart of the computer is the **CPU** or central processing unit, the microprocessor where all of the calculations made by the machine take place. New data can be inputted from the keyboard or imported via the floppy disk drive, the **CD**, or **DVD** drive, or by the Internet along a telephone line.

? How do computers work?

A computer is a device for processing information very rapidly and accurately. It processes words, pictures, sounds, and numbers, and some computers can make billions of calculations per second. Most computers are digital, which means that they convert all the data, or information, entering the computer into the digits 0 or 1.

The heart of a computer is a microprocessor, which contains millions of tiny electronic devices on a silicon chip. Other chips form the computer's memory, where information is stored until needed. Computers vary from small hand-held devices to desktop computers. Large computers used in industry and for military purposes are called mainframe computers.

? How does radar work?

Radar works by sending out a beam of high- frequency radio waves, which are reflected back when they strike a solid object. The radio waves can also be reflected by clouds or other weather features. The reflected waves are collected and used to produce an image. Usually the radar beam is emitted from a rotating scanner, so a complete 360° image is produced. Radar is important in the navigation of ships, aircraft, and weather forecasting.

How is nuclear energy produced?

Nuclear energy is produced by changes in the nucleus of the atom of a radioactive element such as uranium or plutonium. This process is called nuclear fission. The nucleus is split by bombarding the atom with a neutron particle. Each time the uranium atom is split in this way, it releases energy. It also produces three more neutrons, which then go on to split other uranium atoms. This is called a chain reaction because, once started, it will continue the process of nuclear fission while releasing very large amounts of energy.

◀ The atom bomb is such a powerful weapon that it has only been used in anger twice, near the end of World War II, and even testing has now been abandoned. The technology to produce atomic weapons is very complex, and only a few countries have managed to make them.

How do nuclear power stations work?

Once nuclear fission takes place inside a nuclear reactor, the chain reaction has to be controlled, or moderated. The reactor's core of uranium is surrounded with a substance that slows down and absorbs the escaping neutrons. The moderating material becomes heated. In a nuclear power station, steam generated by this heat is used to drive the turbines to produce electricity.

▼ Nuclear power holds out the promise of cheap and unlimited power, but the technical difficulties and safety concerns have limited their use.

How do nuclear weapons work?

Atom bombs are a form of uncontrolled nuclear fission. When a large enough mass of uranium is put together, a fission reaction starts. The flood of neutrons emitted becomes so enormous that a vast amount of energy is released in a very short time, producing an atomic blast.

Hydrogen bombs have an atomic bomb at their heart, but this core is surrounded by a layer of light material. Using the power released from the fission of the uranium or plutonium core, this layer of material causes a fusion reaction like the one in the core of the sun. This nuclear fusion releases more heat energy than a fission explosion, as well as huge amounts of radioactivity.

What is a nuclear reactor?

A nuclear reactor is used to control nuclear fission. In most reactors, uranium is encased in metal tubes that are inserted into the reactor. The tubes are surrounded by a moderator, such as graphite, that slows down the reaction.

In another form of reactor, the fuel rods are surrounded by low-grade uranium, and the neutrons escaping from the reactor strike this material. The radiation converts the low-grade uranium into plutonium, which can be used as a nuclear fuel. This type of reactor, called a fast-breeder reactor, produces more plutonium than it can use as fuel. Although this sounds very useful, plutonium is much more dangerous to handle than uranium, and there are serious safety problems in its use.

Radioactive healing

Radiation from radioactive isotopes is used in medicine to destroy cancer cells. Radiation from an unstable isotope, such as radioactive cobalt, can be focused onto the site of a tumour to destroy the invading cells. Radioactive isotopes with very short half-lives are also used to locate areas of disease.

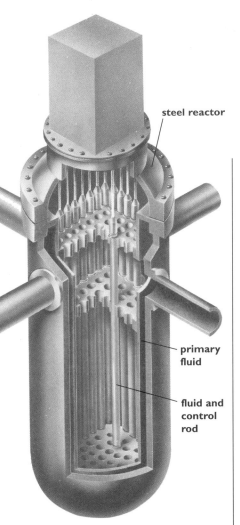

steel reactor

primary fluid

fluid and control rod

◀ In a nuclear reactor, uranium or plutonium undergoes fission, releasing huge amounts of energy. Graphite rods absorb some of the energy and prevent the reaction 'running away' and causing an uncontrolled reaction, which would be very dangerous. The energy generated heats water, which cools the reactor and can be used to power electrical generators.

What does half-life mean?

Particles continuously escape from the nucleus of radioactive elements, in a process called radioactive decay. Half-life is the time taken for half of a substance's atoms to decay into a different element. Uranium-235 has a half-life of nearly 250,000 years, while polonium-214 has a half-life of a tiny fraction of one second.

What are isotopes?

The nucleus of an element normally has a fixed number of protons and neutrons. Some elements exist in different forms, however, with varying numbers of neutrons in their nuclei. A radioisotope is an element that releases radioactivity. Its nucleus is unstable. It can only become stable by releasing radiation and energy in the form of heat and particles. These are split off from the nucleus. Radioisotopes such as iodine and cobalt are widely used in medicine. They are particularly helpful in the study of organ function.

Radioisotopes are known to have a steady rate of decay. This means that we can use them to accurately date fossilized remains. Carbon-14 is used in this way.

What is nuclear fusion?

Nuclear fusion is a means of producing energy that involves fusing together the nuclei of light, non-radioactive substances. This process takes place in an uncontrolled way in hydrogen bombs. Machines called particle accelerators fire tiny particles at a target and produce fusion. It has not been possible to use nuclear fusion to generate power for electrical supplies.

What is light?

Light is a form of electromagnetic radiation. It travels as waves that pass freely through space, even in the absence of air. Like other forms of electromagnetic radiation, light waves have a wavelength, and light is the visible part of these waves.

The actual wavelength of the electromagnetic radiation determines the color of the light. Long wavelengths produce red colors, and very long wavelengths produce infrared light, which we cannot see. Shorter wavelengths produce blue light, or ultraviolet radiation. Strangely, light can also be considered as a form of particle, called a photon, which travels in a straight line. Both descriptions — wave and particle — are correct, and both mean that light is a form of energy.

How fast does light travel?

Light travels faster than anything else known to man — it travels through a vacuum at almost 1,863,000 miles per second. This means that light from the sun takes eight minutes to reach the Earth. It slows down very slightly when it passes through any kind of material, because it collides with atoms. According to Einstein's special theory of relativity, there is nothing else that can travel as fast as light.

▶ **Nearly all of the light and energy reaching the Earth comes from the sun, which is powered by a continuous thermonuclear reaction, like a gigantic hydrogen bomb.**

How is light produced?

Light is given off by atoms that have gained extra energy. This excess energy is released in the form of light or heat. Such atoms become excited by absorbing energy from other sources. Atoms can also become excited when heated. The atoms of the heated material move around rapidly and collide with one another, becoming excited and emitting their extra energy as light. The color of the light produced depends on how much energy is released. A few substances store extra energy and then release it gradually. These substances, such as the glowing paints used on watch faces, are phosphorescent. Other substances only produce light when exposed to other forms of energy; for example, fluorescent substances may glow brightly when exposed to ultraviolet light.

Mirror image

Mirrors are coated with a reflective material, so when a beam of light strikes the surface none of it is absorbed. The beam of light is reflected away again. The light is reflected at exactly the same angle as it struck the mirror, but in the opposite direction. This can be visualized as being similar to a pool ball striking the cushion of the table and bouncing at an angle.

⁇ What is a spectrum?

When light strikes a transparent surface at an angle, its speed reduces and the rays of light bend slightly. The 'white' light we see is actually a mixture of colors: red, orange, yellow, green, blue, indigo, and violet; each of these colors is bent by a different amount. So when a beam of white light passes through a glass prism, the light coming out the other side consists of bands of these colors. You can often see this banded effect around the bevelled edges of a mirror.

This process of refraction, or bending, of light also takes place in raindrops when sunlight strikes them, which is why you see the colors of the spectrum in a rainbow.

⁇ How can light travel along a cable?

Although light travels only in straight lines, it can be made to bend around curves and angles using optical fibers. These are bundles of very thin strands of exceptionally clear glass. The fibers are treated so that their outer surface reflects light. When light is shone in one end of the bundle it passes along the fibers, reflecting from the sides as they curve and eventually emerging at the far end.

Optical fibers carry electronic signals to computers, and they are increasingly used in telephone lines. Optical fibers are very useful in medicine to diagnose disease. A flexible fiberoptic probe can be inserted into the body to view the internal workings of an organ.

▼ As light passes through a prism, it is split into its component colors: violet, indigo, blue, green, yellow, red, and orange. Each color is bent a different amount as it passes through the glass at an angle, so they always appear to be in the same order.

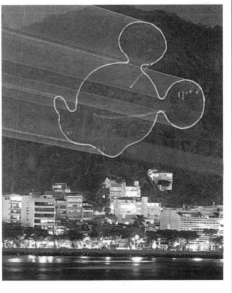

▲ The intense beam of light produced by a laser can be used to produce images for publicity or entertainment purposes. This method of using light is not possible with conventional light sources.

⁇ What are lasers?

Lasers are devices that produce a narrow beam of very strong light. Lasers amplify light by causing photons to be bounced back and forth in a substance (solid, liquid, or gas), which adds extra energy. The result is that intense light is emitted in a very narrow beam.

Lasers are used to cut metal and other solid materials, and even to burn out skin blemishes such as tattoos in a painless way. In CD players, lasers scan a beam of laser light across the CD's silvery surface, reading the tiny changes in light reflected back. They are also used in office printers and scanners. In engineering, the intense narrow beam of laser light is used to measure and align roads and tunnels.

? What is sound?

Sound is a form of vibration passing through the air or some other material. Sound travels in the form of waves but, unlike electromagnetic waves, sound waves cannot pass through a vacuum. The frequency of a sound wave controls its pitch. Long wavelengths produce deep sounds, while short wavelengths produce higher sounds. The loudness of a sound depends on the height of the sound waves, or their amplitude. The higher the amplitude, the louder the sound.

Sound vibrations are received in your ears. They are conveyed to a mechanism inside your ears that first amplifies them, then converts the vibrations into signals that your brain interprets as sound.

? How many sounds can we hear?

Compared to other animals, the human ear is not very sensitive. We can hear sounds with a frequency of up to 20 kilohertz (kHz) — a normal speaking voice is about 1 kHz. Bats, dogs, and some insects can hear sounds that are pitched much higher, which we cannot hear at all. Children can usually hear a bat squeaking, although this sound can sometimes be as high as 120 kHz, but in adults the ability to hear these high-pitched sounds is usually lost. 'Supersonic' dog whistles are used to call dogs, and their sound is so high-pitched that humans cannot hear it at all.

◀ Bats produce a continuous high-pitched squeaking in flight, and the echoes from this sound allow them to navigate in darkness and even to locate the small flying insects on which they feed.

? What is an echo?

Like light, sound can be reflected from certain surfaces. Hard surfaces such as rock or the side of a building reflect sound well; as the sound bounces back, you hear an echo. The delay in hearing the echo is due to the comparatively slow speed of sound. Soft materials absorb sound and will not produce an echo. This is why recording studios are lined with felt material, which prevents any unwanted noise from interfering with the recording.

▼ Concorde is the only supersonic airliner in regular use. The sonic 'boom' it produces, together with noise and air pollution concerns, has limited the development of such aircraft.

? What is the Doppler effect?

You will have noticed that as a car travels quickly towards you, the sound of its engine gets higher, then becomes deeper after the car has passed by. This is called the Doppler effect. What happens is that as the car approaches, the frequency of the sound of its engine increases as the wavelength of the sound decreases. Each successive sound wave is a little shorter as the car comes towards you. Then as the car moves away, the process is reversed; the frequency decreases while the wavelength of the sound becomes longer.

You will not notice the Doppler effect if a supersonic aircraft flies past, because you cannot hear the sound of the plane until it is actually flying away from you.

? What is the sound barrier?

At sea level, sound travels though the air at around 1,100 feet per second, and slightly slower at high altitudes. The denser the substance, the faster sound will travel through it. Sound travels at 4,900 feet per second through water, for example. When traveling at such very high speeds, an aircraft begins to build up a huge wave of compressed air in front of it. This is known as the sound barrier because it was an obstacle to high-speed flight. When the aircraft exceeds the speed of sound, it leaves the built-up waves of pressure behind, and these break away, forming a 'sonic boom.' The speed of sound in air is called Mach 1, and the speed of supersonic aircraft is measured in Mach numbers. Concorde is the only commercial aircraft to have broken the sound barrier.

Shattered

Wine glasses made of very thin glass may be shattered by a loud sound, which causes the glass to vibrate at a certain frequency. This can sometimes be done by an opera singer with a very powerful voice. What happens is that the singer produces a note with the same frequency as the note that would be produced if the glass were struck lightly. This is called the resonant frequency of the glass.

? What causes thunder?

Thunder is produced when lightning heats up the surrounding air very rapidly, causing it to expand faster than the speed of sound. This produces a 'sonic boom' like the one caused by a supersonic aircraft. If you count the seconds between seeing a flash of lightning and hearing thunder and divide this number by 3, it will tell you how many miles away from the lightning you are. Sound travels at about 750 mph, while light from the lighting strike travels so fast that you see it almost instantaneously.

? Can sound hurt?

The loudness of sounds is measured in units called decibels (dB). Ordinary speech has a sound intensity of about 20 decibels, while a noisy room full of people produces about 70 decibels. The quietest sound you can hear is about 20 decibels. Loud music at a rock concert reaches a level of about 125 decibels, while sounds of 140 decibels or more actually cause pain in the ear. This level of sound can produce permanent hearing damage if it continues, which is why people operating noisy machinery have to wear ear protectors.

? How can sound detect submarines?

Sound waves travel very well through water, so they are used to detect submarines or even shoals of fish. A sonar device under a ship sends out sound waves that travel down through the water. The sound waves are reflected back from any solid object they reach, such as a submarine, shoals of fish, or the seabed. The echoes are received by the ship and can be used to 'draw' an image of the object, and its location, on a screen.

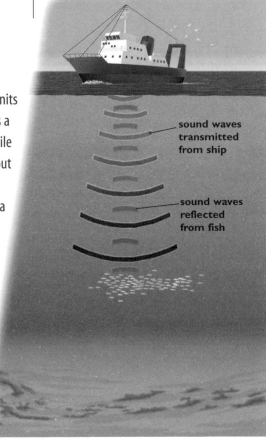

sound waves transmitted from ship

sound waves reflected from fish

▲ Sonar, or echo sounding, is used by fishermen to detect shoals of fish. It can also be used to detect submerged submarines or to find wrecks on the seabed. Sonar works by measuring sound waves reflected from the objects they encounter.

What is a force?

A force pushes or pulls something in a particular direction. Isaac Newton was the first person to make a study of forces. He realized that when an object produces a force on something else, there is an equal and opposite reaction. For example, if you wear roller skates and push against a wall, exerting a force, you will be pushed away with just as much force as you are applying.

▶ **Sir Isaac Newton (1643–1727) was the first scientist to develop the laws of gravity. He supposedly was inspired by seeing an apple fall from a tree.**

What is friction?

Friction is a type of force that stops things from moving when they have to slide past one another. It is the force that you have to overcome if you push something along. Friction also tends to slow down moving objects, which is why a bicycle will not travel very far if you stop pedaling. All forms of moving machinery are subject to friction. Oil is used to reduce the level of friction, and this helps to make machines work more efficiently.

What stops us from falling off the Earth?

Gravity is the force that pulls towards the center of the Earth. No matter where you stand on the Earth's surface, the ground is always 'down.' The force of gravity depends on the mass, or amount of material, of an object - objects feel heavy because of their mass. Isaac Newton realized that gravity not only affects the Earth, but it also controls the movement of the planets and the stars, as well as the orbit of the moon around the Earth.

▼ **Inertia is the force that makes it difficult to start a bicycle moving. Once traveling, friction is another force that will slow it down unless it is overcome by pedaling.**

gravity

path of ball without air resistance and gravity

Why do falling objects keep traveling faster?

Falling objects are subject to the force of gravity, and as they fall their speed increases, or accelerates, by 32 feet per second every second. This increase continues until the friction of the air becomes so great that acceleration stops and the object then falls at a constant speed.

Gravity produces the same force on any object, no matter how heavy or light it is. In a vacuum, a feather would fall and accelerate just as quickly as a brick. When a bullet is fired from a gun, the force of the explosion accelerates the bullet along the gun barrel. This force stops immediately when the bullet leaves the gun, and friction begins to slow the bullet's speed.

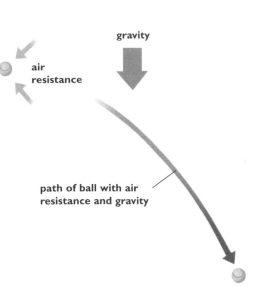

gravity

air resistance

path of ball with air resistance and gravity

▲ When you hit a ball into the air, at first it travels in a straight line. However, the force of gravity soon slows it down and begins to pull it towards the ground. The ball travels in a geometric path called a parabola.

Why is it so hard to start a heavy object moving?

Due to a force called inertia, an object will remain still or travel in a straight line unless some force interferes with it. Friction is one such force. The greater the mass of an object, the greater its inertia, and the bigger the force that will be needed to start it moving. This is why it is very difficult to move a stationary car by pushing it, but much easier once the car starts to roll. A very strong man is able to pull along a railway car once it has started to move. Inertia is the explanation for the magician's trick of pulling a tablecloth off a table without disturbing the dishes and silverware on it.

What is centrifugal force?

When you whirl something around your head on the end of a string, it flies outward and appears to defy the force of gravity. Centrifugal force is acting to pull the object away. The object tries to fly off, and you are applying a force to retain it. This is called centripetal force. The centripetal force stops suddenly when you let go of the string, and centrifugal force makes the object fly away in a straight line. These forces are the reason why you can whirl a bucket of water above your head without spilling a drop.

How does a gyroscope stand up?

A gyroscope is a heavy metal wheel made with ball bearings that reduce friction. Once the wheel is set spinning at high speed in an upright position, the force of gravity will try to topple it. However, the effects of gravity are countered by another force called precession. This force means that a spinning body tends to move at right angles to any force that tries to change its direction of rotation. The effect is to keep the gyroscope in the same position until it has slowed down so much that gravity overcomes precession.

▶ For thousands of years, levers have been used to lift heavy objects. The two upper diagrams show how long levers make it easy to lift a heavy object for a short distance. Using the levers in the bottom diagram would make it much harder to lift the object.

How can you lift very heavy objects without using powerful machinery?

For thousands of years, people have used levers as a way of transferring a force from one place to another, and to change the amount of movement that results.

To move a heavy object, a long lever can help. The lever is free to move about a point called the fulcrum. The shorter end of the lever is placed under the object, and force is applied to the longer end. This will cause the object to be lifted, but the long end of the lever will have to be pushed down a long way to lift the object only a short distance. With a long-enough lever, you could lift a car for a short distance.

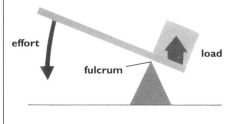

effort
fulcrum
load

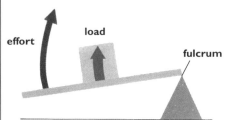

effort
load
fulcrum

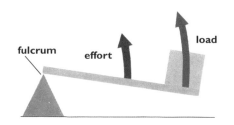

fulcrum
effort
load

? Why do we need to measure time?

People have always organized their lives by the passing of time. The earliest hunters had to hunt during the hours of daylight. When farming had developed, it was important for farmers to understand the seasons in order to plant their crops at the right time.

Long ago, people realized that the movement of the sun allowed them to recognize the time of day. They also realized that the movement of the moon was regular and could be used to give measurements of roughly one month. Modern life is governed much more by time, and we now depend on highly accurate clocks to measure every second of the day.

? What is a sundial?

Sundials are the simplest way to measure time during the day. A simple stick casts a shadow that grows shorter until midday, when the sun is at its highest in the sky. The shadow grows longer again after midday. A sundial simply casts its shadow onto a plate marked with the hours. Sundials have been used for many centuries and are still in use today.

▶ The sundial is a simple device that measures time by casting the shadow of the central spike onto a graduated scale.

? How is time calculated?

The Earth spins on its own axis once every 24 hours, or one day. The Earth orbits the sun every 365$\frac{1}{4}$ days, or one year. Every 4 years, we need to have a leap year with one extra day to make up the difference between the calendar year (365 days) and the time it takes for one complete orbit of the sun. The year is divided into 12 months, which roughly correspond with the time it takes for the moon to complete one full orbit of the Earth.

▶ The Earth rotates on its axis once every 24 hours (top). It also orbits around the sun, taking a year to complete the orbit (middle). At the same time, the moon orbits the Earth in about 28 days, and this measurement is used to describe a month (bottom).

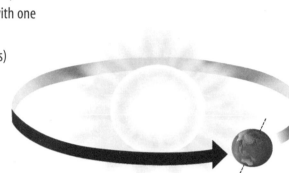

one day

one year

one month

⟨?⟩ How do we measure time accurately?

After the invention of sundials, other means of telling the time indoors were developed, such as hourglasses and burning candles. The invention of clocks, however, allowed far more accurate timekeeping. Early clocks were powered by a weight hanging from a fine chain (a pendulum), but later on springs were used to store energy. Most mechanical clocks and watches now contain a balance wheel that spins backwards and forwards, allowing an escapement wheel to move a very small amount each time it spins. This wheel is driven by the energy stored in the clock spring.

Many watches and clocks are now powered by an electronic timer with no moving parts. It contains a tiny integrated circuit and a vibrating quartz crystal, which measures time with great accuracy.

⟨?⟩ What is Greenwich Mean Time?

In 1884 an international conference decided that the 0° line of longitude, or meridian, would run through the Royal Observatory in Greenwich, England. As you move to the east from the Greenwich Meridian, the time is one hour ahead of Greenwich Mean Time for each degree you move. If you move to the west, time is one hour behind for each degree. Midday is the point where the sun is highest in the sky, whichever time zone you are in.

The amount of daylight varies with the seasons, so daylight savings time, or summer time, was introduced to make maximum use of daylight hours. In the northern hemisphere clocks are reset one hour ahead in spring and one hour back in autumn. (In the southern hemisphere, the seasons are reversed.)

Body clock

People normally have a good idea of the time even without the use of clocks, because we are aware of the amount of time that has passed since daybreak, for example. However, there are other ways in which the body measures time. Humans have an built in body clock that controls many of our functions, such as the flow of hormones into the bloodstream and the time for sleeping.

⟨?⟩ How were calendars developed?

Calendars have been used for thousands of years. The early ones were usually based on the phases of the moon and the movement of the sun. We still depend largely on the natural movements of the Earth, moon, and sun to divide up time. The calendar we use today is based on the Julian calendar, which was introduced by the Romans in 46 B.C. It had 365 days, and the Romans had not yet discovered the need for leap years. By 1582, the Julian calendar was ten days out, and Pope Gregory decreed that ten days would have to go missing from that year. This caused rioting because people felt that ten days of their lives had been stolen.

◀ **Magnetic energy produced by vast storms on the sun's surface strikes the upper atmosphere of the Earth, producing patterns in the sky near the poles called the northern lights or aurora borealis. The same effect in the southern hemisphere is called the aurora australis.**

Why do we need to use numbers?

Numbers are used to describe the amount of things. We can express numbers in words, by hand gestures, in writing, or using symbols or numerals. When we talk about a number, we use words ('five') rather than the numeral (5), but when we write, we use both words and numerals.

Numbers can describe how many objects there are or their position among lots of objects, such as 1st or 5th, for example. Other types of numbers describe how many units of something there are, for example how many pounds (weight) or feet (length). Numbers are just a convenient way to describe ideas.

What is the metric system?

The metric system is a group of various units of measurement. Its name comes originally from the meter. It is a decimal system, which means that each unit is ten times bigger, or smaller, than the next unit. Previously, measurements were difficult to calculate; in measurements of length, for example, there were 12 inches in one foot and three feet in one yard, while weight was calculated using ounces and pounds (16 ounces in one pound).

The metric system was devised in the 1790s in France, and is now used in most countries in the world for all scientific and technical measurements.

What are decimals?

The decimal system describes a numbering system for calculation based on multiples of ten. Multiplying or dividing a number by ten is very easy because only the decimal point needs to be moved. In the decimal system, each number has a value ten times that of the next number to the right. For instance, 5,283 means five thousands, two hundreds, eight tens and three ones. The decimal point simply separates the main number from numbers less than one. The number ten has always been important in mathematics — you can easily count it on your fingers.

How did Roman numbering work?

In some ways, Roman numbering worked like the modern Arabic numeral system where, starting from the left, there are thousands, hundreds, tens, and individual units. However, Roman numerals are quite different. One thousand is written as M, five hundred as D, one hundred as C, fifty as L, ten as X, and five as V.

M	D	C
one thousand	five hundred	one hundred

L	X	V	I
fifty	ten	five	one

▲ Roman numerals were once widely used, but it is very difficult to carry out calculations using them, largely because the Romans did not use zero. Roman numerals are now used only on clock faces and carved into monuments.

Who invented our modern numerals?

Our numbers are called Arabic numerals, although they probably appeared first in India around A.D. 600. By the 800s the Arab numbering system was used throughout Europe because it was much easier to use than the old Roman system. At first, the numbers varied in the way they were written, but with the invention of printing, the numbers became standardized. The basic Arab numbers are 0 to 9, and can be used to write any combination of numbers.

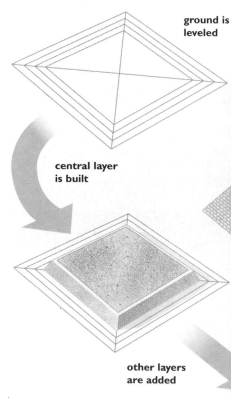

ground is leveled

central layer is built

other layers are added

▶ Pyramids were once built in both Egypt and Central America. These huge structures were very carefully designed and constructed, and it is clear that the builders had a very good knowledge of mathematics and were able to measure very accurately.

What is geometry?

Geometry is a part of mathematics that deals with the shape, position, and size of things of geometric form, such as squares, triangles, cubes, and cones. Its name comes from the Greek words meaning 'earth measuring,' because it was probably originally invented as a means of surveying and measuring land.

The ancient Egyptians also used geometry when constructing buildings and tombs. Nowadays, geometry is important to engineers and architects. It is also essential in navigation because geometry is used to follow charts and maps.

▲ Even using the most powerful forms of radio telescope, there is no visible limit to the universe. According to some mathematicians, it continues into infinity, while others say that if you continued in a straight line for billions of miles, you would eventually finish up where you started, because space is curved.

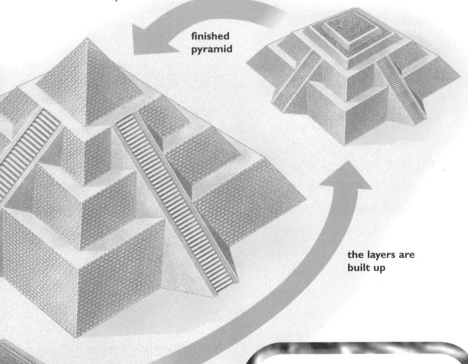

finished pyramid

the layers are built up

Prime candidates

A prime number is a mathematical curiosity. It can be divided only by itself and by 1. For example, the lowest prime numbers are 2, 3, 5, 7, 11, 13, 17, and 19. You can work out other prime numbers for yourself.

What is infinity?

Infinity is a number, or value, which is so huge that it cannot be measured. For instance, the distance to the end of the universe is called infinity, because if there is an end, it is so far away that it could never be measured.

Sometimes infinity can be the result of a mathematical calculation. For example, the formula for calculating the distance around the outside of a circle is pi (π) times the diameter. Pi is a Greek letter, and it represents a value of approximately 3.14159. Pi can never be fully calculated, because you would finish up with a string of numbers extending to infinity.

? How does an airplane fly?

As an airplane moves though the air, the air passes over the surface of the wings. These are shaped with a curved top surface and a flatter lower surface, which means that air passing over the top of the wing has to travel a little faster than that below the wing. This lowers the pressure above the wing, while the air pressure below pushes up. The end result is the lift that keeps the airplane in the air.

The tail surfaces keep the wing at the proper angle to provide the right amount of lift. The power to propel the airplane can come from the engines or, in the case of gliders, from rising air currents.

▼ Air passing over the upper surface of an aircraft's wing reduces in pressure, allowing higher pressure air beneath the wing to exert an upward force, so it can fly. The tail, or stabilizer, holds the aircraft at the correct angle to maintain its altitude.

airflow

airflow

propellor produces thrust

? How do jet engines work?

Like rockets, jet engines propel an airplane with a stream of hot gases. Unlike rockets, which produce hot gas as a result of burning an explosive mixture, jet engines burn fuel in the air that they draw in at the front of the engine.

Air enters the front of the engine and is compressed by a rapidly spinning compressor wheel. Fuel is injected into the compressed air, burns fiercely, and expands. The hot gas rushes out of the jet pipe at the rear of the engine. The hot gas passes through a turbine, which drives the compressor at the front of the engine.

? What is the difference between a gasoline and a diesel engine?

Engines that burn fuel inside them are called internal combustion engines. A gasoline engine injects fuel into a cylinder and ignites it with a spark. The mixture of fuel and air explodes and drives a piston down the cylinder. The piston is connected to a crankshaft, which turns as the piston moves down. As the crankshaft continues to revolve, it pushes the piston up again.

A diesel engine works in the same way, except that a spark is not needed to ignite the fuel. Instead, the engine is spun over by a starter. As the piston comes up the cylinder, it compresses the mixture of diesel oil and air. Compressing the mixture heats it up and it explodes, driving the piston down.

On the right track

Steam powered trains were one of the earliest forms of mass transport during the Industrial Revolution. Today, they are still one of the most effective ways of carrying very heavy loads and large numbers of people. Trains have an advantage because loads can be carried inexpensively, and to carry the equivalent by road would require many trucks or cars. Modern trains are powered by diesel engines or electricity.

Why doesn't a steel ship sink?

A ship, or any other floating object, displaces (pushes away) water. You can see this for yourself if you fill a bowl with water right up to the brim, then float a smaller dish inside it. Water will spill over, and the amount spilled will be the same as the volume of the smaller dish. A vessel will float if it is lighter than the amount of water it displaces.

A very small boat built of steel would probably sink like a stone. However, a very large ship built of steel would be so buoyant that it could also carry huge amounts of oil or other cargo. The capacity of a cargo ship is measured by the weight of water that it displaces.

How does a hovercraft work?

The hovercraft is an ingenious machine that rides on a cushion of air. It looks like a flat-bottomed ship and is usually powered with huge propellers like those of an airplane. Engines draw in a large amount of air, which is pumped out under the hovercraft and kept in by flexible rubber skirts. The craft rises up, supported on the column of air, and is then able to travel quickly over the water or over land. There is little friction because the bottom of the hovercraft does not actually touch the water.

Hovercraft have a number of uses, but have never replaced ordinary ships because they are expensive to run, very noisy, and are unable to operate in stormy seas.

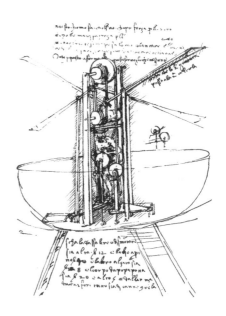

▲ Leonardo da Vinci (1452–1519) drew his plans for a helicopter hundreds of years before people were first able to fly.

How do helicopters fly?

Helicopters are lifted into the air by their large rotating propellers, or rotors. These work like long narrow wings, generating lift as they spin rapidly through the air. The tail rotor generates enough thrust to stop the fuselage spinning.

A helicopter turns by increasing or decreasing the thrust of its tail rotor. It climbs by increasing the angle of attack of the rotor blades. It moves forward by increasing the angle of the blade, moving back on every rotation so that it pushes against the air.

◀ The hovercraft is very useful as a means of transport in shallow waters where a conventional boat would run aground. Because they are flat, hovercraft can hold a large number of vehicles and are often used as car ferries.

? What are communications?

We exchange ideas and messages by communication. Humans, as well as other animals, communicate visually and by sounds. Some animals also communicate by means of smells that convey messages. Humans differ from all other living things because we can communicate by means of symbols. These are compressed pieces of information, such as written letters or numbers, that actually communicate very complex ideas.

▲ Many animals communicate by means of smell. The skunk uses its pungent smell as both a warning and a weapon when it feels threatened.

? What is telecommunications?

Telecommunications is the passing of messages and information over long distances by means of electrical signals. These signals may be carried along wires, like telephone, telegraph, and fax messages, or by radio waves.

? How does a telephone work?

Telephones transmit speech messages along wires by means of electrical signals. Telephones were invented as long ago as 1876. The handset of a telephone includes a loudspeaker and a very small microphone, which contains granules of carbon. When you talk into the microphone, the sound waves of your voice cause a metal diaphragm to vibrate, and it presses against the carbon granules. The vibrations vary depending on the sounds. They change the very small amount of current flowing out along the wires to the receiver of another telephone.

When the electric current carrying the signals reaches the receiver handset, the same variations in the current run through an electromagnet. This causes another diaphragm to vibrate in the earpiece, accurately reproducing the sound of the speaker's voice.

Surf's up

The Internet is an international network linking computers all around the world by means of telephone lines or radio transmission, so they can exchange information. The system was invented during the Cold War, when it was feared that an attack might disrupt communications with any central point. With the Internet, computers are dotted about everywhere, and communications cannot be cut off by damage to any single point.

Recently, the World Wide Web has become accessible to people with home computers. It allows them to connect to an ordinary telephone line and send written messages anywhere by means of electronic mail, or e-mail. People can now buy goods and even carry out banking via the Internet.

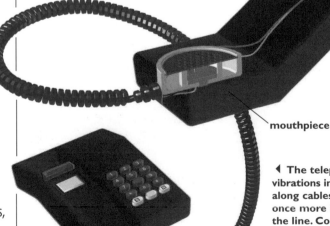

diaphragm

earpiece

wire

mouthpiece

◀ The telephone converts speech vibrations into electrical energy that travels along cables and is decoded into sounds once more in the receiver at the end of the line. Complex switching is needed to allow the call to reach the right person.

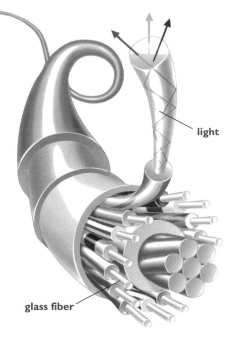

light

glass fiber

▲ Light travels much faster than electricity and is used in optical cables to carry communications for very long distances without electrical interference. The light travels along tiny glass fibers, usually packed into huge bundles capable of carrying many thousands of messages at the same time.

How can television pictures be transmitted by radio waves?

Television cameras break a picture into electrical signals, separating them into three colors (red, blue, and green) and turning them into coded messages. Sound is recorded and coded at the same time. The coded pictures and sounds are transmitted by radio waves, electrical cables, or optical fibers to the receiver. Inside a television receiver, the signals travel to three electron guns — one for each color. The electron guns emit streams of electrons, which are directed at a fluorescent screen. Magnets bend the electron streams so that they scan back and forth from top to bottom, exciting the phosphors in the screen and producing a color image. They scan so quickly that our eyes see the images as a continuous picture.

How do we receive messages and TV pictures from a satellite orbiting the Earth?

Television pictures, radio, and telephone communications are bounced off satellites to cover the greatest possible area of the world. Satellites orbiting the Earth must travel at high speeds to escape being brought down by the Earth's gravity. As the Earth itself is spinning rapidly, there is a point above the Earth's surface where the orbiting speed of the satellite can be matched with the rotational speed of the Earth. At this point — 22,300 miles above the Earth — the satellite appears to stand still and is said to be in a geostationary orbit.

Geostationary satellites can be positioned right over the areas where they are needed. They can also be used as spy satellites, because they remain constantly over a region of interest.

How do mobile phones work?

Mobile phones, which are properly called cellular phones, allow calls to be made wherever the caller happens to be. They are called cellular phones because a territory is divided up into a series of small areas, or cells, each with a small radio station. When a call is made, the telephone sends a radio message to the base station, which in turn passes it to a mobile phone exchange. Here the signal can be routed to the ordinary telephone system, or transmitted back to another mobile phone. Mobile phones use low-powered microwaves to send and receive messages to and from the base station.

What is a modem?

Computers that are connected to a telephone line incorporate a device called a modem. It turns signals into a form that can be transmitted along the telephone line. The name 'modem' comes from the term Modulator-Demodulator. The device modulates, or changes, the digital signal from a computer into an analogue signal, which is the type of signal that travels along telephone lines. The modem decodes, or demodulates, the signals it receives back so they can be read by the computer.

◀ Communication satellites are used to carry communications such as radio, television, and telephone messages around the world. These satellites are 'parked' in an orbit where they will remain in position over the same part of the Earth's surface.

▲ Steel is a form of iron, alloyed with carbon and other metals to make it stronger. It is produced in giant furnaces.

How is steel made?

Steel is made from iron, which is usually mined in the form of iron ore. The ore needs to be smelted in order to extract the iron. Smelting is done in a blast furnace, where coke and limestone are added to the iron ore. This mixture is heated to a very high temperature and air is blown through it. The molten iron is drawn off.

To make steel, iron is mixed with carbon and other metals to give it extra hardness. There is about 1.6 percent carbon in most steel. Other forms of steel contain elements such as chromium and nickel to prevent rusting. Ordinary carbon steel rusts as easily as iron and must be protected with paint or other coatings.

Where does rubber come from?

Natural rubber comes from a kind of tree that originally grew in South America. Its liquid sap, called latex, is drained from the tree by making cuts in the bark. The latex is collected and processed into rubber. Natural rubber is very soft and is used for making the soles of shoes and sandals.

In 1839 Charles Goodyear, an American inventor, found that heating rubber together with sulphur made it much harder. This process, known as vulcanization, made it possible to use rubber for vehicle tires. Rubber is now used for electrical insulation, motor tires, cushions, golf balls, and many other applications.

Since World War II, most of the rubber we use has been produced synthetically. Rubber's properties are based on the way its molecules link up into long chains, making giant molecules called polymers.

Dot to dot

To produce color images, printing presses use inks. These images are made up of four separate types of ink: red, yellow, blue, and black. The color is applied to the paper as tiny dots - the larger the dots, the more intense the color will appear. Your eyes do not really notice the dots because your brain fills in the details to form a complete picture. Television pictures work in a similar way.

▶ Polymers are long chains of molecules consisting of groups of identical smaller molecules joined together. This changes the properties of the basic molecule and may make the substance more flexible, or more rigid, depending on how the molecules are linked.

A POLYMER OF SOFT PLASTIC

What type of materials are plastics?

Plastics are synthetic materials that consist of long chains of molecules called polymers. When the chains are positioned in long rows, the plastic is rigid. When the polymer molecules are tangled together, the plastic is soft and flexible. All plastics can be molded under pressure into complicated shapes. Thermoplastics melt when they are heated, and this means that they can be remelted at any time. There are other forms of plastic, known as thermosetting plastics, which cannot be remelted.

The majority of plastics are made from synthetic resins, which are usually derived from oil. Other types come from sources such as coal or wood. As they do not conduct electricity, most plastics are excellent insulators, so are widely used in electrical wiring. The main disadvantage of plastics is that they are very slow to break down, causing serious environmental problems when discarded.

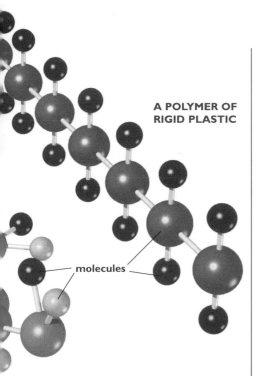

A POLYMER OF RIGID PLASTIC

molecules

❓ What are explosives?

Explosives are substances that release a very large amount of energy in a short time when they burn. They all contain a fuel plus an oxidizer, which is a substance containing sufficient oxygen to burn the fuel. Explosives do not need air to explode, because they contain their own oxygen, and so they can burn in confined spaces or even underwater. Some explosives, such as those in a cartridge detonator, explode violently when hit or heated. Others only cause a violent explosion when confined in a gun barrel or a hole drilled in rock for blasting.

Gunpowder, the first ever explosive, was invented in China over 1,000 years ago. Large amounts of modern explosives are commonly used in quarrying and mining, as well as for munitions.

❓ How does printing work?

Printing is the process by which many copies of words and pictures can be reproduced on paper or other materials. Simple wood blocks with carved letters covered with ink were used to print until around 1440, when Johannes Gutenberg developed movable type (a separate piece of metal type for each character). A machine pressed the inked type against paper.

Most modern printing is carried out by offset printing, or lithography. Images are placed on metal printing plates by a photographic process, and a greasy ink is applied that sticks to the areas where the image will be. The inked image is then transferred to a rubber roller and applied onto paper. Some of the fastest newspaper presses can print at a speed of 2,900 feet of paper per minute.

▼ An explosion is a very violent form of burning. Explosive substances contain all of the oxygen and fuel they need for burning, which allows them to burn very rapidly.

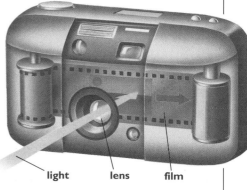

light   lens   film

▲ Light enters a camera lens and is focused on the surface of the film. This is coated with light-sensitive chemicals the change color as the light strikes them. The chemical process of developing makes the image visible and permanent, producing a photograph.

❓ How is a photograph produced?

Cameras work by focusing light in order to produce an image on a light-sensitive surface. Some cameras work by forming the image on light-sensitive film. Sometimes film uses dyes that change color when exposed to light, as happens with film used to make colored slides or prints. Earlier, film or glass plates used a silver compound as the light-sensitive material. To produce a photographic print, the image is projected onto the surface of light-sensitive paper. It is treated with chemicals to make the print visible and prevent further changes when exposed to light.

Digital cameras are a recent development. They convert the image they receive into electrical signals that are stored. These signals can then be read by a computer and used to produce a picture on screen, which can then be printed out.

What do we obtain by mining?

Mining has taken place since the Stone Age, when flints were mined for making stone tools. By 3500 B.C., people were mining for copper, which they soon combined with tin to harden it and make tools and weapons. Today we mine minerals, diamonds, metals, coal, and rock for building material, using a variety of techniques.

How is mining carried out?

The earliest form of mining involved following seams of metal in tunnels driven into the rock. This method is still used today, usually in deep mines where other techniques would be impractical. Tunnels are dug with explosives and with automatic machines. Some of these mines go thousands of yards into the rock, becoming very hot and dangerous.

Placer mining uses huge floating dredgers to extract metals such as tin and copper from submerged mud. It extracts large amounts of metal inexpensively, but causes enormous environmental damage. Strip mining is used to obtain coal and minerals that lie close to the surface. Open pit mining involves blasting into the rock to produce a huge quarry from which material is removed, layer by layer.

▶ **Most of the deposits of coal and other useful minerals near the surface have been used up. Miners have to dig deeper, and modern technology is needed to ensure their safety.**

How is gold mined?

Gold is unusual because it is found in its metallic form, rather than as a chemical compound. Metallic gold, which is easy to identify and shape, has been mined for thousands of years. Most gold is found in what are called alluvial deposits. They consist of river mud containing tiny particles of gold washed out of rock over thousands of years. Water currents are used to wash away the mud and gravel, leaving the heavy gold particles. Gold is mined in many parts of the world, but most modern gold supplies come from countries such as South Africa and Russia.

Gold does not tarnish, and this makes it very valuable. It is used mainly for the manufacture of jewelry and for coating electrical contacts. It is also a very good conductor of electricity.

How is coal formed?

Coal is formed from the compressed remains of plants that lived in bogs 250–350 million years ago. This was during the Carboniferous Period, when primitive animals first appeared on the land. Coal formed from the remains of tree ferns and other primitive trees, which were covered with mud and sand and buried as new rock was laid down. Very gradually, over millions of years, this material turned into coal.

A similar process is taking place today in peat bogs, where the rotting remains of heather form peat. When dried, peat burns in a similar way to coal. In some parts of the world a soft shale, which is called brown coal, is mined. The hardest and most pure form of coal is anthracite, which contains very few impurities.

Fish and ships

Fish and shellfish are a particularly good source of protein and have always formed an important part of the diet of people living near rivers, lakes, and seas. The fishing industry has become highly efficient, using huge nets and long fishing lines to catch the fish, which are then processed and frozen.

Unfortunately, fishing has become so efficient that often not enough adult fish are left to breed. One solution is for fishing fleets to seek new types of fish from polar waters and the deep oceans. Another alternative is to farm fish, either in huge cages or in sheltered sea inlets and freshwater pools, taking away some of the pressure on stocks of fish in the open sea.

? How do we obtain oil?

Oil is thought to have formed from the remains of organisms that died millions of years ago. Billions of tiny organisms lived in shallow water or in the surface layers of the oceans. As they died, their remains settled to the bottom and were eventually buried. The remains were compressed under the weight of rock. They underwent chemical changes due to the high pressure and eventually formed oil and gas, which remained trapped under the rock layers.

Geologists locate deposits of oil, and holes are drilled so the oil can be extracted. Usually, water is pumped into an oil well under pressure, forcing the lighter oil up to the surface.

▶ The energy from the sun can be harnessed to provide power. Solar panels can produce electricity or heat domestic water or the water in swimming pools. The process is not efficient enough to replace conventional electricity supplies, but helps to conserve energy.

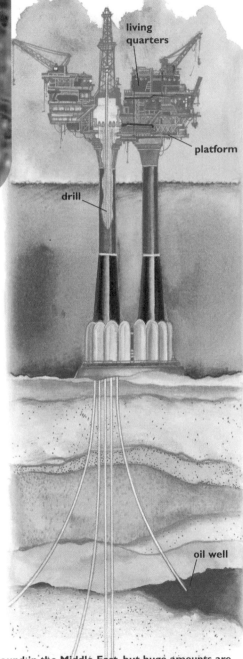

living quarters

platform

drill

oil well

▶ Much of the world's oil is found below ground in the Middle East, but huge amounts are buried beneath the seabed. Oil rigs are huge floating devices that are anchored to the seabed while wells are drilled into oil-bearing rock. These self-contained rigs contain all of the drilling machinery and a helicopter pad for receiving supplies.

? Can sunlight provide power?

As we use up natural resources such as coal and oil, there is a constant search for new sources of energy. The sun gives out vast amounts of energy, of which only a tiny fraction reaches the Earth. If we could use just a small part of this energy, it would fulfill all the world's foreseeable needs for power, but so far it has not been possible to find efficient ways to collect solar energy. We harness the sun's energy with solar panels. This energy is then used to heat water.

? Why is forestry important?

Trees are an important natural resource, because there is a constant demand for timber for building, for paper, and other purposes. In developing countries, wood is used as fuel for cooking. Even waste wood can be chipped and mixed with an adhesive under high pressure to form large flat building boards.

Tree felling in some areas has resulted in large scale deforestation, often followed by erosion. With no tree roots to stabilize it, the soil is washed away by rainfall.

▲ Water exists below even the driest deserts, stored in porous rock and sand. Sometimes the edges of these water deposits are exposed and an oasis is produced where plants will grow and animals can live.

❓ How do we obtain fresh supplies of water?

An adequate supply of clean water is essential for life and for health. Water is often drawn from rivers or may be pumped up out of the ground. Rainwater soaks into the ground and collects in areas where an impervious rocky layer stops the water from draining away. Wells are bored down into this layer to extract the water. A huge mass of fresh water in porous rock beneath the Sahara desert could supply all the water needs of North Africa for hundreds of years. Water from wells is usually stored in reservoirs. Before being used it is purified. The water goes to a settling tank where mud and sediment are removed. Chlorine is added to kill any microbes.

❓ What happens to our waste?

The huge quantities of domestic and industrial waste that we produce cause a major environmental problem. Sometimes waste is buried in vast landfill sites, which are often old quarries. Alternatively, waste can be burned or in some cases recycled.

Waste from our toilets, baths, and washing machines is collected in sewers and carried to a treatment plant. Bacterial action breaks down solid waste into a harmless form, and the waste is stirred in huge pools while this process takes place. After treatment, purified water is run off and can safely be drained into rivers. The solid material remaining is usually processed into fertilizer after further treatment to make sure it contains no dangerous microbes.

▶ Electricity is carried for long distances along cables supported high in the air by pylons. This keeps the current from escaping into the ground and is cheaper than burying the cables.

❓ How is electricity supplied to our homes?

Electricity is generated by burning gas, coal or oil, by water or hydroelectric power, or by nuclear power. The distribution of power to homes varies in different countries. In the United States, voltages from power stations range from 4,000 to 35,000 volts, with the most common being 15,000 volts. The electricity is carried on cables strung between high pylons, where insulators prevent it from escaping to the ground. The cables are interconnected across the United States and Canada to form a single grid. If there is a fault with one power station, power can still be obtained from the grid.

The electricity is drawn off in sub-stations, which reduce it to 120 volts. This voltage is used through most of North America, while in Europe 240 volts are used.

Clever cloth

Weaving fibers into cloth is one of the oldest human skills. Representations of woven fabrics have been found on small Stone Age statues, and by 5000 B.C. the Egyptians were weaving textiles. Cloth is usually made from wool, cotton, flax (linen), silk, or artificial fibers such as nylon. Natural fibers such as wool and cotton are twisted into yarns before use.

All cloth is woven from two sets of yarn. One set of yarn stretches lengthways along the loom (weaving machine), while the other set runs crosswise, over and under the first set of yarn. This process can be done by hand or by high-speed power looms. Some looms produce fabric at a rate of 60 mph.

How does an electric motor work?

Most powered devices in the home contain an electric motor, which turns electric energy into movement. When an electric current passes along a wire in the field of a magnet, it exerts a force to move the wire. Usually the magnet is still, while the coil carrying the current spins around inside it. Domestic motors run on alternating current, and the current in the coil is rapidly reversed so the magnet's poles change direction too, forcing the coil to make another half-turn. This process is repeated very rapidly as the motor turns.

When a motor runs from direct current, which flows in only one direction, a device called a commutator reverses the current and causes the coil to rotate.

How is natural gas obtained?

Natural gas is widely used to supply energy for domestic use and for industrial processes. It was formed millions of years ago by the same process that produced oil. Gas flows or is pumped out of boreholes, often mixed with oil and water. The gas is separated and passes through a refinery. Some of its constituents, such as propane and butane, are removed and liquefied so they can be pumped into cylinders and used as fuel. Liquefied gases held under pressure can be carried all around the world in specially constructed ships.

The remaining gas, which consists mostly of methane, is pumped along pipelines for domestic use. Methane has no smell, so a strong-smelling additive is used to make people aware of gas leaks.

How does a photocopier work?

Most modern photocopiers use a process called xerography, which was invented in 1937. Photocopiers contain a drum, which is coated with a photosensitive substance. It only conducts electricity when light falls on it. The drum is charged with static electricity. An image of the document to be copied is focused onto the drum. Where it strikes the drum's surface, the static electrical charge is removed, leaving an electrostatic image of the document. The drum is then coated with black toner powder, which sticks to the charged areas. It transfers the powder to a sheet of paper, which is heated to make the impression permanent. Some older types of copier use a 'wet' process. These machines are used to make large prints of engineering drawings.

▼ Most electric motors consist of a series of electromagnetic coils that rotate inside a series of magnets. The coils are energized by current passing through a device called the commutator, which rotates past carbon brushes that carry the electricity that powers the motor.

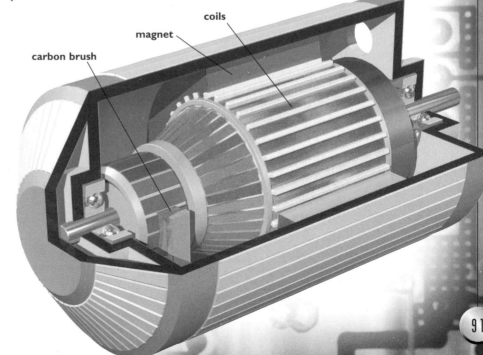

coils

magnet

carbon brush

Discoveries

? Who invented the modern science of astronomy?

Galileo Galilei (1564–1642) built several telescopes and observed the movements of the moon and planets. He was the first person to discover that the surface of the Moon is rough and cratered, and not smooth as had been supposed for centuries. He also found that he could use the swing of a pendulum to measure time.

Galileo got into trouble with the authorities when he claimed that the Earth moved around the sun, rather than the sun moving around the Earth. This idea was thought to be a threat to biblical teaching, and Galileo was placed under house arrest for the remainder of his life.

? Who invented the scientific method?

Archimedes was a Greek mathematician who lived between about 287 and 212 B.C. Unlike many Greek philosophers of the time, Archimedes believed in making experiments to prove that his theories worked. He made practical inventions, such as the Archimedean screw which is still used today to lift water for irrigation. He also worked out the laws that govern the use of levers and pulleys.

Archimedes is most famous for allegedly leaping out of his bath in excitement shouting 'Eureka!' (the Greek for 'I have found it!'). He did this when he realized that his body displaced a volume of water equal to its own volume.

▼ The screw was just one of the inventions of the Greek philosopher Archimedes. It was originally used to pump water and is still used today in some developing countries to irrigate the fields.

▲ Ben Franklin developed lightning rods to protect buildings from storm damage.

? Who first understood lightning?

Ben Franklin (1706–1790) was an American with many talents. He was a printer, scientist, and politician who played an important part in founding the United States. He discovered the nature of lightning while flying a kite during a thunderstorm. Franklin noticed sparks jumping from a key tied to the end of the wet string. This could easily have killed him, but it did not. He went on to invent the lightning conductor, a strip of copper that is run from the top of a building to the ground in order that lightning can earth itself safely.

? Who discovered the double helix?

The scientists James Watson and Francis Crick studied genes in an attempt to find out about their structure. The genetic material DNA (deoxyribonucleic acid) is a complicated molecule, and it had been difficult to understand how DNA could copy itself when cells reproduce. Watson and Crick found that it was shaped like a stepladder twisted into a spiral, and that if the two sides were pulled apart, the 'rungs' of the ladder would automatically reproduce the rest of the molecule.

▶ The electrical nature of the nervous system was discovered after Italian scientist Galvani noticed how frogs' legs twitched when an electrical current was applied to the nerve.

❓ How did frogs' legs lead to an understanding of the nervous system?

Luigi Galvani (1737–1798) was an Italian scientist. He accidentally noticed that severed frogs' legs twitched when the nerve was touched with a pair of metal scissors during a thunderstorm. Alessandro Volta (after whom the volt is named) explained why this happened. It was because an electrical current was produced between two metals, which provided the stimulation to the nerves. This discovery later led to the realization that the nervous system works by means of electrical signals.

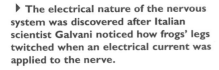

Atomic

Ernest Rutherford (1871–1937) was a physicist who studied radioactivity. He found several different forms of radiation and also discovered that elements change as a result of radioactive decay. He received a Nobel Prize for this work. Rutherford went on to discover the nucleus of the atom, and in 1919, he finally succeeded in splitting an atom for the first time.

❓ Who developed the theory of relativity?

Albert Einstein (1879–1955) was a physicist who was born in Germany but lived in Switzerland and the U.S.A. in later life. He developed the theory of relativity, which led to the famous equation $E = mc^2$ (which very few people actually understand).

Einstein's work is the basis for most of our theories about the nature, history, and structure of the universe. He laid down the rules that govern objects moving close to the speed of light and explained why travel at this sort of speed could distort time itself. His work also proved invaluable in the development of the atomic bomb.

❓ Who discovered the radioactive element radium?

Marie Curie and her husband Pierre began their research into radioactivity in 1895. They soon discovered the new element thorium, and in 1898 they discovered two other elements — polonium and radium. They received the Nobel Prize for physics for this work in 1903, although they shared the prize with Henri Becquerel, who researched the same subject. After her husband's death, Marie continued her research, winning a second Nobel Prize before dying in 1934 of cancer caused by unprotected exposure to atomic radiation. A new element discovered in 1944 was named curium in her honor.

No crops visible

⁇ Who invented the first steam engine?

During the 1st century A.D., a Greek inventor and mathematician, called Hero of Alexandria, produced a device that later led to the development of modern turbines and jet engines. Hero's device was a hollow water-filled ball mounted on a swivel. Two nozzles stuck out on opposite sides, pointing in different directions. When the ball was heated, steam shot out of the nozzles, causing the ball to spin rapidly.

Hero failed to see the practical use of this device and regarded it as an interesting toy. He went on to invent several mathematical formulae, one of which is still used for calculating the area of a triangle.

⁇ Who invented the microscope?

Although he was actually a draper, the Dutchman Antonie van Leeuwenhoek (1632–1723) ground glass lenses and used them to examine the world about him. In the 1670s he made his first crude microscope with a tiny lens, and this allowed him to be the first person to see microscopic life such as bacteria, yeast, and living blood cells. During his career, van Leeuwenhoek ground a total of 419 lenses, and his microscopes became progressively more effective.

⁇ Who invented sound recording?

Thomas Edison (1847–1931) worked with telegraphic printers, but in 1876 he invented the first phonograph, a clockwork device that recorded sound onto a wax cylinder. Edison was a prolific inventor, and only three years later he invented the first light bulb. His kinetoscope was the first machine to produce moving pictures and eventually led to the development of modern cinema. Edison eventually patented 1,097 inventions.

▼ Some microcopes are so powerful they can magnify the smallest objects many thousands of times. This plant cell is invisible to the naked eye.

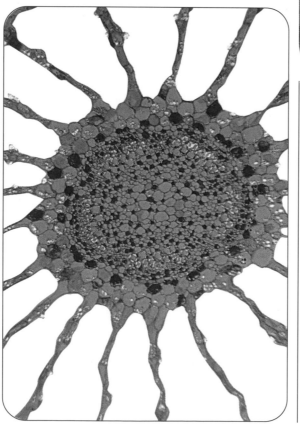

Laughing gas

Sir Humphry Davy (1778–1829) was a British chemist who first described the pain-killing results of inhaling the gas nitrous oxide. This allowed the gas to be used as a dental anaesthetic, although it became famous for inducing fits of laughter in those who inhaled only small amounts of the gas.

⁇ Who invented the first telephone?

Alexander Graham Bell (1847–1922) was born in Scotland but moved to the U.S.A. He realized that sound consists of vibrations, and he began working out a way of changing these vibrations into electrical impulses. These impulses could then be carried along a wire — this was the origin of the telephone. His rival, Thomas Edison, soon produced a much improved version of Bell's telephone. Bell retaliated by devising a better version of Edison's own phonograph.

▲ The Wrights were the first people to invent a practical airplane that could be flown under full control. Although it looked like a box kite, the **Wright Flyer** was a practical and successful aircraft.

Who made the first powered flight?

In 1903, at Kitty Hawk in the United States, Orville Wright made what is said to be the first controlled powered flight of a heavier-than-air craft. People had already flown small airships, but there was now a race to make the first successful airplane. The Wright brothers and other would-be pilots had already built several gliders. The Wright biplane looked like a huge box kite, with a home-made engine that drove two propellers by means of chains — but it flew and it was controllable.

Clément Adler, in France, had flown under power in 1890 in a bat-shaped airplane powered by a steam engine. However, the aircraft was not controllable, so many people do not accept his attempt as the first flight.

Who invented the jet engine?

Frank Whittle designed the first true jet engine between 1928 and 1930, but it was not used to fly a jet aircraft until 1941. Meanwhile, the German engineer Hans von Ohain began work on a similar jet engine in 1936. His engine had flown a Heinkel aircraft by 1939. German developments proceeded more rapidly, and Germany had a jet fighter plane in action before the end of World War II.

Who built the first motor vehicle?

In 1771, Nicolas Cugnot produced what was probably the first self-powered vehicle, driven by steam. In 1801, the Englishman Richard Trevithick ran a steam car along a road in Cornwall, reaching a speed of 7 mph. From then until the end of the 1800s, all successful road vehicles were powered by steam, although there were many experiments with gas engines. Then in 1885, Karl Benz in Germany built the first successful modern motor car, powered by a gas engine.

Who invented the computer?

Various types of mechanical calculators had already been invented when, in 1835, Charles Babbage, a professor of mathematics at Cambridge University, described the principle of an analytical engine. This was the world's first programmable computer, using a system of cogwheels and data entered by means of punched cards. Ada, Countess Lovelace, was also a mathematician, and she wrote several computer programs for Babbage's device. The analytical engine was, sadly, far ahead of its time and was never developed past its first crude form.

The first practical computer was Colossus, a huge mechanical device invented to help break German secret codes during World War II. It was based on the theories of the eccentric mathematician Alan Turing.

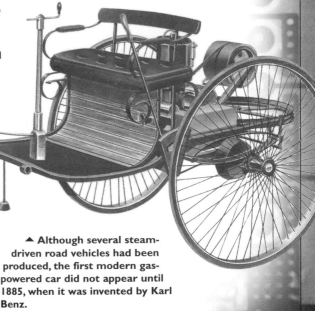

▲ Although several steam-driven road vehicles had been produced, the first modern gas-powered car did not appear until 1885, when it was invented by Karl Benz.

Nature

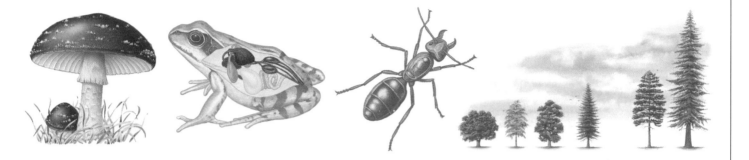

Life has existed on this planet for hundreds of millions of years. No one is quite sure when the first form of life appeared or how this differed from the chemical compounds that formed in the seas covering much of the Earth. But somehow, these chemicals developed the ability to group together into life forms that could grow and reproduce. Some scientists think that this life may have first appeared around the volcanic vents spewing hot material from the interior of the Earth into the chilly waters of the deep-sea abyss. Others believe that life began in shallow seas and pools.

Once life had begun, it flourished everywhere and changed the face of the planet. Due to the growth of microscopic plants, the atmosphere itself was changed from choking poison gas to oxygen-rich air that allowed animals to evolve. Life swiftly spread to the land, and a whole series of new creatures appeared. Some of these were nature's experiments, such as ammonites and trilobites, and though they survived for millions of years, they were unable to successfully adapt to changes in their environment.

Nature is incredibly diverse, and all forms of life are interconnected in some way. Animals feed on each other and on plants; fungi consume dead forms of life and sometimes prey on the living; plants adapt to almost all forms of environment on Earth and provide food and shelter for animals.

We can be attacked by the simplest forms of life, such as bacteria and viruses, but at the same time we can use these organisms to make drugs and vaccines to protect against infection.

❓ What do we mean by 'nature?'

Nature is the term we use to describe all living things and the ways in which they relate to the Earth on which we live.

❓ Why do animals and plants have complicated Latin names?

Most plants and animals have popular names that vary from place to place. Scientific names are given so that the same name is recognized everywhere.

Latin is used for scientific names. Centuries ago, it was the language of learned people. Scientific names are in two parts. The first is the generic name, which describes a group of related living things. The second name is the specific name, which applies only to that living thing.

The specific name may describe the living thing, or it could include the name of the person who discovered it. For example, a human being is called *Homo sapiens* (thinking man). A fossil form of *Homo*, or man, is *Homo habilis* (tool-using man).

▲ **Carl Linnaeus (1707–1778) established the modern scientific method for naming plants and animals.**

❓ Which scientists study nature?

Nature is a subject that involves many different types of scientists. Zoologists study animals, and botanists study plants. There are many other subdivisions within these individual subjects. Paleontologists, for example, study extinct creatures, whereas biologists study living things. Look at the chart below to find out other subject areas that are studied by scientists.

Type of scientist	The study of
Anthropologist	Human beings and their way of life
Bacteriologist	Bacteria
Biologist	Living things
Botanist	Plants
Ecologist	Living things and their environment
Marine biologist	Life in and around the sea
Ornithologist	Birds
Paleontologist	Fossils
Physiologist	The functions of living things and their parts
Zoologist	Animals

❓ What is evolution?

Evolution is the name given to the gradual adaptation of living things to take advantage of the environment in which they live.

This process, which takes place over millions of years, can mean that both animals and plants can change their appearance, size, and habits, and eventually become new species.

❓ How do we know that evolution really happened?

We can see how evolution has changed living things by examining fossils. Fossils preserve the body parts of living creatures from long ago, so we can see how they have changed over millions of years. Sometimes the changes are very gradual, while others seem to have taken place quite rapidly. It is often possible to find a series of fossils, with each one showing a gradual change. This can tell us how a creature has altered due to the process of evolution. For example, scientists have traced the evolution of the horse from a tiny ancestor with normal toes to the large-hoofed animal we see today.

❓ How did Charles Darwin develop his theory of evolution?

The English scientist Charles Darwin (1809–1882) developed his ideas about evolution after years of study and voyages of exploration. He realized that many small and isolated islands had populations of unique creatures. Darwin was able to show how these creatures differed from their close relatives elsewhere. In the Galapagos Islands, for example, he found that finches had adapted to take advantage of the fact that there were few other birds. The finches had evolved into 80 different types, each one adapted to a particular lifestyle. Some had even become predators.

Darwin's islands

The Galapagos Islands have a unique range of animal life, due to their isolation from the South American mainland. Few new animals have been able to colonize the islands, and the original inhabitants have evolved in isolation. In addition to Darwin's finches, the Galapagos Islands now have a population of penguins and fur seals that live together with tropical animals. The marine iguanas (large lizards that swim underwater to graze on seaweed) are unique. A different type of the famous giant tortoise has evolved to live on each island in the group (some are recently extinct). The only natural inhabitant that is not unique to the Galapagos, apart from some bird species, is a small lizard.

(?) Can we see evolution in action today?

Some forms of evolution take place quickly, and we can see evolution in progress in some types of moth.

The peppered moth uses its coloring to hide from predators as it rests on the bark of a tree. Industrial pollution had blackened tree bark, so the light-colored moths became visible to predators and were eaten, while the few dark moths were able to reproduce and replace them. Now industrial pollution is being controlled, and the tree bark is lighter in color. The dark moths stand out and are eaten, while the lighter moths are reproducing to replace them once more.

(?) What is natural selection?

Natural selection is a process that is also known as the 'survival of the fittest.' Every time an animal or plant reproduces, tiny changes in the genes make the offspring slightly different from its parent. Sometimes these changes can make the offspring more successful than its parents. For example, a young giraffe with a longer than normal neck can graze higher in the trees than other giraffes and therefore has access to more food. As a result, it will become healthier and stronger and will be more likely to breed successfully, passing its new genes for longer necks to its offspring. Other genes could be damaging, so the animals carrying them will be less successful and may eventually die out.

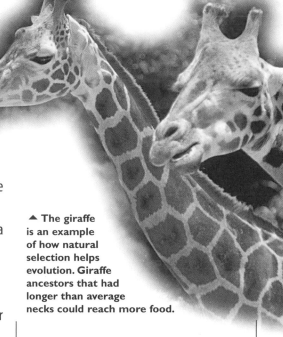

▲ The giraffe is an example of how natural selection helps evolution. Giraffe ancestors that had longer than average necks could reach more food.

(?) Have we changed our views about evolution?

Modern biologists and paleontologists have many examples to prove Darwin's theories.

Fossil discoveries have filled in some of the gaps in our knowledge of the evolution of prehistoric life. Modern genetics has allowed the relationships of living creatures to be uncovered. For example, we now know that 98 percent of our genes are identical to those of the chimpanzee, which shows that we had a similar ancestor in the distant past. Scientists now think that evolution proceeds in a series of small jumps, rather than as a slow, continuous change, as was originally thought.

◀ When Charles Darwin published his theories on evolution, they created a sensation and were soon widely accepted.

What is an animal?

Animals are one of the major groups of living things. The other two groups are plants and fungi.

The cells of animals differ from plant cells because there is no hard cell wall. The cell contents are held together with a flexible membrane. Animals are not able to make their own food, but must obtain food from plants or fungi. Most animals are able to move about and to respond to changes in their environment. About three-quarters of all living things are animals.

What are the two main groups of animals?

The animal kingdom is divided into two groups – vertebrates and invertebrates. The vertebrate group contains all animals with backbones (as well as some that have a primitive form of backbone). Vertebrates include fish, amphibians, reptiles, birds, and mammals. Invertebrates have no backbone. They include worms, molluscs, corals, scorpions, spiders, insects, and crustaceans such as crabs and lobsters. Scientists divide these two main groups into smaller groupings that show the relationship between all these animals.

▶ Phyla are major groups of living creatures that have a number of important characteristics in common. The process of evolution shows how the phyla become more complex over many millions of years of geological time.

What are vertebrates?

Vertebrates have a backbone that provides support for the muscles and protection for the spinal cord. The backbone is actually a series of small bones called vertebrae. They are jointed together and locked with rope-like ligaments to provide a flexible but extremely strong anchor for the back muscles. The spinal cord runs down a channel inside the vertebrae, providing protection from damage. In some primitive fish, such as sharks and rays, the spine is made of a tough rubbery material called cartilage.

▼ Molluscs are soft-bodied animals. Some have snail-like shells while others have two shells that are hinged together.

▲ Annelida, or worms, are a major group of invertebrate animals. Their limbless, tubular bodies are divided into many segments.

▶ Coelenterata are a group of small animals including sea anemones and corals. Most, like jellyfish, live in the sea and have arms covered with stinging cells. They feed on plankton.

▲ Protozoa are tiny single-celled animals with soft bodies surrounded by cell membranes. Most are able to swim.

▲ Fish live solely water. They have scaly skin, and sw using fins. Almost all breathe throu gills, taking oxyge from the water.

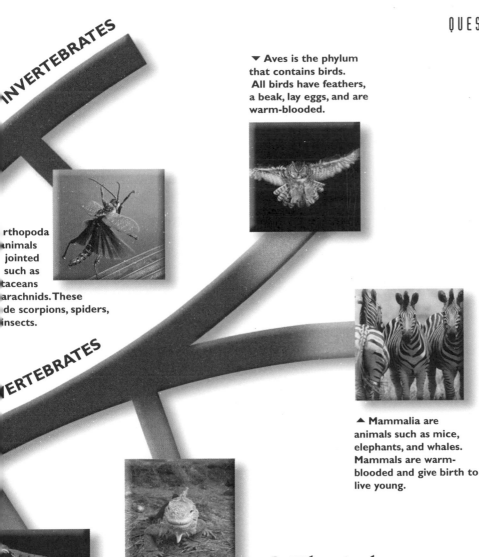

INVERTEBRATES

rthopoda
nimals
jointed
such as
taceans
arachnids. These
de scorpions, spiders,
nsects.

VERTEBRATES

▼ Aves is the phylum
that contains birds.
All birds have feathers,
a beak, lay eggs, and are
warm-blooded.

▲ Mammalia are
animals such as mice,
elephants, and whales.
Mammals are warm-
blooded and give birth to
live young.

▲ Reptilia include
lizards, snakes, turtles,
and crocodiles. All are
cold-blooded and have
scaly skins.

mphibia return to
water to breed.
ir young are larvae
change shape as
become adults.

How are animals related to each other?

The fossil record and modern studies on genetics have shown how animals have evolved from simple worm-like organisms.

The development and relationship of animals can be drawn like a tree, with branches representing each of the major forms of life. This shows that vertebrates probably split off from primitive worm-like ancestors many millions of years ago. Invertebrates, such as insects and spiders, developed along quite a different line of evolution. Many branches of the evolutionary tree were unsuccessful and have died out, for example, the dinosaurs.

How do animals reproduce?

Apart from some of the simplest animals, reproduction requires a sperm to fuse with an egg cell. This fusion produces an embryo that will develop into a new animal. Some simple worms and single-celled animals can simply split in two. However, sexual reproduction is the most common means by which animals produce copies of themselves. Some animals, such as snails, contain male and female cells and can fertilize themselves. A few animals are all female and can reproduce without a male. These include aphids and the greenfly.

Sexual reproduction is important because it mixes genes. This can prevent the deterioration of a species.

What is the advantage of being warm-blooded?

The chemical reactions that power the bodies of animals work best at warmer temperatures.

Warm-blooded animals are able to live and move about at any temperature that they experience in their normal environment. They can do this because their internal temperature is always the same. Cold-blooded animals, however, become sluggish as the temperature around them drops, and many will hibernate or migrate in very cold weather.

Which animals are warm blooded?

Mammals and birds are the main groups of warm-blooded animals. Some very active fish, such as tuna, are also warm-blooded. However, the mechanism that heats their bodies is different from that of mammals and birds.

⑦ What is a mammal?

Mammals are vertebrate animals that nourish their young with milk. All mammals are warm-blooded.

At some stage in their development they all have hair, although this sometimes disappears before they are born.

⑦ Do all mammals give birth to live young?

True mammals all give birth to live young, which are smaller versions of the adult animal.

An unusual group of Australian mammals, called monotremes, lay eggs. Echidnas, or spiny anteaters, are monotremes. The other monotreme is the duck-billed platypus. The appearance of this animal is so strange that when it was first described, scientists assumed that the animal was a clumsy fake! The duck-billed platypus has a leathery bill shaped like a duck's beak, a body similar to an otter and a tail very much like a beaver's. To make things even stranger, it has poisonous spurs on its legs, too!

▲ The duck-billed platypus is perfectly adapted for swimming and lays a single egg from which its helpless young hatch.

⑦ What is a marsupial?

Most mammals nourish their developing babies in the womb through an organ called the placenta. Marsupials do not have this organ.

In marsupials, the baby is born at a very early stage of its development and is usually only a few millimeters long. The baby makes its way slowly up the mother's stomach and crawls into a protective pouch. The baby attaches itself to a teat through which it receives milk while it develops. As the baby grows larger, it is able to leave the pouch, returning to feed. Marsupials are said to be

Save our panda

Several mammals are on the verge of extinction, mostly because of human activities. The most familiar of these mammals is the giant panda, which lives in bamboo thickets in the mountains of China. Due to its isolated way of life, the number of pandas has never been very large. The panda has now become very scarce as a result of hunting, loss of suitable habitats, and its very slow rate of reproduction. The rat, in contrast, is very unlikely to ever become extinct because of its ability to adapt to almost any circumstances it meets.

more primitive than most other mammals. However, they are highly successful in Australia where they have been isolated from invasion by other animals and have survived for millions of years.

▼ **Tigers are usually thought of as animals of the tropical rainforests of Asia, but they are also found in the freezing tundra of Siberia. Siberian tigers are larger than their tropical cousins and have very thick coats to keep them warm.**

◀ The rat is a very good example of adaptation.

Which is the smallest mammal?

Shrews are the smallest kind of mammal. Some weigh less than one ounce. A shrew looks like a mouse with a long snout, but it is not closely related to rodents. Shrews feed on insects and other animals and need to eat almost continuously in order to survive.

Can mammals fly?

Bats are the only mammals that are capable of true flight. Several other mammals are capable of gliding for considerable distances.

Bats are efficient flyers, although their wings have developed very differently from those of birds. A bat's wing is like an outstretched hand with very long fingers, connected by thin skin. Other mammals, such as squirrels and marsupials, are able to glide by means of sheets of skin stretched between their front and back legs. They use these sheets to travel from tree to tree. These animals are not closely related, and yet they have developed the ability to fly quite separately. This is an example of parallel evolution.

What is parallel evolution?

Mammals, like other animals, sometimes develop a body shape or lifestyle that is very similar to that of an unrelated animal living in exactly the same environment.

Dolphins, for example, have a very similar body shape to sharks and to the extinct marine reptile ichthyosaurus, because they inhabit the same environment and have a very similar way of life. In the same way, kangaroos have adapted to a similar lifestyle to antelopes and sheep, grazing in open grasslands. This process is called parallel evolution, and it demonstrates how animals develop in the same way in order to fit in with the available living space and food supply.

Which is the largest land mammal?

The largest living land animal is the African elephant, which reaches a weight of 16,500 pounds and stands 9—14 feet high at the shoulders when fully grown.

However, the African elephant is dwarfed by some extinct plant-eating dinosaurs, which may have weighed at least 80 tons, and reached a length of 98 feet. It was thought that the weight of these huge creatures had to be supported by water. It is now known that they inhabited regions similar to those of elephants.

Which is the most successful mammal on Earth?

We like to think that humans are the most successful animals, but it could be argued that rats are even more successful. Rats are found wherever people live, and they can adapt to live in most environments. The two common types are the brown rat and the black rat. Rats produce up to seven litters per year, each one containing between 6 and 22 young.

Rats are a source of disease, and their droppings frequently contaminate stored food. Black rats were responsible for the spread of the Black Death in the Middle Ages, which killed millions of people in Europe. Rats are very difficult to control because they quickly adapt to the effects of poisons and learn to avoid traps.

Rats are also highly intelligent and are able to exploit new food sources. They climb walls to enter food stores or tunnel beneath walls, and can even bite through plastic or water pipes in order to drink. They are omnivorous, which means that they can live on almost any edible substance.

🄐 How are birds different from mammals?

The structure of a bird is very similar to that of a mammal. Birds differ from mammals in that their front limbs are modified as wings and they possess feathers instead of hair. Birds do not have teeth but use their horny beak to cut, crush, and tear their food, although much of it is swallowed whole. They use a muscular organ called the gizzard to grind their food after swallowing it. Many birds swallow stones that lodge in their gizzard and help this grinding process. Bird wings are based on heavily adapted forelimbs. On each wing, a very small thumb is hidden beneath the feathers. The other fingers are fused together to provide a firm support for the wing.

🄐 Can all birds fly?

Several birds have lost the ability to fly because flight is unnecessary for their way of life. Penguins and ostriches have very small wings and cannot fly. The penguin uses its wings in underwater 'flight,' while the ostrich uses its wings only when displaying to other ostriches. The extinct dodo and the modern kiwi are examples of flightless birds. A rare kind of parrot has also lost the power of flight.

🄐 How do birds fly?

Birds' bodies are very highly modified to give them the power of flight. Their bones are hollow to keep them light. Their bodies are extremely light too, allowing them to glide and to fly with the minimum of effort. For example, an eagle with a wing span of more than 6.5 feet weighs less than 9 pounds. Birds have air sacs linked to their lungs to provide extra oxygen as they flap their wings.

Flying is not just a matter of flapping wings up and down. It is usually a mixture of gliding and powered flight. When the wings are flapped, they move in a complicated path, scooping air downward and backward. The wings twist so that the air is pushed back in the right direction to provide lift. The wings are twisted again on the forward stroke so that they slide easily through the air and do not slow down the bird's flight.

🄐 Which is the largest bird?

The largest living bird is the ostrich. It stands up to 8 feet high and weighs 300 pounds. Two extinct birds, the moa of New Zealand and the elephant bird of Madagascar, stood about 10 feet high and would dwarf even the ostrich. The largest living bird capable of flight is the albatross, which has a wing span of 11.5 feet. However, the largest known flying bird lived about 2 million years ago. It was a condor-like bird with a 16 feet wing span.

🄐 Which is the smallest bird?

The smallest living bird is the bee humming bird from Cuba, which is only 2 inches long and weighs 1 ounce. A long, slim beak takes up nearly half of its length.

Hummingbirds use their long tongue to feed on flower nectar, which they sip while in hovering flight. Their wings beat 80 times per second while they are hovering. Hummingbirds are able to fly backward and sideways as they manuver to find nectar in another flower.

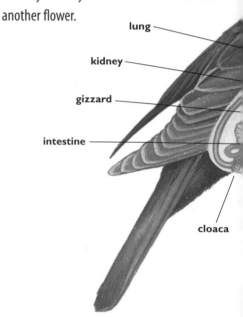

lung

kidney

gizzard

intestine

cloaca

🄐 How far can birds fly?

The longest distance regularly traveled by birds is the annual migration of Arctic terns from the Arctic to the Antarctic. They travel 18,600 miles each year. Even the tiny hummingbird is able to travel enormous distances, and they have been known to cross the Gulf of Mexico, which is a vast distance of 500 miles.

◀ The ostrich cannot fly, but its powerful legs enable it to run at speeds of up to 37 mph.

▶ The hummingbird is the world's smallest bird. It can hover backwards as it feeds on flower nectar.

beak

gullet

crop

heart

liver

◀ Birds are warm-blooded animals with similar organs to those of mammals. They also have a powerful, muscular gizzard which is used for grinding and crushing food. The air passage extends from the lungs into hollow bones, making them extremely light.

? Which is the most common bird?

Some birds live only in certain areas of the world, but the most successful birds are found almost everywhere.

Settlers introduced the starling and the sparrow into most countries. Like rats, these birds are so adaptable that they have increased in enormous numbers. The most common bird of all was the passenger pigeon, which lived in North America in such huge flocks that they darkened the skies for days during their migrations. These birds were hunted nearly to extinction during the 1800s, and the last one died in a zoo in 1914.

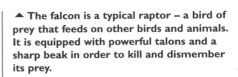

▲ The falcon is a typical raptor – a bird of prey that feeds on other birds and animals. It is equipped with powerful talons and a sharp beak in order to kill and dismember its prey.

? How fast can birds fly?

Most birds fly at speeds of 20-30mph. In general, the heavier the bird the faster it needs to fly in order to stay in the air.

However, a racing pigeon has been timed at more than 90 mph, and it is claimed that the Indian spine-tailed swift can fly at more than 190 mph. The peregrine falcon is a very fast flyer, and is said to travel at more than 190 mph when diving on its prey. Strictly speaking this is not flight because the falcon closes its wings and drops like a stone to pick up speed. The prey is usually killed outright by the strength and speed of the falcon's strike. Powerful muscles in the bird's legs help to cushion the enormous impact of the strike. Afterward, the falcon follows the dead or stunned prey to the ground and often feeds there, as the prey may be too large for the bird to carry it away.

? Which birds hardly ever land?

Swifts and frigate birds spend almost all their life in the air. They never walk on the ground because the length of their wings would stop them from taking off again. Swifts rest by clinging to a vertical surface, and they then launch themselves into the air. Frigate birds are large seabirds that sleep on the wing, using only a section of their brain to keep flying.

Giant eggs

Ostriches lay the biggest eggs, which weigh about 3 pounds. However, in proportion to the bird's huge size, this is not really very large. Smaller birds lay proportionately bigger eggs; for example, the flightless kiwi of New Zealand lays a single egg that can weigh 16 ounces. This may not seem very heavy, but it is equal to one-third of the bird's total weight. The kiwi is a very strange creature. It is a nocturnal bird with a long beak with nostrils at the end, which it uses to probe into the soil to find the small insects.

Reptiles

⑦ What is a reptile?

A reptile is an air-breathing animal with a body structure between that of the amphibians and the birds and mammals. Reptiles are generally scaly and their eggs are fertilized internally.

Living reptiles include crocodiles, tortoises and turtles, snakes, and lizards. There are about 6,000 surviving species. Long ago there were many more kinds of reptiles, such as the dinosaurs and the flying pterosaurs.

⑦ How do snakes move?

Snakes have several ways of moving about. The most common way is to throw their body into loops and move forward by pressing against anything solid in their environment.

Another way in which snakes move is by waves of muscular contraction, which push the body along rather like an accordian being squeezed open and shut. The desert-living sidewinder moves by throwing a loop out to one side, then sliding its body towards the loop while throwing another loop sideways at the same time. The sidewinder looks like a spring rolling along the sand, but this is an effective way of moving on this soft surface. Most snakes are able to swim effectively by using a wriggling motion.

▲ The distinctive markings left by the sidewinder as it slides across the sand make its movements easy to track.

⑦ Do reptiles look after their young?

Most reptiles lay eggs or give birth to live young, which can then immediately live an independent existence.

Crocodiles, on the other hand, care for their young. They bury their eggs in warm sand and guard the nest until the young are ready to hatch. The mother will often carry the baby crocodiles in her mouth to the water, where they will be guarded for several weeks until they are old enough to live independently. However, an adult is quite happy to eat the babies of other crocodiles.

⑦ Why do some lizards lose their tails?

Some types of small lizard often deliberately lose their tails when attacked by predators. This is a defense mechanism, because the predator usually seizes the lizard by the tail as it tries to escape. The lizard's tail may continue to wriggle for a while after coming free, distracting the predator while the lizard escapes. The stump of the tail is quickly sealed over by special muscles that stop the bleeding. A new tail is gradually grown to replace the one that was lost.

⑦ What is a tuatara?

The tuatara is a lizard-like animal, over 2 feet long, that lives only on small islands off New Zealand. Its most interesting feature is a very primitive third eye, which is thought to be sensitive to light.

⑦ Which are the most poisonous snakes?

Every year about one million people are bitten by poisonous snakes, mostly in tropical regions of the world. Between 30,000 and 40,000 of these people die.

There are several groups of poisonous snakes, and their venom can attack the body in many different ways. Venom can attack the blood, the nervous system or, in the case of the rattlesnake, most of the body organs. The danger depends on how much venom is injected into the body through the snake's hollow fangs when it bites.

Rattlesnakes and copperheads are common hazards in North America, while vipers and their relatives, together with cobras and mambas, are common dangers in Africa and Asia. The spitting cobra is most unusual because it sprays venom into the eyes of its victim to blind it, rather than biting. Snake bites on humans are nearly always acts of defense. This is because the snake thinks that it is being attacked.

Super snakes

Giant snakes have been reported in many parts of the world. The largest officially recorded snake is the anaconda from South America, which sometimes reaches a length of 30 feet and is proportionately very thick. There are unconfirmed reports of even bigger specimens. The reticulated python of southeast Asia is a similar size, and both snakes are known to have killed and eaten people. Both these snakes are constrictors, which means that they crush their prey in their coils before eating them whole. Some venomous snakes are also very large. The Asian king cobra reaches a length of 18 feet. The American diamondback rattlesnake is probably the heaviest venomous snake, weighing up to 34 pounds.

◄ The cobra, although dangerously poisonous, rears up and tries to frighten away potential enemies before resorting to biting them. The cobra's hood expands to make it look bigger, and it also carries dark "eyes," which may frighten some predators.

⁇ Which is the largest living reptile?

The sea, or estuarine, crocodile can reach a length of 30ft, although it is usually much smaller. It is one of the most dangerous types of crocodile. Because sea crocodiles frequently enter the sea and travel for long distances, they are sometimes found in areas that were thought to be free of these dangerous animals. Some prehistoric crocodiles reached a length of 50 feet. Surviving relatives include the alligator of North America, the caiman of South America, and the gavial of India. True crocodiles live in Asia, Africa, and Australia.

▲ The Komodo dragon, is a huge monitor lizard found living in Indonesia.

▼ Crocodiles have changed very little since their ancestors lived alongside the dinosaurs. They are a very successful reptile and do not need to evolve further.

⁇ How long can reptiles live?

Giant tortoises are known to have lived for 177 years. Reptiles usually only die because of an accident, disease, or a predator. The chemical reactions powering reptiles' bodies take place very slowly, and this is thought to extend their lives.

⁇ What is the biggest land-dwelling reptile?

The largest surviving land-dwelling reptile is the Komodo dragon, a gigantic monitor lizard living on the small island of Komodo, in Indonesia. This aggressive lizard grows to a length of 9 feet and can weigh up to 300 pounds. It is a carrion eater with a keen sense of smell but it can also hunt and kill larger animals, including humans. This fearsome lizard is known to live for about 100 years. The giant tortoise of the Galapagos Islands is just as heavy as the Komodo dragon, reaching a length of 4 feet.

⁇ Which reptiles live in the sea?

Turtles, crocodiles, and snakes are all found in the sea. Turtles and sea crocodiles lay their eggs on land, but most sea snakes give birth to live young at sea. Many types of sea snakes have extremely powerful venom.

Turtles are found in most warm seas, coming ashore to bury their eggs in warm sand. They feed on animals and plants, and some can grow very large. The leatherback turtle is the largest turtle of all. It can reach a length of 7 feet and a weight of 1000 pounds, and there have been reported sightings of far bigger specimens.

What is an amphibian?

From an evolutionary point of view, amphibians are halfway between fish and reptiles. There are 4,400 living species of amphibian. This group includes frogs and toads, newts and salamanders, and an obscure group of burrowing creatures that are called caecilians.

Which amphibian lives in caves?

The olm is a blind newt-like amphibian that lives in flooded caves in eastern Europe. Like other cave-dwelling animals, it does not have any pigment in its skin and it never leaves the water.

Where do amphibians live?

Most amphibians live in moist places near rivers, streams, or lakes. They have thin, moist skin and cannot usually tolerate dry conditions. Amphibians are thought to be the descendants of the first animals to emerge from the sea onto land. Most amphibians are still partly aquatic, especially in their breeding habits.

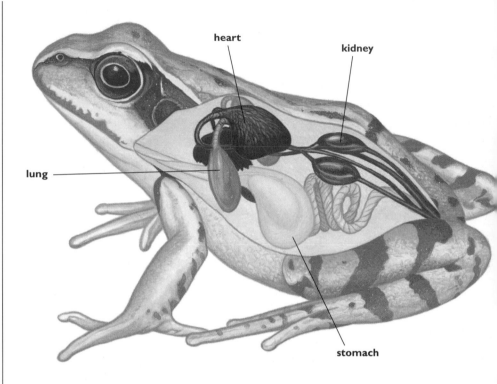

heart   kidney   lung   stomach

▲ The internal organs of an amphibian are typical of vertebrate animals, although their lungs and heart are much simpler than those of mammals and birds.

Why are amphibians important to humans?

Frogs and toads are particularly important in tropical regions because they keep insect pests under control. They eat enormous numbers of insects, and their tadpoles feed on pests such as mosquito larvae. Unfortunately, frogs are increasingly caught as food, and so their numbers are greatly reduced. Their thin skin makes them very susceptible to the poisonous effects of crop sprays, contributing further to their reduced numbers.

◄ A frog's eyes are on top of its head so it can see above the water's surface, watching out for predators.

Fatherly frogs

Frogs and toads have developed some of the most unusual and varied forms of reproduction known among vertebrate animals. The midwife toad drapes fertilized eggs around the hind legs of the male, who returns to the water every night to damp them down. He returns to the water when the eggs are hatched so the tadpoles emerge safely.

The Surinam toad is even more odd. As the eggs are fertilized, the male presses them onto the female's back. They sink into her skin, and each egg forms a small cell in which the tadpole develops. After 80 days, it emerges into the water as a small toad. The eggs and young of the Darwin's frog, found in South America, are brooded inside the male's vocal sac. Some frogs lay their eggs in water-filled holes high up in trees in the tropical forest, while others lay them on the damp ground and sit on them to keep the eggs moist.

? How do amphibians reproduce?

Nearly all amphibians have aquatic larvae called tadpoles, which usually lead an independent existence while they grow. In most amphibians, the male clasps the female and sheds sperm over the eggs as they are laid. The eggs of salamanders and caecilians are fertilized inside their bodies. Amphibian eggs are delicate and must be kept moist. The developing tadpoles may have a large rounded head and body before their legs appear, as in frogs and toads. The tadpoles of salamanders and newts are shaped like the adult animals, but they have feathery gills.

? Can amphibians live in dry deserts?

The bodies of some frogs and toads are adapted to survive in very dry conditions in deserts. During the brief rainy season, their bodies absorb huge amounts of water and become swollen like a bladder. These frogs and toads bury themselves deep in the ground to protect themselves from the heat and sun. They can survive for several years if necessary, until the next rains arrive. Once the rain comes, the amphibians emerge from their underground holes and breed quickly, laying their eggs in puddles. The tadpoles develop very rapidly before the puddles dry up.

? Are frogs and toads poisonous?

The skin of some frogs and toads contains poisons, which are among the most powerful known to humans. In South America, poison from the poison arrow frog is added to the arrow tips used by the Indians for hunting. Common toads contain poison that they exude through their skin if attacked. Dogs and cats commonly experience this poison, however they seldom suffer serious effects from it and quickly learn to avoid these amphibians. Cane toads are very large toads that contain a drug capable of causing hallucinations if it is eaten.

▲ The South American arrow frog is extremely poisonous. It advertises this danger by being very brightly colored.

? Which is the largest type of amphibian?

The giant salamander of Japan is a very strange-looking creature. It grows to a length of 5ft and lives in fast-flowing mountain streams. It breathes through its wrinkled and baggy skin. The giant salamander is a very sluggish animal that cannot move around on land.

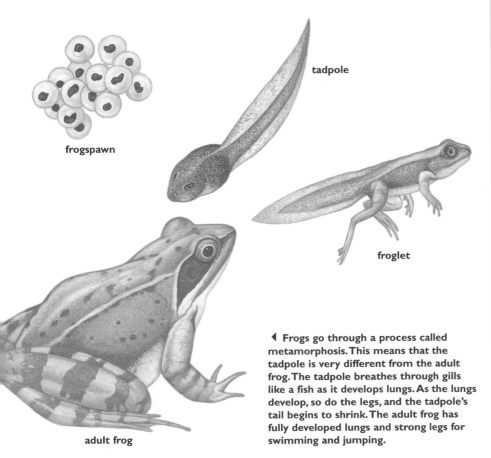

tadpole

frogspawn

froglet

◀ Frogs go through a process called metamorphosis. This means that the tadpole is very different from the adult frog. The tadpole breathes through gills like a fish as it develops lungs. As the lungs develop, so do the legs, and the tadpole's tail begins to shrink. The adult frog has fully developed lungs and strong legs for swimming and jumping.

adult frog

How can fish breathe underwater?

Fish are able to breathe underwater because they have special organs called gills. Gills are bars of tissue at the side of the fish's head. They carry masses of finger-like projections that contain tiny blood vessels. Water enters the fish's mouth and flows over the gills. The gill filaments take in dissolved oxygen from the water and pass it into the fish's blood. In this way, the gills have the same function as the lungs of air-breathing animals.

Can some fish breathe air?

Many fish that live in water containing little oxygen are able to breathe air. They usually have to do this in foul water, when bacterial decay reduces oxygen levels. Some fish have a special breathing organ called a labyrinth, and they rise to the surface every few minutes to breathe air into this organ. Many catfish breathe air in a similar way – they swallow it and it passes into their gut where oxygen is absorbed through the thin lining of the gut wall.

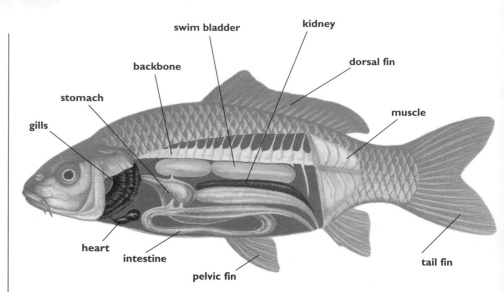

swim bladder · kidney · backbone · dorsal fin · stomach · muscle · gills · heart · intestine · tail fin · pelvic fin

▲ Most of a fish's body is composed of powerful muscles, and its internal organs are squeezed into a small area. Fish have a swim bladder, which is filled with gas in order to keep the fish buoyant in the water. The fins are used to propel and stabilize the fish in the water. Water is passed in through the mouth and over the gills to provide oxygen.

Where do fish live?

Fish have colonized almost every aquatic habitat and are found from the water's surface down to the deepest depths. They even live in warm springs and spring water containing large amounts of dissolved minerals. A fish's shape is modified to suit its lifestyle. Fish such as tuna and sharks are streamlined because they are powerful swimmers. Fish living in mountain torrents are often flat and have suckers to help them cling to stones to avoid being swept away.

Can fish fly?

Flying fish are able to launch themselves above the surface of the water to escape from predators. They support themselves in the air with large, outstretched fins. It is this that gives the appearance of flight.

The lower lobe of a flying fish's tail is extended so the fish can still propel itself along by beating it in the water while its body is above the surface. A single 'flight' above the water can cover a distance of 490 feet, at a speed of 35 mph.

▼ Salmon breed in small freshwater streams but spend most of their life in the sea. To breed, they return to the stream where they hatched. They even leap up waterfalls in order to reach their spawning grounds.

Male mom?

Seahorses and pipefish are very unusual creatures with rigid armored bodies. They lay their eggs and fertilize them in the normal way, but the eggs are then deposited in a groove on the stomach of the male. This groove folds over the eggs to form a kind of pouch. The eggs develop in this pouch and hatch, at which time the male seems to give birth to the young fish.

⟨?⟩ Why don't fish sink?

Most fish have an organ called a swim bladder, which is filled with gas to make them buoyant. The amount of gas in the swim bladder can be altered so that when the fish swims in deep water, and the pressure squeezes the swim bladder, more gas is pumped into it to compensate. When fish are caught in very deep water and pulled quickly to the surface, their swim bladder expands rapidly and may burst. Some fish, such as sharks and tuna, do not have swim bladders. They have to keep swimming so that they do not sink.

⟨?⟩ Can fish make electricity?

Electric eels are well known, and they can stun their prey with a powerful shock. Other fish can also produce electricity to kill their prey or to defend themselves. They include electric rays, which are common in many warm seas and also electric catfish living in African rivers. Fish called mormyrids, which live in very muddy waters in Africa, use electrical fields as a form of radar. This allows them to move about safely and to find food. They can also communicate by means of these electrical signals.

Sharks do not produce electricity, but they possess organs in their skin that can detect tiny electrical currents produced by the muscular movements of other fish. In this way they can hunt without being able to see their prey.

⟨?⟩ Which is the largest fish?

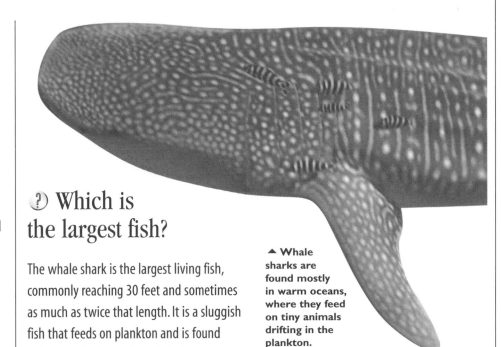

The whale shark is the largest living fish, commonly reaching 30 feet and sometimes as much as twice that length. It is a sluggish fish that feeds on plankton and is found only in tropical seas. One of the largest freshwater fish is the arapaima of South America, which reaches a length of almost 8 feet. The European catfish grows to a length of 15 feet and weighs around 600 pounds.

▲ **Whale sharks are found mostly in warm oceans, where they feed on tiny animals drifting in the plankton.**

▼ **Piranhas are aggressive fish, and can be dangerous in large numbers.**

⟨?⟩ Which is the most dangerous fish?

Sharks kill several people every year, probably because they mistake swimmers for seals, which are often their normal prey.

The small piranha can also be extremely dangerous. Piranhas live in rivers in South America. They are stocky disc-shaped fish, about 12 inches. in length, with a blunt head. Piranhas feed by biting out a crescent-shaped piece from their prey with razor-sharp interlocking teeth. They can give a nasty bite, but are not really dangerous unless they attack in large numbers. Piranhas are supposed to be able to strip all the flesh from a pig or cow in a few minutes, but they are probably not dangerous to humans unless they are attracted by blood.

⁉ What are arthropods?

Arthropods are animals with a hard external skeleton like a suit of armor. The skeleton is jointed to allow movement. Arthropods have evolved in a different way to vertebrates, and even their blood is chemically different, and so it is not red. They do not have a brain and spinal cord like vertebrates. Instead, they have a nerve cord running along the underside of their body and small thickenings of this nerve cord instead of a brain. Arthropods have efficient eyes, but these work in a different way from those of vertebrates. Arthropods such as spiders may have many eyes.

⁉ How does an arthropod grow?

The rigid shell of arthropods cannot stretch to allow the animal to grow, so the shell must be discarded. When the shell splits open, the animal emerges and withdraws its legs and antennae. The newly emerged animal is soft and can now increase in size. A new hard shell forms within a few days. The animal is vulnerable to predators during this period, and must hide away while the new shell develops.

◀ A spider's web is incredibly strong and forms a deadly trap for many small insects.

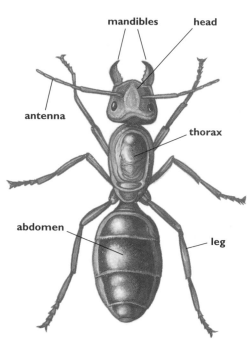

▲ Ants are typical arthropod animals, with a hard outer shell to protect their organs and joints to allow free movement.

⁉ How do spiders make their webs?

Spiders spin their webs from silk. It is pumped out from tiny nozzles at the back of the abdomen, which are called spinnerets. As the silk is stretched by the spider into a thread, it hardens. For its thickness, the thread becomes proportionately stronger than steel. Some of the threads are sticky, while others simply support the web. The spider is able to feel the vibrations of the web when an insect flies into it, and it runs quickly across the web to capture and subdue the prey. Usually, the insect is wrapped in silk before being eaten by the spider.

⁉ Are spiders insects?

Together with scorpions, ticks, and mites, spiders are part of a group called arachnids. They are not insects. The body of an arachnid is divided into two parts, while the body of an insect is in three sections. Arachnids have four pairs of walking legs, while insects have three pairs. Spiders are the most common members of this group of arthropods, and they are all carnivores. They capture their prey in webs or by running after them, paralyzing them by injecting poison from their jaws. Spiders cannot swallow solid food, instead they inject digestive juices into their prey, which liquefy it. They are then able to suck in the digested food through their jaws.

scorpion

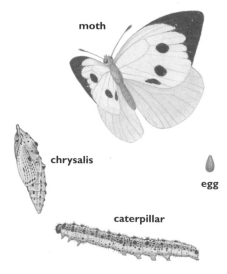

moth

chrysalis

egg

caterpillar

▲ Caterpillars develop from the moth's egg. After feeding for a while, they form a hard chrysalis. Within this, the animal's structure reforms, or metamorphoses, into a new moth. The moth emerges from the chrysalis to mate and begin the cycle again.

What's crawling up that tree?

Several types of crabs live on land and only return to the sea when they mate. The robber crab, a relative of the hermit crab, is also able to live on land, but it differs from all the others because of its size. The robber crab is huge — no less than 3 feet long and weighs 37 pounds. It can climb up trees and also lives on fallen coconuts, which it crushes with its enormous pincers! Although it obviously needs very careful handling, this crab is a favorite food for people living in the Pacific and Indian Ocean regions.

▲ This hover fly mimics a wasp, though it has no sting. It is an excellent flyer and can hover or fly backwards or sideways if necessary. It feeds on flower nectar.

What are insect larvae and pupae?

Insects such as grasshoppers and locusts emerge from eggs as miniature adults. Other insects go through a complicated development during which they completely change their shape and structure. Houseflies, bees, wasps, butterflies, and moths go through various stages of development. First they produce a larva, such as a grub or caterpillar, which lives an independent existence for some time. Next, the larva goes through a process that is called metamorphosis. This is when the animal rests in a protective cover called a pupa. Inside the pupa, the insect's internal structure is gradually rearranged into the adult form. Finally, the pupa splits open and the adult insect breaks out - it looks totally different from its larval stage. At first its body is very soft and vulnerable to predators, but the hard exterior skeleton soon forms. The adult is now ready to breed.

How do insects fly?

Insects have had 340 million years of experience in flying, which they now do very efficiently. Insects have two pairs of wings, which are flapped using a different kind of mechanism from birds. There are several ways in which the wings can beat, but usually they are raised by the contraction of a muscle. The wing then snaps down powerfully due to the spring-like properties of the insect's external skeleton. This mechanism allows the wings to beat very fast – 250 times per second for bees, and as many as 1,000 times per second for some midges (which accounts for the high-pitched whine these insects make).

How can flies walk on the ceiling?

The feet of a fly are adapted so that they can stick to almost any surface by means of a combination of tiny hooks and sticky pads. A fly's feet can even grip on shiny surfaces such as glass. When a fly lands on a ceiling, it flies up towards it, then somersaults into a half-loop so that it finishes in an upside-down position, ready to grasp the ceiling.

What is a crustacean?

Crustaceans are aquatic arthropods such as crabs, lobsters, and shrimp. They have a very tough, jointed external skeleton and jointed walking legs. Their body is divided into a region that contains most of the internal organs, covered by a shell called the carapace, and a muscular tail section that is usually folded under the body. Many crustaceans have powerful pincers that they use to capture and break up their prey and to signal to others of their species. Crustaceans live in the sea and in freshwater habitats.

How big can crabs grow?

The biggest crab is the giant spider crab found in the Pacific Ocean, near Japan. The crab lives at a depth of up to 980 feet. When its claws are outstretched, they can span as much as 11 feet. The giant spider crab's body is actually quite small and is only 14 inches across, but the whole animal may weigh as much as 40 pounds.

❓ What are invertebrates?

Invertebrates, or animals without backbones, make up 97 percent of all animals. This group of animals includes all the arthropods such as spiders, insects and crustaceans. The remaining invertebrates are mainly soft-bodied animals, although many of them have shells. They include animals such as sponges, corals, shellfish, worms, sea urchins and starfish and many less familiar animals.

❓ Are all worms similar?

Most long, thin-bodied animals are called 'worms', but they are not all closely related. Roundworms are the most common type of worm. At least 15,000 different types of roundworm have been described, and there could be as many as 500,000 species altogether. Many roundworms live in the soil, and there may be millions in one cubic metre of soil. They feed on dead and decaying material. Other worms are predators or parasites, which live inside the bodies of other animals.

Worms are found in almost any damp environment. Some marine worms live in tubes made of sand, sieving the water with flower-like tentacles. Leeches are aquatic worms that may suck blood. Most leeches are aquatic, but some live in tropical rainforests and wait on the surface of the vegetation until they can attach themselves to a passer-by. They drop off after feeding.

❓ How do cuttlefish and squid 'talk' to each other?

Cuttlefish and squid have a visual language in which they communicate by changing their body colour and patterns. This change happens extremely quickly. Waves of colour and complicated patterns pass over the animal's body when it is frightened or hungry, or trying to escape from danger.

❓ How long can a worm grow?

Ribbon worms are marine worms that can grow as long as 30 m. They capture their prey by shooting out a spiked organ called a proboscis. It impales the prey so the worm can haul it in and eat it.

❓ Are any invertebrates intelligent?

The octopus has been studied in the laboratory and has proved to be highly intelligent. Experiments have shown that the octopus can recognize shapes and colours, and can remember experiences. This means that it can be trained to some extent. The octopus also demonstrates its intelligence by escaping from captivity by climbing out of almost any tank in which it is kept.

Killer cones

The cone shell is a marine snail found in the Indian and the Pacific Oceans. Cone shells are beautifully marked and often brightly coloured so they are much prized by shell collectors. However, one of these shells packs a fearful defence. It can shoot out a long tubular tentacle, which stabs into the prey or the hand of a person who tries to pick it up. This tentacle injects powerful venom that causes agonizing pain and can produce paralysis very quickly. Several people have died within just a few hours from cone shell stings.

▼ The octopus has very efficient eyes, though they have developed quite differently from those of vertebrates. This means that evolution has invented the eye several times.

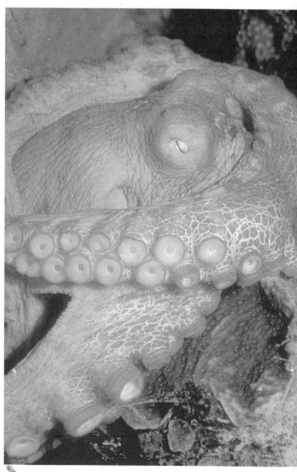

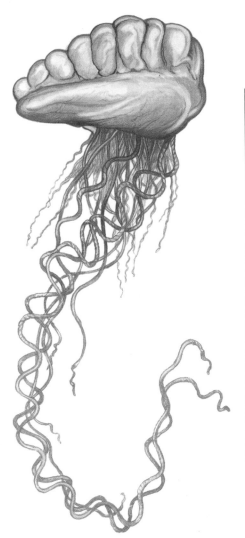

▲ The Portuguese man-of-war is a colony of many tiny animals. Some of these animals group together to form stinging tentacles to capture their prey, while others form a bladder-like float that drifts on the surface. The tentacles can cause a painful sting to nearby swimmers.

How do jellyfish sting?

The long arms that trail beneath the umbrella section of a jellyfish carry thousands of microscopic stinging cells. These cells have triggers, which cause the stinging cell to fire out a sharp thread when they are touched. The thread injects venom into any creature that contacts the stinging cells. Once the jellyfish's tentacles have gripped the prey and the stings have immobilized it, the prey is drawn up to the jellyfish's mouth and eaten.

Which animals make coral reefs?

Coral reefs are built up from the skeletons deposited by millions of tiny invertebrate animals. These coral animals live only in warm water, feeding on plankton and also living on food substances produced by microscopic plants living inside their tissues. The reef builds up over thousands of years. Eventually the coral skeletons form complete islands that are colonized by plants and land animals.

Why are starfish like sea urchins?

Both starfish and sea urchins move about on tiny tube feet. These creatures have the same internal structure. Imagine the sea urchin as a starfish rolled up and joined along the edges of its arms.

Which is the largest invertebrate?

The giant squid is by far the largest invertebrate known. This monstrous creature lives in the ocean depths, and is only occasionally washed ashore. The specimens found so far have been 20 m in length, and their eyes are 40 cm across (these are the largest eyes known).

Squids have tentacles like an octopus that surround a powerful beak. Two of these tentacles are enormously long, with gripping suckers at the end. The giant squid's suckers have a ring of sharp teeth around them to help grip their prey. These suckers leave scars on the sperm whales that feed on them, and some of these scars are from suckers nearly three times bigger than those on the largest squid found so far. So there are much larger giant squids still to be discovered!

▲ Most starfish have five arms, or multiples of five arms. Their underside is covered with thousands of tiny feet with which they creep about or grasp their prey of shellfish.

⑦ Why do animals become extinct?

According to the theory of evolution, some animal species become extinct because they are less successful than other species that gradually replace them.

These so-called 'failed' animals are also unable to adapt to changing circumstances. Humans have accelerated their extinction by changing the environment so rapidly that animals do not have time to adapt. For example, the destruction of Indonesian rainforests has left nowhere for the orang-utan to live. It would take millions of years for the animal to evolve into a ground-living creature. Hunting is the reason for the reduced numbers and probable extinction of animals such as the tiger, the blue whale, and the giant panda.

⑦ Why are turtles a threatened species?

Turtles are threatened because of hunting and loss of habitat. They have been a favorite food for thousands of years, and their population is unable to sustain the present level of hunting. The worst threat comes from the disturbance and destruction of the turtles' breeding sites. The ideal beaches for turtles to lay their eggs on are also the ideal beaches for vacationers. The result is that hotels have been built near these beaches, roads carry cars whose headlights confuse turtles heading for the beach at night, and tourists disturb the turtles as they lay their eggs.

⑦ Does keeping pets threaten the survival of some animals?

The desire of some people to keep exotic pets threatens many parrots and wild cats. Spectacular parrots like the macaw are captured in large numbers and exported for the pet trade. This practice has greatly reduced their numbers in the wild, and this trade is now strictly controlled in most countries. Captive breeding programs have been set up to avoid the need to capture wild parrots. Hawks are subject to the same pressures, and are protected in many countries.

Some of the smaller wild cats, such as the ocelot, are popular among the wealthy as prestigious pets. However, these creatures are not really suited to captivity.

⑦ Will whales disappear from the oceans?

All the larger kinds of whale are threatened with extinction. Although whales are protected from hunting by international law, there are many loopholes that are exploited. A new threat comes from the commercial exploitation of krill, the tiny crustaceans that form the bulk of the diet of the huge blue whales and some of smaller relatives. Krill are being harvested in huge quantities by fishing boats, for use as fertilizer and as food. If their stocks are reduced, the whales will have no alternative food sources.

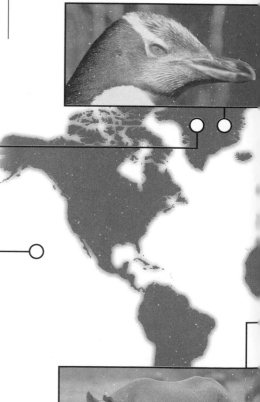

Yellow-eyed penguins are threatened by man's activities, especially by oil spills. There are only 3,000 left in the wild.

There are about 40,000 polar bears living in northern regions. Scarce food resources limit their numbers.

The humpback whale was hunted almost to extinction, and its numbers dropped from 100,000 to 3,000 today. It is now generally protected.

Poaching has reduced the number of black rhinos to 2,550. Most survive only in protected game parks.

Dead or alive?

It is generally thought that all the large animals have been discovered, but many surprises still turn up. The okapi is a large forest-dwelling relative of the giraffe. It was found in the Congo as late as 1900, to the amazement of the scientific world. The enormous megamouth shark was found only accidentally when the first specimen became tangled in an underwater cable. Scientists were stunned when the first coelacanth was discovered. This primitive fish with 'legs' was thought to have become extinct 70 million years ago, when its last fossils were found. However, it turned up alive and healthy off the Comores Islands near South Africa in 1938, and has been caught there regularly ever since.

❔ What happened to the dodo?

The dodo was a large, flightless relative of the pigeon that once lived on the island of Mauritius in the Indian Ocean.

It was discovered in 1507, but by 1681 it was extinct, although some relatives living on nearby islands survived for a few more years. The dodo was very large and fat, weighing around 50 pounds, so sailors hunted it for food. Being a very trusting and slow-moving creature, it was easy to catch. The dodo also suffered from attacks by introduced animals such as pigs and rats, which destroyed its eggs and young.

❔ Are there still 'wolves' in Tasmania?

There are no large marsupial predators living in Australia today, but the thylacine 'wolf' only became extinct recently. There may still be a few survivors in Tasmania.

The thylacine was a large, dog-like animal with striped sides and an enormous mouth lined with fierce teeth. Sheep farmers hunted it to the edge of extinction in Tasmania in order to protect their flocks. The last known thylacine died in a zoo in 1936, but there are still occasional reports of their being seen in the thick bush.

The thylacine was once common throughout Australia, but it was pushed out by the success of the dingo, a semi-domesticated dog introduced into Australia by the Aborigines when they colonized this country.

❔ Which extinct giant animals were familiar to prehistoric humans?

There is evidence from prehistoric cave paintings, and from bones showing signs of cooking or carving, that humans lived alongside some very large extinct animals.

Just after the last ice age, woolly mammoths, woolly rhinoceroses, and giant cave bears lived in Europe. They were hunted by humans, and together with the warming climate, this may have led to their extinction. The giant ox was also prey for hunters. It became extinct in 1627, having survived in the forests of eastern Europe.

The red wolf became extinct in the wild in 1980, but small numbers of captive specimens were bred. There now are 200 in captivity.

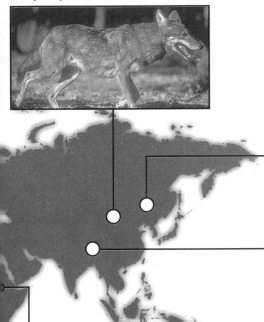

Giant pandas were never plentiful but farming has now destroyed much of their habitat in China. There are less than 1,000 giant pandas remaining.

Tigers have been hunted for centuries, as trophies. There are only about 2,550 tigers living in the wild.

Ivory poaching reduced the number of African elephants from 1.3 million in 1980 down to 610,000 by 1990. The ivory trade has now been controlled by international convention.

Animal Behavior

❓ What are parasites?

Parasites are animals that live at the expense of other animals. They rob the host animal of food and can make it become sick. However, in other forms of relationship, different animals can help one another. Some hermit crabs place sea anemones on their shells, hiding under their protective stinging tentacles. At the same time, the sea anemone benefits because it shares the crab's food. Similarly, a species of shrimp digs a burrow that it shares with the small goby fish. The fish benefits from being able to hide in the burrow, while acting as a lookout to warn the shrimp of approaching predators. This kind of relationship can only be revealed by the careful study of animal behavior. Most true parasites are very simple animals, because they do not need complicated organs to digest their food. Some parasites are simply a mass of reproductive organs.

▼ Leeches are parasites that live on the blood of other animals. Unlike many parasites, they do not live permanently on the surface of their host and drop off after feeding with their sucker mouths.

❓ How do scientists study animal behavior?

Scientists used to study just the appearance and structure of animals, but in recent years the study of their behavior has become just as important.

The new science of ethology measures and records animal behavior. We can now describe behavior in terms of what the animal actually does and not as a result of guessing what is going on in an animal's mind. These studies have shown, for example, that animals such as birds have many inbuilt types of behavior, which are inherited and not learned from other birds.

▼ Herd animals pack closely together and move in unison. This makes it difficult for a predator to catch an individual animal.

❓ Why do some animals live in large groups?

Predators usually live singly or in small groups, but their prey animals often group together in large numbers.

The most important reason for this behavior is that there is safety in numbers. A predator will often become confused by a large, rapidly shifting group of prey. For example, a tuna will find it very difficult to select one target fish from a closely packed shoal containing several thousand fish. Similarly, a lion will usually not try to catch one of a panicking herd of wildebeest, but will attack stragglers or injured animals.

Sometimes a herd has a defensive function. Adult buffalo and musk ox group together to form a protective circle around their vulnerable youngsters when a predator is near. The predator will not usually attack a fully-grown adult.

Two legs or four?

Why do kangaroos hop on two legs? Because these marsupials are more primitive than advanced mammals, it has been assumed that their method of getting about was not very efficient. Apart from a few small hopping rodents, very few mammals apart from marsupials use this form of traveling. But it has recently been found that kangaroos use less energy when hopping than other mammals use when running. There is a limit to the size of any animal that moves in this way, which is why no giant kangaroos ever evolved.

What do cleaner fish do?

Cleaners are tiny fish living in coral reefs. They regularly clean parasites from much larger fish. Even large predatory fish queue up to be cleaned of skin parasites. The cleaner fish (or sometimes a shrimp) even swims into the predator's mouth and gills without being eaten.

Birds can do a similar job. A basking crocodile opens its jaws so small birds can pick pieces of food and parasites from between its teeth. Small birds ride on the backs of grazing animals on the African grasslands, picking out skin parasites and feeding on insects as the animal feeds. At the same time the birds act as an early warning system for the host animal, by flying away when danger is near.

What is a pecking order?

Among animals that live in groups, one becomes the clear leader. In chickens, this means that one bird dominates all of the other birds. The next one down in the 'pecking order' can dominate all except the leader, and so on, until the bird at the bottom of this process can be bullied by the entire flock. This can also be seen in families with dogs. The dog remains at the bottom of the pecking order, and submits to the human members of the family. Sometimes an aggressive dog tries to raise its status by snarling at a new baby that threatens its position in the family.

Why do some animals care for their young?

Care of the young is important because it ensures that the young will grow up and be able to breed to continue the species. Animals that do not care for their young, such as many kinds of fish, produce huge numbers of eggs in the hope that a few will survive and reach maturity. Similarly, babies that do not receive care from the parent become independent at an early stage. A newborn deer is able to stand and run about within a few hours, while a human baby takes many years of care before it is independent. Parental care is often easier among animals that live in groups. Lionesses, for instance, may share responsibility for care of their young, and so do gorillas and chimpanzees. Meercats, a small type of mongoose, have a system of care where a family of 'aunts' look after the babies for the whole troop.

▲ Apes like this gibbon give birth to helpless young that need careful parental care for a long time.

How can we study wild animal behavior in the home?

Although they have been domesticated for thousands of years, cats and dogs still retain many aspects of their wild ancestors.

The domestic cat has never lost its hunting instinct. Like most solitary predatory wild cats, it eats whenever the opportunity arises. When it is not eating, it spends the majority of its time sleeping.

The ancestors of dogs were pack animals, and the modern dog has adopted the family as its pack, accepting its owner as the pack leader. Even the dog's habit of turning round and round before going to sleep is a relic of the habit of flattening a sleeping place in long grass. The dog still marks its territory by urinating on trees and lamp-posts to warn other dogs to keep away.

◀ Dog fights do not usually cause too much damage. The loser will usually submit by lying down, which reduces the level of aggression in the dominant dog.

Animal Migration

What is migration?

Migration is the mass movement of groups of animals. It is caused by the animals' need to find food, by climatic changes during the year, and by the need to breed. Sometimes migrating animals travel enormous distances at a time.

▲ Caribou usually live in small numbers. However, they form herds of up to 3,000 animals when on their migratory routes.

Which mammals migrate?

Caribou and lemmings are migratory animals. Caribou live in herds in the cold northern regions, feeding on lichen. Each year, when snow buries their food supply, they migrate south to warmer regions. The caribou return when the snow thaws.

Lemmings are small rodents that live in similar regions to the caribou. After a year of abundant food, they breed in such enormous numbers that their food supply runs out. The lemmings then migrate toward the coast in search of more food. Many drown while crossing rivers, but Arctic foxes and predatory birds eat most of them.

Do fish migrate?

Many fish migrate, in both fresh water and the ocean. Tuna make some of the longest migrations. The need to migrate is due to sea temperature, since these fish need the correct temperature in order to breed. They migrate along the coasts of the Atlantic and the Pacific, traveling thousands of miles. Herrings migrate in the North Sea, moving south to warmer water in winter.

How do migrating animals find their way?

Migrating animals navigate in a variety of ways. Fish use their sense of smell to recognize their migration paths and are guided by changing water temperatures. Birds use the position of the sun to orient themselves. Some birds have magnetic particles in their ear mechanism that can act as a compass. Mammals rely on their memory. Some elephant trails have been in use for hundreds of years.

Travel sick

Regular migration means that hunters take advantage of these movements in order to catch their prey. It is well known when fish migrate up rivers to spawn, and nets and lines are set to catch them at the same time each year. Whales and large oceanic fish are at risk during their migrations because hunters know exactly where to find them. Thousands of birds are killed as they travel along their routes. In just a few decades, hunters wiped out passenger pigeons, once the most common bird in the world.

▲ Birds may migrate for thousands of miles every year, seeking food or travelling to traditional nesting sites. Even our common garden birds may migrate to equatorial regions in the winter when food is scarce.

Where do swallows go in the winter?

Every autumn, swallows gather in large flocks to rest before they begin their long migration to Africa. Swallows and their relatives, swifts and martins, all migrate to Africa when the weather becomes too cold for them to catch their insect prey. They return in the spring when the weather in northern Europe begins to warm up.

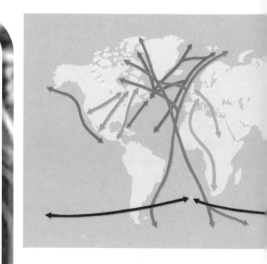

Do insects migrate?

Many insects migrate, sometimes for thousands of miles. The monarch butterfly migrates from North America to Mexico in the winter, a distance of almost 2,000 miles. Here they spend the winter in a state of semi-hibernation. Incredibly, most of the butterflies die during the journey, and the grandchildren of the original butterflies arrive back exactly where their grandparents hatched. Sometimes it takes three or four generations before the migration is completed. In spring, the butterflies begin the journey north again.

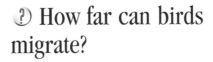

◀ This map shows the migratory routes of some animals. The Arctic tern travels many thousands of miles along a single route.

■ Blue whale

■ Wandering albatross

■ Arctic tern

■ Cuckoo

■ Monarch butterfly

What is a locust swarm?

For thousands of years, locust swarms have devastated farmland throughout Asia and Africa. A typical swarm can be 30 miles long and contain more than 100,000 million locusts. These animals are large grasshoppers that normally live a solitary and harmless existence. When their population builds up to a high level, they begin to mass together and migrate in search of food. These migrations can cover many thousands of miles.

Locust swarms can now be predicted by monitoring the insects' behavior. Locusts can be sprayed with pesticides to prevent them from swarming.

How far can birds migrate?

The Arctic tern makes the longest-known migration of any bird we know, by traveling from the Arctic to the Antarctic and back again.

One tern was ringed in the north of England and arrived in Australia 115 days later, having flown an average distance of 99 miles per day. The short-tailed shearwater, which breeds on offshore islands near Australia, has an annual migration all round the Pacific. It passes through Japan, Alaska, Canada, and Fiji before returning home again to breed.

▲ A swarm of locusts can turn the sky black, with up to 100,000 million insects in a single swarm. A swarm of this size can wreak terrible damage on farmers' crops.

Do some animals return to their birthplace to breed?

Like migratory birds, there are many animals that return to their birthplace to breed. Even frogs and toads migrate back to the ponds where they first grew up.

Salmon carry out long migrations to return to their birthplace. Young salmon, which hatch in small streams, travel down rivers to the sea as they develop. They spend nearly all of their adult life at sea. When it is time to breed, the salmon migrate back toward their birthplace, sometimes traveling for thousands of miles. They somehow manage to enter exactly the same river and travel upstream to find the same tiny stream in which they hatched. Here they lay their eggs to repeat the cycle. The adult salmon die after breeding.

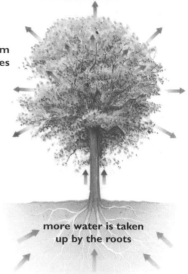

water evaporates from
the leaf surfaces

? What is a plant?

Plants are organisms that use light as a source of energy and to produce the food they need in order to live and grow. Plant cells have a tough outer wall made of a substance called cellulose, which makes the wall rigid. This explains why plants are able to move only very gradually, unlike animals whose cells have no rigid wall.

? How did plants lead to the appearance of animal life on the Earth?

The Earth's original atmosphere contained poisonous gases. The lack of oxygen meant that no animals could survive on the Earth. The earliest plants or plant-like bacteria began the process of photosynthesis, which releases oxygen as a waste product. This gas gradually built up in the atmosphere as the plant life spread, making it possible for oxygen-dependent animals to evolve.

? How do plants survive cold weather?

Plants survive the cold by shutting down most of their normal processes. Some plants die back as soon as the weather becomes cold, storing food in their roots or in special organs such as bulbs. The plants are ready to grow back when the weather warms up again. Woody plants cannot do this, so they usually lose their leaves because they do not need to photosynthesize. These plants become inactive, or dormant, until the spring. Some plants have tough leathery leaves that can withstand the cold, so they just slow down their internal processes and wait for warmer weather. Some plants do not survive the winter at all, but their continuation is guaranteed because they produce resistant seeds that grow quickly in the spring.

? How do plants use sunlight?

Plants use a process called photosynthesis in order to change sunlight into food. Their cells contain packets of a green pigment called chlorophyll that carry out this process. During photosynthesis, water and carbon dioxide from the air are converted into sugars that nourish the plant.

Carbon dioxide is taken in through the stomata, and oxygen is given off.

◀ **Plants absorb water through their roots, which combines with carbon dioxide in the leaves to form sugars. This is called photosynthesis. At the same time, the plant releases oxygen into the air. These gases enter and leave through holes in the leaves, called stomata.**

more water is taken
up by the roots

▲ **Energy from the sun evaporates water from the leaf surface, through the stomata. This reduces pressure in the channels carrying water from the roots, so more water is drawn up the stem.**

? What are leaves for?

The process of photosynthesis takes place mostly in the leaves of a plant. Leaves are large and flattened so that a large area of chlorophyll is exposed to the sunlight. Leaves are also used in a process called transpiration, which helps draw water and dissolved minerals up the plant's stem from the roots, where these substances have been absorbed from the soil. During transpiration, water evaporates through tiny holes in the leaves. More water is drawn up through a thin tube extending down the plant's stem.

The underground greenhouse

A small African plant called Fenestaria, which looks like a cactus, lives underground to protect it from the glare of the sun. The only part of the plant that shows on the surface is a small transparent window, which allows light to enter so that the plant can carry out photosynthesis. Beneath this window are filter layers that reduce the damaging ultraviolet light and provide the right light levels for photosynthesis to take place.

light
energy
from the
sun

water is taken in through the roots

▲ Cacti are modified to minimize water loss in the hot deserts where they live. They do not have leaves, and photosynthesis takes place in the swollen barrel-like stems, which are often covered with protective spines.

▲ The Venus's-flytrap has a trap which looks and smells like a flower to the insects. When they land on it and touch a trigger hair the trap slams shut, and they are digested by the plant.

How can plants live in dry areas?

Plants living in very dry regions are specially adapted to stop them from losing too much water. They have smaller leaves, which are often thin and spiny, or they may have no leaves at all as in the case of cacti. The chlorophyll in a cactus is concentrated in the plant's fattened stems.

Desert plants also conserve water by having a thick waxy coat over their leaves and stems, and by storing water after the rain. Some desert plants have fat, swollen leaves or stems that are filled with water. Desert plants also have extremely long roots that burrow deep into the soil.

Can plants move?

Many plants are able to move their leaves slowly to keep them facing the sunlight. In some plants, this movement is very fast. The sensitive plant suddenly collapses all its leaves when touched, and looks as though it is dead. This is to help protect it from grazing animals. Other forms of movement happen when a plant distributes its seeds. Some plants can "fire" their seeds for a considerable distance, making sure that the new plants do not grow too close.

How can plants store food and water?

Plants store food and water over the winter, or in dry conditions. Underground storage organs develop from roots, stems or leaf bases, and we use many of these plant organs as foods, for example potatoes and carrots. Bulbs and corms are common storage organs, which are familiar in many garden plants. Above the ground, desert plants have swollen stems or leaves in which they store water.

Can plants catch animals?

Plants growing in bogs and peaty areas often need to supplement their food supply by catching insects. Bog water contains very little nitrogen, but some bog plants can obtain this substance by catching and digesting insects. They are known as insectivorous plants. Some have vase-shaped structures, into which insects are lured by bright colors and scents, like flower nectar. They fall into a slippery funnel and drop into a pool of liquid containing digestive juices. Other insectivorous plants are covered with sticky tentacles that trap flies. The most remarkable is the Venus's-flytrap plant. It has two clawed plates that slam together when a fly walks over them and touches a trigger hair.

Other insect-eating plants are aquatic, catching tiny crustaceans in bladder-shaped underwater traps. Some of the largest insectivorous plants live in the tropical rainforests of southeast Asia. They produce hanging, vase-shaped traps as big as a fist.

When did the first plants appear?

Scientists believe that the first primitive plants appeared about 1,000 million years ago. It is difficult to be certain about the date, because simple organisms do not usually leave fossils. However, these primitive plants are thought to have laid down fossil deposits, rather like coral reefs, in shallow seas.

What are algae?

Algae are the most primitive form of plant life. Most algae are aquatic, and they range in size from microscopic single-celled organisms to seaweed that is several yards long. Algae photosynthesize, like other plants, and they are responsible for providing most of the world's oxygen. Algae are varied, but even the large forms, such as kelp and other seaweeds, lack the true leaves, stems, and roots found in other plants. Not all algae use the green chlorophyll found in other plants in order to photosynthesize; some use red or brown pigments for this purpose.

▲ Algae in the form of seaweed grow on exposed surfaces in the sea, below the high-water mark. They do not have roots, but grip the surface with an organ called a holdfast.

Which primitive plants are often found as fossils in coal?

The impressions of fossilized leaves are commonly found in coal. The most common fossils are of ferns, mosses and horsetails, all of which still grow on the Earth today. Coal was formed in shallow bogs, where plants died and were gradually buried by more material, until pressure and time converted them into coal. The oldest coal was formed 350 million years ago, and the process still continues in swamps and bogs. Peat is the earliest stage in the formation of coal. It has not yet been subjected to the pressure that will eventually turn it into a hard material.

Which is the biggest kind of algae?

Giant kelp looks like a kind of seaweed, but it is in fact the largest-known kind of algae. It grows in very long strands up to 70 yards in length, and is fastened to the seabed with a root-like organ called a holdfast. Small air bladders help to keep the kelp floating upright and spreading across the water's surface. Kelp is harvested and used for various industrial purposes. One substance extracted from it is called algin and is commonly used to make ice cream.

How do ferns differ from flowering plants?

Ferns differ from flowering plants mainly in the way that they reproduce. They have fronds instead of true leaves, and some ferns grow into a tree-like form that can be 26 yards tall. Microscopic spores are produced on the underside of the fronds, and these are scattered by the wind. When the spores land in a suitably damp area, they sprout and grow into a tiny flat plant that develops small reproductive structures. Sperms fertilize the egg cell, which begins to grow as the tiny plant shrivels and dies, and the complete fern begins to develop. Ferns' delicate reproductive parts can only survive in a moist atmosphere, so these plants only grow in damp places.

Creeping clump

Slime molds are simple organisms that live on rotting wood. When they are ready to reproduce, thousands of separate mold cells clump together into a single organism that may be 2 inches across. It produces a stalk and bears spores, which are carried on the wind, while the original organism dies.

▲ Ferns are primitive plants that have existed for millions of years. They do not have seeds but reproduce by means of microscopic spores.

What are lichens?

Lichens are peculiar organisms in which algae and fungi live together. They are usually flat and crust-like, with no roots, and often grow on roofs, rocks, or tree branches. They are frequently brightly colored. The main structure of a lichen is the fungal part, but it also contains algae cells that contribute food through photosynthesis. Reindeer moss is a form of lichen that is very common throughout the Arctic. It forms the main diet of the caribou and other grazing animals. Lichen grows very slowly, but can eventually cover very large areas. Some individual ones are extremely old, and some lichens growing in rocks in Antarctica are thought to be 10,000 years old – they are the oldest living organisms.

▼ Lichens are a mixture of algae and fungi. Many grow like a mat over rocks or tree trunks, while others look like a small branched plant.

What are fungi?

Fungi used to be considered part of the plant kingdom, but they are now thought to be quite different. The main part of the fungus is a mass of tiny threads called a mycelium. Fungi live on other organic matter. In the soil, fungi are the most important agent in the breakdown of dead plant and animal material, recycling it so that plants can use the nutrients. Fungi live in damp areas or in water because they have no method of preventing their fragile threads from drying out – they cannot survive dry atmospheres. Some fungi are parasites, attacking animals or plants.

Mushrooms are the reproductive organs of some types of fungi, in which the threads of the mycelium compact together to produce the familiar umbrella-shaped mushroom. Microscopic spores, which are produced on the underside of the mushroom cap, spread in the wind to start new fungal colonies.

What is a 'fairy ring?'

A fairy ring is a circular pattern that is produced by fungi growing in grassland. As the fungus grows out from a central point, it forms a circle, and at the edges of this circle the grass changes color. Meanwhile, the original fungus dies off, so all that is left is the expanding ring of fungus growing beneath the surface. Sometimes a ring of mushrooms also appears. These fairy rings keep growing for many years, perhaps even for centuries. They can reach a very large size unless they are disturbed, for example, when the land is plowed.

▲ Mushrooms and toadstools are the reproductive organs of tiny, threadlike fungi that usually live unnoticed in the soil. The mushroom is a device for making and distributing the microscopic fungal spores.

Are most toadstools poisonous?

A few mushrooms and toadstools are extremely poisonous, but most are harmless or simply do not taste good. All types of cultivated mushrooms are perfectly safe to eat. However, expert knowledge is needed to identify wild mushrooms accurately, so it can be very dangerous to experiment with them.

Why are fungi usually found near trees?

Sometimes fungi attack the roots of a tree, eventually killing it. More often, however, the fungus and the tree depend on one another for food.

Most fungi that produce mushrooms live alongside the roots of trees or other plants. The tree roots nourish the fungus, and the fungus in return provides nutrients to the tree by breaking down dead leaves.

⑦ Why do some plants have flowers?

Flowers are a plant's sexual reproduction organs. They have evolved in such a way to ensure that fertilization takes place and that seeds are produced.

⑦ What are the main parts of a flower?

All true flowers contain the same basic parts, although they may look very different from one flower to another. Flowers contain male organs called stamens and female organs called pistils, which contain the egg cells. Most flowers contain both types of organ, but some are either male or female. Flowers have other large and often brightly colored parts, which we usually think of as petals. However, sometimes these parts are actually structures called sepals or even modified leaves.

⑦ Why are flowers brightly colored and scented?

Flowers are colored and perfumed to attract insects, which play an important part in pollination. Some plants also produce a sugary liquid called nectar, on which bees feed .

▶ Bees are attracted to the color and scent of a flower. They feed on the nectar in the flower and gather pollen, which they store in sacs on their legs to take back to the hive. As they visit other flowers they transfer the pollen to the stigma of the flower and fertilize it.

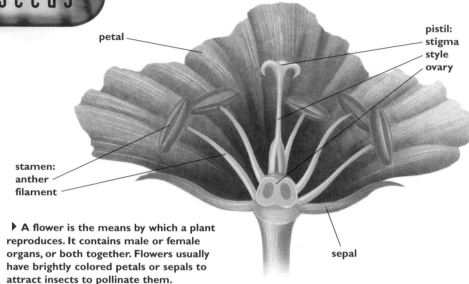

petal — pistil: stigma, style, ovary

stamen: anther, filament

sepal

▶ A flower is the means by which a plant reproduces. It contains male or female organs, or both together. Flowers usually have brightly colored petals or sepals to attract insects to pollinate them.

⑦ What is pollen?

Pollen is the plant's equivalent of an animal's sperm. It carries the male reproductive genes.

Pollen consists of tiny grains, each with a tough coat that is often patterned with characteristic ridges and spikes. When inhaled, the fine pollen causes allergies, such as hay fever, in some susceptible people. Pollen can be found in fossil deposits, making it possible to identify the plants that were living then – even though no actual plant fossils may be found.

▼ Millions of microscopic pollen grains are produced by a flower. Pollen grains have a pattern, allowing the plant to be identified.

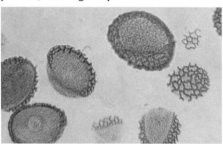

⑦ How are flowers pollinated?

Pollination takes place when a pollen grain is deposited on the tip of a pistil. It then grows a long tube down inside the pistil that fuses with the egg cell and completes the process of fertilization.

Sometimes pollen is blown by the wind, and a single pollen grain is accidentally deposited on the pistil. In other flowers, insects do the same job, carrying pollen stuck to their bodies as they travel from flower to flower. In some plants, the flower is modified to force the insects feeding on nectar to brush past the stamens, collecting a large amount of pollen on their bodies as they pass by.

Smelly giants

The biggest flower of all is the rafflesia, a parasitic plant that does not photosynthesize. It grows in the rainforests of southeast Asia. The plant grows underground and is not visible until a huge bud appears, like a cabbage. This opens up into a leathery flower 3 feet across and weighing up to 124 pounds. The flower looks and smells just like a huge lump of rotting flesh, and it attracts thousands of flies, which pollinate the flower as they walk on it. The berry contains sticky seeds that are spread by rodents.

What are seeds?

After fertilization takes place, the egg cell develops into a seed from which a new plant can develop. The seed contains an embryo from which the new plant will grow. It also contains a food store to nourish the embryo until it has developed roots and leaves. The seed is enclosed in a tough coat to protect it from drying out.

▼ Seeds are the main means by which flowering plants reproduce and spread, though many can also spread by underground runners and shoots.

Can seeds fly?

Many seeds are carried by the wind. Some have a fluffy 'umbrella,' which is carried for long distances. Others have wings that allow the seed to glide or spin around like a helicopter blade. The wings slow the seed's descent so that the wind can carry it further away. One particular seed, from a tropical tree called *Zanonia*, glides so effectively it was used as the model for the wings of early planes.

▼ The origins of the enormous seed of the coco de mer was a mystery for centuries until the palm tree that produces it was discovered in the Seychelles.

Which is the biggest seed?

The biggest seed is the coco de mer, a kind of coconut that grows in the Seychelles, a group of islands in the Indian Ocean. The coco de mer seeds weigh 40lbs each, so it can be dangerous to walk beneath the parent tree. These giant seeds take 10 years to develop on the tree.

Strangely, the coco de mer does not grow close to the beach, so how the giant seeds reach the sea is still not understood.

How do animals help plants spread their seeds?

Animals eat plant fruits, the fleshy wrappings around seeds. Seeds spread in this way can resist the digestive processes of the animals that feed on the fruit. They pass right through the animal's gut without injury. The seeds start to grow when they are deposited in the animal's dung, which often acts as a fertilizer.

How long can seeds survive?

Many seeds can survive for hundreds of years, providing they are kept in dry conditions. In 1954, a seed was found buried in frozen mud in Canada. The seed was 10,000 years old, yet it still grew when it was planted. Seeds kept for research purposes are stored in refrigerators to provide similar cold, dry conditions.

How do mangroves stop their seeds from floating away?

Some mangroves produce seeds that spear themselves into the mud. While the seed is still attached to the tree, a long root emerges. The seed drops like a dart and the root sticks in the mud, anchoring the plant firmly as it develops.

The young mangroves trap tidal mud and, in this way, the whole bank of mangroves gradually grows in size.

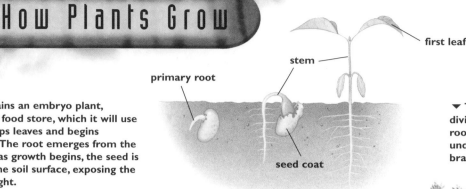

primary root

stem

first leaf

seed coat

▶ A seed contains an embryo plant, together with a food store, which it will use before it develops leaves and begins photosynthesis. The root emerges from the seed first, then as growth begins, the seed is carried above the soil surface, exposing the new leaves to light.

▼ The roots of a tree fork divide beneath the ground. The roots of most trees spread out underground just as far as the branches do above the ground.

⍰ How does a seed grow?

The embryo in a seed contains everything that the seed needs to grow. The seed will not start to germinate until conditions are right. This usually means that the seed must be warm and moist. The embryo starts to grow, using its stored food supply, and soon bursts the seed coat. Usually the root emerges first, growing downwards in search of water, and the shoot follows. The first leaves to emerge are often fleshy organs that are part of the food store, and the leaves that appear later do not resemble them.

⍰ How do roots find water?

Several outside factors influence the way in which roots grow. They grow away from light and are pulled downwards by gravity, as you can see in simple experiments with large seeds such as beans or peas. This downward growth naturally takes the roots towards water in the soil. Some roots seek water more actively, for example, trees such as willows. They send out roots that extend well beyond the spread of their branches; these roots may enter the joints of water pipes and sewers in search of water.

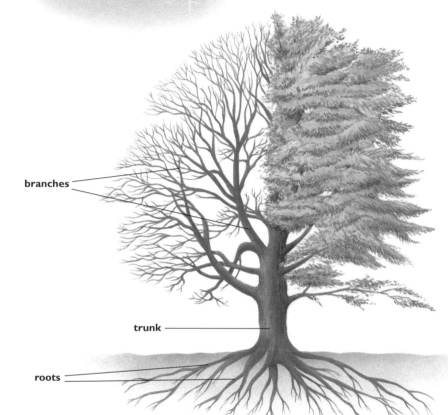

branches

trunk

roots

⍰ Why do shoots grow toward the light?

Hormones called auxins are responsible for a plant growing toward the light. Auxins cause the cells of a shoot to lengthen. They are also destroyed by light, so if the plant leans over, auxins collect on the shady underside. They cause the cells on the underside to grow longer, pushing the shoot upright, usually toward the light. Plant shoots are able to grow away from the pull of gravity.

⍰ How does water travel to the leaves?

Water reaches the leaves by several methods. Transpiration is the evaporation of water through the leaf's surface. As the water evaporates, more water is drawn up the plant's stem. The other method consists of water and dissolved minerals being pumped up the stem under pressure from the roots. A tree trunk 'bleeds' when it is cut because the sap is pumped out under pressure until the cut dries over.

Chemical control

Fertilizers are used to make crops grow larger and faster. They can be made of natural, or organic, materials such as rotted manure or straw, but most farmers use chemical fertilizers. Crops are also regularly sprayed with pesticides and herbicides. These chemicals interfere with the body chemistry of insects and with the growth of certain weeds, reducing expensive crop losses. Many people are becoming concerned about the widespread use of chemicals, because traces of them remain in our food supplies. There are fears that the chemicals could cause health problems for the people who eat them. Crops grown without the use of artificial chemicals are known as "organic".

What are fertilizers?

Fertilizers contain some of the essential chemicals that plants need to stay healthy. Nitrogen is one of the most important chemicals, and it is in constant demand from the plant. Nitrogen cannot easily be obtained from the air, except by plants that have organs containing nitrogen-fixing bacteria. Fertilizers used on crops and garden plants usually contain nitrogen, phosphorus, iron, potassium and several other minerals that can boost the plant's rate of growth.

▶ **In the fall, many leaves change color and drop from the tree. This is because the tree will not need to grow in the winter, so it conserves its energy by losing its leaves.**

What are perennial plants?

Perennial plants survive from one year to the next. They usually grow quite slowly, and can afford to build up their strength before they need to produce seeds. Another group of plants, called biennials, grow in one year and flower in the following year before dying.

Why do leaves change color in the fall?

Plants that are about to lose their leaves in the fall conserve their food supplies by withdrawing all the nutrients from the leaves. Chlorophyll is broken down in the leaves, causing their color to change. Eventually all the nutrients are removed from the leaves and they wither and turn brown.

What are annual plants?

Plants that cannot survive the winter are called annuals. They grow very quickly when their seeds geminate in the spring, because they have to complete their entire lifecycle in a short time.

Why do plants sometimes wilt?

A non-woody plant is held upright by the pressure of water in its cells. These cells are tightly expanded like balloons. If too little water reaches the cells, as happens in a drought or if the stems are damaged by disease, the cells soften and the plant sags or wilts. Usually it can stiffen up again when water is available, provided the plant has not dried out too much. Woody plants can also wilt at the tips of their shoots.

coast redwood

Corsican pine

? What are deciduous trees?

Trees that lose their leaves in winter are called deciduous trees.

? What is a conifer?

Conifers produce their seeds without the aid of flowers, whereas deciduous trees are actually flowering plants. Conifers produce cones, which are whorls of papery scales packed tightly together to protect the seeds developing inside them. Male and female cones are produced separately, and pollen shed from the male cones fertilizes the egg cells and leads to the production of seeds. The seeds, which are usually winged, are released in dry weather when the scales of the cone open up and release them. Most conifers keep their needle-like leaves throughout the winter, although a few types are deciduous.

? Can tree roots grow above the ground?

Some trees that grow in soft, wet ground or very thin soil sometimes develop buttress roots, which stop them from blowing over inn strong winds. These roots are like very large, flattened plates that stiffen the base of the tree. Some trees that grow in very stony ground produce roots that actually run over the surface of the ground in search of softer soil. In this way, they grip the rocky surface to stabilize the tree against the effects of winds.

? Which is the largest tree?

Trees are the largest living organisms on Earth. The biggest tree is the Californian giant redwood, which grows nearly 328 feet high and can have a trunk that is 36 feet thick. The total weight of one of these trees is more than 2,000 ton, which is more than 10 times heavier than a blue whale.

These ancient giant trees have very few branches and leaves and are often scarred by fire and lightning strikes.

▲ The Californian giant redwood is one of the oldest and largest living things on Earth.

? How can you tell the exact age of a tree?

Every year as a tree grows, it deposits a new layer of cells on the outside of its trunk, beneath the bark. This new layer is called an annual ring.

By counting the annual rings, it is simple to work out the exact age of a tree. Even in the case of a living tree, it is possible to drill into the trunk and remove a sample in order to date the tree without causing any permanent damage.

Which is the oldest tree?

The oldest known trees are bristlecone pine trees. They grow in the White Mountains in California, in the U.S. Although they are quite small, some of these gnarled trees are more than 4,500 years old. The oldest tree is named *Methuselah*. It is thought to be more than 4,600 years old.

Norway spruce

English elm

silver birch

evergreen oak

▲ Most conifers are tall, slim trees that naturally grow close together, straight toward the light. Deciduous trees are usually less densely packed and have a more spreading habit. Deciduous trees such as the oak and ash can be readily recognized by their characteristic shape.

Blaze of glory

The talipot palm that grows in some Asian countries flowers only once in its lifetime, then dies a year later. Before it dies, it produces a mass of flowers up to 43 feet across, followed by more than 50 million fruits, each about 1 inch long.

Why don't trees grow on top of mountains?

Mountaintops are usually bare of trees because growing conditions are not suitable for them. The soil is usually very thin on mountaintops, and the location is too cold and exposed for trees to grow without damage. Some trees can grow there, but they are usually dwarfed and flattened by the wind. Sometimes, although they are trees, they look more like mosses.

What are bonsai trees?

Bonsais are decorative miniature trees that were first developed in Japan.

They are grown in shallow dishes, and the shoots and roots are carefully trimmed to stunt their growth. Some of these trees are very old and are perfect miniatures, even producing tiny flowers or cones. Most bonsai trees are extremely valuable because of the length of time it takes for them to grow.

How are straight trees grown in order to make telephone poles?

Trees always grow directly toward the light. In tree plantations, this property is used in such a way to make sure the trees grow very straight.

The young trees are planted very close together, and in order to reach sufficient light, the trees grow straight up, without putting out many side branches. As they get larger, some of the trees are removed to give the remaining ones more space in which to grow.

What have trees to do with making paper?

Paper is made from wood pulp, which in turn comes from shredded trees.

The main trunk is usually used for timber, and smaller sections and branches are shredded up. They are treated with chemicals that break down the structure of the wood into thin fibers. The fibers are pressed flat and dried to make paper. Whole forests are grown to satisfy the huge worldwide demand for paper.

▲ Some bonsai trees can live for hundreds of years if cared for properly .

What lives in a puddle?

Rain puddles may look as if they contain only clear rainwater, but they also contain millions of tiny organisms. Most of these are too small to be seen with the naked eye. Microscopic plants and animals lie in the dust, where they are protected inside spores to stop them drying out. These organisms will resume their life within a few hours of rain falling, and if the puddle lasts, it will be teeming with life within one or two days.

Much of this microscopic life consists of algae and single-celled animals that are called protozoa. It also contain rotifers, which are very tiny animals with complicated feeding arms that eat the other smaller organisms.

What are protozoa?

Protozoa is the name given to the whole group of single-celled animals. All protozoa are very tiny, and most are able to move about, usually by means of beating hairs, which are called cilia. Protozoa do not have any organs, but regions inside their jelly-like body have special functions, such as feeding and catching prey. Some protozoans are parasites and can cause diseases such as dysentery and malaria.

Most protozoa are aquatic, because they do not have an outer coat to keep them from drying out. Protozoa can be found living in every puddle you see, feeding on bacteria and debris.

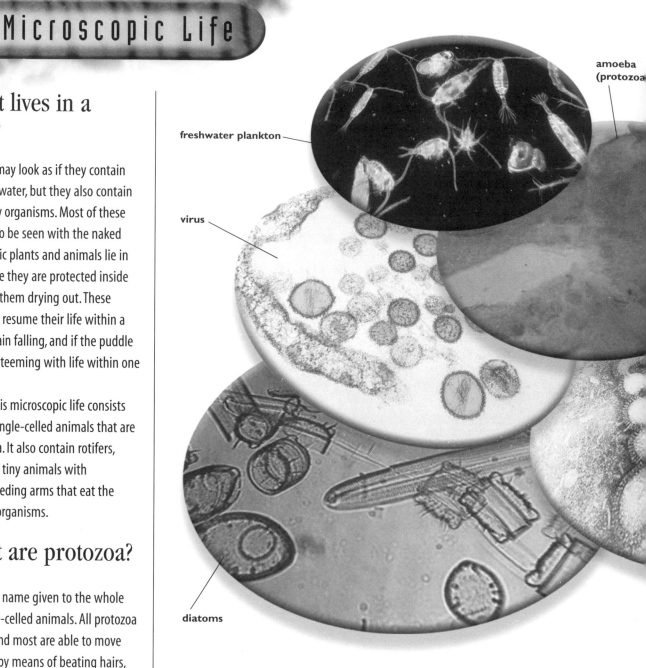

freshwater plankton

amoeba (protozoa

virus

diatoms

What is an amoeba?

An amoeba is a tiny, shapeless animal that is composed of a single cell. It has no real body shape, and it moves by flowing around slowly. If you have extremely good eyesight, you could just about see an amoeba as a very tiny speck. Amoebas feed by flowing over their food and absorbing it. They live mainly on other small creatures and bacteria.

What are plankton?

The surface layers of the sea are filled with tiny life forms. Many of these are the young of fish, crustaceans, worms, and other forms of sea life.

All these creatures, together with algae, make up the plankton that is the main food resource of the seas. Plankton is found in large amounts in the cold polar seas where whales are most common.

amoeba

bacteria

influenza virus

◀ **Microbes come in various shapes and sizes and can be found living almost everywhere. Tough organisms such as bacteria can even live in hot mineral springs or in the ocean depths.**

What are bacteria?

Bacteria are the simplest living organism. Unlike other living cells, bacteria do not have a nucleus. Instead, their genes are scattered throughout their interior. Bacteria have a thick protective cell wall. There are thousands of bacteria in every cubic yard of air you breathe, and everything you touch is loaded with bacteria. They even live inside your body.

Although bacteria can cause disease, the majority of them are completely harmless and carry out the vital function of breaking down dead and waste materials. Bacteria in the gut, for example, help the body's digestive processes.

Are viruses alive?

Viruses are even smaller than bacteria, but strictly speaking they are not alive. To be 'alive,' an organism must be able to grow and reproduce. Viruses cannot do this themselves, and the only way they can reproduce is to enter a living cell and take control of it. The cell then becomes a living factory that produces more viruses.

How do we use microscopic forms of life?

We use bacteria and fungi to make food and for other useful purposes. Yeasts are used to ferment alcohol, while the bacteria living in milk change it into yogurt. Molds give some cheeses their characteristic color and taste, and even the soy sauce used in Chinese cooking is made by fermenting soya beans. Experiments are taking place using specially bred bacteria to break down waste materials and to clear up oil spills on beaches. Microscopic algae and bacteria are used to break down sewage and make it harmless.

How can bugs make drugs?

Penicillin was the first antibiotic that was made from a mold. Since then, many other drugs have been produced from molds and bacteria. No one knows why these substances are produced, but they may help to defend the host organism from other microscopic invaders. Most antibiotics work by damaging the ability of bacteria to reproduce and form new cell walls. In this way, the body's own defenses can kill off the bacteria.

Microbes probably help make antibiotics and other substances to defend themselves against other organisms. They are able to evolve very quickly, changing their body chemistry to produce new substances to suit changes in their environment or threats to their existence.

Jewels of the sea

Microscopic diatoms, which are sometimes called "jewels of the sea," are tiny algae floating in almost all waters. They have a hard shell made from silica (a glass-like substance), which is marked with elaborate patterns. These patterns are so characteristic that the inspection of diatom shells is sometimes used to test the quality of microscope lenses. Diatoms contain a globule of golden oil that hides the green color of the chlorophyll they use for photosynthesis. Diatoms form a major part of the ocean's plankton population.

⍰ What is ecology?

Ecology is the study of how living creatures relate to one another and their environment. It is a comparatively new branch of science, but it has shown how interfering with a small aspect of a living community can lead to unforeseen consequences. Killing off one type of predator to protect livestock, for example, can cause prey animals to multiply in huge numbers and devastate crops.

⍰ What is a food chain?

A food chain is a sequence that demonstrates how one organism forms the food for another. It begins with the simplest animals and plants and continues until the top of the chain is reached. Humans or predator animals are often at the top of food chains.

▼ Plants such as grass and trees are toward the bottom of the food chain. Grazing animals browse on these plants, and these animals are in turn eaten by predators such as lions. Their dung fertilizes the soil, encouraging the growth of more plants, so the food chain actually becomes a circle.

⍰ Which communities live in hot deserts?

The plants and animals living in hot deserts have all developed ways of conserving or storing water. Cactuses and other succulent plants store water in swollen stems and leaves. Some cacti grow to a huge size and can live for 100 years or more. Other desert plants have tiny leaves that reduce water loss and spines that protect the plant from grazing animals. Their roots may go down as far as 33 feet to reach water.

Reptiles are common inhabitants of deserts because they are cold-blooded and need heat if they are to remain active. Most other desert animals are either small burrowing rodents or birds and animals that hide from the sun among bushes or rocks at the hottest times of the day.

⍰ Which communities live in the tundra?

Tundra is the cold, partly frozen region near the North Pole. It is covered with grasses and other low-growing plants, including the lichen known as reindeer moss. Many familiar trees, such as willows and birches, live in the tundra too, but they are stunted and low growing. Despite the cold, the tundra is covered with flowers in the spring, and huge numbers of flies pollinate them. Mosquitoes are present in vast numbers, biting the mammals that live in this region.

Killer toads

An ecological community is a very finely balanced system, and changing one element can alter the whole community. This fact was discovered when giant African cane toads were imported into the West Indies and into Australia to control the rats and mice that damaged sugar cane crops. Unfortunately, the greedy toads ate the local wildlife instead. They have severely damaged the communities of ground-living birds, reptiles, and mammals, some of which were already under threat.

A similar situation arose when the mongoose was introduced to help control rats. It promptly wiped out some species of bird instead. Rats and mice breed in such huge numbers that they can always outbreed the appetite of any predator introduced to control them.

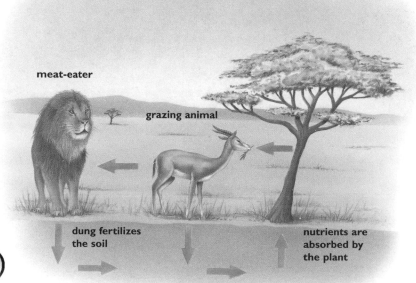

meat-eater

grazing animal

dung fertilizes the soil

nutrients are absorbed by the plant

What lives in conifer forests?

Conifer forests cover huge areas of cool parts of the world. They are not rich in plant life apart from the trees, because the deep shade of the forested areas prevents most other plants from growing.

Various kinds of squirrels, burrowing rodents that feed on fallen cones, and many types of birds inhabit conifer forests. Eagles, hawks, and owls prey on the small rodents. Deer graze on the bark of young trees, and the huge moose lives in wet areas, paddling around the edges of lakes and streams and feeding on water plants.

What lives in tropical rainforests?

Tropical rainforests contain the most varied mixtures of animals and plants of any habitat on the Earth. They contain large and small predators and a bewildering variety of birds. All these animals are supported by huge numbers of trees that produce fruit to feed them and their prey all year round. Because there is no true winter in tropical rainforests, there is no need for the cycle of eating and storing food that takes place in cooler climates.

▲ Bears are typical forest-dwellers. They are omnivorous and able to eat roots, fruit, nuts, fungi, and any animals or eggs that they find. They fatten themselves up and then hibernate through the winter when food is scarce.

What lives in deciduous forests?

Temperate forests contain far more varieties of trees and shrubs than are found in conifer forests. Because the shade in these forests is not so great, there is far more undergrowth and larger clearings between the trees. During the lifetime of a tree such as the oak, large branches fall off and rot on the forest floor, providing a rich habitat for fungi and small animals. Other fungi live naturally in association with tree roots, and their mushrooms are eaten by mice and squirrels. Foxes are common predators in temperate forests. Deer graze in the clearings and feed on young trees. Many types of small seed-eating birds live in temperate forests, hunted by predators such as hawks.

◀ Rainforests contain the bulk of the world's species of plants and trees, and many of these have still not been described scientifically. Each year new plants are discovered, and new and valuable plant chemicals are found.

What lives on coral reefs?

Coral reefs are the marine equivalent of rainforests. They are home to huge numbers of a great variety of animals. Unlike some other habitats, few plants grow on coral reefs because fish and sea snails graze them. Ocean currents carry most of the food to the reef. Plankton is the basic food that powers the whole reef system. The small animals that feed on plankton are eaten by large crustaceans and fish, and so on up the food chain to predators such as sharks.

If a coral reef continues to grow, it may begin to rise out of the water, becoming a coral island. The sea helps to break up the coral growths and pile them up. Creatures such as calcifying algae cement the pieces together to form a solid structure. If soil lodges in the coral, vegetation often begins to grow on the surface. Many of the Pacific islands were formed in this way.

▲ Coral reefs have the most diverse forms of life of any habitat. They are home to thousands of species of fish and invertebrates, all living in a complex balance that makes the reef system an extremely stable environment.

⁇ Which are the main plants grown as crops?

About 150 types of plants are regularly cultivated as food crops, although thousands more are eaten in local areas. The most important crops are cereals (grass-like plants), especially maize, rice, and wheat. Root crops such as potatoes are commonly grown in temperate climates, and sweet potatoes, yams, and cassava are grown in tropical parts. The seeds of the pea family, known as pulses, include beans, soy beans, chickpeas, and lentils. They are a particularly valuable source of protein, especially in some parts of the world where meat is in short supply and malnutrition may be commonly encountered.

⁇ What is the main crop grown on the prairies?

The prairies in Canada and the U.S.A. are enormous grassy plains, which were once the home of huge herds of bison.

Today, the prairies are covered with enormous fields of maize, supplying most of the world's needs for this important food crop. The agriculture here is true factory farming, where the crops are planted, treated, and harvested with vast machines and using very little manual labor.

▶ **The three main crops grown throughout the world amount to nearly 2,000 million ton every year. The vast amounts grown are more than enough to feed the world's entire population. However, vast stock piles of food go wasted.**

⁇ Why is deforestation damaging the world's ecology?

The world's tropical rainforests are being lost at an alarming rate, and already the effects of this loss can be seen. Rainforest trees are cut down to provide timber as well as land for grazing and raising crops. The remaining scrub and branches are usually burned, providing a rich source of fertilizer for one or two years. Then the land becomes barren. Rainfall washes away the topsoil, leaving bares rock in which very little grows.

The results of deforestation are seen in countries such as Bangladesh, where heavy

▲ **Removal of trees to make new farmland means that the soil soon becomes infertile. Rain and wind remove the topsoil, and within a few years, the land is barren.**

rains are no longer soaked up by the forests in the foothills of the Himalayas. Instead the rainwater sweeps down the valleys, causing enormous flooding and loss of life.

World crop production

Thousands of metric tonnes		
Wheat	Corn	Rice

Frozen strawberries?

You might think of Iceland as a land of snow and ice, but it is also a land of volcanic activity and hot springs. The Icelandic people have made this work for them in an ingenious way by building underground greenhouses that are heated by hot water pumped out of the ground. The greenhouses have clear plastic roofs to let in the light. This free energy allows the Icelanders to grow crops such as strawberries, which are normally grown in warm climates and are only grown successfully when the summer weather is good.

▲ Many crops can be picked by machine, but tea picking must be done by hand. The pickers remove the soft shoot tips from the tea plants and place them in baskets carried on their backs. The tea is later dried and ground.

How have we changed animals and plants?

Most of the farmed animals and crops that we use today are extremely different from their wild ancestors. Wild wheat was only a large form of grass, while maize produced small, hard kernels instead of the juicy cobs we like to eat today.

The wild boar is also very different from the friendly pigs we see on modern day farms. Cattle were once long-legged, lean and dangerous to approach—unlike today's slow, placid animals.

All dogs, however, are still exactly the same species despite the many differences in their shape and size. In 12,000 years of constant breeding, humans have still not succeeded in producing a new species of dog, in other words, one that cannot breed with its ancient ancestors. Modern dogs are still able to breed successfully with wild wolves and dingoes.

What are domesticated animals?

There is a long list of animals that have been domesticated by human beings.

The dog was probably the first animal used by humans, around 12,000 years ago. It was followed by goats, cattle, and sheep about 5,000 years later. Pigs, horses, donkeys, and poultry all followed later.

Which animals no longer live in the wild?

Several animals are partly domesticated and probably no longer exist in the wild. Indian elephants live a semi-wild existence in the jungles of Asia, where they are still used as beasts of burden. They cannot be completely domesticated, however, because the males are too aggressive to be handled in the breeding season. Camels and llamas are both partly domesticated, as are the Asian water buffalo and the yak.

Where do tea and coffee come from?

Tea is made from the leaves of a species of camellia plant. It is widely grown in cool regions of China and India. Coffee was originally grown in Ethiopia, but it is now grown throughout the world. The coffee plant is a small evergreen shrub, and the coffee bean is the seed at the heart of a fleshy red berry.

How has over-fishing affected the seas?

Modern fishing methods are capable of sweeping up almost all the fish in a particular area. In addition, these methods destroy those fish that are not caught by damaging their habitat.

This damage has become apparent when trawlers stir up the seabed as they tow along huge nets. The nets destroy young fish and the shellfish on which the adults normally feed. When too many fish are caught, the young may never grow big enough to breed, and the fish population will suddenly become very depleted. This happened in recent years when herring and cod were overfished in the Atlantic Ocean.

Large fish such as tuna and sharks have been almost wiped out in some regions because of over-fishing. The main culprit has been giant gill-nets, sometimes many miles in length. These can catch literally all of the fish in a large area, and at the same time, cause the death of air-breathing dolphins by drowning them.

? What did Cuvier contribute to biology?

Baron Georges Cuvier (1769-1832) stated that an animal's structure and function are the result of its relationship with its environment, which is more or less the same as Darwin's view. However, Cuvier also insisted that all animals are exactly the same as they were at the time of the Creation, and that change (or evolution) is not possible. Cuvier was very skilled in identifying the bones of dinosaurs.

? Where did potatoes, maize, and tomatoes come from?

These familiar plants were cultivated in America for centuries before being found by the early European explorers. Potatoes were brought to Europe in the 16th century, and were a great curiosity. They originated in the Andes, in South America, where they had been cultivated for 1,800 years.

Tomatoes were brought to Europe at about the same time and were quickly adopted as a basic food by the Spanish and Italians. In northern Europe, it was a long time before tomatoes were accepted as a safe food because they are close relatives of the poisonous nightshade plants. Maize was also introduced by the early explorers and is now widely grown .

? How was the first rubber produced?

Rubber is produced from a white, milky liquid called latex, which oozes from cuts made in the trunk of the rubber tree. This tree originally grew in the jungles of Central and South America, but although rubber was in great demand, it was in short supply because the trees grew wild. Eventually some rubber tree seeds were brought back and grown at the Botanical Gardens in Kew, England.

The young trees were distributed around the British Empire, and large plantations were established in countries such as India, Malaya, and Sri Lanka. A huge international rubber trade quickly developed, and there is still a great demand for natural rubber even though synthetic substitutes are now widely used almost everywhere.

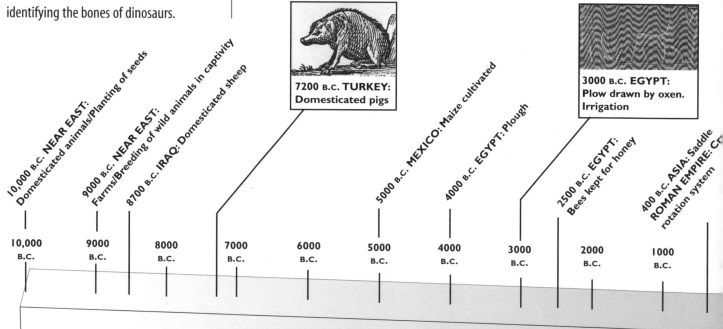

10,000 B.C. NEAR EAST: Domesticated animals/Planting of seeds

9000 B.C. NEAR EAST: Farms/Breeding of wild animals in captivity

8700 B.C. IRAQ: Domesticated sheep

7200 B.C. TURKEY: Domesticated pigs

5000 B.C. MEXICO: Maize cultivated

4000 B.C. EGYPT: Plough

3000 B.C. EGYPT: Plow drawn by oxen. Irrigation

2500 B.C. EGYPT: Bees kept for honey

400 B.C. ASIA: Saddle ROMAN EMPIRE: Cr rotation system

| 10,000 B.C. | 9000 B.C. | 8000 B.C. | 7000 B.C. | 6000 B.C. | 5000 B.C. | 4000 B.C. | 3000 B.C. | 2000 B.C. | 1000 B.C. |

Horse play

Horses first evolved in North America and spread to Asia across the land bridge that once connected Alaska and Siberia. From there, horses spread as far as Europe. For some unknown reason, horses died out in America between 8,000 and 10,000 years ago. When the first Europeans explored this new continent, they reintroduced the horse, which was by then completely unknown to the Native Americans.

▲ The marine iguana, found only on the Galapagos Islands, is the only lizard that can swim. It browses underneath the water in search of seaweed. The lizards crawl ashore to bask in the sun before the cold water makes their temperature drop too low.

? What led Darwin to develop his theory of evolution?

In 1831, Charles Darwin (1809–1882) set out on an exploratory voyage in the ship *Beagle*, heading for South America. The voyage lasted five years, and during this time, Darwin kept careful notes of everything he saw, and especially of the strange animal life in the Galapagos Islands. In 1858, Darwin published his theories in a book called *The Origin of Species*. It caused a great sensation. The book was almost immediately accepted by the scientific world. It is now generally agreed that evolution takes place along the lines that Darwin suggested. Some scientists believe that changes take place in a series of steps rather than a continuous gradual process.

? Who first studied genetics?

Gregor Mendel (1822-1884) was a botanist and monk who lived in what is now called the Czech Republic. He was interested in finding out how changes took place in an organism as it reproduced. He studied the garden pea plant, breeding plants with different colored flowers, different shapes of seed pod, and other characteristics. Recording the effects, Mendel formulated simple rules that allowed him to predict how many plants would resemble one or both parents, and how many would combine characteristics of each parent.

Mendel's studies formed the basis of modern genetics. Although he altered some findings to fit with his ideas, his theories are still important to the study of biology.

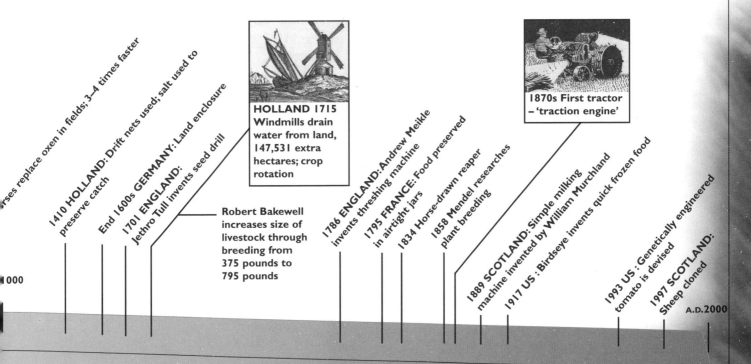

...rses replace oxen in fields; 3–4 times faster

1410 HOLLAND: Drift nets used; salt used to preserve catch

End 1600s GERMANY: Land enclosure

1701 ENGLAND: Jethro Tull invents seed drill

HOLLAND 1715 Windmills drain water from land, 147,531 extra hectares; crop rotation

Robert Bakewell increases size of livestock through breeding from 375 pounds to 795 pounds

1786 ENGLAND: Andrew Meikle invents threshing machine

1795 FRANCE: Food preserved in airtight jars

1834 Horse-drawn reaper

1858 Mendel researches plant breeding

1870s First tractor – 'traction engine'

1889 SCOTLAND: Simple milking machine invented by William Murchland

1917 US : Birdseye invents quick frozen food

1993 US : Genetically engineered tomato is devised

1997 SCOTLAND: Sheep cloned

000

A.D.2000

Prehistoric
Life

During Earth's long history, many millions of species have appeared, thrived for a time, and then died out. Dinosaurs are the example that most people think of, but there were many other creatures just as spectacular, such as colossal sea lizards and giant sharks far bigger than any similar predators living today. But of all these extinct animals, the dinosaurs were the most successful, living for 150 million years and colonizing almost every part of the land surface. They were so successful that the biggest mystery about them is why they disappeared at all.

Dinosaurs ranged from small chicken-sized creatures that scuttled about in the ferns and mosses, to the gigantic plant-eaters and predators that we see reconstructed in films. Because generally only their bones survive, there is much that we do not know about dinosaurs and their habits. There is also a lot that can be deduced from their remains, which show us that they often laid eggs in carefully constructed nests, lived in herds, and carried out long migrations. What we don't know is what colors they were, if they had a 'voice,' or even if they were warm-blooded like modern mammals and birds.

After the extinction of the dinosaurs, the small shrew-like mammals that took over also went through a period of evolutionary growth. This produced monstrous grazing animals and sloths so big they could push trees over in order to feed on them. Mammoths, woolly rhinoceroses, and sabre-tooth cats appeared and later became extinct, but by this time, humans had emerged from their ape-like ancestors and contributed to the extinction of the animals they killed for food.

The Dawn of Life

How did life first appear?

No one knows exactly how life on Earth began. Most scientists think that it started as a result of reactions taking place in the soup of chemicals dissolved in the ancient seas. The atmosphere contained poisonous gases, and fierce electrical storms raged.

In laboratory experiments, conditions such as the ones above can produce the substances found in living creatures. Some of these substances have been found in freshly fallen meteorites, so they are also being created elsewhere in the universe.

What can we learn from the fossil record?

Since life began, parts of animals have been preserved as fossils. When the animals died, their remains were covered with mud and sediment that slowly turned to rock. When scientists examine layers of ancient rock, the oldest layers are at the bottom, and new rock is laid down on top of them. So unless the rocks have been disturbed by movements of the Earth's crust, the deeper the fossil is found, the older it is.

By studying rocks and the fossils they contain, it is possible to decide how old fossils are, and to identify creatures that lived at the same time but in different parts of the world.

Usually only the hard parts of extinct animals are fossilized, but recently some fossils have been found showing internal organs, and there are even fossils of jellyfish.

Do fossils prove evolution took place?

There are gaps in the fossil record, so it is not possible to prove that evolution took place. In order to do this, fossils of every single change in a species would need to be preserved. However, enough fossils exist to show the relationships of all modern animals, allowing scientists to deduce their probable ancestors from the fossil record. New fossils are constantly being found, gradually filling in gaps in our knowledge.

Are there fossils of all extinct animals?

The fossil record has very large gaps in it, so there are periods where we know little about the life that once existed. Conditions may have changed long ago, making it unlikely that fossils were preserved. Also, changes on the Earth's surface may have worn away rocks that contained fossils.

Fossil shells are quite common, but fossils of larger animals are very rare. It is even more unusual to find a complete skeleton of an animal such as a dinosaur because its carcass would have been partly eaten by scavengers and the remains scattered. Some of the best fossils were formed in shallow lakes or mudflats, where the animal has been preserved because it was quickly covered with protective silt. Preservation of a delicate animal in fossil form requires ideal conditions, such as soft mud where there is no oxygen present, so scavengers cannot destroy the carcass.

Did all the ancient life forms turn into the animals we see today?

Evolution seems to have carried out some very strange experiments. Some of the earliest forms of animal life did not lead to further evolution, so they died out quickly. A few creatures have survived almost entirely unchanged, such as brachiopods. These look like small clams, although they are unrelated. They appear in the oldest fossil beds and survive in exactly the same form to this day, living in ocean depths.

Some of the oddest failures in evolution were found in a layer of rock called the Burgess Shale, in Canada. This rock preserved the tiny remains of soft-bodied animals, which is an extremely rare occurrence. The animals amazed scientists because most of them had no relationship to any other known life form.

How is the Earth's time broken up?

Scientists break up the earliest history of the Earth in several ways, according to the forms of life that existed. The time we consider in this book is split into the Palaeozoic Era, when most modern life forms developed, and the Mesozoic Era. During this period, many life forms evolved further and mammals and birds gradually began to appear. Dinosaurs also evolved during the Mesozoic Era and lived throughout three distinct periods, called the Triassic, Jurassic, and Cretaceous periods.

Ancient fossils

The fossil record begins about 550 million to 600 million years ago, in a time known to scientists as the Late Precambrian Period. There may have been simple animals around even earlier, but they have left no traces. Soon after, in the Cambrian Period, there was an explosion of life, and many life forms left behind shells that are well preserved. Usually there is little clue to the soft parts of these ancient creatures, so it is hard to reconstruct how they looked and behaved.

▼ Geological time covers many millions of years, and can be conveniently broken up by describing the typical animals living during each period. These geological periods are generally not exact, and there is some overlap, except with creatures such as dinosaurs, trilobites, and ammonites that died out quite suddenly.

Quaternary	1.64 million years ago
Tertiary	65 – 1.64 million years ago
Cretaceous	145 – 65 million years ago
Jurassic	208 – 145 million years ago
Triassic	245 – 208 million years ago
Permian	290 – 245 million years ago
Carboniferous	362 – 290 million years ago
Devonian	408 – 362 million years ago
Silurian	439 – 408 million years ago
Ordovician	510 – 439 million years ago
Cambrian	570 – 510 million years ago

⁇ Which ancient creatures may be the ancestors of modern animals?

Animals such as fish, amphibians, reptiles, birds, and mammals have a backbone. It supports their body and serves as an anchor for muscles. These animals are called vertebrates. Some of the ancestors of vertebrates are found in old fossils. They have traces of a stiffening rod to support their back, which is thought to have later evolved into a proper spine.

⁇ How did the Earth look in ancient times?

The Earth's surface looked similar to its appearance today, although the continents did not exist because they were still joined together in one supercontinent called Pangaea. When Pangaea broke up, the continents were formed, and they drifted about on the Earth's crust to their present positions. Ancient plants were very different, and flowering plants and modern trees have developed comparatively recently (about 100 million years ago). Plant-eating animals would have fed on ferns, horsetails, and primitive trees called cycads.

Swamp and bogs covered large areas, and mountains were much higher than they are today, because they had not yet been worn down by erosion. Volcanic activity was greater too, and this would have caused earthquakes and eruptions, which may have influenced the extinction of some animals.

What is an ammonite?

Ammonites were members of the same class of animals as the modern octopus and squid. They were tentacled animals that lived in a flat, coiled shell. There were many thousands of different types of ammonite. The shells of some ammonites were as much as 3 feet across, but most were much smaller. The animal lived in a small, horny cell, constructing a new cell as it grew. The cells contained gas, probably making the shell buoyant and allowing the animal to swim freely. Later, the shells of some ammonites became partly straightened out. Ammonite shells have been well fossilized. They are commonly found on beaches, where they have been washed out of the soft rock by wave action.

▲ Ammonites were relatives of the modern octopus and squid. They secreted a hard shell, living in a small compartment. A new compartment was added as they grew larger, eventually producing a spiral shell. The nautilus is a modern member of this group, living in a similar shell. It is not closely related to ammonites.

What are trilobites?

Trilobites are another of the great groups of animals that lived 500 million years ago but have now disappeared. They looked rather like large flattened woodlice (pill bugs). Some trilobites were predators, but most were scavengers that scuttled around on the seabed on their many jointed legs. Some grew to a length of 17 inches. and weighed about 10 pounds, but most were much smaller. Like woodlice, trilobites could roll up into a ball when threatened. The name 'trilobite' comes from the animal's appearance — its body was in three lobes. Trilobites were arthropods (animals with jointed skeletons), and like modern crabs and lobsters, they had to split their rigid shell and emerge before they could grow bigger.

Which is the largest scorpion ever known?

Among the earliest large inhabitants of the seas and shallow waters were giant relatives of the scorpions and spiders. Some of these creatures were around 4 inches in length, but others were enormous — up to 6.5 feet long. These fearsome creatures had a flattened armored body, and claws tipped with sharp spines for catching their prey. As well as ordinary jointed walking legs, they had large paddle-shaped limbs with which they rowed themselves along. They could swim by beating their tails up and down. These creatures were the largest predators living in the seas 450 million years ago.

What did the first fish look like?

The earliest fish were very small. They were heavily armored to protect themselves from attacks by the invertebrate predators that were common in the seas 450 million years ago. Most of these fish seem to have lived by feeding on small animals and algae in the mud on the seabed. Some of the earliest forms had a third eye, and all of them differed from modern fish because they had no jaws. The mouth was a simple hole or slit, which limited the types of food they could eat. The descendants of these primitive fish are modern lampreys and hagfish. These eel-like creatures resemble their ancestors in that they have no jaws. However, they are either parasites living off other fish or scavengers feeding on dead fish.

Killer fish

As fish developed jaws, they were able to hunt other animals. Soon they evolved into large creatures, sometimes with armor to protect them. The most fearsome fish grew to 30 feet in length.

Dinichthys (also known as *Dunklosteus*) had a long, powerfully built body, with fins like an eel. Its 6.5 feet long head was covered with bony armour, and could be raised to allow it to open its mouth wide. *Dinichthys* did not have teeth, but its jaws were edged with great plates of jagged bone that cut through its prey like knife blades.

❓ What was the largest shark that ever lived?

The modern white shark reaches a length of 19 feet, making it one of the most feared predators of the seas. But an extinct shark may have been 40 feet long, and weighed around ten times as much as the white shark. This shark, called *Carcharocles*, lived about 15 million years ago, and its bulk was the size of a bus. Only its huge teeth have survived, allowing paleontologists (scientists who study fossils) to calculate its actual size. The jaws of the megatooth shark would have been large enough to swallow a car.

❓ What is the Burgess Shale?

In 1909, a fossil bed was found in Canada high up in the Rocky Mountains. Examination of the tiny fossils in this rock revealed very small creatures. The fossils found here are unique, and no animals like these have been discovered anywhere else. Special conditions in the shallow seas where these animals lived allowed their delicate structures to be preserved, buried in mud. Many of these animals crept about on the seabed, feeding on small organisms in the mud. Some were active predators. *Anomalocaris* was about 2 feet long and a powerful swimmer. It was armed with grasping claws and a circular mouth lined with cutting blades, enabling it to make short work of its far smaller prey.

◀ The ancient seas contained many fearsome predators, but none was as terrifying as *Carcharocles*, the giant shark that could have tackled any other creature it encountered. Its fossil teeth show that it was very similar to the modern white shark, but far bigger.

? What was the first form of life on land?

Plants were the first to colonize the land, starting with very simple plants such as algae. Then mosses and liverworts developed, followed by ferns and other larger plants. Animals did not leave the sea until plants had become established – otherwise there would have been no food for them. Relatives of the spiders and scorpions were probably among the first animals to leave the sea and colonize the land. At first these animals would have been quite small and probably returned to the sea to breed, like modern land crabs. Later they evolved into larger and more complex forms of life like modern insects.

? When did fish leave the sea?

Around 400 million years ago, ancestors of the coelacanth began to creep out of the water onto the land. Many fish are able to wriggle along on land, but in order to lift their body clear of the ground, ordinary fins are not strong enough. The relatives of the coelacanth had leg-like fins reinforced with bones, which allowed them to slither along like a modern crocodile even though they did not walk properly. They were still fish, however, and had to return to the water to breed. It is thought that these early four-legged animals, known as tetrapods, lived in shallow freshwater pools, like modern lungfish. They needed to develop lungs in order to breathe when oxygen levels in the stagnant water fell.

? Why did fish come out onto the land?

The main reasons for an animal to change its habit are to obtain fresh food supplies and to escape from its predators. Many modern fish, such as those commonly found around tidal rockpools, leave the water briefly for these reasons. Their ancient ancestors probably also did this, spending more and more time on land as they evolved.

? Can fish breathe on land?

Many ancient fish, together with their surviving relative the lungfish, developed simple lungs that they used instead of their gills when out of the water. Modern lungfish hibernate in a mud cocoon when the pools in which they live dry up. Lungfish can also migrate overland to other pools, using their leg-like fins to help pull them along.

Attack of the amphibians!

During the Carboniferous Period some 300 million years ago, amphibians multiplied rapidly and developed into many different forms. All of these amphibians were predators, feeding on insects, spiders and other land animals, and probably on each other. They were mostly shaped like salamanders, with long, flexible bodies and short legs, and they probably all lived near water.

A few amphibians returned to the water and became completely aquatic, although they managed to retain some of the adaptations they developed to survive on land. Some had huge armoured heads, and a few lost the use of their limbs. These amphibians probably had a moist, smooth skin like their modern relatives, but some may have had scaly skin. They were much larger than surviving amphibians, and some reached more than 6.5 feet long.

▼ Early fish, related to the surviving coelacanth, began to creep out of the water about 400 million years ago. This may have been to seek new food sources, or to escape from aquatic predators. As they evolved into amphibians, they developed lungs and their fins gradually changed into limbs.

⍰ What is a coelacanth?

Primitive fish with leg-like fins are thought to have become extinct during the period when dinosaurs lived. Later they were found, alive and well, living in the Indian Ocean. One of these fish is the coelacanth, a large fish up to 3 feet long with strange leg-like fins. It was found to contain bones that were very like those of land-living vertebrate animals.

The first of these unknown fish was caught off the Comores Islands in the 1930s. It was later found that coelacanths were common enough to be a popular food. They have since been found in other places, always living in very deep water. Because they have hardly changed over many millions of years, coelacanths can be described as true "living fossils".

⍰ What are amphibians?

As fish evolved into land-living animals, they had to change their body form. Water supports the body, but on land the animals needed to evolve a strong spine and ribs to stop their body from collapsing. They needed to develop muscles to support the body and to move the limbs. New bone structures had to evolve to support the limbs. Other changes were the perfection of lungs for breathing air, and sense organs, which would work well on land. Despite adaptations, these animals still needed to keep moist and to return to the water to breed. They are known as amphibians, which means "living on land and in water".

⍰ What are the modern amphibians?

Frogs, toads, newts and salamanders are amphibians which survive today. There are also some other unusual types of amphibian, such as blind cave-dwellers. All modern amphibians produce aquatic tadpoles from their eggs, which are laid in water or kept moist by special body modifications. It is thought that their ancestors reproduced in the same way.

Amphibians such as frogs and toads are valuable because they eat huge amounts of damaging insect pests, but their numbers have been drastically reduced in recent years. They are sometimes used for food, and they are also susceptible to the many insecticides used by farmers.

? What are reptiles?

Reptiles evolved from amphibians, but there are several important differences between these two kinds of animal. The most obvious difference in the living animals is that reptiles have scaly skin to prevent their bodies from drying out, while amphibians have thinner, moist skin. Reptiles also have a more efficient heart and kidneys to equip them for living on land, and they have evolved more efficient ways of walking. It is not so easy to tell the difference between reptiles and amphibians when examining fossils because the soft parts of the body are not preserved. However, there are important structural changes in the skeleton that can be observed.

? How do reptiles differ from amphibians?

The development of eggs with protective shells was the single thing that freed reptiles from the watery environment that amphibians needed to reproduce. The egg of a reptile contains membranes, which surround the developing embryo. They provide a protective pool of liquid and food stores for use while the embryo grows. The young reptile completes its development inside the egg and emerges perfectly formed as a miniature version of the adult.

Reptiles also differ in having a scaly skin that helps protect them from predators, in contrast to the thin, naked skin of amphibians. Their heart and circulation is also improved to allow them to have a more active lifestyle.

? Which were the first reptiles?

The earliest known reptiles were small lizard-like animals only a few centimeters long. They appeared about 330 million years ago and are known to have lived in the rotted stumps of fallen trees. They probably fed on insects and other small creatures living in fallen trees. Reptiles quickly adapted to live in habitats that were not suitable for the amphibians. They spread across many parts of the Earth's surface and developed into flying forms as well as many types of land dweller.

? What did early reptiles look like?

Unlike the amphibians, reptiles were able to exploit all the available food sources, and many of them adopted a vegetarian diet. These reptiles were not dinosaurs, but many looked like the dinosaurs that would follow.

Carnivorous reptiles developed with long fangs to stab and tear their prey. These animals were lightly built and fast moving in order to hunt. Others were herbivores, developing teeth capable of grinding vegetation and huge barrel-like bodies to contain the massive digestive system needed to cope with a vegetable diet.

Although some of these reptiles looked like the dinosaurs, scientists know from studying the structure of their hip bones and limbs that most would have been more clumsy when walking or running.

? Reptiles or mammals?

As the reptiles multiplied, they became more diverse. Among them were mammal-like reptiles called the synapsids. One of these, *Dimetrodon*, had a sail-like structure on its back. The sail may have helped control body temperature. By turning the sail to face the sun, these cold-blooded reptiles could absorb heat. *Dimetrodon* was a large, 9-foot-long predator with saber-like teeth. Other mammal-like reptiles, called dicynodonts, are thought to have become warm-blooded to gradually evolve into true mammals.

Legless lizards

Snakes are thought to have evolved from lizard-like reptiles that gradually lost their legs. Pythons are modern snakes that still retain a tiny trace of their legs in the form of two small claws near the rear of their body.

▲ *Dimetrodon* was a typical reptile of the Permian Period, with some mammal-like features. It had a huge crest along its back of uncertain function, although it may have been used to regulate the animal's temperature.

⑦ What were archosaurs?

Archosaurs were a whole group of reptiles that appeared during the Triassic Period. Most of them were predators, and they gave rise to animals such as the dinosaurs, the crocodiles and their relatives, and the flying pterosaurs. The archosaurs were the group of animals in which the modification to the hips and legs developed. This modification led to the dinosaurs being able to support their own weight and to stand upright. Because they were able to move more efficiently and most were fierce predators, it is thought that they may have killed off the mammal-like reptiles and other early relatives.

⑦ Which reptile had the longest neck?

One of the most remarkable looking reptiles that ever lived was called *Tanystropheus*. It was about 9 feet long, but almost 7 feet of this length was its neck! Tanystropheus was quite lightly built, and its neck was probably not very flexible because it contained only a few vertebrae. No one is quite sure just how this creature lived or why its neck was so incredibly long, but the shape of its teeth suggests that it might have been a fish eater. Its long neck could have been extended like a fishing pole to help it catch its fish prey.

▶ *Tanystropheus* has puzzled many scientists, because no one is sure why it had such an extraordinarily long neck. It is thought that is neck might have helped the animal to fish for prey.

149

❓ What were dinosaurs?

Dinosaurs were reptiles that evolved into the most varied kinds of any living creature. They ranged from tiny bird-like animals to monstrous beasts that were the largest animals ever to live on land. The dinosaurs survived for about 150 million years. They were not all the meat-eating killers familiar from films and books; neither were most of them gigantic creatures. In fact, most dinosaurs were peaceful, browsing animals about the size of modern farm livestock.

❓ What do we know about how dinosaurs' bodies worked?

Although dinosaur remains are few, we know or can deduce quite a lot from their fossilized skeletons. For example, we can calculate a dinosaur's weight by studying its bones. Heavy animals have massive bones to support their weight, while swift-moving hunters usually have very light, hollow bones. Muscles are firmly attached to bones, and although no trace of the muscles remains in fossils, the attachment points can be seen on the bones. These tell scientists how big the muscles must have been.

We know that a bulky digestive system is necessary to digest vegetable matter. The herbivores would have had massive barrel-shaped bodies, while carnivores would be slimmer. The shape of the teeth tells us what type of food the dinosaur ate.

❓ Why did dinosaurs become so successful?

The main thing that distinguishes dinosaurs from other reptiles is the way their body is supported by their legs. The legs of ancient and existing reptiles stick out sideways, so the body drags on the ground for most of the time. It is raised briefly when the animal runs. This is very obvious with crocodiles, which can run very fast for short distances. The skeletons of dinosaurs developed so the legs were beneath the body, raising the whole body off the ground. This allowed them to stand erect and to walk and run with long strides. These developed predators could run faster than more primitive reptiles, which soon became extinct.

▼ *Brachiosaurus* was a typical long-necked dinosaur with a barrel-shaped body and powerful legs to support its enormous weight. We can only guess at the structure of its internal organs, but the points where its muscles are attached to bones can be clearly seen, so it is possible to reconstruct its shape very accurately.

vertebrae

lung

heart

gizzard

large intestine

knee

ankle

⍰ Were dinosaurs stupid?

How do you measure the intelligence of an extinct animal? What we can say is that the intelligence of dinosaurs must have been sufficient for their way of life – otherwise they would not have survived for millions of years. Some plant-eating dinosaurs certainly had very small brains in proportion to their size. However, a large brain is not important in an animal that is too enormous to be attacked and has little to think about apart from grazing. On the other hand, some of the predatory dinosaurs had quite large brains, presumably because they needed to think quickly as they pursued their prey.

In comparison to their size, the brains of the smallest dinosaur predators were the biggest, because they needed to be agile and fast moving.

⍰ How do we know how dinosaurs moved?

We can reconstruct the shape and habits of dinosaurs from their remains. Dinosaurs also left behind other evidence, in the form of their footprints.

These were imprints in mud that were later covered by flood waters and became fossilized. Some of the dinosaur footprints give us a good idea about how these animals lived and moved. By measuring the distance between each footprint, we can measure the stride of the animal, and from this we can calculate how fast the dinosaur moved. Footprints also show that dinosaurs sometimes moved in herds or small family groups, and they show evidence of dinosaurs being hunted by predators.

⍰ How many different types of dinosaur were there?

There were thousands of different species of dinosaur, and we have discovered only a small proportion of these. It is important to realize how rare fossils are. A few dinosaur species must have been very common, for example *Iguanodon,* which left many fossils. Others were probably scarce when they were alive or lived in regions where fossilization was unlikely, and so there are few remains of these dinosaurs.

Herbivores often lived in groups or herds, but carnivores were usually more solitary and their fossils are therefore more rare. Many of the most interesting dinosaurs are known from a single fossil, or sometimes from just one or two bones. Paleontologists must deduce the shape and size of the animal from these few remains.

High pressure heart

Modern reptiles have an inefficient heart. It mixes blood that contains oxygen with blood that is low in oxygen. This is quite adequate, because modern reptiles are not very active, and so their hearts do not have to work hard to pump blood around their bodies. Giant reptiles such as dinosaurs, however, were much more active. They stood on two legs, which meant that their hearts had to work harder. The heart of a giant long-necked sauropod had to pump at very high pressure to get blood up to its brain. This makes it likely that a dinosaur's heart was able to pump effectively.

▲ *Iguanodon* was a typical plant-eating dinosaur, living in large herds. It would have eaten huge amounts of plants and probably needed to migrate to reach fresh grazing.

? Why did many dinosaurs walk on two legs?

The hip bones of many dinosaurs evolved in such a way that walking upright on two legs became an efficient way to travel. Dinosaurs that walked in this way developed long legs, which allowed them to walk and run very efficiently. Scientists used to think that they walked in an upright position with their tail dragging on the ground, but we now know that the tail stuck out horizontally to balance the forward-leaning body. These dinosaurs were able to stand upright while grazing.

? Which dinosaur was bone-headed?

The *Pachycephalosaurus* had a reinforced skull, which was probably used when rival males fought each other.

Pachycephalosaurus was a medium-sized dinosaur, up to about 26 feet long, although many of its relatives were much smaller. They all had an enormously thickened domed skull, and their spine was strengthened. Scientists think that adult males could ram each other with force when competing for a mate.

Despite its fierce appearance, *Pachycephalosaurus* was a plant-eater. In many forms, the skull was decorated with spikes and knobs of bone.

? What was *Iguanodon*?

Iguanodon was a plant-eating dinosaur that stood 16 feet high and was 33 feet long. It was very common throughout Europe and the U.S.A., and is thought to have lived in large herds. Unlike many similar plant-eaters, *Iguanodon* sometimes walked on two legs or dropped down onto its front legs and walked on all four legs. We know this from its fossil footprints. Despite its size, *Iguanodon* was often attacked by large flesh-eating dinosaurs. It defended itself using a large horny spur on its hand. Early paleontologists thought that this was a horn, and they reconstructed the animal to look like a rhinoceros. *Iguanodon* was a very successful animal and survived for about 30 million years. The remains of 39 *Iguanodon* were found in a single site in Belgium, where a whole herd appears to have perished. Unusually, many of these skeletons are complete.

? How small were some dinosaurs?

Some dinosaurs were about the size of a chicken, or even smaller. *Compsognathus* was only about 28 inches long and was very lightly built. It was an agile and fast-moving creature, and is thought to have lived on insects and small animals. Specimens of *Compsognathus* have been found with the fossilized remains of their last meal – a lizard – still preserved. The skeleton of *Compsognathus* is very similar to that of a modern bird.

Like modern flightless birds, it probably scuttled about in the undergrowth to protect it from larger predators, feeding on any small animals it could capture.

▲ Often called the 'bone-headed dinosaur', *Pachycephalosaurus* and its similar relatives had a massive bony lump on its skull which it is thought was used for defense or for battles between rival males.

⟨?⟩ Which dinosaur behaved like a rhinoceros?

Triceratops and its relatives were large plant-eating dinosaurs very similar to the modern rhinoceros. They even had large horns like the modern animal. Members of the *Triceratops* family were large, bulky animals that walked on all fours. They are thought to have lived in herds. As well as their huge horn, they had an enormous bony frill. It extended from the back of the head and over the shoulders, often with more spikes and horns attached. *Triceratops* reached a length of 10 yards and a weight of about 6 tons.

 Triceratops and its relatives probably used their horns in defense against attacks from flesh-eating dinosaurs. The frill might have been used by rival animals to create a threatening display.

⟨?⟩ Did plant-eating dinosaurs stand upright?

The giant sauropod dinosaurs walked on all four legs, but many plant-eaters walked on either two legs or four. Scientists used to think that the dinosaurs that spent most of the time on two legs walked in an upright position. The tail dragged along the ground or was used as a support when the animal reached up to browse from trees. We now know that these dinosaurs carried their bodies in a more horizontal position, so their shorter front legs could easily reach the ground. Their tail was used to balance the body, often sticking out stiffly. In some cases, the tail was made more rigid because it was supported by bony rods – these would have prevented the tail from bending easily.

⟨?⟩ Did dinosaurs have beaks?

Many of the plant-eating dinosaurs had a horny beak with which they cropped the vegetation that they ate. Unlike modern grazing animals, which use their lips to grasp food and pull it into their mouths, reptiles have no lips. The dinosaurs had to cut and tear their food with their beak, before grinding it up with rows of teeth at the back of their mouth.

 True beaked dinosaurs evolved at about the same time as the appearance of the first modern flowering plants, so the parrot-like beak may have been an adaptation that allowed them to take advantage of this new food source.

▼ *Triceratops* was one of a large family of plant-eating dinosaurs that all had spiked skulls and a frill of bone covering their necks. They lived in herds and probably had a similar lifestyle to the modern rhinoceros.

Dinostrich!

Many medium-sized dinosaurs resembled ostriches and similar birds in their shape, habits, and the way they walked. Most of the dinosaurs that lived on the open plains, like modern ostriches, were tall, long-legged, and had long necks. They could stretch their necks up above the undergrowth to see if any predators were nearby.

What were sauropods?

Sauropods were a group of dinosaurs that were all built to the same general design. They all had a short barrel-shaped body to accommodate the huge gut needed to digest their vegetable diet, a very long neck and tail, a comparatively tiny head, and peg-like teeth for grazing. The other important feature of the sauropods is that they were all enormous. They were extremely heavy, and because they lived in large herds, they churned up the ground as they moved about. It is still possible to see the damage caused by their movements in the ancient rock layers where fossils of the sauropods have been found.

Why did the sauropods have such long necks and tails?

The long neck of the sauropods is thought to be an adaptation to help the animals feed on tall trees, like the modern giraffe. The whole structure of these dinosaurs is a very clever piece of engineering, because their long neck, which was usually held out horizontally, was balanced by the weight of the tail. The vertebrae were shaped to allow the attachment of powerful muscles and rope-like tendons and ligaments, which held the whole structure together like a suspension bridge. Despite the great length of the neck and tail, they were not as flexible as we might think. They were usually stretched out almost in a straight line.

Which was the biggest sauropod of all?

Scientists cannot agree on the maximum size of these giant dinosaurs. *Brachiosaurus* is usually said to be the biggest, weighing about 85 tons. A recently described dinosaur, provisionally called *Ultrasaurus*, is thought to have been about 99 feet long and to have weighed as much as 140 tons. This would make it by far the heaviest land animal ever to have existed. Even the mighty blue whale is small in comparison to these huge prehistoric creatures.

What happened to the *Brontosaurus*?

Most people have heard of the *Brontosaurus*, which is the sauropod described in many books and films. This term is no longer used, however. It was discovered that the fossil originally called *Brontosaurus* had already been described, and was called *Apatosaurus*. This latter name is the one now officially recognized by scientists.

Which was the tallest sauropod?

Brachiosaurus used to be considered the tallest of the dinosaurs. It was 82 feet long, but it stood more erect than other sauropods because its front legs were so much longer than the rear ones. Its head was very small, but it reached up to 43 feet above the ground.

Recently, another dinosaur called *Sauroposeidon* has been described. This huge animal stood 56 feet high, making it three times the height of the tallest giraffe. Each of the vertebrae in its neck was more than 3 feet long, and its bones were filled with tiny air cells that helped to reduce its weight.

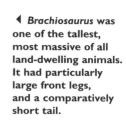

◀ *Brachiosaurus* was one of the tallest, most massive of all land-dwelling animals. It had particularly large front legs, and a comparatively short tail.

▶ Much smaller than the true giant sauropods, *Saltasaurus* was protected from predators by armored plates across its back.

? How were sauropods armored?

Most of the great sauropods relied on their huge size to prevent attacks from predators. *Saltosaurus* was not as large as many of the other sauropods, but as compensation for this, its back was covered with armored plates. These plates were ridged and packed close together to provide extra protection. The fossils of *Saltosaurus* found so far are incomplete, so we don't know exactly how far this armor extended over its body. Most of the sauropods were well able to defend themselves with a large clawed toe on the inside of the front foot, and they probably also trampled any attackers using their great weight.

? Did sauropods have any natural enemies?

It is unlikely that a predator could bring down an adult sauropod because of its huge size. However, the young sauropods may have been more at risk.

Sauropods such as *Diplodocus* had a large claw on the front foot, and were probably able to rear up and use this claw to defend themselves. Some scientists believe that they could swing their huge long tail as a weapon. It would have struck the attacker with great force, like an enormous whip.

? How did sauropods digest their food?

We do not know what the structure of the sauropod digestive system looked like, but there are some clues about it in fossil specimens. These show that there were large numbers of smooth, well-worn stones inside the animal's body. Scientists think that these were held in a muscular gizzard organ, like that of a bird. The stones churned and ground the plant food to aid digestion.

◀ A relative of *Apatosaurus*, *Diplodocus* was much lighter in build and very much longer, with a slim neck and whip-like tail.

? Did the dinosaurs live in groups?

Almost all modern grazing animals live in herds or large family groups, and there is no reason to suppose that dinosaurs were any different. Animals living in herds are able to alert each other to the approach of threatening predators, so this behavior helps with survival.

Fossil footprints show us that plant-eating dinosaurs traveled in groups made up of both large and small individuals. Sometimes large groups of fossils of the same species are found tumbled together. Scientists think that sometimes a herd may have died when overwhelmed by a flood, for example when crossing a river.

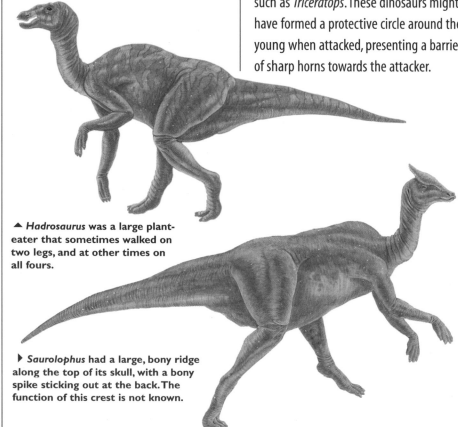

▲ **Hadrosaurus** was a large plant-eater that sometimes walked on two legs, and at other times on all fours.

▶ **Saurolophus** had a large, bony ridge along the top of its skull, with a bony spike sticking out at the back. The function of this crest is not known.

? How might plant-eaters have defended themselves from attack?

The smaller bird-like dinosaurs were as fast and agile as most of their predators, and would simply have run away when attacked. The giant sauropods were well able to defend themselves by rearing up and trampling any attacker with their huge weight. They also defended themselves with the claws that many of them had on their front legs. They may have used their tails and long necks as weapons, too.

The young sauropods would have been very vulnerable, and it is probable that the adults guarded them. This may also have happened with bulky horned dinosaurs, such as *Triceratops*. These dinosaurs might have formed a protective circle around the young when attacked, presenting a barrier of sharp horns towards the attacker.

? How did meat-eaters hunt their prey?

The bodies of meat-eating dinosaurs varied considerably, so their hunting methods would also have been very different. Small agile dinosaurs would have pursued their prey, catching them as they ran and dodged. Some of them probably hunted in packs.

The very large carnivores probably lived alone and attacked their large prey by ambush. We do not know enough about dinosaur anatomy to say whether they chased their prey for long distances or whether they made short dashes like modern reptile predators, such as crocodiles and monitor lizards.

? How did the plant-eaters feed?

The food of plant-eating dinosaurs depended on their type of mouth. Some dinosaurs had broad mouths like a duck's bill, and they probably grazed on a mixture of plants. Dinosaurs with narrow jaws probably selected particular plants to eat.

The long-necked sauropods probably grazed on leaves and shoots. Large herds of sauropods would have caused tremendous devastation by feeding in this way, and may have used their great weight to push trees over so they were easier to reach. A herd of sauropods would have cleared great areas of trees, creating large expanses of open land where smaller dinosaurs could graze. Dinosaurs with cutting beaks probably cropped the vegetation very short.

Multi-colored dinosaurs?

No one knows for certain what colors these animals were, because pigments do not survive in fossils. Although dinosaurs are usually illustrated in a dull green or grey color, it is likely that many of them were brightly colored and patterned like modern lizards. These colors and patterns would have concealed the plant-eaters from their predators, and hidden the lurking predators from their prey.

Did dinosaurs migrate?

From the evidence of fossil footprints and the distribution of the remains of dinosaurs, it seems likely that the plant-eating species migrated according to the seasons. In the Jurassic and Cretaceous Periods when the dinosaurs flourished, there would have been variations in the seasons just as there are today. Like any other grazing animal, the dinosaurs would have migrated to where they could find food. *Maiasaurus* is thought to have lived in herds containing thousands of individuals. These herds migrated along regular paths, flattening the ground with their great weight as they traveled.

How long did dinosaurs live?

Many scientists believe that the largest dinosaurs, such as the sauropods, may have lived for as much as 100 years. This can be calculated because of the time it would take for an animal to reach the enormous body weight of these sauropods. This calculation takes into account their vegetable diet, which was not very nutritious.

The world would have been a very dangerous place for young dinosaurs. We do not know which dinosaurs cared for their young. However, young dinosaurs probably developed quickly in order to become independent and able to look after themselves. The modern crocodile is one of the few reptiles that looks after its young until they are able to avoid predators.

Did dinosaurs have voices?

There are some very strong clues that some plant-eating dinosaurs could produce a lot of noise, although we cannot be sure about this. Many duck-billed dinosaurs had a large bony structure on their head, which was probably used to amplify sound, like the body of a guitar. Hollow air passages in the bony structure allowed the dinosaur to produce low, booming cries. In some species, the shape of the crest and the sounds produced varied between individual animals, helping herd members to locate each other. Males might have used their individual sounds in mating displays. A duck-billed dinosaur called *Parasaurolophus* had a crest that swept back in a long curve, while others had a crest that bulged forwards.

▼ **The extraordinary crest carried by *Parasaurolophus* appears to have acted as an echo chamber, giving this dinosaur a loud booming cry.**

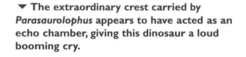

? What do we know about dinosaur breeding habits?

As far as we know, all dinosaurs laid eggs rather than giving birth to live young. Many of these eggs have been fossilized, but it is sometimes difficult to find out which animal produced them. Sometimes the eggs contain the remains of an unhatched baby dinosaur. Occasionally the fossil of a newly hatched baby is found near the eggs, showing which species they belong to. Dinosaur eggs were laid in clutches, like those of today's birds. We think that dinosaurs, like birds, would have had courtship behavior, built nests, and cared for their young until they were old enough to look after themselves.

? How did dinosaurs look after their young?

Originally it was thought that dinosaurs laid their eggs in isolated places, but in 1978 a remarkable find was made in Montana, U.S.A. Fifteen *Maiasaurus* babies were found scattered around a large mound-shaped structure, together with many broken eggshells. The babies were not newly hatched because their teeth were partly worn. The nest was about 6.5 feet across, and covered with vegetation. In the Gobi desert, the pig-sized dinosaur *Protoceratops* dug holes in the sand and buried her eggs. She left them to hatch in the heat of the sand while she guarded them from predators.

? What did dinosaur eggs look like?

Dinosaur eggs looked very much like bird eggs and were surprisingly small. Most were about the size and shape of a large potato. Their small size means that the hatchling would also have been small and would have needed plenty of care from its parent.

? Did dinosaurs return to their nest sites?

There is good evidence to show that dinosaurs such as the *Maiasaurus* migrated back to its traditional nest site every year, where it laid up to 20 eggs. Scientists have found nest sites containing masses of eggshells, together with the remains of babies of various ages, showing that the dinosaurs re-used the sites over the years.

? Did different types of dinosaur nest together?

When *Orodromeus* nests were discovered, other dinosaur eggs were found between them. These eggs were smaller and were laid in straight lines. It has recently been found that they are the eggs of a small predator, *Troodon*. It appears to have laid its eggs in the *Orodromeus* colony to gain protection from other predators. This habit is similar to that of modern cuckoos and their relatives, although they also use another species of bird to rear the young.

▼ **Very large numbers of remains of *Protoceratops* have been found in the Gobi desert, including eggs and nestlings. These animals seem to have nested in very large groups and probably cared for their young.**

▼ *Maiasaurus* **was a large plant-eating reptile that lived in herds and laid large clutches of eggs in circular nests. They returned to the same communal nest site each year.**

▲ **Eggs of *Orodromeus* have been found broken open from the inside as the young hatched out. The baby dinosaurs are thought to have foraged for their food while being guarded by adults.**

⑦ Were dinosaur eggs buried like those of a turtle?

The eggs of *Protoceratops* have been found laid in nests in the Gobi desert. The eggs were arranged in careful circles, in layers. Presumably the mother dinosaur turned herself above the nest as she laid each egg.

⑦ Where did dinosaurs build nests?

The first dinosaur nests were discovered in the 1920s in the Gobi Desert, proving that *Protoceratops* was an egg layer and nest builder. However, it was not until the 1980s that a huge number of nests and hatchling dinosaurs was uncovered in Montana, U.S.A. These remains were of several types of duck-billed dinosaurs. The area where they were found had originally been on uplands, probably because this was a less hazardous environment for the young than the low-lying areas where adults spent most of their time. The layers of nests and eggs showed that the dinosaurs migrated to the same nesting site every year.

▼ *Oviraptor* **was an odd dinosaur that probably lived entirely on the eggs of other dinosaurs. It was bird-shaped, with a powerful beak for crushing eggs, and did not have any teeth.**

⑦ How big were nesting colonies?

Dinosaurs like the *Maiasaurus* lived in huge herds, probably containing many thousands of individuals. Their breeding colonies were probably also very large. Their nests were placed about 7.5 yards apart, which is roughly the length of an adult *Maiasaurus*. This arrangement allowed the dinosaurs to crowd together without getting in each other's way. These great nesting sites gave some protection from predators. Also, by grouping the young together, it was relatively easy for the parent to find its own offspring after going off to forage for food.

⑦ Did dinosaurs need to guard their young?

The meat-eating dinosaur *Velociraptor*, which was featured in the film *Jurassic Park*, fed on small dinosaurs. A *Velociraptor* skeleton has been found entangled with the remains of a *Protoceratops*. Both animals had died in a struggle over the eggs and young of the *Protoceratops*. Another dinosaur called *Oviraptor* fed on dinosaur eggs, which it cracked with a powerful beak. It also used two sharp bones inside its mouth to crack the tough eggshells. Although many plant-eating dinosaurs had nests and looked after their young, nothing is known about the breeding habits of the giant sauropod dinosaurs or the meat-eaters.

Dino-graves!

Some extraordinary mass graves have been found, filled with the remains of dinosaurs of varying ages. The dinosaurs had all been killed together in some ancient disaster, probably while trying to cross a river. In Canada, one such herd contained the remains of at least 300 *Centrosaurus* of all ages, both adult and young. In Montana, U.S.A. the remains of a herd of more than 10,000 *Maiasaurus* was found. The herd had been overcome by volcanic gas and ashes.

? How did slow-moving dinosaurs protect themselves?

Plant-eating dinosaurs had three ways to escape from fierce predators. First, a plant-eater might simply be too big to be brought down and eaten, for example the sauropods. Second, a plant-eater might run away very fast, like many of the bird-like dinosaurs. Finally, a slow-moving dinosaur may have been covered with spikes and horns to help deter potential attackers.

Triceratops and its relatives had long horns and bony shields over its head and shoulders. Some dinosaurs developed a hard jointed skeleton as a defense, rather like modern armadillos. Often the bony plates covering the dinosaur's back were interlocking, making it difficult for a predator to reach the soft flesh. Many of the ankylosaurs had long spikes on their body, providing extra defenses.

? Did dinosaurs have scales?

The bodies of modern reptiles, such as lizards and snakes, are covered by overlapping scales. Dinosaurs, however, had leathery skin that was often studded with small lumps, or nodules. We know that dinosaur skin looked like this because impressions of the skin is sometimes found with fossils.

? Why were ankylosaurs usually a match for predators?

Ankylosaurs such as *Euoplocephalus* had heavily armored backs, like a military tank. However, they did not rely only on this to protect them from attack. A huge club of bone grew on the end of the tail, and the *Euoplocephalus* could use it as a fearsome weapon if attacked. Meat-eating dinosaurs walked on two legs, so they would have been very vulnerable to a blow from the club on the tip of an ankylosaur's tail. Such a blow would easily have shattered a leg and left the animal helpless. Other ankylosaurs such as *Edmontonia* were not only heavily armored, but they had long shoulder spikes facing forwards. These spikes would have caused very deep wounds if the ankylosaur lunged at its attacker.

▲ *Triceratops* was a huge animal with heavy armor around its head and shoulders. The horns would have been used as a defense against predators.

▲ As well as being covered with jointed armor and defensive spines, *Euoplocephalus* carried a massive club on the end of its tail which would have crushed any predator.

◄ The sharp spikes along the edges of the body of *Sauropelta* would have stopped any predator from getting at its soft underbelly.

❓ When was it a good defense to lie down?

For many ankylosaurs, some of which had no tail club, lying down prevented the predator from reaching its soft underparts. In many of these animals, such as *Sauropelta* and *Hylaeosaurus*, the sides of the body were edged with heavy spikes. A predator would have found it very uncomfortable to try to turn its prey over. The interlocking bony plates on the ankylosaurs' back meant that there were no gaps in its armor. Even if it was tipped over, an ankylosaur called *Minmi* had armor underneath its body to protect its soft belly.

❓ What were stegosaurs?

Stegosaurs were related to the ankylosaurs. They were plant-eaters, and most of them were large. Stegosaurs all had extremely small brains, and had to develop a mass of nerve tissue near the base of their spine to help control the movement of their hind limbs. Their appearance was extraordinary, because they had two lines of very large bony plates standing on end all the way down their back. In addition, stegosaurs had long spikes on the tail, which might have been used in defense. Various bony plates were studded about the vulnerable parts of their body. Although most stegosaurs were very large, there were other types about the size of a small pony.

❓ How did stegosaurs use their armor?

Scientists cannot agree on the function of the plates on the back of the *Stegosaurus* and its relatives. Some people think that they were used in display to rival animals, while others believe that they helped to regulate body temperature. Fossils show that there was a rich blood supply to these parts of the body. When it turned sideways to face the sun, the stegosaur's body would have been heated up by the sun's rays. When it turned itself away from the sun, the stegosaur's body would have cooled down as a result of the increased heat loss. It has even been suggested that the plates could have folded flat to make a sheet of armor over the animal's back.

Armor plated

The whole head of an ankylosaur was covered with protective plates, and this cover even extended to the eyes. Bony plates could drop down inside the eye socket like a metal shutter, so vulnerable areas were not accessible to attackers.

These animals probably did not need to rely on such defenses because most of them were quite capable of looking after themselves. In addition to their body armor and protective spikes, the club on the tail of some ankylosaurs would have broken the legs of any attacker, even the fearsome *Tyrannosaurus* or its relatives.

▲ Although the sides of its body were less heavily armored than many of its relatives, the underside of *Minmi* was well protected by being covered with tough bony plates.

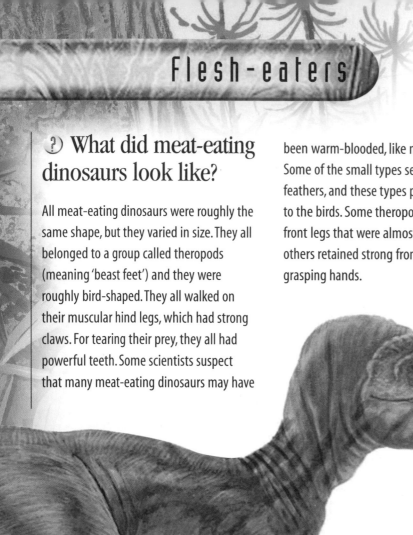

What did meat-eating dinosaurs look like?

All meat-eating dinosaurs were roughly the same shape, but they varied in size. They all belonged to a group called theropods (meaning 'beast feet') and they were roughly bird-shaped. They all walked on their muscular hind legs, which had strong claws. For tearing their prey, they all had powerful teeth. Some scientists suspect that many meat-eating dinosaurs may have been warm-blooded, like mammals. Some of the small types seem to have had feathers, and these types probably gave rise to the birds. Some theropods had small front legs that were almost useless, while others retained strong front limbs with grasping hands.

◄ **Tyrannosaurus rex, usually just called T. rex, was the largest and most fearsome land-living predator ever to have existed. It probably stunned its prey by simply charging at it with its mouth wide open, then tore it apart with its huge teeth.**

How did meat-eaters attack their prey?

Giants like *T. rex* probably ambushed their prey, charging at them with jaws wide open. They could run at a speed of 20 mph, although probably for only a very short distance. The impact of eight tons of dinosaur hitting its prey with a jagged mouthful of teeth would probably kill most animals outright. Many similar but smaller theropods retained powerful front limbs and claws, and could cling to their prey while biting it.

Which was the biggest meat-eater?

Tyrannosaurus rex (*T. rex*) is usually thought to have been the biggest meat-eating dinosaur – and the biggest land-living carnivore ever to have existed. It was about 40 feet long and weighed about 8 tons. No one is quite sure why its front limbs were reduced to such a tiny size, with only two claws. The limbs were so short that they could not even reach the dinosaur's mouth, so they were not used in feeding.

Baby killers!

Baby meat-eaters would have been easy prey for other predatory dinosaurs, and in some cases adults even ate the young of their own species. Remains of a small predator called *Coelophysis* have been found with the remains of *Coelophysis* babies fossilized inside it. Even the giant *T. rex* may have been a cannibal, according to remains recently found. Parts of a *T. rex* skeleton had been torn away, and part of a tooth from another *T. rex* was embedded in these remains.

▲ *Baryonyx* is the only known fish-eating dinosaur, and uniquely it carried huge claws on its front limbs.

⁇ Which remarkable 'new' dinosaur was found in 1983?

In 1983 an amateur fossil hunter found a huge claw, 13 inches long, in a Surrey clay pit. When the site was excavated, it revealed an entirely new type of meat-eating dinosaur, which has been named *Baryonyx*. Although this animal looked similar to other meat-eaters, it had some unique features. A huge claw was attached to each thumb, and its head looked rather like that of a modern crocodile. Fish scales were found inside the skeleton, so it is now thought that this was the only known fish-eating dinosaur.

The first mammals

The first mammals lived alongside the dinosaurs, but in comparison with the reptiles they were tiny and insignificant. Most were only a few centimeters long and looked like modern shrews, with a long nose and teeth adapted to eating insects and other small creatures. At some point, these ancient mammals stopped laying eggs like their reptile ancestors and gave birth to live babies, like the kangaroo and other modern marsupials.

⁇ How could small meat-eaters bring down large dinosaurs?

Some smaller dinosaurs may have hunted in packs, like modern wolves. By working together they would have been able to kill much larger animals.

Deinonychus was about the size of a human adult male, and was lightly built so it could run fast.

⁇ What was a *Velociraptor*?

The fierce raptors shown in the film *Jurassic Park* actually existed, although they were not as large as the ones depicted in the film. Like *Deinonychus*, *Velociraptor* had a large ripping claw on its hind legs, and may have hunted in packs. It had a much slimmer head than *Deinonychus*, and probably had a less powerful bite.

This hunter had a very stiff tail, which it probably used to steer itself and change direction quickly while chasing its prey. Like other theropods, *Deinonychus* had very sharp teeth, and it also had powerful arms with grasping claws. The most unusual feature was a large upturned claw on its foot, which could be swivelled downwards so that it could slash its prey with its muscular hind legs. This probably killed the prey due to loss of blood.

◄ Standing about as tall as a man, *Deinonychus* was a fast and intelligent predator that grasped its prey with clawed front limbs before ripping it apart with the huge claw on its hind foot.

▼ Many remains of the fast and agile *Velociraptor* have been found in the Gobi desert. This raptor was small but heavily armed with a ripping claw on its hind leg. It probably hunted in packs.

❓ Which plant- and meat-eating dinosaurs had a crest all the way down their backs?

The plant-eater *Ouranosaurus*, a close relative of the very common *Iguanodon*, and many similar large dinosaurs walked mostly on two legs. *Ouranosaurus* was different because it had a large sail-like crest down its back. The purpose of this crest is not certain, although as this animal lived in hot regions, the crest may have been used as a heat regulator. A similar dinosaur was *Spinosaurus*, a typical meat-eater which had a crest 6 feet high running down its back. It was a very large predator, about 39 feet long and weighing nearly 4.5 tons. *Spinosaurus* would have been rather unwieldy as a hunter, so it may have scavenged the carcasses of dead animals.

❓ Which dinosaur had the largest claws?

A claw found in Mongolia from the hand of an unknown dinosaur measured no less than 27.5 inches in length. As the horny outer part of the claw was missing, it would have been even longer. Almost nothing is known about the rest of this extraordinary animal, which has been given the name of *Therizinosaurus*. We do know that it was a theropod and must have been a ferocious predator.

▲ Although in many ways *Ouranosaurus* was a typical plant-eating dinosaur, it had a remarkable sail-like crest running down its back and along its tail. Its function is unknown.

❓ Which dinosaur had a head like a parrot?

Oviraptor was a dinosaur that specialized in eating the eggs of other dinosaurs. It cracked them open with its powerful beak. *Oviraptor* was only the size of a modern domestic dog, but had long, powerful legs for its size. It would have needed to be able to run fast to escape the dinosaur whose nest it was robbing. *Oviraptor* also had large hands with long claws, which it would have used to dig into dinosaur nests and remove their eggs. Some relatives of this dinosaur had strange, helmet-like growths on their heads, rather like modern hornbills.

❓ Were dinosaurs an unsuccessful experiment in evolution?

Dinosaurs thrived on Earth for 180 million years. Since their extinction, mammals have ruled the world for just 65 million years. Together with other reptiles, dinosaurs lived in almost every available habitat and evolved into thousands of different forms. For these reasons, they must be considered an extremely successful biological experiment. The experiment eventually failed only because these animals could not adapt quickly enough when conditions on Earth suddenly changed. It is interesting to speculate on how dinosaurs might have developed if these mass extinctions had not taken place. Possibly they could have evolved to parallel the ways that modern mammals have developed.

The cleverest dinosaur

The theropod *Troodon* was about the size of a large domestic dog, with grasping hands and eyes that faced forward like human eyes. Its brain was very large in proportion to its size, and it could probably run very fast, swerving and ducking to catch its prey. One paleontologist has suggested that, had the dinosaurs survived, this big-brained animal could have evolved into an intelligent form of life rather like human beings.

◄ **Could *Troodon* have evolved into an intelligent form of life? It had all of the right physical attributes, but became extinct along with the other dinosaurs.**

Which dinosaur had a head like a bull?

Carnotaurus, a meat-eating theropod found in Argentina, had a number of puzzling features. It looked rather liked *T. rex*, but was smaller and had even tinier arms, which probably had no function at all. *Carnotaurus* had a massive head and short horns like a bull. Its back and sides were covered with knobbly scales.

▼ **The feeding habits of *Segnosaurus* are a complete mystery. Did it eat termites, fish, or plants? There are arguments for all of these possible diets.**

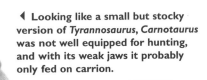

Which theropod dinosaur was not a meat-eater?

Segnosaurus is an odd dinosaur that scientists have found difficult to classify. It seems to be related to the meat-eating dinosaurs, but it would not have been able to run fast and does not have the right kind of teeth for a meat-eater. Because the front legs of *Segnosaurus* have powerful claws, it has been suggested that this dinosaur fed on termites, like the modern anteater. Alternatively, *Segnosaurus* could have been a plant-eating dinosaur, although it would have been the only theropod to do this.

Which giant sauropod dinosaur was able to defend itself well?

Most of the sauropods were too enormous to be successfully attacked by predators. Some of the smaller sauropods developed their own defenses. *Saltasaurus* had body armor, while *Shunasaurus* had a tail club like the ankylosaurs. *Shunasaurus* was found in China. It was about 33 feet long and weighed about 3 tons. Other sauropods could defend themselves adequately by using their enormous tail as a whip, wielded with enormous force. The largest sauropods would have reared up and trampled any predator with their front legs.

◄ **Looking like a small but stocky version of *Tyrannosaurus*, *Carnotaurus* was not well equipped for hunting, and with its weak jaws it probably only fed on carrion.**

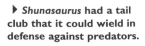
▶ ***Shunasaurus* had a tail club that it could wield in defense against predators.**

◄ **Descriptions of the mythical sea serpent sound remarkably like those of the plesiosaur, with its barrel-shaped body and long, snaky neck. These animals rowed themselves along with flattened flippers.**

? Which were the biggest marine reptiles?

Pliosaurs were relatives of the plesiosaurs, but they had shorter necks and massive skulls armed with enormous teeth. They were the largest and most powerful predators ever known. Some types, such as *Liopleurodon*, reached a length of 14 yards. The head of another species, called *Kronosaurus*, was nearly 8 feet long. These pliosaurs played a similar role in the seas to that of modern killer whales.

Super turtle!

Turtles developed at about the same time as many of the dinosaurs. Unlike modern turtles, the early forms did not have a complete shell. The largest was called *Archelon*, and was 4 yards in length. Its shell was made of flattened plates that were not completely joined together, making them lighter and allowing the animal to swim rapidly. This feature would have been important because there were many powerful predators in the sea at that time.

? Which marine reptile had the most flexible neck?

Some of the plesiosaurs evolved very long necks, and *Elasmosaurus* was one of the most extreme examples. Its neck contained up to 70 vertebrae, and it would have been able to coil its neck around itself two or three times.

? What were plesiosaurs?

Although dinosaurs did not return to the sea, plenty of other reptiles did. Some of the most familiar are the plesiosaurs, large animals with a barrel-like bodies and long snaky necks. Plesiosaurs lived on fish, capturing them with a mouthful of spiky teeth. Their flexible necks could probably shoot out like a striking snake to catch their prey. Some species had an enormously long neck that was as flexible as a snake's. Plesiosaurs did not have flexible bodies. They rowed themselves along by waving their fin-like front and rear limbs up and down.

? How did plesiosaurs breed?

Unlike ichthyosaurs, which have been found with embryos inside their remains, there is little evidence of how plesiosaurs reproduced. They probably bred like modern turtles, hauling themselves out of the water with their flippers and laying eggs in the sand.

Unfortunately, although their fossilized remains are not uncommon, neither eggs nor newly hatched babies have yet been found, so their breeding habits remain a mystery.

? What were mosasaurs?

Mosasaurs were relatives of the modern monitor lizards, but they differed from monitors in being up to 11 yards in length. Mosasaurs had a long snaky body, which was flattened to help them swim, and paddle-like limbs. These animals were so modified to suit their marine environment that they could probably not venture onto the land. They are known to have fed on ammonites, because mosasaur teeth marks have been found on the fossil shells of these creatures. Mosasaurs died out at about the same time as the dinosaurs.

⑦ What were ichthyosaurs?

Ichthyosaurs are an interesting example of what is known as parallel evolution (when unrelated animals sharing the same habit come to look very similar). In this case, ichthyosaurs, dolphins, and sharks evolved into almost the same shape. Ichthyosaur fossils are very common, and there were many different types. They all had long beaks lined with shark teeth for feeding on fish. The largest types were 11 yards long. Although some other marine reptiles probably laid their eggs on beaches, the streamlined fish-like ichthyosaurs were completely aquatic and gave birth to live young. Unborn babies have been found inside their remains. One odd feature of the ichthyosaurs is the large ring of bony plates around their eyes.

⑦ Did any ancient reptiles feed on shellfish?

Placodus was a very large, heavily built reptile that probably lived on shellfish. It had spade-like teeth at the front of its mouth for chipping shellfish off rocks. The broad blunt teeth at the back of its mouth were used to crush the shells before the meat was swallowed. *Placodus* was a stocky, clumsily built animal that would have found it awkward to move about on land. Some species developed heavy armor like that of a turtle.

▲ The ichthyosaurs looked very much like modern dolphins but were totally aquatic reptiles that gave birth to live young.

▼ *Mesosaurus* was a small ancestor of the crocodile. Its remains have been found in both North and South America.

⑦ Are crocodiles dinosaurs?

Crocodiles are not dinosaurs, although they both evolved from the same type of reptilian ancestors at about the same time. Crocodiles have changed very little over millions of years, because their body is very well suited to their lifestyle and has not needed to evolve. Fossil forms range from tiny crocodiles of less than 1 yard up to 17.5 yard-long giants. This is more than twice as long as any crocodiles still living today.

▶ The stocky *Placodus* was a large marine reptile that has no exact modern parallel. It probably fed on shellfish, chipping them from rocks with its chisel-like teeth.

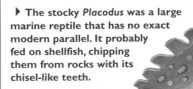

? What were pterosaurs?

Various reptiles have developed the ability to glide, but the pterosaurs were the only ones to develop true flight. The arms of a pterosaur were quite short, and its entire wing was supported by an enormously long fourth finger, leaving the other fingers free to function as a hand. A thin, skin-like membrane was stretched from the elongated finger to the sides of the body, and sometimes to the hind legs.

The whole body of the pterosaur was extremely light, with hollow bones. In several forms, the head was larger than the entire body. Some pterosaurs had tails, while others were tail-less. Some fossils even show signs of hair covering the body. Many pterosaurs lived a similar life to the modern seagull or albatross.

? How big were pterosaurs?

As with most other extinct animals, new discoveries about pterosaurs are constantly being made. The size of pterosaurs that have been discovered has increased enormously in recent years. One of these, *Quetzalcoatlus*, had a wing span greater than 16 yards, which is larger than that of many light planes. Its body was about the size of a human's, but much lighter.

Paleontologists have difficulty in understanding the diet of *Quetzalcoatlus*. This pterosaur has been found in inland fossil deposits, so it would not have been a fish-eater. Some people think that it may have been a scavenger, like a vulture. However, it is difficult to imagine such an enormous and awkward creature scrabbling around on a carcass on the ground.

? What did pterosaurs feed on?

All pterosaurs were carnivorous, and most are thought to have fed on fish because of their long, pointed teeth. As the pterosaur swooped low over the water, it would have snatched fish from the water's surface. Some toothless pterosaurs may have had a pouch in which small fish could be trapped, like that of the modern pelican.

One extraordinary form called *Pterodaustro* had a long, upturned curved beak filled with hundreds of fine bristles. These were probably used to sieve tiny shrimp from the water, like the beak of the modern flamingo.

▼ Scientists were astounded when the remains of *Quetzalcoatlus* were found. It proved to be the largest flying creature ever to have existed, with a wing span greater than many modern light aircraft.

◀ *Rhamporhyncus* was a moderate sized pterosaur with a 2 yards wing span. Its long tail was tipped with an unusual diamond-shaped piece of skin, which may have helped stabilize it in flight.

⑦ How did pterosaurs get around on the ground?

The experts are unable to agree about how pterosaurs moved about on the ground. We know for certain that their huge wings could not be folded away as neatly as those of a modern bird, and they would have been very ungainly on the ground. Most paleontologists think that pterosaurs scuttled around on their hands and on the feet of their hind legs, with their wings folded and trailing behind them. A different view is that some pterosaurs may have scuttled about upright, running on their hind legs.

⑦ How did pterosaurs fly?

Scientists used to think that pterosaurs were unable to flap their wings and fly like a bird. Instead they probably launched themselves off cliffs and glided on upward currents of air. More recently it has been suggested that pterosaurs were actually very efficient flyers. Some of the smallest types would not have been effective gliders and must have fluttered their wings like modern birds. This would not have been possible for the giants, which must have been pure gliders.

⑦ How small were some pterosaurs?

Pterodactylus had a wing span 16 inches across. This means that it would have been a fast and agile flyer.

▲ *Pterodactylus* was a very small flying reptile, smaller than a modern pigeon and much lighter in build.

⑦ Did pterosaurs have feathers?

Pterosaurs did not have feathers, because their large wings were more like those of a bat than a bird. However, pterosaurs did have fur! Fossils have shown that the body of many types was densely covered with hair, and even the wings were lightly furred. This seems to suggest that pterosaurs were warm-blooded, as there would be no point in the body of a cold-blooded creature, such as a modern reptile, being insulated.

⑦ Did pterosaurs evolve into birds?

Despite their apparent similarities, pterosaurs were quite different in structure to birds, and they never developed the powerful breast muscles needed to beat their wings in the same way as birds. Similarly, they could not fold their wings away like modern birds, so would always have been clumsy when moving on the ground.

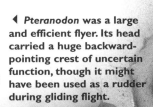

◀ *Pteranodon* was a large and efficient flyer. Its head carried a huge backward-pointing crest of uncertain function, though it might have been used as a rudder during gliding flight.

⑦ Which is the first known bird?

A single fossilized feather was discovered in a German quarry in 1860. It was identical to the feather of a modern bird, and a year later *Archaeopteryx* was discovered, also in Germany. This find caused a sensation, because Darwin's theory of evolution had just been published and was causing enormous interest. *Archaeopteryx* looked like a small dinosaur, but there were clear impressions of feathered wings and a tail. It had teeth in its jaws, a long tail and fingers extending from the front of the wing. It appeared to be a true "missing link".

Modern birds never have teeth, and their tail is reduced to a small stump; the "parson's nose". *Archaeopteryx* had clearly evolved from a reptile, but the type of reptile is still a matter for dispute.

▲ *Archaeopteryx* is a strange mixture of reptile and bird, leading some scientists to think that its fossilised remains were a fake.

⑦ Which fossils have been confused with *Archaeopteryx*?

One recent fossil of *Archaeopteryx* was identified as *Compsognathus*, a small theropod dinosaur, until it was later re-examined. The problem had arisen because there were no obvious feather impressions, which shows the similarity between dinosaurs and birds.

⑦ Why was *Archaeopteryx* thought to be a fake?

Ever since its discovery, scientists have argued about *Archaeopteryx*. In 1985 some scientists expressed the views that the fossils (several had been discovered) were nothing but an elaborate hoax. They claimed that the feather impressions had been printed over the remains of a small dinosaur. Detailed re-examination proved this claim to be false, and there is no doubt that *Archaeopteryx* did have true feathers. Whether it was a dinosaur or a bird is open to argument, however.

⑦ Which recent discoveries have changed views on the origins of birds?

Many recent discoveries show how birds may have evolved. A fossil found in Madagascar had a sickle-shaped claw on its foot like the predatory theropods *Deinonychus* and *Velociraptor*. It also had hollow bones like a bird, and traces of the points where feathers would have been attached. Fossils of a whole range of feathered dinosaurs are now being found in many countries, and especially in China. All these creatures were built along the same lines as birds. Some were undoubtedly dinosaurs and would have used their feathered forelimbs to help them run, rather than to fly.

◀ The small predatory therapod dinosaur *Compsognathus* resembles *Archaeopteryx* so closely that the remains of the two animals have been confused in the past, making clear the dinosaur ancestry of birds.

? How might flight have developed?

The evolution of birds has met with more argument than almost any other part of paleontology. The reason why flight developed will probably never be proven. Some scientists suggest that small feathered dinosaurs ran along the ground flapping their arms to help them catch their prey. Others suggest that flight started when the ancestors of modern birds climbed and leaped about in trees, using their feathers to extend their leaps and eventually to glide.

The simple structure of the wings of *Archaeopteryx* means that it would have been an extremely clumsy flyer. It probably needed to use the fingers that were attached to its wings to help it scramble about in the trees.

? Why is there so much argument about the origin of birds?

The difficulty in explaining the evolution of birds is that there are so few fossils. Bird bones are very fragile and honeycombed, with small air spaces. They crumble away very easily after death, and consequently bird fossils are extremely rare.

The only fossils of ancient birds are those where the animals fell into shallow freshwater lagoons and were covered very quickly with mud, which prevented decay or scattering of the remains by predators or scavengers. These special conditions appeared only occasionally, however. Until more types of bird fossils are found, it will be difficult for scientists to fill in the evolutionary gaps and find out more about the origin of birds.

? Are there any living clues to the ancestors of birds?

A South American bird called the hoatzin may have some of the characteristics of the very early birds. The young hoatzin has claws on the front of its wings like the *Archaeopteryx*, which it uses to scramble about in the branches. The adult birds are very clumsy flyers. Unlike all other birds, the hoatzin does not have a specialized gizzard in which food is ground up. Instead it grinds its food inside a large muscular crop. This feature is regarded as being very primitive.

▼ The ungainly and primitive hoatzin lives in South America. Its young show their reptile ancestry by having claws on their wings with which they clamber about in the branches.

? When did the dinosaurs die out?

Dinosaurs lived for an enormously long time — some 150 million years — before they died out about 64 million years ago. During their time on the Earth, they dominated the land, while other reptile relatives were the dominant forms of life in the sea and in the air. Before the dinosaurs finally disappeared, there were two mass extinctions when a large number of species died out. The dinosaurs survived, however, until the end of the Cretaceous Period.

▼ Many people believe that dinosaurs became extinct as a result of climate change after a huge meteor or a small asteroid struck the Earth. Huge meteor craters still exist, though most become eroded after millions of years and are not as obvious as this crater in Arizona, U.S.A.

▲ Crocodiles stopped evolving in the time of the dinosaurs and have changed very little. No one knows why they survived while the dinosaurs were wiped out.

? Could dinosaurs have continued to evolve?

Until they mysteriously disappeared, more and more strange forms of dinosaur were still evolving. Some types disappeared and were replaced by newer forms. This rapid rate of change is in stark contrast to animals such as crocodiles, which hardly altered after the first ones appeared. There is no reason to suppose that dinosaur evolution would not have continued. It might eventually have led to a form of life just as intelligent as human beings.

? Was the Earth struck from space?

There is plenty of evidence that the Earth was struck by huge comets and possibly by great stony asteroids. These objects would have devastated huge areas of the land and changed the Earth's climate for many years. At the time of the dinosaurs' extinction, there is evidence to suggest that an asteroid or comet struck the Yucatan Peninsula in the Gulf of Mexico. It produced tidal waves and global dust clouds that shut out the sun's light. Large amounts of the rare element iridium have been found in rocks deposited at this time. Iridium is believed to be characteristic of comets and meteorites.

⁇ How did climate change affect the dinosaurs' extinction?

During the late Cretaceous Period, the world's continents were drifting into new positions. This constant shifting within the crust led to a huge increase in volcanic activity. Volcanoes spewed out hot lava and gases, which could have built up in the atmosphere to such high levels that they affected dinosaurs and their plant food.

▲ The extinction of the dinosaurs coincided with a period of high volcanic activity, which could have contributed to their extinction.

◀ Climatic changes like ice ages may have wiped out many species of dinosaurs, which could not adapt to the cold.

⁇ What other animals became extinct?

The extinction of the dinosaurs was not an isolated event. At the same time, most marine reptiles and pterosaurs also died out. Also, tiny plankton whose shells form chalk deposits became extinct, as well as ammonites and the remaining species of trilobites. It is very difficult to imagine the causes of this extinction. For example, why did turtles survive, while marine reptiles, well adapted to their environment, such as ichthyosaurs, died out?

A dying breed

All the dinosaurs disappeared at about the same time. However, whether this happened over a few days, a few years, one or two centuries, or even over a few thousand years is impossible to say. Geological time cannot be measured with such accuracy. Dinosaurs had been in decline for millions of years before their final extinction, and many types had evolved and then disappeared again during their history.

⁇ Can dinosaurs ever be re-created?

It has been suggested that dinosaur DNA (the substance found in all cells) might have survived in the remains of blood-sucking insects preserved in fossilized tree resin, or amber. The film *Jurassic Park* was based on this appealing idea. However, we have to be content with the dinosaur descendents that still exist, such as birds, because only tiny and incomplete traces of DNA have been found in this way.

❓ When did mammals first appear?

A group of mammal-like reptiles preceded the appearance of the dinosaurs. However, these early mammals gradually disappeared during the Triassic Period and were replaced by the true mammals. It is difficult to decide exactly which of these extinct animals was a reptile and which had become a mammal. It is quite likely that the later reptiles had hair and other mammal-like characteristics.

❓ Which was the biggest mammal of all?

The first mammals were small and inconspicuous, and they were vulnerable to all the fierce dinosaur predators. Once the dinosaurs died out, the mammals were able to develop and evolve. Eventually the mammals grew into forms that were almost as gigantic as their dinosaur predecessors. *Indricotherium*, which was a member of the rhinoceros family, developed into something resembling the giant sauropods but with a shorter neck and tail. It grew to a height of 16 feet at the shoulder and weighed 16.5 tons. It probably grazed on trees like the modern giraffe. *Indricotherium* had four large teeth, two in the upper and two in the lower jaw. It also had three toes on each foot. In many ways it resembled a gigantic tapir.

❓ Which modern mammals are 'living fossils?'

Marsupials, like the kangaroo, are said to be primitive mammals because they give birth to tiny undeveloped young. The young are raised in a pouch until they are developed enough to live on their own. Two surviving kinds of mammal, however, still lay eggs like their reptile ancestors. Both the duck-billed platypus and the spiny anteater, or echidna, live in Australia. They lay eggs, and the hatchlings are placed in a primitive pouch on the mother's stomach. Unlike the young of reptiles, these babies are nourished with their mother's milk. These two peculiar animals give us some indication about how the earliest mammals may have developed.

❓ What were sabre-tooth cats?

Sabre-tooth cats survived until as recently as 10,000 years ago, and must have been encountered by prehistoric humans. The best known of these cats was *Smilodon*, which was more massive than a lion. It had a pair of canine teeth up to 8 inches long. It used these teeth to slash and stab its prey, and it could open its jaw very wide to allow the teeth to be used in this way. *Smilodon* probably brought its prey down using its considerable weight and sharp claws before stabbing with its enormous teeth.

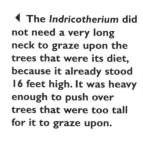

◄ The *Indricotherium* did not need a very long neck to graze upon the trees that were its diet, because it already stood 16 feet high. It was heavy enough to push over trees that were too tall for it to graze upon.

▶ **Thylacosmilus** was a typical example of the sabre-tooth cats, with long canine teeth that were used to stab the prey.

⏀ What are placental mammals?

cental mammals give birth to ll-developed young, unlike the marsupials. ese animals are called placental mammals ause their babies are nourished inside mother's body by a large fleshy organ ed the placenta. It extracts food and gen from the mother's blood and passes o the developing young, removing waste ducts at the same time.

⏀ What was *Glyptodon?*

This odd creature looked very much like some of the dinosaurs. It was a giant armadillo-like animal, with a shell 5 feet long. Its head was covered with armored plates, and the tail was also armored. In many types, the tail was tipped with a huge bony club or massive spikes that the creature could swing to defend itself.

⏀ What was *Chalicotherium?*

Although it was related to the horse and the rhinoceros, *Chalicotherium* was a very strange-looking beast. Its body was something like a horse's, but its front legs were very long and powerful and were armed with large claws. It probably used these claws to dig up roots from the ground on which it fed.

The first mammals

The first mammals lived alongside the dinosaurs, but in comparison with the reptiles they were tiny and insignificant. Most were only a few centimeters long and looked like modern shrews, with a long nose and teeth adapted to eating insects and other small creatures. At some point, these ancient mammals stopped laying eggs like their reptile ancestors and gave birth to live babies, like the kangaroo and other modern marsupials.

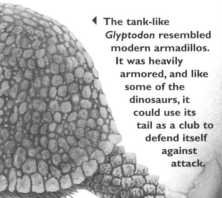

◀ The tank-like *Glyptodon* resembled modern armadillos. It was heavily armored, and like some of the dinosaurs, it could use its tail as a club to defend itself against attack.

175

❓ How did horses evolve?

Animals with hooves carry all their weight on the middle toe of the foot. This was not always the case, however. The evolution of horses shows how they changed from five-toed creatures to single-hoofed animals. Early relatives of the horse were about 12 inches tall and lightly built for fast running. There were four toes on the hind legs and three on the front legs; each toe had a small hoof. As horses grew larger, the number of toes gradually reduced until *Merychippus* appeared some 23 million years ago. It had several toes but carried all its weight on the large central toe, which had a hoof. *Merychippus* stood about 3 feet high at the shoulder and looked like a small horse. The development of the horse from its primitive ancestors is one of the best examples of evolution, because unlike many other animals, the development of the modern horse and its specialized hooves can be seen in detail in the fossil record.

❓ How did whales develop?

Whales evolved from sea lion-like ancestors that returned to the sea. We do not know what the whale's land-dwelling ancestors looked like. Early whales were mostly like huge dolphins or killer whales. One of these, called *Basilosaurus*, was a slender predator about 69 feet long.

Fossil remains of whales are very scarce and not much is known about these animals. The early forms did not have the echo-sounding ability of modern whales and dolphins, which did not evolve until much later.

They are thought to have swum with an eel-like motion and may not have propelled themselves with the flattened fluke found in modern whales. Some early whales still had rudimentary hind legs, but these were so small that they could not have played any part in swimming. When whales die, their remains usually sink in deep water where they are unlikely to form fossils.

❓ Did prehistoric sloths live up trees?

Modern sloths are all slow-moving tree dwellers, but some of their ancestors were very different. Ancient ground sloths grew to an enormous size. They had a massive body, a short tail, and a small head, and some grew to a length of 23 feet. Their forearms were massive and had very large claws, which the sloths used to pull down the branches on which they fed. The back legs were short, and it is thought that these animals propped themselves up on their muscular tail while feeding from trees. They would have been strong enough to push over most trees.

Giant sloths survived in the Americas until approximately 10,000 years ago. Pieces of their skin, which have been found preserved in dry caves, show that the sloths' skeleton contained extremely tough nodules of bone. It is this bone that probably helped to protect these giant creatures from predators.

▲ Also known as *Zeuglodon*, *Basilosaurus* is the most commonly found of the ancient fossil whales. It was a predator like modern dolphins.

Giant elephants

There are now only two types of living elephant, but in the past there were many different types. *Deinotherium* was like a giant elephant, 13 feet high at the shoulder. It had huge, downward-curving tusks in the lower jaw, which it probably used to dig up roots to eat. Other forms had tusks in both upper and lower jaws, and the hoe-tuskers had tusks in the lower jaw that were flattened into a shovel-like shape.

Mammoths were very like modern elephants in shape. They survived in cool climates, spreading throughout Europe, Asia, and North America. The closest surviving relative of the elephant is the hyrax, a small and agile African animal that looks more like a rodent than its huge modern relative.

▲ Mammoths closely resembled modern elephants but were covered with thick, coarse hair and were adapted to live in the cold tundra regions, feeding on scrub and small trees. They survived in northern Arctic regions until well after the appearance of man, who hunted them to extinction.

⁇ What were killer birds?

After the death of the dinosaurs and before the development of large mammals, birds were the main predators. Some of these were fearsome and very similar to some of the dinosaurs they replaced. *Diatryma* stood 9 feet tall, with massive legs and talons. It was flightless, with the lightweight bones of a bird. These allowed it to run and to manuver itself quickly. With its huge slashing beak it would have been able to tackle prey such as the ancestors of modern horses. These birds died out when the first predatory mammals appeared. These small, fast mammals probably ate the eggs and chicks of this flightless monster, which was obliged to nest on the ground and would have been very vulnerable.

▼ Giant flightless birds like *Diatryma* were important predators and could tackle almost any prey with their massive beaks.

⁇ How did animals survive the ice ages?

Several ice ages occurred as the world's climate changed and glaciers moved away from the North and South Poles. Many animals migrated to warmer climates or simply died out, but others adapted to live in this new and cooler climate. Woolly rhinoceroses and woolly mammoths appeared. They were able to survive in cold climates, as did great cave bears, hyenas, and many other animals.

⁇ How did dogs evolve?

Dogs appear to have evolved from small mammals such as the mongoose, which appeared about 30 million years ago. This family proved very successful, and even the very early forms were similar to the modern dog. The early animals probably hunted in packs like modern animals of this group, enabling them to bring down large prey.

Reconstructing the Past

⑦ When were the first dinosaurs discovered?

Many people must have noticed old bones in the ground, but they did not attract much attention. In the 1500s, dinosaur fossils were thought to be the remains of animals or human giants that had perished in the Biblical flood.

The first proper scientific investigation took place after a huge pair of jaws was unearthed in the Netherlands in 1770. The jaws were identified by the great anatomist Cuvier, who recognized them as the remains of a marine lizard. The creature was christened '*Mosaurus.*' Many other fossil finds followed, and by 1830 five major groups of extinct reptiles had been recognized.

▲ **This skeleton of the early reptile *Dimetrodon* is unusually complete. Most fossil remains consist only of fragments, which must be pieced together.**

▶ **Excavating a large fossil reptile is a long and painstaking business. The surrounding rock must be carefully removed to expose the skeleton, which is usually removed for preservation while still partially embedded in slabs of rock.**

⑦ Why do paleontologists disagree about dinosaurs?

Scientists have found very few examples of some of the more interesting and puzzling types of dinosaur. It is very rare to find a complete skeleton and even rarer to find other clues, such as the animal's last meal or traces of its fur or feathers.

As a result, paleontologists often guess at the appearance of an extinct animal, based on a few clues and on similar living animals. This method leads to strong disagreements. For example, some experts say that dinosaurs must have been warm-blooded, in order to move quickly and to live in such varied habitats. Others insist that they were cold-blooded animals, like modern reptiles.

⑦ How are dinosaurs preserved and reconstructed?

It is rare that you can just pick up dinosaur bones. They are usually embedded in very hard rock, and it can take weeks of painstaking work to chip them out carefully and release the whole skeleton. Usually the bones were scattered before fossilization, so paleontologists often have to excavate a wide area around the first finds in order to make sure that they have not missed any important parts. The remains may be taken to a museum still embedded in a block of stone. Once the rock is removed, the fossil bones are reconstructed on a metal frame. These bones have now turned to stone and so they are very heavy and brittle. As a result, many museums make castings of the bones in plastic, which can then be jointed together for display.

Dinosaur discovery

Fossils are found all over the world, wherever sedimentary rocks were laid down. However, there are some places where large numbers of dead animals accumulated or were particularly well preserved.

Shallow muddy lakes provided the best conditions for fossilization, because animals that died there sank quickly into the mud. The lack of oxygen in the mud reduced bacterial decay, leaving the remains very well preserved. Some deposits from such lakes in China have clear impressions of feathers, which have helped to explain the evolution of birds. Other deposits even retain clear impressions of soft-bodied animals such as jellyfish.

? How are fossils found?

Fossils are usually first revealed by the process of erosion, or by quarrying. They are found in sedimentary rocks that have been formed from mud and sand laid down millions of years ago. The remains of animals and plants are buried in the layers of rock. These sedimentary rocks are often buried deep beneath layers of other rocks that do not contain fossils. They are often exposed in sea cliffs, where the rock is worn away by the waves. Mining and quarrying also expose the deeper layers of rock, and many fossils are found in the loose material at the foot of rock faces.

? Could we ever reconstruct an extinct animal?

We know that it is very unlikely that a dinosaur can be brought to life because its DNA is no longer complete. However, there are other possible ways of re-creating more recent animals.

Woolly mammoths are often found buried in the permanently frozen ground of Siberia and Alaska, and attempts have been made to extract DNA from the carcasses. It is hoped that this material could be inserted into the egg cells of a modern elephant, so a mammoth could be born again.

? Where are most dinosaurs discovered?

Most fossils have been found in Europe and North America, but they have also been found in most other parts of the world. In recent years, huge numbers of new and exciting fossils have been discovered in China, including huge new sauropods and several of the small dinosaurs that seem to have given rise to modern birds.

Fossils of mammals are not as old as those of the dinosaurs, and they are found in other regions. In particular, fossils of early man and the ancestors of mankind have been found in Africa.

▶ Now that the habits of dinosaurs are becoming better understood, museums are able to mount their fossilized remains in realistic poses that show people how they lived.

? Could a giant sauropod walk on its front legs?

Some fossil footprints of *Apatosaurus* caused puzzlement when scientists realized that they were the imprints of only the front legs of this vast reptile. They realized that the *Apatosaurus* must have been wading along in shallow water, pushing itself along with its long front legs while its hind legs floated clear of the muddy bottom.

At one time scientists thought that sauropods were far too large to have walked on land and that they must have lived entirely in swamps where the water would support their weight. We now know this is incorrect and that these giants were normally land-dwellers. In fact, they would probably have become stuck in soft mud due to their enormous weight and preferred to live on dry land.

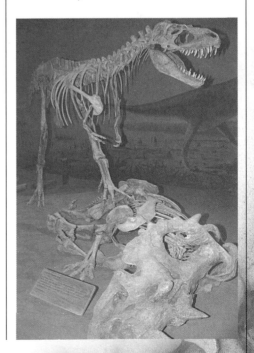

▲ *Ramapithecus* was a small ape that may have been a distant ancestor of man.

▲ *Australopithecus* was an early ancestor that walked upright but still had many ape-like features.

▲ *Homo habilis* was an early form of man that began to use simple tools like flints.

▲ *Homo erectus* was the first of our ancestors to walk completely upright, and he looked very like modern man, though with a heavy jaw and bony eyebrow ridges.

Who were our first ancestors?

Humans belong to a group of mammals called primates. It includes apes, monkeys, and several much smaller animals such as lemurs and bush babies. As much as 50 million years ago, back in the Eocene Period, there were traces of primate-like animals. They were small and looked rather like squirrels, but their eyes faced forward like modern monkeys, and they had grasping hands and feet.

These animals evolved into monkey-like animals, but remains of primates are scarce, and the fossil record contains many gaps. Those few remains that have been found are of tree-living monkeys that are very similar to monkeys living today.

Where did humans probably evolve?

The early ancestors of humans were called hominids, and they appear to have evolved in Africa where many of their remains have been discovered.

The earliest remains of what were probably our ancestors are those of human-like apes called *Australopithecus*, which date back more than three million years. These creatures walked erect and looked similar to us, but their brain capacity was small. Several forms of *Australopithecus* have been found. All of them were much shorter than modern humans, and their teeth show that they had a vegetarian diet.

What remains of ancient humans have been found?

The first true human appeared around two million years ago in Africa. It has been named *Homo habilis* ('handy man') because it used primitive stone tools. It was still rather ape-like, however, and was soon replaced by *Homo erectus*, which looked very much like us. It had a much heavier jaw, bony ridges over the eyes, and a sloped-back forehead. *Homo erectus* appeared about 1.6 million years ago. Only a few incomplete fossils of these early humans have been found, but their tools have been discovered in large numbers

▲ The Neanderthals lived alongside modern man. They were heavily built but probably just as advanced as modern man, but they soon died out.

▲ Modern man probably appeared first in Africa and spread rapidly throughout Europe and Asia.

? When did our ancestors begin to walk upright?

Some of the earliest remains of our ancestors are more than three million years old. They show very clearly that these creatures walked upright. The development of an upright posture, walking on two legs, is thought to have followed climatic changes. As the forest areas retreated, our ancestors were forced to live on open grasslands. An upright posture would then be an advantage, because it allows an animal to travel more quickly. It also frees the hands for carrying food, babies and, eventually, weapons and tools.

? How closely related are we to modern apes?

Research shows that 99 percent of our genetic material is identical to that of the chimpanzee, which means that we not only resemble one another, but often share the same diseases. Some of the tropical diseases emerging from Africa are thought to have crossed over from chimpanzees to humans very recently. In addition to the physical resemblance, chimpanzees share with us the abilities to develop social systems and to communicate complex messages. Some of them have also developed the ability to make and use simple tools. We do know from fossilized teeth that there was once a huge ape called *Gigantopithecus* that was around three times the size of modern gorillas.

? Who were the Neanderthals?

The Neanderthals are a puzzle, because they appear to have lived alongside modern humans for a very long time. Their remains are found throughout Europe and the Middle East, dating from between 100,000 and 35,000 years ago. The Neanderthals were more primitive than humans because they still had a massive jaw and bony brows, but they used tools and buried their dead. Some people think that they were wiped out by modern humans. It has even been suggested that some may still survive, giving rise to accounts of the Abominable Snowman of the Himalayas.

? When did the first modern human appear?

Modern humans appeared between 300,000 and 150,000 years ago, probably in Africa. The first ones were known as the Cro-Magnons, and they rapidly migrated throughout Asia and Europe. They did not reach North America until 12,000 years ago. Some of these ancient humans were the artists who made cave paintings showing extinct animals such as the mammoth and the cave bear. They were also almost certainly responsible for the extinction of many of these ancient animals, which quickly followed their migration into new hunting areas.

❓ Where can we see dinosaurs?

Most modern museums are very different from the early scientific exhibits of the 1800s. This was the time when popular interest in prehistoric life grew and fossils of dinosaurs and other extinct creatures were first put on display to the public.

Today there are thousands of exhibits in natural history museums. Scientists have been able to reconstruct, in painstaking detail, how prehistoric creatures would have looked in real life. This gives us important information about the probable habits of these animals, instead of simply showing a mounted skeleton or fossil.

Wherever you live, take the time to look at the fossil remains in your nearest museum. By using your imagination, try to picture these extinct creatures as they once would have roamed the Earth.

❓ Can you bring dinosaurs home?

Yes, if you have access to the Internet. It's really easy to find interesting information about dinosaurs from home or school. Simply use a search engine on your computer and type in 'dinosaur.' Or, if you have a particular interest in a certain dinosaur, you can type in its name. There are thousands of interesting Internet sites available all around the world.

▼ Geological time groups together typical plants and animals. The earliest living things were all small and aquatic, and as they evolved, they became larger and more complex. The age of the dinosaurs continued for many millions of years through the Triassic, Jurassic, and the Cretaceous Periods, while man's ancestors only appeared in very recent times, in geological terms, during the Quaternary Period.

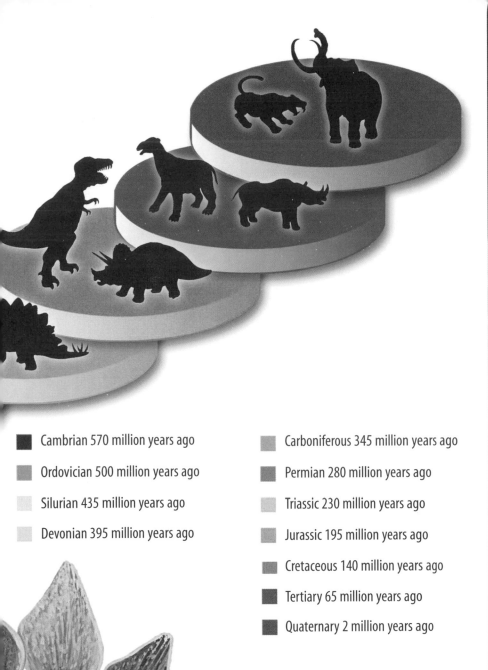

- Cambrian 570 million years ago
- Ordovician 500 million years ago
- Silurian 435 million years ago
- Devonian 395 million years ago
- Carboniferous 345 million years ago
- Permian 280 million years ago
- Triassic 230 million years ago
- Jurassic 195 million years ago
- Cretaceous 140 million years ago
- Tertiary 65 million years ago
- Quaternary 2 million years ago

Fossil hunter!

Fossil hunting can be fascinating. It can also be very frustrating when you cannot find anything. You can look for fossils near any cliff or area where sedimentary rock is exposed, searching among the debris where rock has been broken away. But you must be very careful. You don't want to get buried under a rockfall while you are poking about.

Here are some simple rules to help you find fossils.

■ Look for irregularities in the rock. A color change or an unusually regular pattern may indicate a fossil.

■ Do not expect to see a dinosaur sticking out of the rock! You are far more likely to find shells that look much the same as modern seashells.

■ Soft shale is a likely place to look for fossils. This is grey, flaky material that can easily be split into sheets and often contains fossils such as leaves and twigs.

■ If you find something that looks unusual and you think it might be an exceptional find, make sure that you can remember exactly where you found it. Report your find to a local museum, which may want to excavate to see if there are any more remains.

■ Don't try to chip the rock away from any fossil you find. This is a very skilled job that requires special tools and knowledge.

■ When you do find a fossil, just reflect on its age. Remember that its survival and your discovery are a huge coincidence, because millions and millions of its fellow organisms disappeared without trace. Every fossil is an irreplaceable piece of ancient history.

◀ With the dinosaurs, nature and evolution combined to produce some of the wildest experiments in prehistoric life. Even today, no one is entirely sure why *Stegosaurus* had these huge bony plates along its back, or even if they were arranged liked this. There is so much we still don't know, but extra pieces of the jigsaw come to light almost every week. New and even more fascinating species are discovered, and more detailed information is found about the species already known.

The Human Body

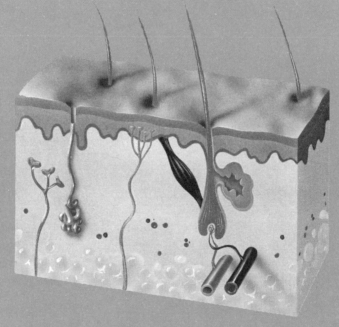

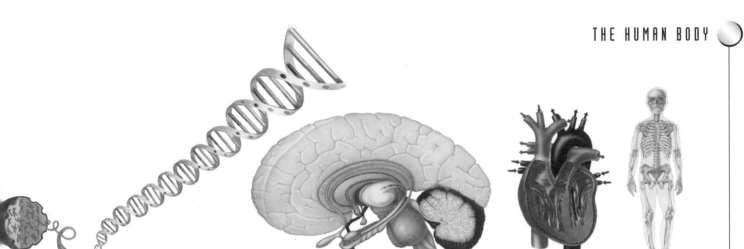

It is easy to take our own bodies for granted. We feed ourselves, keep ourselves clean and warm, and are reasonably careful to avoid injury, but otherwise we don't think about how our bodies work, though we are concerned about our outside appearance. But inside, our bodies are miraculous living machines capable of growth, self-repair, and reproduction, while at the same time carrying around the most sophisticated computer that has ever been developed – the human brain.

Like other animals, our bodies are constructed from billions of tiny cells, each behaving like a separate little animal, but each also containing the blueprint for an entire person. Masses of similar cells are grouped together into tissues, and different tissues are combined together into organs with specific functions, such as a gland or an eye. The complexity does not stop there. Organs form parts of systems that run the body. The circulatory system, for example, consists of the heart, lungs, blood, and blood vessels, while the excretory system contains kidneys and bladder, together with various connecting tubes.

This whole massive and complex collection is kept running by the brain and the nervous system, which connects to all parts of the body and monitors and controls its functions. Sub-systems allow parts of the body to run themselves, using chemical messengers to switch organs on and off like machines in a giant factory that must be kept running smoothly.

What is the body made of?

More than half of the human body is made of water. The rest of the body is built from a huge number of complicated chemicals. These chemicals, together with water, are assembled into tiny building blocks called cells. Each cell is self-contained and has a particular function in the body. There are more than 50,000 billion cells in your body.

What's inside a cell?

Cells consist mostly of a watery jelly-like material called cytoplasm. Each cell is held together by a very thin, flexible membrane, rather like a balloon filled with water. Inside the cell the cytoplasm is organized into special areas called organelles. These control the functioning of the cell, for example, the production of essential substances called proteins. Tiny grains called mitochondria use oxygen to break down food and release the energy that powers the cell. An area called the nucleus contains 46 thread-like chromosomes that control the working of the cell. Some cells, such as those lining the intestines, only live for a few days, while other nerve cells within the brain can survive throughout your entire life.

What do cells look like?

The shape and appearance of a cell depend on what job it does. Nerve cells are long and thread-like so they can carry messages around the body along the nervous system. Red blood cells are like flattened discs that are pinched in at the center. White blood cells are shapeless so they can squeeze between other cells and attack invaders such as bacteria.

◀ **Cells consist of jelly-like cytoplasm, surrounded by a membrane. Nutrients pass through this membrane, and substances produced by the cell leave.**

What are tissues?

Millions of cells that do the same job are grouped together into tissue, so they can be put to work by the body. There are many different types of tissue, for example, muscle tissue. Muscle is built up from millions of thread-like muscle cells.

Super cells

Red blood cells are among the smallest in the body and are only 0.01 mm across. The largest cell is the egg cell, or ovum, which is 0.2 mm across. It can just be seen with the naked eye. The longest cells are the nerve cells that run along your legs. They are up to 1 m (approximately 1 yard) in length, but they are very thin.

What do cells need to survive?

Cells need food, oxygen, and a watery environment in order to survive. Food and water are supplied by the blood and other body fluids, which also carry away wastes. Blood also contains all of the food substances and chemicals needed by the cell.

What are organs?

Organs are made up of different types of tissue that are grouped together to carry out a particular body function.

The heart, for example, is a collection of muscle tissue, connective tissue and nervous tissue. These tissues, work together to pump blood around the body.

Different types of organs are in turn grouped together to form systems, such as the circulatory system. It includes the heart and all the body's blood vessels. The digestive system includes the mouth, gullet, stomach, and intestines, while the nervous system includes the brain, spinal cord, and nerves extending throughout the body. The human body also has a skeletal system, a muscular system, an endocrine system (glands), a respiratory system, a urinary system, and a reproductive system.

▼ The body is composed of billions of living cells. When cells of one type are grouped together, they form organs.

cell membrane

cytoplasm

mitochondria

nucleus

Breathe easy

Respiration is a process during which substances such as sugars are broken down in the body, with the help of oxygen, to produce energy. Respiration is also the term for breathing, which provides the body with the oxygen that it needs to stay alive. Oxygen is taken in through the lungs.

What is metabolism?

Metabolism is the term for all of the chemical activity that takes place inside the cells. Metabolism breaks down more complicated substances obtained from food. This allows these substances to be changed into other materials that the body needs.

What are the essential substances the body needs for life?

Apart from oxygen, the human body needs food. Your food contains fats, proteins, carbohydrates, and fiber, as well as vitamins and minerals. You need all these substances to stay healthy. They are first broken down in the process of digestion. They are then built up again inside the cells to make useful substances.

What are glands?

Glands produce substances the body needs to maintain itself. Salivary glands in the mouth produce saliva that wets food so you can swallow it. Other glands produce substances called hormones. These help control conditions within the body.

▲ Our metabolic rate rises during vigorous exercise. This means that we are using energy provided by food in a more efficient way.

Why is the body so complicated?

If we were simple single-celled animals, we would not need a complicated body system to stay alive. Single-celled animals absorb oxygen directly from the water around them, and they get rid of waste in the same way. Many feed by simply crawling over food material and absorbing it, or by letting food pass through the flexible membrane around it.

Human cells operate in a similar way. Our organ systems simply provide the basic conditions that the billions of individual cells in our bodies need to survive. In general, the bigger an animal is, the more complicated its body needs to be in order to survive and reproduce.

Skeleton and Joints

Why do I need a skeleton?

Bones provide the framework that holds the whole body together. Without a skeleton you would simply flop about, and you would not be able to move. The skeleton also gives protection to delicate organs such as the brain, heart, and lungs. It acts as a support to the soft parts of the body. The skeleton also provides a system of levers on which your muscles can work, enabling you to make all your movements.

Which is the largest bone in the body?

The thigh bone, or femur, is the largest single bone in the body. It is also the strongest bone, because it has to support all of our weight. An adult male who is 6 feet tall has a femur 1.5 feet in length.

Which is the smallest bone in the body?

The smallest bone in the body is called the stirrup. It is in the middle ear and is part of the system that carries sound signals to the brain. At only 3 mm long, the stirrup is about the size of a grain of rice. It is connected to two other very small bones called the hammer and anvil. All three of these bones are joined to the eardrum, where sound is collected before it is sent in the form of nerve signals to the brain.

What are bones made of?

Bones are made of hard minerals that are supported by tough fibers called collagen. Most of the substance of a bone is made of a stony material called calcium phosphate. It is a hard but brittle material. The collagen strands reinforce this brittle material to prevent it from breaking easily.

Are bones alive?

Bones consist of a solid stony material that is laid down in layers by living bone cells. New bone is constantly being reabsorbed and then replaced, to keep it healthy. The surface of a bone is covered by a skin that is full of nerves, so it hurts when you bruise or break a bone. Inside the bone are blood vessels and marrow, a soft material in which new blood cells are produced. When people get old, their bones may become very spongy and weak, and so they are more prone to breakage.

How do bones grow?

The bones of a baby inside its mother's womb are made up of a rubbery material called cartilage. As the body grows, this cartilage is gradually replaced by hard bone. The long bones of the body, such as the thigh bone, grow from the ends. This explains why teenagers suddenly increase in height during a growth spurt.

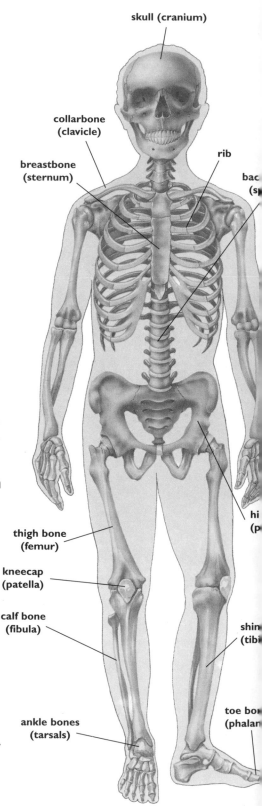

skull (cranium)

collarbone (clavicle)

rib

bac (s

breastbone (sternum)

thigh bone (femur)

kneecap (patella)

calf bone (fibula)

ankle bones (tarsals)

hi (p

shin (tib

toe bor (phalan

▲ The skeleton provides support and protectio for the body, the delicate organs in the abdome and the brain in the skull. It also provides a firm anchor for muscles, allowing us to move freely.

How can bones heal themselves after a break?

Bones are alive, and so the bone cells can gradually replace and repair the solid bone when it is broken. The damaged material is gradually absorbed back into the body, and the bone cells secrete more hard bone. This eventually builds up into a thickened area on the repaired bone, which is actually stronger than the original bone.

What are joints?

A joint is the point where two or more bones come together. Joints can be fixed, such as those that hold together the rounded part of the skull, or they can allow movement, such as your knees and elbows. Straps of tough flexible material called ligament hold together the bones in a joint.

Vanishing bones

Adults have about 206 bones. The number varies a little because some people have extra rib bones or more bones in their hands or feet. A newborn baby has more than 300 bones, but some of these fuse (join) together as the baby grows. The skull is actually made up of 29 bones. Most of the skull bones are firmly joined together in adults, allowing only the jaw to move.

Bones in space

Constant use keeps the bones strong, so lack of exercise is one of the reasons why older bones can become weak. Astronauts orbiting the Earth for long periods lose a lot of their solid bone. They can lose as much as one ounce of bone in a month. In order to keep their bones healthy, astronauts have to take regular exercise even though they are weightless.

How do joints work?

The ends of most bones are covered with tough, rubbery cartilage, which cushions them from impact as we move.

Many joints are lubricated with an oily liquid called synovial fluid so they can bend freely. Synovial fluid is held in a bladder between the layers of cartilage on the ends of the bone. These lubricated joints can move freely and without friction.

Can joints wear out?

Joints can become diseased or wear out after a lifetime of use. When this happens, the cartilage or the fluid inside the joint gradually disappears. The joint becomes hard to move and may be very painful.

How many joints do I have?

The human body has more than 100 joints. Some joints move like a simple hinge, such as those in the elbows and knees. Other joints move in all directions, such as the shoulder joint or the base of the thumb. Joints in the spine allow only a small amount of movement between the vertebrae that protect the spinal cord. Joints such as the bones of the skull and those joining the two sides of the pelvis are locked firmly together so they do not move at all.

▼ The knee is a typical load-bearing joint. The ends of the bone are cushioned by a pad of cartilage to cushion them from impact. Wear and tear is minimized by a lubricant called synovial fluid.

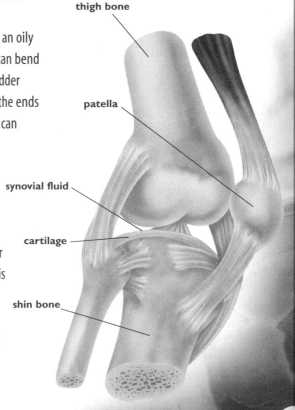

thigh bone

patella

synovial fluid

cartilage

shin bone

Muscles

❓ What job do muscles do?

Muscles are needed for all body movements. Muscles move the bones, pulling them into position as they move about their joints. Some muscles just move soft parts of the body, for example, the face muscles that allow you to smile.

You can control many of your movements by using voluntary muscles. Other muscles, called involuntary muscles, work automatically to maintain the body. The heart, for instance, beats without your being aware of it. The muscles that squeeze your food along inside the intestines also work automatically.

❓ How are muscles joined to bone?

Muscles are attached to bone by long ropy strands called tendons, which are made of collagen. You can feel these tendons on the inside of your wrist when you flex your hand and fingers.

❓ How are muscles constructed?

Muscles are built up from millions of thread-like cells called muscle fibers. These fibers are gathered into bunches. Nerves instruct the muscle fibers when to shorten, or contract, causing the whole muscle to become shorter in length. The shortened muscle then pulls on the tendon and the bone to which it is joined.

❓ Which are the strongest muscles?

Although it is not very big, the strongest muscle in the body, for its weight, is the masseter muscle in the jaw. It allows you to have a powerful biting action. The largest muscle of all is the *gluteus maximus* (a Latin name, like many medical terms). It runs from the buttocks down the back of the thigh. The longest muscle is the sartorius, which runs from the hip bone, or pelvis, right down to just below the knee.

❓ What is muscle tone?

Muscles need constant work to keep them strong and healthy. When two muscles work against each other, they will always be slightly contracted and under tension. This is called muscle tone. The fitter you are, the more strongly these muscles will pull against one another, even while you are relaxed.

❓ How do muscle fibers shorten?

Muscle fibers contain tiny rod-like structures that overlap. When the fiber receives a nerve signal that tells it to contract, these rods slide over one another, making the fiber shorter. As the fibers shorten, the whole muscle contracts. All the fibers do not contract together. The harder the muscle needs to pull, the greater the number of fibers that will contract at the same time.

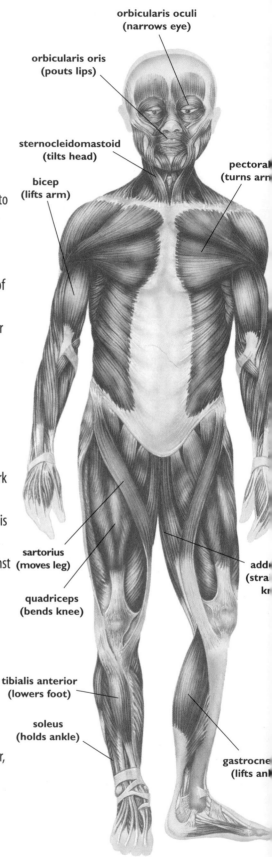

orbicularis oculi
(narrows eye)

orbicularis oris
(pouts lips)

sternocleidomastoid
(tilts head)

bicep
(lifts arm)

pectoral
(turns arm

sartorius
(moves leg)

quadriceps
(bends knee)

add
(stra
kn

tibialis anterior
(lowers foot)

soleus
(holds ankle)

gastrocne
(lifts an

▲ Movement is controlled by the contraction of muscles. Muscles are capable of growing according to the demands placed on them. This is why athletes are so muscular.

Special muscles

The involuntary muscles that automatically keep your body working have a different structure from voluntary muscles. A type of muscle called smooth muscle is mostly found in thin sheets wrapped around internal organs. Smooth muscle contracts quite gently. The bladder, for example, is a balloon-like structure that stores urine until there is sufficient to be discharged from the body. The smooth muscle that covers the bladder then contracts and forces the urine out. Smooth muscle is also present in the iris of the eye.

❓ Can I make my muscles grow?

Muscles react to frequent exercise by growing more muscle cells, or fibers, making the muscle thicker and more bulky. The more fibers there are in a muscle, the stronger it will be. This explains why athletes who constantly exercise develop very large muscles.

❓ How many muscles do I have?

You have about 650 muscles in your body. There are more than 50 muscles in your face alone.

❓ Why do many of my muscles work in pairs?

A muscle can only pull in one direction. It needs another muscle to pull in the opposite direction in order to return a bone to its original position.

When you lift your forearm, the biceps muscle shortens to lift the bone. When you straighten your arm, the triceps muscle pulls it back again and the biceps relaxes. The same action takes place in your legs when you walk and run and when you move your fingers and toes.

❓ What causes muscle cramps?

Cramps are caused by the build-up of a waste substance called lactic acid. When a muscle works harder than usual, it starts to break down stored food without using oxygen. This process is called anaerobic respiration. It produces lactic acid as a waste product.

As the lactic acid builds up, it interferes with muscle action, making the muscle feel tired, until the acid is flushed away by the blood. If too much lactic acid builds up, it makes the muscle contract very sharply and painfully, causing a cramp.

❓ How does regular exercise help the muscles?

Muscles are able to adapt gradually to the amount of work they have to do, so regular exercise can build them up and make them healthier. Exercise strengthens the muscles and improves muscle tone. It can also improve your body shape and posture, as well as strengthen your heart and improve your blood flow. It will generally make you feel much better and help you to sleep soundly.

▼ The muscles that raise and lower our arms work in pairs. They are called the biceps and triceps. One muscle pulls as the other relaxes, causing the arm to bend or straighten. The biceps muscle that lifts the arm is the stronger of the two.

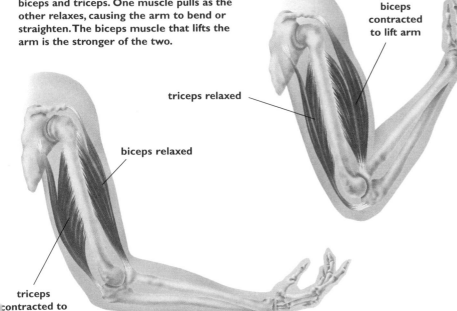

triceps relaxed

biceps relaxed

triceps contracted to straighten arm

biceps contracted to lift arm

biceps relaxed

▲ Exercise improves muscle strength and endurance and keeps the body supple.

? How do I breathe?

When you breathe, you draw air in through the nose and mouth and into the lungs. Air consists of 79 percent nitrogen and about 21 percent oxygen, with small amounts of carbon dioxide and other rare gases. Air travels down a tube called the trachea that forks into other tubes called bronchi, which lead into the lungs. From here the air passes into a series of smaller air passages and eventually into tiny air sacs, or bladders, called alveoli. Oxygen is absorbed through the thin walls of the alveoli into the blood, and waste carbon dioxide is released to be breathed out as a waste product.

? How big are the alveoli?

Each alveolus is about 0.2 mm across. The walls of the alveoli are very thin — only one cell thick — so oxygen and carbon dioxide can easily pass through. There are probably 300 million alveoli in the lungs.

? Can I breathe out all the air in my lungs?

Normally you only breathe out about 10 percent of the air in your lungs. If you are running and panting very hard, you may use up to 60 percent of the air, but at least 20 percent will always be permanently trapped in the alveoli. You breathe faster and deeper when you exercise in order to get more oxygen into your body. This helps to break down sugar and provide energy for your muscles to work.

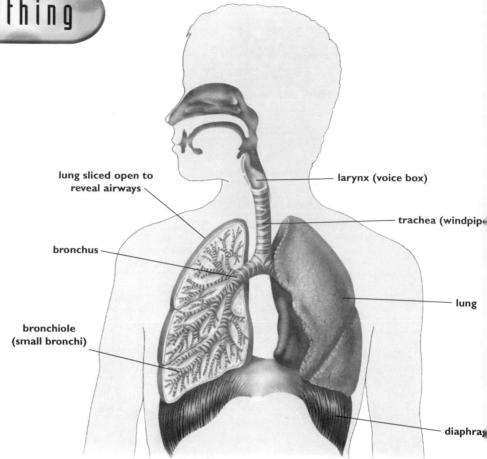

lung sliced open to reveal airways

bronchus

bronchiole (small bronchi)

larynx (voice box)

trachea (windpipe)

lung

diaphragm

▲ The delicate lungs are protected by the rib cage. Air is drawn in and out of the lungs by contractions of the muscular diaphragm, and to a lesser extent by movement of the ribs.

? How is air passed in and out of the lungs?

Most of the airflow in the lungs is caused by the contraction of a sheet of muscle called the diaphragm. It is a curved muscle sheet that separates the contents of the chest from the abdomen. As the diaphragm contracts and flattens, the volume of the chest is increased. This causes the pressure inside the lungs to drop, so air rushes in. When the diaphragm relaxes, it becomes curved again and forces air out of the lungs. The chest also helps in breathing when you exercise vigorously, and the ribs are moved in and out by muscles that run between them.

? How long can you hold your breath?

Most healthy people can hold their breath for about 90 seconds, but it soon becomes very uncomfortable. You normally breathe automatically and never have to think about it. This is because there is an area in the brain that controls breathing. Normally the brain detects the build-up of waste carbon dioxide if you exercise. It speeds up breathing to get rid of it quickly by flushing it out of the lungs. If you try to hold your breath, you can override this mechanism for a while. However, the brain will not let carbon dioxide build up too much and will soon force you to breathe.

Why do I sometimes cough?

Coughing is the way in which the lungs dislodge anything that blocks the air passages. Usually these are only minor blockages caused by a build-up of mucus when you have a cold or chest infection. When you cough, your vocal cords press together to seal off the air passages. At the same time, your chest muscles become tense, raising the pressure in your lungs. When you release the air, it rushes out, carrying the obstruction with it.

How does smoking harm the lungs?

Smoking damages the natural cleaning mechanism of the lungs, and also poisons the cells that line the lungs. Tobacco smoke paralyzes the tiny beating hairs inside the air passages of the lungs. These hairs normally clean out any material that is inhaled. Tar from the smoke accumulates inside the lungs, together with small grains of soot and chemicals that can sometimes cause cancer. These substances are absorbed into the blood and can cause damage to the heart and circulation.

Regular smokers often suffer from lung diseases such as bronchitis, which are caused by irritation of the lungs by tobacco smoke.

Achoo!

Sneezing is caused by irritation of the delicate membranes in the nose. Just like when you cough, the body tries to blow the irritating material away. In a sneeze, however, the tongue blocks off the air flow. Instead of all the material passing out through the mouth, some of it rushes up the throat into the back of the nose. A sneeze can blast bacteria in a cloud of water droplets from your nose and mouth at about 99 mph.

Why should I breathe through my nose?

Breathing through your nose filters and warms the air that passes into the lungs. The air breathed into the passages behind your nose flows over thin bones. These are covered with sticky mucus, in which dirt particles are deposited and later swallowed. This stops your lungs from getting filled with dirt that cannot be removed. Sometimes people such as coal miners breathe in so much dust that it cannot all be filtered out. This can sometimes cause lung disease, such as emphysema.

Why is it harder to breathe when you are on a mountain?

At high altitudes, the air is thinner, so there is not so much oxygen in it. This means you will breathe heavily if you exert yourself by climbing. Some mountaineers carry oxygen cylinders to help them breathe. In aircraft, air is pumped in under pressure so that passengers can breathe at high altitudes.

▲ When you sneeze, a cloud of tiny water droplets is ejected violently through the mouth and nose, carrying with it any microbes present in your lungs. This is how colds and influenza are spread.

How can people breathe underwater?

You can breathe through a snorkel if you are swimming on the surface. It would not be possible to suck air down a snorkel if you were 3 feet under water. The pressure of the water would prevent your lungs from expanding enough to draw the air in. Divers use compressed air to breathe. It is fed to them by a valve that automatically provides air at exactly the same pressure as the surrounding water. No matter how deeply they dive, they can breathe easily.

Some divers who need to work at great depths have to breathe a special mixture of gases, because nitrogen and oxygen become poisonous at very high pressure. The mixture of gases is adjusted automatically to provide the correct amounts.

Heart and Circulation

❓ What is blood?

Blood contains red and white blood cells that float inside a liquid called plasma. It also contains thousands of different substances needed by the body. Blood carries all these things around the body and also removes waste products. It is part of the body's communication system, carrying chemical messengers called hormones that switch organs on and off as required.

Blood carries the white cells and chemical substances that attack invading bacteria and viruses. It also helps control body temperature. Red blood cells carry oxygen collected from the lungs to all parts of the body, releasing it where required. White blood cells help protect the body from infection. They can produce disease-fighting substances called antibodies.

❓ What are blood groups?

A blood group is a particular type of blood that may not match with other blood types when given in a blood transfusion. Blood groups differ from person to person. There are four main blood groups: O, A, B, and AB. These letters refer to chemicals on the surface of red blood cells that are recognized by the body's defenses. When a person receives a blood transfusion, the blood groups need to be carefully matched to make sure that they are compatible.

❓ How does the heart work?

The heart is a fist-sized muscular organ that pumps blood around the body. It is actually two pumps that are joined together. At the top of each side of the heart is a thin-walled chamber called the atrium. It receives blood that returns to the heart through the veins. Once the atrium is filled, it contracts and squeezes its blood into a much more muscular chamber called the ventricle. The ventricle contracts in turn and forces blood at high pressure along the arteries and off to the lungs or the rest of the body. A system of one-way valves stops the blood from leaking back into the heart. The left side of the heart pumps blood around the body, while the slightly smaller right side pumps blood to the lungs to collect more oxygen. The blood circulation actually works in a figure-eight shape.

▼ The heart consists of a pair of similar pumps. On each side of the heart, blood returning along veins collects in the atrium, then is pumped out along arteries from the muscular ventricle.

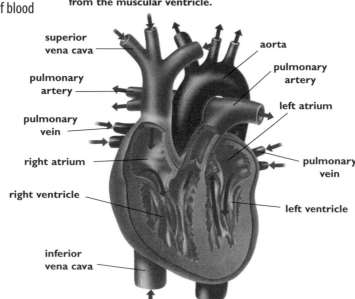

superior vena cava

pulmonary artery

pulmonary vein

right atrium

right ventricle

inferior vena cava

aorta

pulmonary artery

left atrium

pulmonary vein

left ventricle

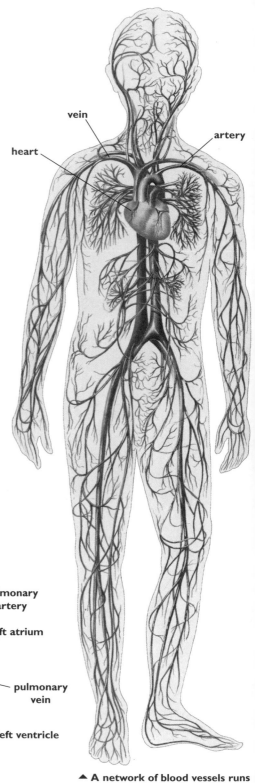

vein

artery

heart

▲ A network of blood vessels runs throughout the body. Arteries carry blood away from the heart, and veins return the blood to the heart.

What are blood vessels?

Blood flows around your body inside a network of tubes called blood vessels. There are three types of blood vessel: arteries, veins, and capillaries. The blood in arteries comes straight from the heart and is pumped under pressure, so the artery walls are thick and muscular. Blood moves from arteries to veins through tiny capillaries, which are about one-tenth the thickness of a human hair. Capillaries are so narrow that red blood cells have to squash themselves up to pass through. Veins return blood to the heart, and because the pressure is now lower, they have thinner walls than arteries.

What is circulation?

Blood is pumped continuously around the body's circulatory system. It is pumped in a continuous flow from the heart through the arteries, then through the tiny capillaries and back through the veins to the heart.

Electrical signals

An electrocardiograph, or EKG, measures the electrical signals that the heart produces as it beats. These signals change when a person is suffering from certain medical conditions that affect the heart. The signals can be measured by attaching wires to the chest near the heart. A doctor can study results as printed information.

Why can too much cholesterol be bad for you?

Cholesterol is a natural fatty substance that is found in many foods such as dairy products, eggs, and meat. It is also produced naturally in the body. High levels of cholesterol in the blood can sometimes collect on the inside of arteries. This gradually reduces the blood flow and can lead to the formation of a clot that may break off and block smaller arteries. Sometimes an artery becomes almost completely blocked by these cholesterol deposits. It becomes so narrow and rigid that it cannot expand to let enough blood pass through. This kind of blockage usually happens in the legs, and is a common result of cigarette smoking.

What keeps the heart beating?

Your heart is a muscular pump that never stops beating. It has its own timing device that produces tiny electrical signals. These signals cause the heart muscle to contract rhythmically. This mechanism allows a heart to be transplanted from one body to another, because the heart will continue to beat when put into another person's body. The heart can be stopped for a short time during heart surgery, then restarted by giving it a small electric shock.

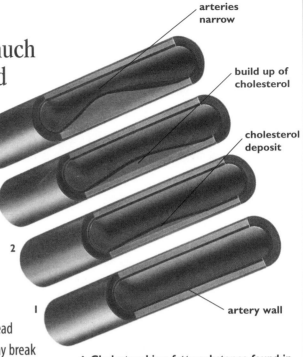

arteries narrow

build up of cholesterol

cholesterol deposit

artery wall

▲ Cholesterol is a fatty substance found in blood and some fatty foods. It can be deposited on the walls of arteries, narrowing them and causing a blockage.

What is the pulse?

The pulse is the throbbing beat that can be felt on the inside of your wrist and in the side of your neck. This regular beat is caused by the expansion of arteries near the surface of the skin. It happens each time the left ventricle in the heart contracts and sends another spurt of blood along the arteries.

What is the heart rate?

Heart rate is the number of times that the heart contracts in one minute. You can measure this yourself by finding the pulse on your wrist, then gently holding your finger on it and counting the number of beats per minute. Don't do this with your thumb because it has its own pulse!

Why do I need food?

Your body is built and maintained by substances that you obtain from your food. These substances are broken down and absorbed into the body during the process of digestion. They are then rebuilt into useful body-building materials.

Which foods give me energy?

Carbohydrates are substances that the body breaks down to produce energy. Starchy foods such as bread, potatoes, and sugars contain carbohydrates. The body also uses some types of fat to provide energy.

Why is protein important?

Protein is an essential body-building substance that you obtain from meat, cheese, eggs, fish, and several vegetable sources. Proteins are broken down in the body into amino acids that can be easily absorbed. Later, these amino acids are reassembled into useful proteins. A large part of the protein you eat is converted into muscle tissue.

Why should I eat fiber?

Fiber is the part of vegetable food that your body cannot digest. It provides the bulk in your diet. Fiber, or roughage, helps food to pass easily through the digestive system. It also helps to keep the system healthy and to prevent some serious diseases.

Why do I need minerals and vitamins?

You only need small amounts of these substances, but they are important in many of the processes that keep the body healthy. If you eat a healthy variety of foods

▼ To stay healthy you need to eat a balanced diet.

you will be taking in plenty of vitamins and minerals. This is called a balanced diet. If you eat lots of junk food this can mean that you are not taking in enough vitamins. You may need to eat more fresh fruit and vegetables.

How much should I eat?

The amount of food you need each day depends on your age, size, sex, and activity level. Older people need less food because they have stopped growing. A teenager who plays a lot of vigorous sports will need extra food to provide enough energy. Babies also need lots of energy to help them grow rapidly.

Why do I have different types of teeth?

Teeth have different shapes so they can carry out different jobs. Incisor teeth at the front of the mouth are flat and shaped like chisels. You use them to cut your food. The canines are the pointed teeth just behind the incisors, and you use them to tear food. The back teeth, called molars and premolars, are flattened so they can grind the food into small pieces ready for swallowing.

What are teeth made of?

Teeth are made of a hard material that is similar to bone. They are covered with shiny enamel to protect them from attack by bacteria. Teeth are hollow and contain blood vessels and nerves. They are rooted into the jaw. Teeth start to grow before you are born, and begin to appear through the gums at about the age of six months. Adult teeth begin to replace baby teeth at about six years of age.

Rumbling stomachs

When you eat, you always swallow some air. The stomach starts to churn as soon as you begin to eat, ready to start digestion. The rumbling you sometimes hear is caused by the digestive juices and the air sloshing around as they wait for the next batch of food. Sometimes this air bubbles back up the food pipe, or esophagus, making a sound called a burp.

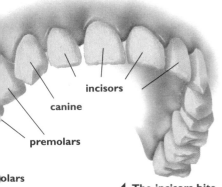

incisors

canine

premolars

olars

wisdom teeth

olars

premolars

canine

incisors

◀ The incisors bite and cut food, while the premolars and molars grind it up. Canines are used to tear food.

? What happens to food in the stomach?

Food in the stomach is churned up with acid and digestive juices that start to break it down. This is the beginning of digestion. The stomach wall is covered with a layer of mucus that stops it from digesting itself. The acid in the stomach helps digestion and also kills bacteria that have been swallowed with the food.

? What is the appendix for?

The appendix is probably a leftover from our very ancient ancestors, and in humans it has very little use. In animals that eat a lot of plant material, such as rabbits, the appendix is large and contains bacteria that help digestion. The human appendix is a tiny finger-like projection from the lower part of the gut. It sometimes becomes inflamed and has to be removed surgically.

? What happens in the small intestine?

Most of the process of digestion takes place in the small intestine. Food is broken down into simple substances that can be absorbed through the gut wall into the blood. Most of these food substances are carried in the blood to the liver, a large organ in the abdomen. The liver stores them until they are needed. The liver has many other useful functions in cleaning the blood and removing old red blood cells. It breaks them down into a greenish liquid called bile, which is used to help the body digest fats. The digestive processes in the small intestine and the rest of the digestive system depend upon having the right amount of acid or alkali present.

? How do I swallow food?

Swallowing is a complicated muscular process. Your tongue forces food to the back of your mouth and into the throat. At the same time, the soft part of the roof of your mouth closes off the air passages to your nose, and a small flap called the epiglottis closes off the passage to your lungs so you do not inhale the food.

You can actually swallow upside down because the food is carried along the digestive system by muscular waves. Astronauts are able to swallow when there is no gravity to help carry the food down their food pipe.

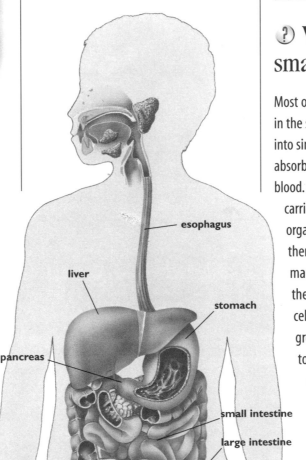

esophagus

liver

stomach

pancreas

small intestine

large intestine

appendix

anus

◀ Food reaches the stomach where digestion begins in a corrosive mixture. Digestion continues in stages as the food moves along the intestines, bathed in digestive juices that break it down so nutrients can be absorbed.

How does the body keep itself working properly?

Millions of chemical reactions take place in the body, and because they can influence one another, they all need to be kept in balance. This process is called homeostasis, and it ensures that the whole complicated system works smoothly and that problems are usually overcome before they can cause illness. The brain monitors what happens within the body and controls everything by means of nerves and chemical messengers, called hormones, that switch chemical reactions on and off as needed.

What is excretion?

Excretion is the removal of waste material from the body. Most of this material is removed from the blood by the kidneys, but waste carbon dioxide produced by the activity of the cells is removed by the lungs. Other waste is excreted as sweat through the skin. The liver gets rid of many poisonous materials by making them harmless and passing them on to the kidneys.

What is urine?

Urine is the liquid produced in the kidneys and discharged from the bladder when we pass water. It contains waste materials.

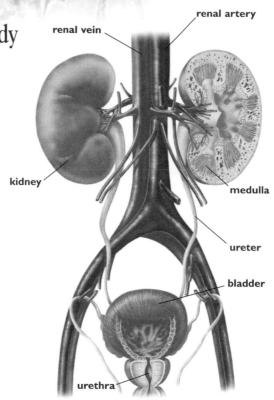

renal vein

renal artery

kidney

medulla

ureter

bladder

urethra

▲ Blood containing waste products is filtered in the kidneys, where waste is removed. Urine containing this waste drains into the bladder where it is stored before being discharged.

What job do the kidneys do?

Kidneys are very effective at removing most of the waste from our blood.

Blood is pumped through groups of tiny tubes inside the kidneys, and harmful waste material passes out through the walls of these vessels and down a long tube called the ureter, into the bladder. Here it is stored until ready to be discharged from the body as urine. The kidneys have a very important function in controling the amount of water in the body. Water balance needs to be kept at exactly the right level if the body cells are to remain healthy.

What is a kidney machine?

If the kidneys become diseased and stop working, it is necessary to use a kidney machine to remove waste from the blood. This machine process is called dialysis. It involves pumping blood from a tube in the person's arm into thin tubing that runs through a tank of sterile liquid. Waste passes from the blood through the walls of the tubing, and the cleaned blood is returned to the body. This has to be done throughout the person's life, unless a new kidney can be provided in a transplant operation. Dialysis needs to be carried out frequently – several times a week – to stop wastes from building up to dangerous levels.

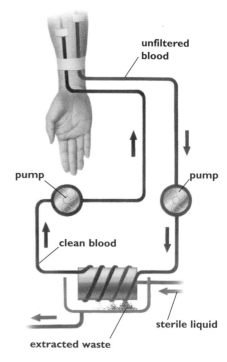

unfiltered blood

pump

pump

clean blood

sterile liquid

extracted waste

▲ A kidney machine takes blood from a patient and filters out waste. It passes the clean blood back into the vein.

? How does the body keep at the proper temperature?

The body has several systems to keep itself at the right temperature. Heat is produced by the breakdown of food substances stored in the body. The chemical reactions in the body will only take place properly if the body is kept at the ideal temperature, so any extra heat has to be removed. Heat leaves the body through the lungs, as you breathe out warmed air, and also through the skin. If you are very hot, the blood vessels near the skin's surface open wider to increase the blood flow, so you look a bit pink. The extra blood means more heat leaves the skin surface, cooling your body.

▶ **Vigorous exercise means the body needs to generate extra energy. Some of this is produced as heat. Excess heat is removed by sweating.**

Cell life

Cells have a fixed lifespan and are replaced automatically as they die off. The more active the cell, the shorter the time it will live. Some white blood cells live for a very short time, and some types that consume dead cells and bacteria survive for only 30 hours. White cells that fight disease live for two to four years. Cells lining the intestine live for about five days before being replaced.

- Skin cells live for 19 days.
- Sperm live for 2 months.
- Eyelashes live for 3 to 4 months.
- Red blood cells live for 4 months.
- Liver cells live for 8 months.
- Scalp hairs live for 2 to 4 years.
- Bone cells live for 15 to 25 years.

? Why do people sweat?

Sweating removes excess salt and wastes through the skin. It also helps to keep you cool because sweat takes heat away from the body as it evaporates on the skin. If you have been exercising and are very sweaty, and then stand in a draft, you will notice this cooling effect very quickly. Sweat is a watery liquid, but other skin glands release an oily substance called sebum that helps to lubricate the skin and keep it supple.

? Why do I need to sleep?

You spend about one-third of your life asleep, but no one is sure why this is necessary. During deep sleep, the body produces large amounts of growth hormone that help to repair or replace damaged cells and tissue. Sleep also speeds healing. While you are sleeping, the brain remains very active. The body goes through stages of being very limp and relaxed, and other stages when the eyes move about beneath closed eyelids. Dreaming takes place during this rapid eye movement period, called REM sleep. Dreaming is very important. If you prevent someone from dreaming by waking them every time they enter REM sleep, that person can become very disturbed and ill after several dreamless nights.

? How does the body repair damaged tissues and cells?

Cells are able to divide very quickly to replace those that are old or have died. Nerve cells are the only ones that cannot be replaced. However, even nerve cells can sometimes grow new connections if the long fibers along which messages are passed become damaged. Dead and dying cells are removed by white blood cells in the blood stream, which actually eat them. The liver is also able to break down red blood cells, which are only able to survive for a short time.

Skin, Hair, and Nails

❓ Why does the body have skin?

Skin is a flexible, waterproof covering that protects us from the outside world. It prevents harmful germs from entering the body. Skin is your largest organ, and it is sensitive to touch, temperature, and pain. Your skin tells you what is happening around your body so you can avoid injuring yourself. Also it helps to prevent damage from the sun's harmful ultraviolet rays. Skin also helps to regulate body temperature by sweating and flushing to lose heat when you get too hot.

❓ How do cuts and grazes heal?

When you cut or graze yourself, the blood clots to prevent bleeding. Clotting is caused by substances in the blood. Together with small particles called platelets, these substances produce masses of fine fibers when they are exposed to air. They block the wound and prevent more blood loss. New cells grow rapidly into the wound, replacing the damaged tissue. Soon the clotted material, called a scab, falls off and clean, new skin is revealed underneath.

❓ Why do people have different skin colors?

Skin color is caused by a dark pigment called melanin in cells below the skin's surface. Melanin filters out harmful ultraviolet light from the sun, preventing damage to the tissues beneath the skin. People originating from hot countries have developed extra melanin in their skin for sun protection, so their skin is darker.

❓ Is skin alive?

All the skin cells that you can see are dead! Your body is constantly producing new skin cells from beneath the surface skin layer that you can see. As new cells push upwards towards the surface, the older cells on top become flattened and eventually die. The dead cells form a protective layer that constantly flakes away like dust.

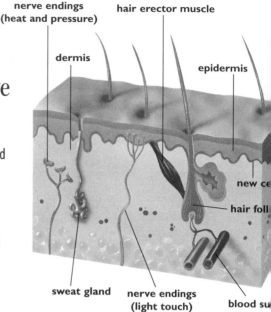

nerve endings (heat and pressure)   hair erector muscle

dermis

epidermis

new ce

hair foll

sweat gland   nerve endings (light touch)   blood su

▲ The skin is composed of several layers and is filled with nerve receptors, muscles, hair follicles, and sweat glands.

◀ Skin coloration developed to protect people from the damaging effects of sunlight.

❓ How does skin tan?

Skin develops extra melanin when it is exposed to strong sunlight. Tiny grains of melanin are produced in the skin cells and spread to produce an even suntan, which helps to protect against sun damage. This even happens in people with naturally dark skin. You can get sunburn if you are exposed to the sun's rays for too long, because the damage will be done before the protective melanin can develop. You should always use protective sun screen and limit the amount of time you spend in the sunshine.

blood escapes

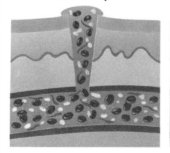

blood begins to clot

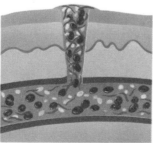

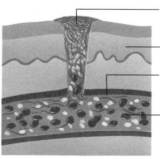

scab forms

skin

platelets

red blood cells

◀ Blood begins to clot as soon as it is exposed to the air. This quickly plugs a wound. White blood cells gather around the wound to kill invading microbes, and new skin cells grow into the healing wound beneath the scab.

▲ Straight hair grows from rounded hair follicles.

▲ Hair growing from oval follicles will be wavy.

▲ Flattened hair follicles cause the hair to be very curly.

? Why do I have hair?

Hair originally helped prevent heat loss from the body. It no longer has that function, although it does help to protect your head. Each hair grows from a pit in the skin called a follicle. The hair itself is made of a tough material called keratin, and it grows continuously from the follicle. The hair shaft contains pigment that gives the hair its color. In older people, air may enter the hollow hair shaft, making it look grey.

? Why is some hair curly?

Hair is straight or curly depending on the shape of the follicle from which it grows. Straight hair grows from completely round follicles, while wavy hair comes from oval follicles. Very curly hair grows from flattened follicles.

? Why do some people go bald?

A substance called testosterone affects hair growth in men. It is responsible for the tough facial beard grown by men. Changes in testosterone levels affect the amount of hair growing on a man's head.

? Why do I have nails?

You need nails to provide a firm support for the sensitive skin on the fingertips. If you cut your fingernails too short you will notice how difficult it is to pick up small objects. Nails grow continuously from an area called the nail bed, or quick. Because your nails are transparent, you can see right into the tissue below the nail, which is always pink because it contains blood. Nails grow at a rate of about 0.1 mm per day. They are made of keratin, the same material as hair. Because nails are not living material, they do not hurt when you cut them.

At your fingertips

Your fingertips are covered with tiny ridges that are caused by patterns in the deeper layers of skin. These ridges probably give a better grip when you pick things up.

As long ago as 1823 it was realized that each person's fingerprint is unique, and fingerprints are now widely used for identification of criminals and sometimes as personal identification. Many hospitals take a footprint from newborn babies, because feet carry similar identifying patterns. This is a good form of identification.

? What are freckles?

Freckles are patches of melanin that are concentrated together instead of being spread evenly throughout the skin. Some people with very fair skin and lots of freckles do not tan evenly. They are particularly likely to develop sunburn unless they protect themselves from the sun.

? What is acne?

Acne is a common skin condition causing pimples and blackheads. These appear during adolescence when the skin produces large amounts of an oily liquid called sebum. The skin's pores can become blocked, and the sebum builds up to produce a pimple or a blackhead. Sometimes the trapped sebum becomes infected and causes an inflamed spot, which is acne.

? What is a bruise?

Bleeding under the skin after a bump causes bruises. The blood spreads in the tissues beneath the skin, and at first look purplish. As the red blood cells break down and become absorbed into the bloodstream, the bruise changes color before disappearing.

What is the nervous system?

The nervous system is made up of billions of tiny nerve cells that carry electrical signals throughout the body.

It consists of two parts: the central nervous system and the peripheral nervous system. The central nervous system is the brain and the spinal cord, which extends from the base of the brain all the way down your back. It is protected by rings of bone in your spine, called vertebrae. The peripheral nervous system is the network of small nerves that extends to all parts of the body. The nervous system is the body's main communication network, helping the whole system to work properly.

What are nerve cells?

Nerve cells, or neuron, make up the nerves that carry messages around your body. They have a star-shaped body containing the cell nucleus, with a long thread-like fiber called the axon. The tip of the axon is branched and touches other neuron, to which it delivers messages or nerve impulses. Neuron have many smaller threads and branches called dendrites, which receive messages from other neuron.

▶ A long thread or axon extends from the body of a neurone, and it is along this that nerve impulses are carried.

Are there different types of nerve cell?

There are three types of neurons with different functions. Motor neurons control the way our muscles work. Sensory neurones carry messages from your sense organs. Connector neurons pass messages between different parts of the nervous system.

How are messages passed through the nervous system?

Nerve impulses that pass through the nervous system are able to jump from one neuron to the next. Inside the nerve fiber, the nerve impulse travels as an electrical signal. When it reaches the end of the long fiber, it jumps across to the next neuron by means of a chemical called a transmitter. This chemical is released from the branched ends of the fiber. As this transmitter substance contacts the next neuron, it starts another nerve impulse. This whole process is very fast, and nerve impulses travel along the largest nerve fibers at 295 feet per second. Messages travel along smaller nerves such as those in the digestive system at a slower rate.

▶ Many nerves are named from the bones that are near them. For example, the femoral nerve is near the femur.

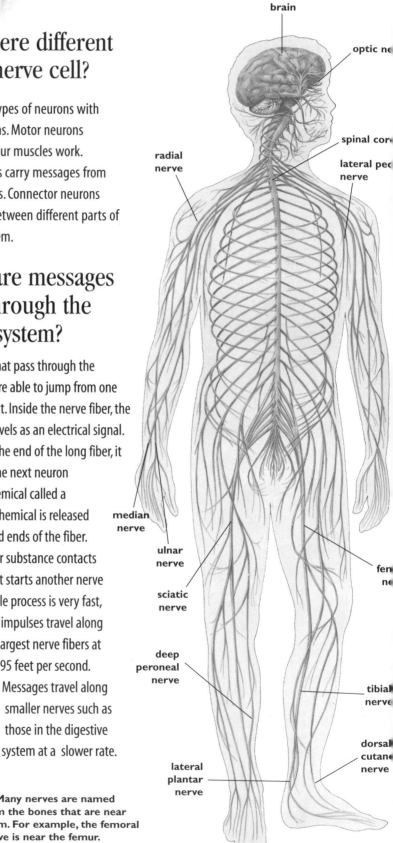

brain

optic ne

spinal cor

lateral pe
nerve

radial
nerve

median
nerve

ulnar
nerve

sciatic
nerve

fen
ne

deep
peroneal
nerve

tibia
nerve

lateral
plantar
nerve

dorsa
cutane
nerve

What is a synapse?

The point where the tiny bulbs on the tips of a nerve fiber contact another neuron is called the synapse. It is the point where transmitter substances carry the electrical signal from one neuron to the next. Some transmitter substances can switch off a nerve signal.

What are nerve impulses like?

A nerve impulse is like a very simple message: either 'on' or 'off.' Because there are so many neuron that are connected to one another, this simple signal is enough to carry the most complicated messages throughout the whole of the body's nervous system.

▼ As a nerve impulse arrives at the junction between two nerve cells, it is carried across the gap or synapse by chemicals called neurotransmitters. These contact sensitive areas in the next nerve cell, and the nerve impulse is carried along.

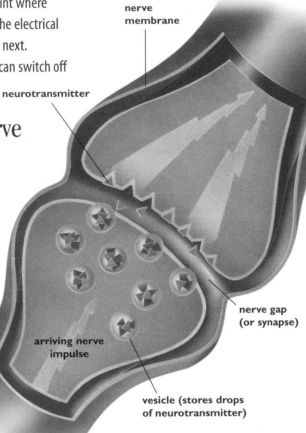

nerve membrane

neurotransmitter

arriving nerve impulse

nerve gap (or synapse)

vesicle (stores drops of neurotransmitter)

What is a reflex?

Reflexes are automatic reactions that take place without your needing to think about them. If you prick you finger, you jerk your arm away instantly, even before your brain is aware that some damage has taken place. These reflexes take place in the spinal cord, where instructions are given to the muscles to pull your arm away as soon as the nerves have detected pain or damage. Reflexes also take place inside the body, maintaining normal conditions. A reflex starts the flow of digestive juices as soon as food enters the stomach. Another reflex causes a cough if you inhale a piece of fluff, or a blink when you get dirt in your eye.

Do nerve impulses travel straight through the nervous system?

It takes more than one nerve impulse to fire off another neuron. Each neuron receives messages saying 'Fire' and 'Don't fire,' and it will only fire off the nerve impulse if it gets more instructions to fire than to stop firing. It works a bit like the principle of voting, where a large number of votes are needed in order for a message to be passed on.

Which are the longest nerve fibers?

The nerve fibers that run down into the leg are the longest cells in the whole body. They can be up to one yard long.

Are nerves insulated?

A nerve impulse is an electrical signal, and so it needs to be insulated if it is not to leak away. Most nerve fibers are covered with a fatty layer of insulation to stop the signal from leaking away. In diseases such as multiple sclerosis, some of this insulation disappears and the nerves no longer work properly. Some small nerves do not have this insulation. Although these smaller nerves can still pass a message, it travels much slower than in an insulated neuron.

Reflex action

There is a well-known reflex that you can demonstrate on yourself. Sit upright and cross your legs loosely. Now tap sharply on the leg you have crossed over, just below the kneecap. Your leg will kick gently. This is because the tap will have stretched the tendon in the front of the knee, and touch receptors interpret this as needing a leg movement to correct the position of the leg. A reflex is immediately set in motion and your leg gives a kick.

Eyes

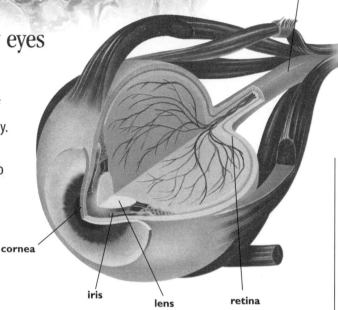

optic nerve

optic chiasma

cornea

iris

lens

retina

▲ **The eye works like a sophisticated video camera, tracking moving objects and focusing automatically. The amount of light entering the eye is controlled by the iris.**

❓ How do my eyes work?

Your eyes are tough balls of tissue that contain clear jelly. They work by producing an image that is transmitted to your brain as 'sight.' A transparent layer, called the cornea, covers the front of each eye. Below this is the iris, which is a flattened ring of muscle surrounding the pupil.

Light enters the eyeball through the pupil and passes to the lens behind. As the light rays pass through the lens, they are bent and focused to form a clear image on the retina. The retina detects this image and turns it into nerve impulses. These impulses travel along the optic nerve to the brain. The brain interprets them as a picture that you can see.

❓ What makes our eyes colored?

Eye coloring is caused by melanin in the iris. This is the same substance that your skin produces when you tan in the sun. Eyes can be various shades of brown, blue, grey, or green, depending on how much melanin they contain. Brown eyes have much more melanin than blue eyes. You inherit your eye color from your parents. The color of the iris is very individual, and it has been suggested that it could be used to identify people in the same way as fingerprints.

❓ Why do I blink?

Blinking cleans and lubricates the surface of the eye. The cornea is very sensitive and must be protected from infection and from drying out. Every time you blink, which is normally every few seconds, a film of tears washes the eye's surface clean. It wipes away bacteria and dust and leaves behind a moist, lubricating layer that also contains substances to kill bacteria.

Blinking is a protective reflex of the body. You can over-rule it for a time and try to stop yourself blinking, but very soon your brain will decide that blinking is essential and you will not be able to stop it from happening. The flow of tears increases when your eyes are irritated, or if a draft causes the surface of the eye to become dry. Excess tears drain away through a duct in the corner of the eye and pass into the nose.

❓ How do the eyes focus?

The lens bends light to make an image on the retina. The lens can change its shape to make this image sharp. The lens is flexible, and tiny muscles pull on it to alter its shape and focus the image. Your lens is almost round when you are looking at something close up, but it becomes flatter when you look at a distant object.

❓ How do I see in color?

The retina is packed with a layer of tiny cells called rods and cones. These cells contain colored substances that react when light falls on them, triggering a nerve impulse. Rods are slim cells that are responsible for black and white vision. They work even in very dim light, seeing everything in shades of grey. Cone cells give us color vision. They contain different light-sensitive substances that respond to either red, yellow-green, or blue-violet light. Together with the grey images produced from the rods, cone cells give you the colored picture that you see. Cones only work in bright light, which is why colors are difficult to see in dim light. You have 125 million rod cells and 7 million cone cells in each eye.

Moving pictures

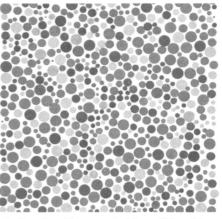

Film and television images consist of a series of rapidly changing still images, yet we see them as continuous motion. There is a slight delay between each of the images that appear on the screen. However, because this delay is so short, our brain is able to fill in the gaps and provide a complete picture of what is happening.

Do my eyes see upside down?

The image that forms on the retina when light passes through the lens is upside down. This is because of the way in which light rays are bent by the eye's lens. The brain automatically turns the image the right way up, but you are never aware that this is happening.

▼ The rods and cones that respond to light entering the eye are buried in the retina, with the nerves connecting them running along the surface. These receptor cells are connected in a regular pattern like electric wiring.

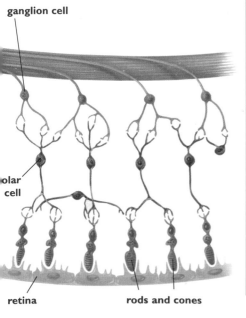

ganglion cell

olar cell

retina

rods and cones

What is color blindness?

True color blindness is when people cannot see any color at all, but it is very rare. More commonly, many people cannot see true colors accurately. The most common form is red-green color blindness, where people find it difficult to distinguish between red, green, and brown. It affects about one in every 12 men, but is less common in women.

Color blindness is measured using special charts in which patterns are made up with colored dots. A person who has a color defect will see these patterns in a totally different way than someone who has perfect color vision.

Why do some people need glasses?

If the eye is not exactly the right shape, or the lens cannot focus properly, you cannot form a clear image on the retina. In this case, you may need to wear glasses to correct your vision. For a short-sighted person, distant objects look blurred because the image forms in front of the retina. A short-sighted person can see nearby objects very clearly. For a long-sighted person, the image tries to form behind the retina, so it is blurred while the lens tries to focus on a nearby object.

In another sight problem, called astigmatism, the cornea is not evenly curved and vision is distorted. The different sight problems can be overcome with the use of glasses.

▲ People with normal vision will be able to see two shapes in this diagram. Those who are color-blind will only be able to see colored dots.

How do contact lenses work?

Contact lenses are thin plastic discs that rest on the surface of the cornea. They act like the lenses of ordinary glasses. Most modern contact lenses are made from very soft material that does not cause discomfort to the eye. Some lenses are worn for just one day and then thrown away. It can be difficult to get used to wearing contact lenses and to put them in the eye without scratching the delicate cornea. However, many people prefer them to wearing glasses.

Why do some older people need reading glasses?

As people get older, the lenses of their eyes grow harder and cannot change their shape to focus close up. Reading glasses provide sharp vision close up. Some people wear bifocal glasses, where a small area of the lens is shaped for close-up vision, while the rest of the lens is suitable for distant vision.

? What part of the ear is inside the skull?

The delicate ear mechanism is inside the skull, close to the brain. The hard skull protects it from damage. When sound enters the ear it first meets the eardrum, which is at the end of the short tube connected to the outside ear. The sound waves vibrate the eardrum. This vibration moves a series of three tiny bones, called the hammer, anvi, and stirrup (because of their shape), that increase the movement. These bones are enclosed in a chamber called the middle ear. They pass their movements to another part, the inner ear. This contains a coiled structure shaped like a snail's shell, called the cochlea, where the sound is detected.

▼ The ear mechanism allows sound vibrations to be turned into electrical nerve impulses that are sent to the brain.

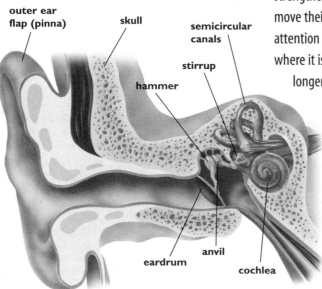

outer ear flap (pinna)
skull
semicircular canals
stirrup
hammer
anvil
eardrum
cochlea

▶ Any sound louder than 100 dB can be uncomfortable. If you are exposed to loud noise continuously, it can cause permanent damage to the sensitive ear mechanism.

? How is sound carried to the brain?

Receptor cells in the cochlea turn sound vibrations into nerve impulses and pass them to the brain. The liquid-filled cochlea amplifies sounds as they pass down the spiral. Sensory cells that line the cochlea have small hairs. These are bent as the sound wave vibrates the liquid, causing them to produce nerve impulses. The impulses are passed to the brain along the auditory nerve.

? Why do I have an ear flap?

The part of the ear on the side of your head is called the pinna. It collects and directs sounds into the inner part of the ear. The pinna contains rubbery cartilage to strengthen it. Many animals are able to move their ears in order to focus their attention on a particular sound and decide where it is coming from. Human beings no longer have this ability. Instead of moving our ears we turn our head toward a sound that interests us.

? What sounds can I hear?

Sound is measured in decibels (dB). You can hear sounds ranging from a low rumble up to a high-pitched whistle. The lowest sounds can sometimes be felt in the chest, while very shrill sounds may be so high that you cannot hear them. A bat's squeak is at the limit of what humans can hear, and many people cannot hear this noise at all. Human hearing is not very sensitive compared to animals such as dogs who can hear very high-pitched sounds. Dogs are able to respond to a supersonic whistle that cannot be heard at all by humans.

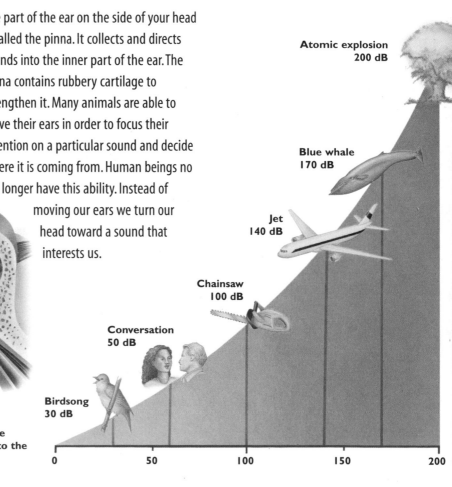

Atomic explosion 200 dB

Blue whale 170 dB

Jet 140 dB

Chainsaw 100 dB

Conversation 50 dB

Birdsong 30 dB

0   50   100   150   200

Hearing without the ears

Many people suffer from hearing impairment. When children are born with this problem, it may be difficult for them to learn to speak clearly because they cannot hear the sounds they produce. Deaf children can be taught to speak with the help of a balloon that is held between the face of the child and the teacher's face. As the teacher speaks, the child can feel sound vibrations in the balloon. Profoundly deaf people can learn to communicate by sign language. They are able to 'speak' clearly to other people trained in this technique.

What is perfect pitch?

Most people have perfectly adequate hearing, but a few people have exceptional hearing abilities. People who can identify and remember a sound exactly are said to have perfect pitch. They are usually able to sing or play any musical note without being prompted.

Why do my ears pop?

When you go up in an elevator or fly in a plane, your ears may pop as the air inside them expands. If this did not happen, your eardrum would burst as the air trapped inside your ear expands with the lower pressure. As the air expands, it leaks out through the Eustachian tube, which leads to your throat. It is this change in pressures that causes the popping sound.

Why do I have wax in my ears?

The ear canal is lined with cells that produce wax to protect the delicate ear mechanism. Wax traps dirt and bacteria, but it can sometimes build up and block the ear causing temporary deafness. When this happens, the wax may have to be syringed out with warm water.

How do my ears tell me where I am?

The ears contain the organs of balance. These are three curved, liquid-filled tubes that are attached to the cochlea. The tubes, called semicircular canals, contain tiny grains of chalky material. As you move and turn your head, the liquid swirls though the tubes, carrying the particles with it. The chalky grains trigger sensory cells that produce nerve impulses. These impulses are then passed to the brain, telling it the exact position of your head at any time.

Why is loud music bad for you?

Loud music can cause permanent loss of hearing, especially when it is fed directly into the ears through a personal stereo. Loud noise is one cause of deafness in later life. Hearing can usually be restored in deaf people by using a tiny amplifier, which is fitted either in or behind the ear. If the deafness is caused by damage to the nerves, hearing aids will not work and the hearing loss is usually permanent.

What makes me dizzy when I twirl round?

Twirling round for too long causes the liquid in the semicircular canals to swirl around too. When you stop, the liquid keeps on swirling, confusing the brain and making you dizzy. If you watch a dancer spin, you will see their head does not move continuously, but remains still then jerks around and stops again as their body turns. This reduces the swirling effect. Astronauts have to cope with the dizzy effects caused by the movement of liquid through their balance mechanism.

? How does the sense of touch protect the body from injury?

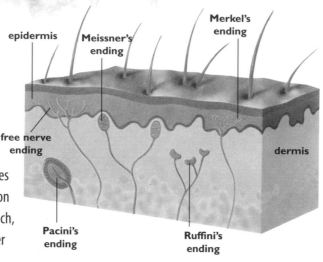

epidermis
Meissner's ending
Merkel's ending
free nerve ending
dermis
Pacini's ending
Ruffini's ending

▲ Tiny sensory receptors in the skin provide our sense of touch. They measure touch, pressure, pain, heat, and cold and keep the brain updated about the state of our environment.

Your skin continuously passes huge amounts of information to the brain. It monitors touch, pain, temperature, and other factors that tell the brain exactly how the body is being affected by its environment. Without this constant flow of information, you would keep injuring yourself accidentally, which is what happens in some rare diseases where the skin senses are lost.

Sensations in the skin are measured by tiny receptors at the ends of nerve fibers. There are several different types of receptor. Each type can detect only one kind of sensation, such as pain, temperature, pressure, touch, and so on.

? Why are some parts of the body more sensitive than others?

Receptors are grouped together according to the importance of their function. There are large numbers of receptors in the hands and the lips, for example, where the sensation of touch is very important. Receptors are present in much smaller numbers over other parts of the body, which are less sensitive to touch, for example, on the back.

? How do pain-killing drugs work?

Pain-killing drugs, or analgesics, work in two different ways. Some drugs, such as aspirin, work by preventing the sensation of pain from reaching the brain. More powerful pain-killing drugs prevent the brain from reacting to the nerve impulses that it receives from pain receptors.

? What is a phantom limb?

When a damaged limb has to be removed surgically, a person may feel as though the limb is still attached to the body. This happens because the nerves that once led from the limb are still in place. They keep producing nerve impulses that trick the brain into thinking that the limb is still part of the body.

? How do we taste things?

Most of the sense of taste takes place on the tongue. The tongue is covered with small bumps, called taste buds, that are grouped together in areas with different functions. These taste buds react to some simple tastes and pass messages to the brain. Taste buds on the tip of the tongue detect sweet tastes, and those at the back of the tongue detect bitter taste (the 'aftertaste' you get after swallowing something bitter). Groups of taste buds at the side of the tongue measure sour and salty tastes. The taste of any food is a combination of these four basic tastes. You have about 10,000 taste buds on your tongue. You will gradually lose them as you grow older, which is one reason why elderly people may no longer enjoy their food so much.

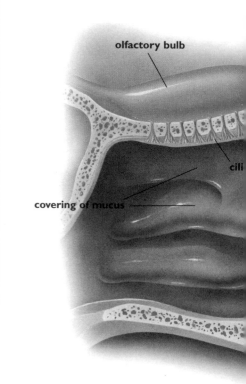

olfactory bulb
cili
covering of mucus

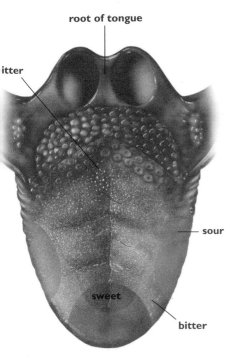

root of tongue

itter

sour

sweet

bitter

▲ There are distinct regions on the tongue where the main tastes are recognized.

Super sniffer

The human sense of smell is very poor compared to that of animals such as dogs. Some dogs are able to identify and follow the smell of a person's perspiration, even though it may be several days old. These so-called sniffer dogs are often used to find people buried beneath an avalanche or in houses destroyed in earthquakes. They can identify just a few molecules of human perspiration.

Vultures can smell a decaying body from several miles away. Even the human nose can detect tiny amounts of some substances. One of the smelliest substances known is called mercaptan, and humans can detect a single molecule of it. Scientific tests have shown that mothers can identify the smell of their own babies.

⁇ Why do hot foods taste better?

Hot foods taste better because the heat causes more of the pleasant smells to rise into the nose. These abundant smells contribute to the total taste of the food.

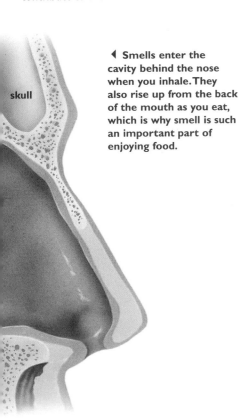

skull

◀ Smells enter the cavity behind the nose when you inhale. They also rise up from the back of the mouth as you eat, which is why smell is such an important part of enjoying food.

⁇ How does the sense of smell work?

The sense of smell is probably the oldest of our five senses. As you breathe in, air passes through a cavity behind the nose. It contains patches of millions of smell receptors called olfactory cells. Sensory hairs stick out from the surface of these receptor cells. The hairs detect smells and pass information along nerve fibers to the brain. Substances that you recognize as having an odor dissolve in the layer of mucus covering the sensory cells, stimulating them to produce a signal.

Most people are able to detect about 4,000 different smells. However, people whose work is based on their ability to smell, such as chefs, perfume makers, and wine tasters, can distinguish as many as 10,000 different smells.

⁇ Are smell and taste the same?

The taste of food is a mixture of both taste and smell. As you eat, tiny food particles drift up into the nasal passages from the back of the mouth. The smell of the food contributes to the simple tastes detected by the tongue. This explains why food tastes odd when the nasal organs are inflamed or covered by thick mucus when you have a heavy cold – the sense of smell is temporarily smothered. When you eat very spicy foods, such as curry or chilli, mild pain also forms a part of the characteristic taste. If these foods did not burn the mouth, they would not taste like curry or chilli at all. If we were to lose our sense of smell, almost all taste sensation would be lost as well. This means that we would not enjoy the taste of our food nearly so much.

Body Defenses

? What is the immune system?

Unlike most of the other body systems, the immune system is scattered throughout the body. The main defense against invaders such as bacteria and viruses are white blood cells called lymphocytes. These blood cells are made and stored in the body's lymphatic system, which is a network of thin tubes running throughout the body. It contains a watery liquid called lymph, which it drains from the tissues and returns to the blood. At intervals along the length of the lymph vessels, are small lumps called lymph nodes. Lymphocytes are stored in these lymph nodes. Waves of lymphocytes are released when the body is injured or when invaders are detected, and the lymphocytes swarm to the damaged area.

? How are invading germs destroyed?

Special T-lymphocytes attach themselves to any invading organisms and destroy them. The T-lymphocytes release special substances that attract another type of white blood cell which consumes the invaders. B-lymphocytes are also stored in the lymph system. They release a flow of substances called antibodies. These lock on to invading organisms. Each antibody attacks a particular type of invader, clumping them together so they are destroyed by the white blood cells. When a new infection is found, the B-lymphocytes make an antibody to attack it.

? Can our bodies attack themselves?

Sometimes the immune system mistakes some harmless material for an invader and this can cause illness.

Grass pollen and dust are harmless materials that are often inhaled. In some people the body mounts a fierce attack on them. The immune system releases the substances normally designed to fight infection, and their effects can cause illnesses such as hay fever and asthma. Sometimes the immune system attacks normal tissue or organs, causing a condition called auto-immune disease. This can produce serious illness, but fortunately it is quite rare.

? Why can the body reject a transplant organ?

All your body cells carry a 'label', or marker substance, on the outside of the cell. This marker is recognized by the immune system, which will not attack it. In some very serious illnesses, when a person's organ has failed completely, an organ from another individual may be transplanted. The donated organs carry different marker substances, so the immune system treats them as invaders and will mount an attack on them called rejection. These attacks from the immune system can be reduced or prevented by the use of powerful drugs.

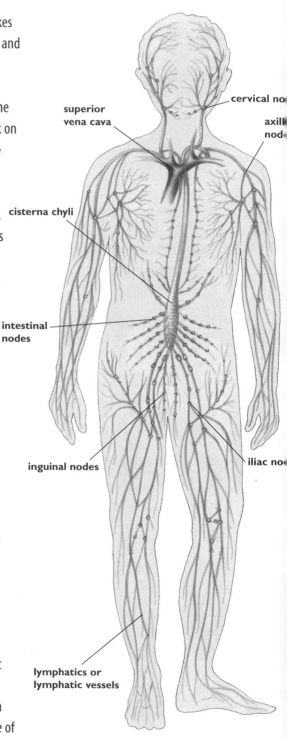

▼ Lymph is a milky liquid drained from the tissues along a system of tubes called the lymphatics. The lymph vessels and the small swellings or lymph nodes, are where most of our immune response takes place.

cervical no

axill
nod

superior
vena cava

cisterna chyli

intestinal
nodes

inguinal nodes

iliac no

lymphatics or
lymphatic vessels

The immune system

It is possible to harness the immune system to protect us from diseases before we ever encounter them. You could be inoculated with a very mild infection that would cause the immune system to produce antibodies without making you ill. A vaccine could contain enough dead germs, or parts of germs, that would trick the immune system into making antibodies.

? Why is AIDS such a serious illness?

AIDS is a unique disease because it attacks the immune system that is intended to defend the body against infection. The HIV virus that causes AIDS destroys lymphocytes so the body cannot fight off infection. The HIV virus does not cause the symptoms of the disease, but the body is now defenseless and can be attacked by other disease organisms. Some powerful drugs can now delay the destructive effects of infection by the HIV virus.

▼ **Many newborn babies are fed on their mother's milk. This contains special antibodies that help boost the baby's immune system.**

? What are bacteria and viruses?

Bacteria and viruses are the most important causes of disease. Bacteria are simple plant-like organisms that can divide very quickly. They cause many common infections such as boils and acne. Viruses are very much smaller, and technically they are not alive at all. They can take over the functioning of an infected cell and turn it into a factory producing millions more viruses. Viruses are responsible for many common diseases such as colds and influenza.

? What happens if the immune system doesn't work?

Very rarely, a baby is born without a proper immune system. It will have no resistance to infection. When this happens, the baby has to live in a plastic bubble from which all germs are kept out. Sometimes the immune system recovers as the child grows, so they can be released from the bubble.

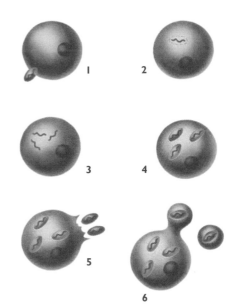

▲ **As viruses invade a cell (1) they shed their outer layer (2) and take over the genetic material in the host cell in order to reproduce themselves (3). They begin to construct protein coats around the new viruses (4) and eventually burst out of the host cell (5) or leave it in an envelope (6) ready to infect new cells.**

? How are babies protected from infections?

A newborn baby is protected from infection by antibodies that were present in its mother's blood. The mother's blood contains antibodies to the infections to which she has become immune during her life. These antibodies are transferred to the baby's blood via the placenta that nourished the baby in the womb.

The antibodies continue to protect the baby for several weeks, while its own immune system develops and begins to work properly. This period of protection is increased if the mother breast feeds her baby, as her milk will also contain these antibodies. Bottle fed babies do not have this natural immunity.

Chemical Control

❓ What job do hormones do?

Hormones are chemical messengers that are produced in one part of the body and have an effect on another part.

Hormones switch body processes on and off, and they regulate most of the body's activity. The nervous system also helps in these processes, giving rapid instructions along the nerves. The body's endocrine system uses hormones that work much more slowly. The majority of hormones are carried around the body in the bloodstream, reaching all the major organs and tissues.

❓ How many hormones does the body have?

The body has more than 30 different hormones. They are mostly produced in organs called endocrine glands.

These glands discharge the hormones directly into the bloodstream. Other types of glands pass their secretions through ducts to the point where they are needed. Endocrine glands are found in the head, neck, and torso. The amount of hormones in the body is regulated by a feedback system. This means that once hormones are produced, the body measures them, and once they have reached the required level, their production is switched off again. Sometimes this mechanism does not work properly, and over or underactive glands such as the thyroid can produce illness.

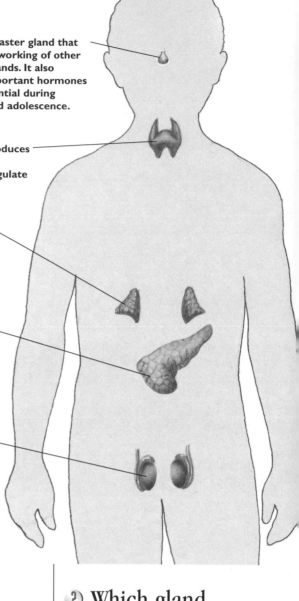

Pituitary
This is the master gland that controls the working of other endocrine glands. It also produces important hormones that are essential during childhood and adolescence.

Thyroid
The thyroid gland produces several important hormones used to regulate body energy usage.

Adrenals
The adrenal glands are attached to the kidneys. They produce hormones that alert and get the body ready for instant action.

Pancreas
In addition to its function in producing digestive enzymes, the pancreas is an endocrine gland that produces the hormones that regulate the amount of sugar in the blood.

Testes
The male testes make the hormone testosterone, which controls many of the functions of a man's body. The female ovaries regulate menstruation and the processes leading to conception and pregnancy.

❓ Which is the 'master gland?'

The pituitary gland, in the base of the brain, is the most important endocrine gland. Although it is only tiny, it produces hormones that regulate the effects of the other glands. The pituitary gland is connected directly to a region of the brain called the hypothalamus, and so provides the link between the brain and the endocrine system. The pituitary gland produces many important hormones, including growth hormone as well as hormones that cause the sex glands to start secreting their own hormones.

❓ Which gland controls the way the body uses energy?

The thyroid gland produces hormones that control the rate at which chemical reactions take place in the body. The gland is in the base of the neck. Thyroxin is one of the hormones produced by the thyroid gland. It speeds up the production of energy from the food you eat. An underactive thyroid can mean that a person becomes slow and sluggish. Other hormones from the thyroid control the amount of calcium in the bones.

Danger glands

Occasionally glands do not function properly and can produce too much or too little hormone. Diabetes is a common example of under production of the hormone insulin. The malfunction of the pituitary gland has more obvious results. Too much growth hormone from an overactive pituitary gland during adolescence has resulted in people growing to over 9 feet tall.
Lack of growth hormone in childhood and adolescence produces very short people whose bones do not grow properly. The thyroid gland needs iodine to produce hormones properly.

▼ The sudden rush of adrenalin produced during any dangerous or violent activity, such as bungee jumping, can be very exciting, although it is really intended to prepare the body for fight or flight.

⑦ What is diabetes?

Diabetes is an illness that is caused when the body does not produce enough insulin. The result is that large amounts of glucose build up in the blood and the person has to urinate frequently to get rid of it. At the same time the loss of fluid makes the person very thirsty. A diabetic person may lose weight, because the body breaks down body fat when it cannot get energy from glucose. Sometimes the insulin shortage can be corrected by drugs or, in the case of severe diabetes, by having regular insulin injections of insulin.

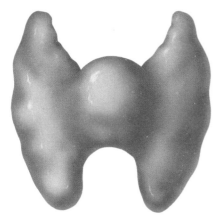

▲ The thyroid is a large butterfly-shaped gland. Its hormones accelerate the release of energy from food.

⑦ What happens when I am frightened?

When you are frightened, hormones help to prepare you to fight or to run away. This is a primitive reaction that all human beings still have, and it can affect our day-to-day behaviour. A hormone called adrenalin is released from the adrenal glands, which are small glands attached to the kidneys. Adrenalin readies the body for instant action. It makes your heart beat faster and you breath more deeply. The increased blood flow releases energy from the stored food materials, ready to provide power for the muscles to work.

Adrenalin causes the pupils of the eye to open wider, improving vision. Also, it makes digestive processes stop, allowing energy and blood to be channelled to other important areas. Blood is channelled away from the skin, so you become pale, and tiny muscles in the skin contract making your hairs stand on end, causing "goosebumps."

⑦ Which gland helps with digestion?

The pancreas is an important gland that helps with digestion. It also controls sugar levels within the body. The pancreas produces digestive enzymes that flow into the intestine during the process of digestion. The pancreas also functions as an endocrine gland, releasing the hormone insulin into the blood. Insulin helps the body's cells to use glucose, which is essential in the production of the energy that powers cells.

⑦ Which hormone affects growth?

Growth hormone, one of the most powerful hormones in the body, is produced in the pituitary gland. Growth hormone causes growth throughout childhood and adolescence, and it also affects the way that food substances are used to build new tissues. It stimulates cells throughout the entire body, and also causes the liver to produce special substances that activate bone and muscle growth.

Growth hormone is produced in differing amounts during adolescence, which is why children have a series of "growth spurts" when they grow very rapidly. In adults, growth hormone acts mainly to maintain and repair the tissues.

❓ What are the female sex organs?

The female sex organs are inside a woman's lower abdomen. The womb, or uterus, is a pear-shaped muscular organ from which two 'horns' run out sideways, ending with the fallopian tubes. The neck of these tubes is funnel-shaped, and the funnels are cupped around the ovaries where the egg cells are produced. The neck of the womb leads to a short tube called the vagina, leading outside the body. Urine passes out through a short tube, the urethra, near the mouth of the vagina.

▼ **Egg cells produced every month from the ovaries pass into the fallopian tubes and move toward the uterus. If they are fertilized, they become attached to the wall of the uterus and pregnancy will begin.**

❓ What are the male sex organs?

The male sex organs are the testes and the penis. The two testes are contained in a skin sac called the scrotum, hanging beneath the groin. A tube called the urethra, which is connected to both the bladder and the testes, runs through the middle of the penis. The urethra is used to pass urine and also, at a different time, to pass sperm out of the man's body. During intercourse, the penis becomes stiff as blood is pumped into a cavity called the corpus cavernosum.

▼ **Sperm produced in the testes pass along the vas deferens and are stored before leaving the body during intercourse. Liquid from the prostate gland is added to the sperm to make semen, which is ejected along the urethra running through the penis.**

❓ How are sperms made?

Sperms, the male sex cells, develop in the testes. They are stored for several days until needed. The testes contain long tubes called the seminiferous tubules, which are tightly coiled. Sperms are produced continuously in these tubes, then passed to the epididymis and stored in a large duct called the vas deferens. Here liquid is added to the sperm to make a milky fluid called semen. It is stored in pouches called seminal vesicles. During sexual intercourse the seminal vesicles contract and force out the sperm. It passes out of the penis and into the female sexual organs.

❓ How many sperms are there?

Up to 100 million sperms are produced every day by the male. If they are not released, they are soon destroyed and replaced. Sperms look like tiny tadpoles, with rounded heads and long lashing tails. They use their tails to swim at a speed of about one cm per minute. The head of the sperm contains the nucleus, which will join with the egg cell during fertilization.

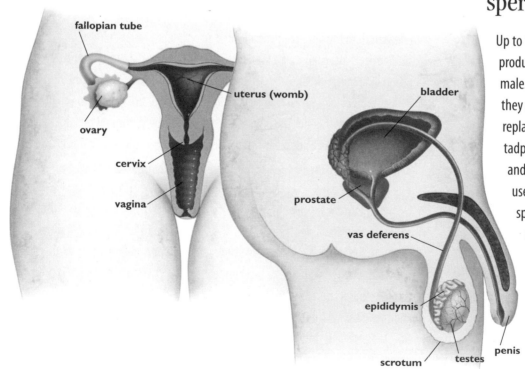

fallopian tube
uterus (womb)
ovary
cervix
vagina
bladder
prostate
vas deferens
epididymis
scrotum
testes
penis

The fertile human

Humans and other primates, such as apes and monkeys, are unusual in that they are able to mate at any time. This is not the case with most other animals. Some have a very brief breeding season, usually at a time of year that ensures there will be plenty of food for their young. This is not necessary for us because we are no longer dependent on the seasons. We can give birth and care for babies at any time of the year.

? What is a human egg cell?

The ovaries of a newborn baby girl contain about 250,000 egg cells. By the time she reaches maturity, there will be about 10,000 remaining. However, only a few of these eggs will be used – one each month throughout the years when she can have a baby. Every 28 days, a swelling appears on an ovary. This releases the egg cell in a process called ovulation. The egg cell then enters the fallopian tube. The swelling it emerged from produces hormones to prepare the womb to receive the egg.

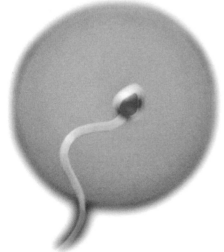

▲ If a sperm penetrates an egg cell, fertilization can take place.

? What is a period?

Each month, an egg cell is released from a female's ovaries. When this happens, the lining of the womb changes so that it is ready to receive the egg if it is fertilized.

If the egg is not fertilized, the womb lining breaks down, and blood and tissue pass out through the vagina. This process is called a period, and it happens about every 28 days. The time from one period to the next is known as the menstrual cycle. Hormones from the pituitary gland and the ovaries control the menstrual cycle, which may be irregular. However, it usually settles into a regular cycle.

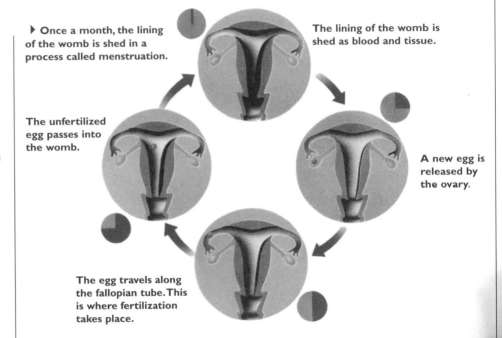

▶ Once a month, the lining of the womb is shed in a process called menstruation.

The lining of the womb is shed as blood and tissue.

The unfertilized egg passes into the womb.

A new egg is released by the ovary.

The egg travels along the fallopian tube. This is where fertilization takes place.

? How does fertilization take place?

It takes two days for an egg cell to travel along the fallopian tube. During this time, it may be fertilized. The male's penis places sperms in the vagina, and about 300 million sperms are released. Some sperms pass through the neck of the womb and swim up into the uterus. They enter the fallopian tube where some will meet the egg. Only one sperm may wriggle inside and fuse its own nucleus with the nucleus of the egg.

? What is contraception?

Contraception prevents fertilization from taking place. There are several different contraceptive methods. One method involves a contraceptive device called a condom. It is a rubber covering, or sheath, that is worn over the penis to stop the escape of sperms. The contraceptive 'pill' is a drug taken regularly by a female. It prevents the ovaries from producing ripe eggs, or stops the eggs from developing.

? What happens after fertilization?

The fertilized egg begins to divide as it travels down the fallopian tube towards the womb. By the time it enters the womb it has divided into a ball of about 100 cells. It settles on the wall of the womb and sinks into the surface, becoming firmly fixed. At this point, the female is pregnant.

? What is an embryo?

For the first eight weeks of a pregnancy, the developing egg is called an embryo. A liquid-filled bag develops around the embryo to protect it. By the fourth week of pregnancy, the embryo is the size of a grain of rice. It has a head and a tail and the beginning of limbs, and its tiny heart begins to beat. The placenta is the embryo's life-support system. It is a red, flattened organ that becomes deeply embedded in the wall of the womb. The placenta extracts food substances from the mother's blood and passes waste material from the embryo back to the mother for disposal. The placenta is connected to the developing baby by a thick umbilical cord, which contains large blood vessels.

? What is a fetus?

After the first eight weeks of pregnancy, the developing baby is called a fetus. By now, all of its major organs have formed, and it is growing at a very fast rate. By the 16th week, the fetus starts to move about, and by the 20th week it may already have eyebrows and fingernails. It weighs approximately 12 ounces.

? What is a baby like just before birth?

At the 26th week, the baby is big enough to survive if it is born prematurely. It weighs about 3 pounds, and from now on it increases in weight, ready to be born. Soon the baby turns over into a head-down position ready for the birth, which usually takes place at around the 38th week.

? How is a baby born?

The mother starts to feel strong tightening pains, called contractions, in her womb when the birth is near. These contractions become stronger, and the neck of the cervix starts to open. As the contractions continue, the baby's head moves down. The membrane around it breaks, releasing fluid out through the vagina. After hard pushing, which can last for several hours, the baby emerges through the cervix and the vagina. The baby is still attached to the umbilical cord, which is tied off to prevent bleeding. Soon after, the placenta is pushed from the mother's womb.

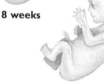

4 weeks

8 weeks

12 weeks

20 weeks

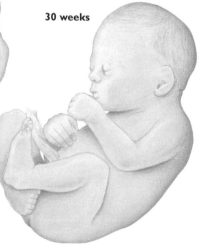

30 weeks

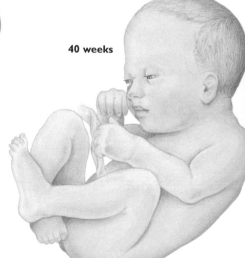

40 weeks

▲ **After five weeks, the embryo has a pumping heart and tiny limbs and is about 1 cm in length. By nine weeks it has become a fetus, and is recognizable as a tiny baby. It begins to move. For the rest of its development, the fetus will increase in size until it is born.**

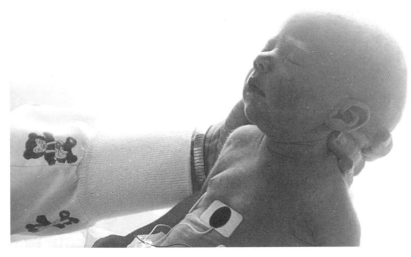

▲ Newborn babies lack coordination of nerves and muscles, so they are unable to support the weight of their own head.

?) What is a caesarean section?

Sometimes a baby cannot be born normally through the vagina, and so it has to be surgically removed from the mother's womb. This operation is called a caesarean section, and it is normally only carried out when there is a risk to the baby or the mother. A common reason for carrying out a caesarean section is when the umbilical cord becomes wrapped around the baby's neck during the birth. There is a risk to the baby's life if it is not born very quickly.

Test-tube babies

Sometimes it is not possible for a male and female to have a baby in the normal way. The male's sperms may be faulty and unable to swim well, or they may be few in number. A female may not produce egg cells or the fertilized egg may not develop properly.

Various techniques are used to help these people. Many involve taking a ripe egg cell from the female and sperm from the male, and completing fertilization in artificial conditions. The embryo is implanted back into the female to complete its development normally. Sometimes several embryos are implanted to increase her chances of becoming pregnant. Occasionally all the embryos develop, and she has a multiple birth, producing quads, quints, or even more babies.

?) How are twins produced?

Twins may be absolutely identical or only as similar as a typical brother or sister. Identical twins are produced when the embryo splits into two in the early stages of its development. This produces two identical children of the same sex. Non-identical twins are produced when two eggs are released at the same time and both are fertilized. They can be the same sex, or brother and sister. One in 83 pregnancies results in twins. Identical twins look so alike they can only be told apart by fingerprints.

?) Why does a new baby have a hole in the top of its skull?

Even a tiny baby's head is too large to pass through the gap in the mother's pelvis. A baby's head is flexible so it can be squeezed out of shape as it passes through the pelvis. This is made easier because some bones in the baby's head are not knitted together, and some of them are still made of rubbery cartilage. The tip of the baby's head is the last place where the bones join. For weeks or months after the birth there is a soft patch on top of the skull where the bones have not yet fused together.

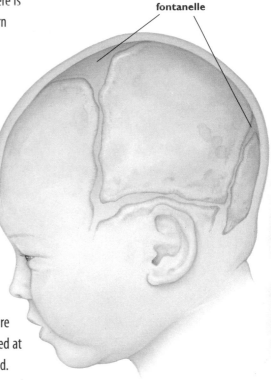

fontanelle

▲ The bones of a baby's head are not fully fused at birth, allowing the skull to pass though the mother's birth canal. The bones gradually become joined, but a gap at the top of the skull, called the fontanelle, may not close up for several months.

What are chromosomes?

Chromosomes are tiny threads that are present in all cells apart from red blood cells. They contain all the information for an entire person to develop. There are 46 chromosomes in each cell. They come in 22 pairs, plus another special pair that determines a person's sex. Chromosomes are found in the cell nucleus, but they are not normally visible under the microscope except when a cell is dividing.

What are genes?

Genes are short sections of a chromosome. Each gene carries the instructions for a specific characteristic, such as eye color, each carries the instructions for making a protein that will form a part of a living cell.

Many of these genes work with other genes, so it is difficult to say what effects they will have. Scientists are currently studying all the genes in a human cell, which will give them the complete blueprint for a human being.

What is Down's syndrome?

Down's syndrome is a condition caused by the appearance of an extra chromosome in the embryo. This extra chromosome is repeated in all the body cells. A child with Down's syndrome has 47 chromosomes instead of the usual 46, and this difference causes physical and mental changes.

How do I inherit genes from my parents?

Sperms and egg cells contain only half of the normal number of chromosomes. During fertilization these chromosomes combine to make up the usual total of 46 chromosomes. This means that half of a baby's genetic information comes from the mother and half from the father, mixing together their characteristics in a random order. In this way you develop a mixture of characteristics from both parents.

Are there such things as 'bad' genes?

Some genes cause us to inherit a harmful condition. The disease haemophilia is an example of such a 'bad' gene. It is handed down through the male side of the family, but the disease is carried on the female, or X, chromosome. This means that women pass the disease on to their sons, even though they are not affected themselves. Hemophilia will not affect a female unless both parents have the gene, which is a very rare occurance.

What are X and Y chromosomes?

The 23rd pair of genes determines the sex of a baby. These are X and Y chromosomes. A woman has two X chromosomes, while a man has one X and one Y chromosome. When the chromosomes join together in fertilization, if the sperm contains an X chromosome, it will combine with the X chromosome of the female to produce XX – a girl. If the sperm contributes the Y chromosome, the baby will have one X and one Y chromosome and will be XY – a boy.

strand of chromosome

What is a mutation?

Mutations are changes in the DNA inside a cell that affect the genes and chromosomes. Mutations arise because of errors in the DNA molecule when it divides and re-forms in the new cells. When this happens in sperms or egg cells, it causes changes that can be passed on to a child. The appearance of hemophilia is an example of a mutation in a single gene.

chromosomes

nucleus of cell

▾ All of the instructions for growing a new human being are coded into the **DNA** molecule. It is shaped like a ladder twisted into a spiral. The two long upright strands are joined by a series of rungs of pairs of amino acids, which can only join together in a limited number of ways. The pattern in which these pairs appear is the code built into the **DNA** molecule, and groups of these connections form genes. Each **DNA** molecule is built up of between 100,000 to 10 million atoms.

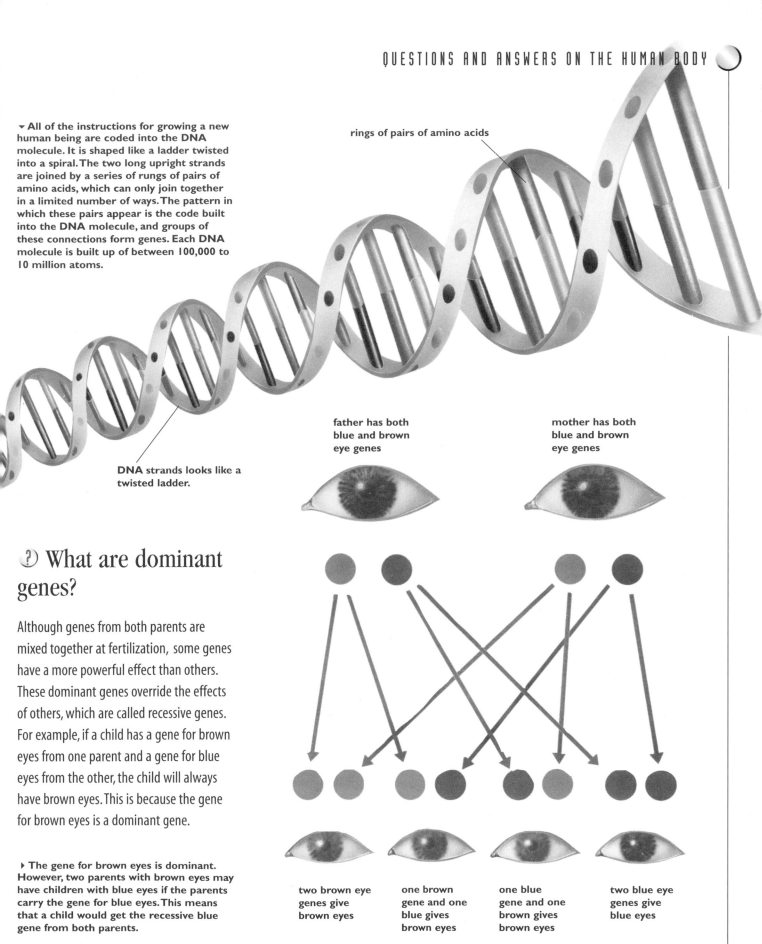

rings of pairs of amino acids

DNA strands looks like a twisted ladder.

father has both blue and brown eye genes

mother has both blue and brown eye genes

☡ What are dominant genes?

Although genes from both parents are mixed together at fertilization, some genes have a more powerful effect than others. These dominant genes override the effects of others, which are called recessive genes. For example, if a child has a gene for brown eyes from one parent and a gene for blue eyes from the other, the child will always have brown eyes. This is because the gene for brown eyes is a dominant gene.

▸ The gene for brown eyes is dominant. However, two parents with brown eyes may have children with blue eyes if the parents carry the gene for blue eyes. This means that a child would get the recessive blue gene from both parents.

two brown eye genes give brown eyes

one brown gene and one blue gives brown eyes

one blue gene and one brown gives brown eyes

two blue eye genes give blue eyes

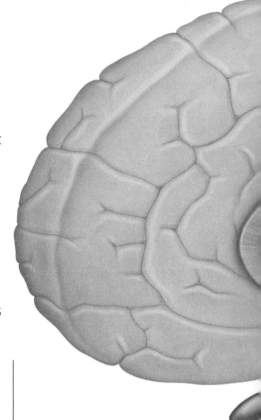

❓ What job does the brain do?

The brain is the body's control center. It coordinates all the messages that pass through the nervous system, giving us the ability to learn, reason, and feel. It also controls the body's automatic functions such as breathing, heartbeat, digestion, growth, and blood pressure.

❓ Does the brain think like a computer?

The brain resembles a computer because it has a memory and generates millions of electrical signals. However, it works in quite a different way from a computer.

A computer can calculate accurately, but it can only use the information programmed into it. The brain is able to learn and grow in complexity from the day you are born. Unlike most computers, it is able to make decisions without necessarily having all the information that a computer would need. The brain has powers of imagination and reasoning, but computers are only just acquiring these abilities.

❓ Which is the oldest part of the brain?

The brain stem is sometimes called the oldest part of the brain. This is because it keeps the whole body alive. Even if the other parts of the brain are destroyed, the brain stem often keeps a person alive for some time.

❓ What are the main parts of the brain?

The brain is divided into three main regions, each with different functions . The large part at the top is the cerebrum. This is where most of our reasoning, thinking, and memory is controlled. The cerebellum is a smaller area at the back of the brain where accurate movement and coordination are controlled. The brain stem is a small region at the base of the brain where most of our automatic body functions are controlled. It is connected to the spinal cord.

❓ Why does the brain have two sides?

The cerebrum is divided lengthways into two halves, called cerebral hemispheres. Each side of the brain controls the opposite side of the body. For example, if you move your right leg, the instructions for that movement come from the left side of the brain. The nerve cells that carry messages from the brain cross over at the base of the brain. In most people, the left side controls speaking, writing, and logical thought, while the right side controls artistic abilities and creative thinking. Most people seem to use one side more than the other. This is why some people seem to be more artistic than others or are better at scientific and mathematical thinking. Usually the left side of the brain is more dominant as far as movement is concerned, which is why most people are right-handed. About 10 percent of people are left-handed.

▲ The brain is immensely complicated. In general, the parts at the back and base of the brain are important for controlling the basic functions needed to support life, while the large cerebral hemispheres control thinking, movement, and memory.

Brain mapping

Scientists have produced maps showing how electrical activity in one part of the brain can cause a movement or other reaction. This mapping has been done during brain surgery. Because there are no sense organs in the brain, some operations are carried out on people who are fully conscious but feel no pain. Tiny electrical currents are applied to the brain's surface, and the person is able to describe what he or she feels. Sometimes the current causes a forgotten memory to resurface, or sound to be heard. This means that when a person has a brain injury, the symptoms can show which area of the brain is affected.

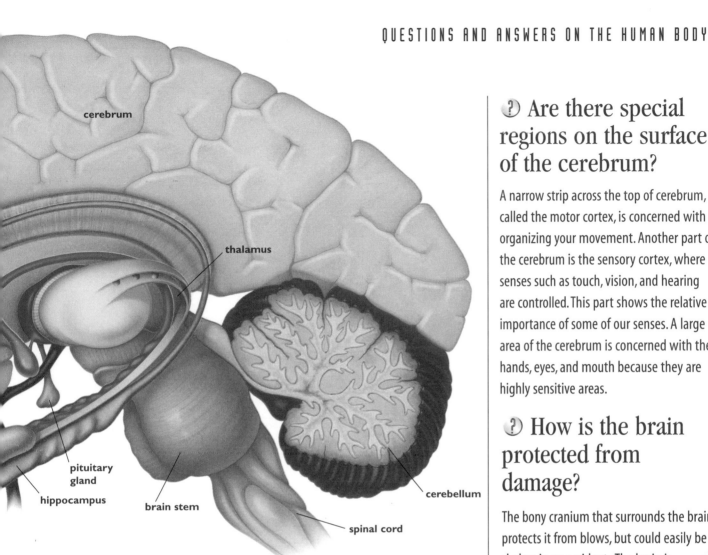

cerebrum

thalamus

pituitary gland

hippocampus

brain stem

cerebellum

spinal cord

? Are there special regions on the surface of the cerebrum?

A narrow strip across the top of cerebrum, called the motor cortex, is concerned with organizing your movement. Another part of the cerebrum is the sensory cortex, where senses such as touch, vision, and hearing are controlled. This part shows the relative importance of some of our senses. A large area of the cerebrum is concerned with the hands, eyes, and mouth because they are highly sensitive areas.

? How is the brain protected from damage?

The bony cranium that surrounds the brain protects it from blows, but could easily be shaken in an accident. The brain is cushioned by three layers of tough membranes called the meninges. They are filled with liquid in which the brain floats.

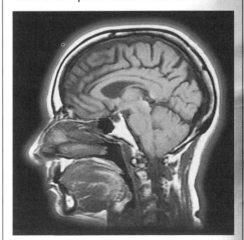

▲ Cavities inside the brain are filled with liquid so that the soft tissue does not flap about.

? Which part of the brain makes me different from animals?

The cerebrum is the part of your brain that gives you your intelligence and emotions. It makes up about 85 percent of the total brain weight of 8 pounds. In proportion to the size of the human body, it is by far the biggest cerebrum in any living creature. Its grey surface is made up of millions of nerve cells. The white layer beneath is mostly made of the nerve fibers connecting them. The surface of the cerebrum is wrinkled and looks rather like a cabbage.

? How does the brain allow us to make careful movements?

Fine movements are possible because the cerebellum filters instructions from other parts of the brain to the muscles. It monitors these instructions and ensures that the muscles work together. The cerebellum is part of the brain that is well understood. Its neuron are arranged in a regular pattern, and it has been possible to trace the electrical circuits from one neuron to another. This part of the brain works very much like a computer.

Learning and Memory

? How do I remember things?

Memory is the ability to store things that you experience and learn, ready for future use. Some things are remembered easily, such as a dramatic event in our life. However, more ordinary things need to be rehearsed in the mind several times before they "stick". This is why revision is necessary when studying for an examination.

? Are there different types of memory?

There are three different ways in which memory can be stored. Sensory memory is very brief. It tells you what is happening around you and allows you to move around without bumping into things. Short-term memory lasts for about 30 seconds. It allows you to look up a number in a phone book and dial the number without forgetting it, but after a minute or so it will have vanished. Long-term memory is for things that you have carefully memorized and learned. It may last for years, and some memories can last throughout your life.

? What is conditioning?

A conditioned action is one that becomes automatic after being repeated many times. You become conditioned to feel hungry when you smell cooking, or to feel thirsty when you hear someone pull the ring off a soft drinks can.

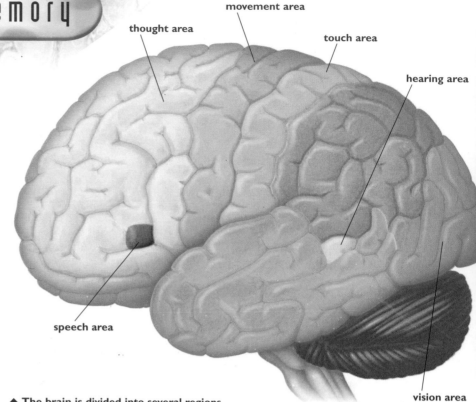

movement area
thought area
touch area
hearing area
speech area
vision area

▲ The brain is divided into several regions according to their function. It is possible to map the functions of a living brain by stimulating the brain surface with tiny currents and observing the effects on a person.

? Can the brain alter to help people to learn?

The structure of the brain can alter slightly as you learn new memories and activities. The number of connections between neurones can increase as you learn a repetitive task, making it easier for nerve impulses to travel through and retrieve a memory. This is why once you have learned a task like riding a bike or swimming, you never forget how to do it. You don't have to think about it at all once you have learned the skills that are needed. Catching a ball is an example of this. Young children cannot coordinate their hands and eyes well enough to catch a ball at first, but after many fumbles they will learn to catch every time.

? Are brain circuits already in place in a newborn baby?

Brain circuits are already in place to maintain the body of a newborn baby, but they continue to develop as the child grows. It is not possible for a very young child to learn language because the brain is not sufficiently well developed. All children, in any culture, start to learn a language in several distinct stages as they grow. By the age of two years most children have an extensive vocabulary of several hundred words, and by the age of four years they understand the simpler rules of grammar. For this reason, some scientists suggest that the brain is "pre-wired" for learning language.

▲ The smell of something like a bonfire can bring back strong memories.

? What is a mnemonic?

Although a memory is stored in the brain, sometimes you cannot find the route to retrieve it. The memory remains hidden. Mnemonics are simple tricks developed to help us remember. Often these are in the form of rhymes, which are seldom forgotten, such as "Thirty days hath September..." to remind you of the number of days in each month. Another example is "Roy G. Biv" to remind us of the colors of the rainbow. Other people associate the thing they want to remember with something completely unrelated but which sounds similar. Most people develop mental tricks of this sort. They can be useful for remembering important facts during exam revision.

? Can a smell bring back a memory?

The sense of smell has powerful effects in retrieving memories. Often a smell can suddenly trigger a memory from many years ago. Sounds and tastes do not seem to work in the same way.

? What is a photographic memory?

A few people have the ability to remember a scene or picture just as though they were looking at a photograph. They can recall all the details in the picture, or remember where a particular word is on a page.

? Where are memories stored in the brain?

Memories are not stored in any one area of the brain. Because the neurones in the brain are connected in a network, parts of memory can be stored in different places . It seems that for short-term memory, things you have seen are stored near the part of the brain that deals with vision, while sounds are stored near the part of the brain dealing with hearing, and so on. Longer-term memories are stored in a small circuit of several connected nerve cells.

? Why does relaxing help you to remember?

When you struggle to remember something this often seems to make it even harder to recall. When you relax, your brain tends to explore alternative routes to find the lost piece of information without you being totally aware of it. It is rather like finding a different way around a maze. You will usually be thinking about something completely different, when the piece of information you were trying to recall suddenly comes to mind. Even though you were not consciously looking for it, your brain will have been continuing to seek out the information you wanted.

Special brains

People used to think that large brains were a sign of intelligence, but years of scientific research have shown that this is false. In fact, you only use a section of your brain, so its size does not really matter. The largest healthy brain that was ever recorded weighed more than I pound, but this did not mean that its owner was especially intelligent.

The brain of a genius such as Einstein cannot be shown to be any different from the brain of an ordinary person. So intelligence must be based on learning, rather than on the number of neurones present in the brain.

Maintaining Health

⚡ What is health?

Being healthy involves far more that simply not being ill. If you feel in good health, your organs will be working properly and you will have the energy to live life to the fullest. This feeling of well being affects your mind and your body.

⚡ How can I keep myself healthy?

The environment you live in, your diet, and your lifestyle affect your health. Physical fitness is an important part of health, and this means that your heart, lungs, skeleton, and muscles all work together smoothly to carry out your daily activities. Fitness involves strength, stamina and suppleness, and you need regular exercise to maintain all these conditions. Careful exercise develops a healthy heart and lungs, and gives you the strength and stamina that allow you to run, cycle, and swim. A sensible diet and sufficient sleep also help you to keep healthy.

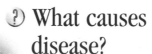

▶ Regular exercise helps to tone up the muscles and the circulatory system.

⚡ Can the environment harm my health?

Air pollution is an environmental factor that can damage health. Exhaust fumes from motor vehicles contain substances that can cause asthma and other breathing problems. In hot climates, smog can also develop, trapping these air pollutants and making the health risk greater.

▲ Air pollution is a serious health risk, which is why lead has been removed from gasoline. However, cars and other vehicles still produce huge amounts of fumes that can cause lung damage.

⚡ What causes disease?

Many diseases are infections that are caused by bacteria or viruses. Other illnesses are caused by failure of some of the body's organs or tissues. Sometimes parts of the body wear out or are not replaced properly, but most health problems are caused when the body simply fails to maintain itself. Joints can wear out, causing arthritis, or the digestive system may not work as efficiently, causing various types of stomach upset. Other diseases may be caused by a person's own lifestyle, for example, lack of exercise or poor eating habits. Smoking is now known to be a contributary factor in many diseases.

⚡ Why is smoking harmful?

Cigarette smoking is known to be the main cause of lung cancer. It also causes bronchitis, heart disease, and other problems with the circulation. Cigarette smoke contains many harmful substances, which are all deposited straight into the lungs. The smoke contains tiny particles of soot that can clog the air passages. The tar in smoke contains substances that can cause cancer. The nicotine in cigarettes is a strong addictive drug that can affect the heart and circulation. However, this addiction can be very difficult to break.

The harmful effects of cigarettes may only appear after many years of smoking. However, even when a smoker gives up the habit, it can be years before these health risks are cancelled out.

Alternative medicine

Modern medicine is based on the scientific study of diseases and drugs to treat them. Alternative medicine is based on different theories that are not provable scientifically but which seem to give relief to many people. Acupuncture is one such form of medicine, in which needles are inserted into the body following instructions developed thousands of years ago in China. Hypnosis is used to treat some conditions by the power of suggestion.

Other forms of alternative medicine involve massage or herbal remedies. The reason that alternative medicine seems to work is that the mind can very often control the way the body works. However, most people try conventional medicine before experimenting with alternative techniques.

Are all drugs dangerous?

People take so-called recreational drugs, such as cannabis and heroin, because of the effect they have on the brain. (These drugs are different from medical drugs that people take when they have an illness or disease.) Recreational drugs can be a danger to health. Some of them make people feel excited and full of energy. Others make them feel sleepy, and some drugs can make people experience hallucinations. All these drugs cause the brain to malfunction, and if taken regularly, they can cause permanent damage to health.

Some of these drugs are addictive. This means that they cause changes in the brain that make people crave them, even though the pleasant effects may wear off.

How do medical drugs work?

Many medical drugs work by correcting the chemical reactions within the body that are responsible for disease. For example, insulin injections replace insulin that is not being produced by the pancreas, so sugar can be used properly by the body. In depression and mental illness, drugs can restore the balance of chemicals in the brain. Aspirin is often given to cure a headache, but it can also neutralize the inflammation that causes pain in the joints of people suffering from arthritis.

Modern drug research studies the cause of diseases, then designs molecules that interrupt or reverse the disease process. All drugs cause some unwanted effects, and scientists try to find new drugs that relieve disease without causing further problems.

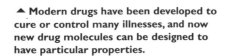

▲ Modern drugs have been developed to cure or control many illnesses, and now new drug molecules can be designed to have particular properties.

What is an antibiotic?

Antibiotics kill bacteria by interfering with the way in which bacteria reproduce. Antibiotics are produced naturally by many simple plants and even other bacteria. Antibiotics are useful because they seldom have any bad effects on the person taking them. The use of antibiotics has meant that many diseases that were usually fatal can now be cured.

Antibiotics work by damaging bacterial reproduction rather than killing the bacteria outright, and so it is important to take the full course of the drug. Often you will feel better within a couple of days of starting treatment, but if you stop too soon, the bacteria can recover. When you keep taking the drug, after several days the bacteria die and are cleared away.

How was penicillin discovered?

Penicillin was the first antibiotic to be discovered, by Alexander Fleming. He was searching for substances that would kill bacteria when he noticed some mold growing on an experimental dish. The mold killed the colonies of bacteria that were growing around it. Penicillin was extracted from this mold, and its use has saved millions of lives. Many other antibiotics have since been discovered or made artificially.

? Why do people grow old?

Aging is a result of the gradual failure of the body's cells and organs to replace or repair themselves. This is because there is a limit to the number of times that each cell can divide. As the body's cells begin to near this limit, the rate at which they divide slows down. Sometimes the new cells that are produced have defects or do not carry out their usual task effectively. Organs can then begin to fail, tissues change in structure, and the chemical reactions that power the body become less efficient.

▲ People are now living far longer and often remain healthy into very old age.

? How does the body change with increasing age?

Elderly people are no longer growing, and so they are not as active as they used to be. For this reason, they do not need to eat as much, and quite often become thinner. The body loses muscle as well as fat, and sometimes older people become unsteady on their feet.

? Why do older people get shorter?

The spine becomes shorter in older people because the pad of cartilage between the bony vertebrae grows thinner. Elderly people often lose bone in a condition called osteoporosis. This usually affects elderly women, although it can also appear in men. The bone becomes spongy, and when it affects the vertebrae in the spine, they may collapse. This causes pain, and also makes the person's spine shorter and curved. Osteoporosis can be treated with drugs, and a diet containing the mineral calcium can also help. Calcium is plentiful in milk and cheese.

? Why does the skin become wrinkled?

The skin becomes looser as people age. As skin sags, it forms into wrinkles and creases. This happens because the fibers of collagen that normally provide support to the skin become weaker. Smoking and over-exposure to the sun can make skin more likely to wrinkle.

? Do people become forgetful in old age?

It is very common for older people to become forgetful, although many retain perfect memories from long ago.

Many things can cause forgetfulness. Sometimes the blood supply to the brain is not effective. The brain cells become starved of oxygen and nutrients, leading to dizzy spells and forgetfulness. Dementia is a condition where forgetfulness becomes a serious problem, and the person may not be able to look after himself or herself. Alzheimer's disease is the most serious form of dementia. For most older people, memories bring great pleasure. Strangely, even though recent events may be forgotten, people often clearly remember events that took place in their childhood.

▲ With age the skin becomes less elastic and gradually forms into wrinkles.

Survivors

How long can a person live? The answer to this is difficult because many of the people who claim to have lived for a great number of years come from societies where accurate birth records were not kept. Some claims are obviously fantasies. The former Soviet state of Georgia has a very small population, but claims to have more than 2,000 people over 100 years old. Some of these people are certainly very old and still healthy, but it is unlikely that they are all as old as is claimed. In Britain, about 20 men over 100 years old die each year, and about 100 women. Very few people survive beyond the age of 110, and 120 years is probably near the maximum age.

? How can older people keep healthy and mobile?

Exercise is important because it keeps bones, joints, and muscles healthy. You cannot expect an older person to take vigorous exercise, but walking and even swimming help the circulation and keeps the joints supple. If seniors are receiving medical treatment, it is important that their doctor advises on the proper level of exercise to avoid doing any damage to the body.

▲ There have always been some long-lived individuals, but nowadays there is a much larger elderly population than in the past due to better diets and improved standards of living.

? Can we help older people to have an active life?

Elders sometimes need to be helped to live their lives to the full. Loneliness is one of the most common features of an elderly person's life, particularly if the person has lost a partner. Most people no longer live in large families within one house, and a single older person can feel very isolated. Although they may not be physically strong, almost all older people can and should exercise.

Most seniors enjoy the company of younger people. Keeping both the mind and body active will help an elderly person's general health and well being. Above all, the company of other people is the best tonic they can have.

▲ Seniors have time to take up interests that will keep them active.

? What is a healthy diet for older people?

It is very important that elderly people eat fresh food. The elderly need to eat protein, fat, and carbohydrate, which form the basis of any healthy diet. They need plenty of fresh fruit and vegetables.

? How long do people live?

People are living longer and longer, and most of us can expect to live to the age of 75 years or more. We can also expect to be reasonably healthy for almost all of this time. Because so many of the diseases that caused people to die young are now being controlled, and people have a far better standard of living, most of us are living much longer than our ancestors.

We are also staying much healthier right up until the end of our lives. This means that a growing number of healthy and active older people are working part-time to occupy themselves and to provide an extra income. This activity helps to keeps their minds and bodies active.

In 1997 a French woman died at the age of 122 years. She was the world's longest-lived person.

History

Many places and events in history seem only remotely related to the world around us today.

If we look at history as a process rather than a series of events, we can see how each event has produced ripples that spread out to affect other cultures and societies. The consequences are with us today. The Saxons probably lost the Battle of Hastings in 1066 because they were so exhausted from a previous successful battle with the Vikings further north. If King Harold had survived and the Normans had been driven back into the sea, millions of people around the world would not be speaking English today, with its odd mixture of French words mixed up with the original Saxon.

It is interesting to think of how the world would have changed if some individual events had happened differently. What would Britain have been like if the Spanish Armada had been successful? Suppose Germany had won World War II? Would Japan have entered the War if the Americans had intercepted the fleet on its way to attack Pearl Harbor? What if the Emperor Constantine had not made Christianity the official religion of the Eastern Roman Empire? Suppose China had never adopted Communism? The world as we know it could have been a completely different place.

When world events are reported in newspapers or on television, it is worth speculating what their effects will be on future history. The flow of history will continue, but the direction of this flow can easily be altered by a single local event.

⑦ What do we mean by history?

History is the study of things that happened in the past. History can be very recent, or it can extend back to the earliest times from which any sort of records can be obtained. History cannot be understood properly by the study of a single event. It is necessary to understand the culture of the people among whom the event took place, and that of any other countries that could have affected the event. An understanding of history can only be obtained by piecing together knowledge from a whole range of sources to provide a broad picture.

⑦ How do we know about the past?

Our knowledge of the past comes from a wide range of sources of information. Sometimes historians record their own version of recent history. Other information is obtained from material that was written down and contained passing references to people and events. A tablet recording the taxes levied on an ancient civilization in the Middle East, for example, can tell us what crops were grown and the type of economy that existed.

History can sometimes be reconstructed even though information was never written down. For example, myths and legends containing historical truths can survive for hundreds of years, and the remains of some buildings can tell us how people lived in earlier times.

Time capsule

To mark an important occasion, such as the completion of a new building, people bury time capsules. They contain various items that represent the period. The items may be dug up by an archaeologist in the future. A typical modern time capsule would contain things such as newspapers, state-of-the-art electronic items, the latest medical drugs and award-winning novels.

⑦ What does an archaeologist do?

An archaeologist reconstructs the past by studying buildings and objects that have survived. Sometimes historical remains are astonishingly well preserved, for example, the Roman cities of Pompeii and Herculaneum, which were overwhelmed by the eruption of Mount Vesuvius. Many tiny aspects of Roman life were preserved, including graffiti on the walls. Such perfect preservation is very rare.

Archaeologists usually need to make a painstaking reconstruction, carefully excavating the remains of ruined buildings. Sometimes only the post-holes of a wooden building are left, but even they can provide useful clues about the type of building. The oldest archaeological remains come from the Stone Age. The remains of flint tools and weapons have survived, together with bones that show which animals were hunted and eaten.

⑦ Who were the first historians?

The first true historians were ancient Greeks, who wrote long accounts about historical events. However, they also wove fanciful events into their stories to make them more interesting, and it is sometimes difficult to separate truth and invention. The problem with ancient historians is that they put across a particular viewpoint. Often they were trying to glorify a local king or ruler. Sometimes a straightforward account of a particular event was written down. For example, Viking explorers recorded their voyages. In more recent times, detailed diaries provide a valuable source of information. Some modern history has been deliberately rewritten for political reasons.

▼ The volcanic eruption that buried the city of Pompeii, Italy in A.D. 79, was so sudden that it gives us a complete overview of Roman life.

▶ Carbon that forms a part of living things loses its radioactivity at a steady and predictable rate. Archaeologists use this information to determine the age of organic remains. After about 70,000 years, organic material has lost all of its radiocarbon.

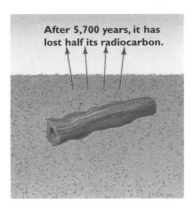

Newly cut wood begins to lose its radiocarbon.

After 5,700 years, it has lost half its radiocarbon.

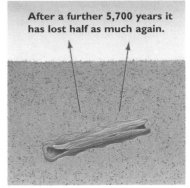

After a further 5,700 years it has lost half as much again.

❓ How are dates measured?

Accurate dating of archaeological remains is a relatively recent science. Wooden objects up to 8,000 years old can be dated by examining the growth rings in the wood. By studying the rings of very old, but still living trees, they can be dated very accurately, so surviving wooden implements and utensils can be dated exactly.

Radiocarbon dating takes us back much further. A radioactive form of carbon decays at a very slow rate, which can be measured exactly. By measuring the amount of carbon-12 and carbon-14 in a small piece of organic material, objects as old as 50,000 years ago can be dated.

Buried objects are often dated by looking at, and dating, nearby objects buried at the same time.

▶ Ancient Egyptian hieroglyphic writing had long been indecipherable. The discovery of the Rosetta stone provided the key to understanding the ancient Egyptian script.

❓ How can you find out about local history?

History is still happening all around you, and local history is an important field of study. It shows how ordinary people lived and worked. It is not difficult to find out what happened in your own area in the recent past. Most towns and cities, for example, have local museums that preserve items of interest. Libraries may hold stocks of old newspapers.

You could construct a family tree to trace the history of your own family. Usually parents and relatives can provide information about recent family members, but after a few generations you will need to check local records. In many countries, churches kept records of births, christenings, marriages, and burials, and these records can be studied.

❓ What is the Rosetta stone?

The discovery of the Rosetta stone in 1799 near Alexandria, in Egypt, was the key to unraveling the language of the ancient Egyptians. Hieroglyphics, a form of picture writing used by ordinary people in ancient Egypt, had puzzled archaeologists and historians for hundreds of years. The discovery of the Rosetta stone, which contained the same inscription in hieroglyphics and in Greek, allowed the meaning of the complicated hieroglyphic pictures to be understood. In turn, this allowed thousands of surviving ancient Egyptian inscriptions to be translated.

? Where were the first cities?

The first known cities were established in the Middle East, as much as 10,000 years ago. These ancient cities were built from stone and mud bricks. One city was destroyed to provide building materials for the next city on the same site, making it confusing to try to reconstruct them. Other ancient cities were built in present-day Turkey and China.

? Who were the Sumerians?

The Sumerians developed the first known civilization, in 3500 B.C. They lived in Mesopotamia, a region between the Euphrates and Tigris rivers in what is now modern Iraq. The Sumerians built large and elaborate cities, developed tax systems and a government, and produced irrigation systems to water their crops.

Excavations of one major city, called Ur, showed signs of a great flood, which is thought to have been the flood described in the Bible. The Sumerian civilization lasted for about 1,000 years.

? When did metal working first develop?

Metal working seems to have been developed independently in several places in about 3500 B.C.

It appeared in China, India, Egypt, and Mesopotamia at around this time. Bronze was the first metal to be worked.

? Why did the Egyptian civilization develop?

The Egyptian civilization grew up as a result of the annual flooding of the River Nile. This provided a green and fertile strip of land that could be cultivated, even in an area that is mostly desert. Every year, when the Nile flooded, it deposited rich, fertile silt along its banks. The ancient Egyptians grew crops of barley, wheat, and flax in the fertile soils. They used the flax to make linen for their clothes.

The river also provided the Egyptians with papyrus reed. They harvested the reed and used it to make a form of paper known as papyrus. It was easy to keep detailed written records on papyrus.

? Why were pyramids built?

Pyramid building developed only slowly in ancient Egypt. The first pyramids were simple structures called mastabas, which were platforms built over the tombs of important people. Over the years, further levels were added, until a structure called a step pyramid was produced.

In later pyramids, the steps were filled in to produce the smooth conical shape of the famous Pyramids at Giza that we can see today. Pyramid building became an important part of the Egyptian civilization. Egyptians believed that the pyramids offered a pathway to heaven for their rulers, the pharaohs, who were buried with items they might need for the afterlife.

▼ Over the centuries, the Egyptians constructed pyramids as tombs for their pharaohs. The Sphinx was constructed near the greatest of these pyramids, outside modern Cairo.

▼ Civilizations sprang up at similar times in different parts of the world. One very advanced civilization was in the Indus Valley, in modern Pakistan and India. The remains of Harappa have been excavated, revealing a large city, with multi-storeyed buildings and carefully laid-out streets.

⑦ What were the Indus civilizations?

Several large civilizations developed in the Indus Valley, in what is now Pakistan and India. These civilizations built houses made from baked mud bricks. They also built toilets, wells, and even bath houses. High protective walls surrounded the cities. Outside the cities, the people of the Indus civilizations cultivated cereal crops and dates and also made weapons and other items in bronze. Stone seals from the Indus civilizations have been found along the Persian Gulf and in the ruins of the city of Ur. The seals show how these ancient peoples developed extensive trade links. These civilizations collapsed in about 3500 B.C., because of invading tribes.

▲ Hieroglyphics were a system of writing used by the ancient Egyptians, using drawings rather than the shapes we use in modern script. They gradually became more stylized to resemble modern forms of writing.

⑦ Who developed the earliest writing?

No one knows how the first writing system developed, because no records remain. The earliest known writing was recorded in the form of picture symbols on clay tablets by the ancient Sumerians, in around 3500 B.C. Hieroglyphics were a similar form of picture writing, and the oldest examples date from around 3000 B.C. Picture symbols were also used in the ancient Chinese writing that appeared in 1500 B.C. It is likely that all writing started this way, before shapes and letters were used to indicate sounds.

? Who were the Indo-Europeans?

About 4,000 years ago, a race of people living in southern Russia began to migrate westwards. These people are now known as Indo-Europeans, or Aryans. However, the language they spoke can be traced all along the routes of their migration. This has meant that some almost identical words have persisted throughout Asia and Europe.

Some of the Indo-European people migrated south into India and Persia, while others continued westwards into Turkey, Greece, and Western Europe. Eventually, the Indo-Europeans gave rise to the Celts.

? What are hill forts?

Hill forts were enormous circular earthworks, which were built on high ground. They were built by the Celts, who were a warrior race. When attacked, the Celts retired to their hill forts.

The banks of the hill forts were surrounded by deep ditches, and were probably topped with defensive wooden spikes. The defenders repelled attackers with showers of stones thrown from slingshots. Many regions formerly occupied by the Celts, such as Britain and France, still have the remains of hill forts.

▼ The Celts often constructed their settlements on hilltops, which could be easily defended. They are identified by circular defensive ditches that still survive in former Celtic areas.

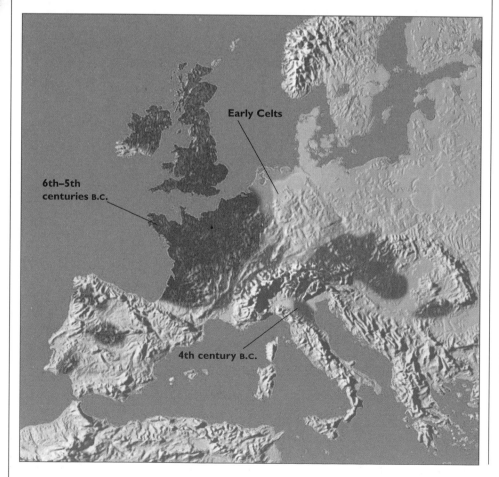

Early Celts

6th–5th centuries B.C.

4th century B.C.

? Have any Celtic cultures survived?

The Celts retreated westwards from the Romans and later invaders. They soon vanished from most of the huge territory that they had originally occupied. Today true Celtic cultures exist only because of their language. They can be found in Scotland, Ireland, Wales, and Brittany. Other Celtic languages recently died out in Cornwall and the Isle of Man.

◄ By about 500 B.C. the Celts had spread across Europe from Ireland in the west to the Black Sea in the

▶ Ancient Celtic traditions persisted into Christian times. Carvings on this cross show characteristic patterns of Celtic art.

? What was the Celtic religion?

There was no single religion throughout the Celtic regions, but there was a common priesthood. These priests were known as druids. We know very little about the Celtic religion because it was ruthlessly put down by the Romans. We know that the Celts worshipped many different gods and goddesses, and they probably had a form of nature worship.

The druids were responsible for religious rituals. These rituals were never written down, but they were preserved by word of mouth and in songs and poetry.

▲ We know little about the druid religion, due to Roman intolerance.

Celtic warriors

The Celts were very lightly armed warriors who did not use armour. In fact, sometimes they fought naked, using large swords, spears, slingshots, and bows and arrows. The Celts did not fight according to any battle plan, but relied on mass charges, which were easily stopped by the well-disciplined Roman troops. Celts decided some battles by single combat between champions from each army.

? Who was Boudicca?

Boudicca (Boadicea) was the queen of the Iceni, a tribe of Celts living in eastern England. Her husband was a governor, who worked with the Romans. After his death the Romans tried to take control. Boudicca led a rebellion, which sacked the towns of Colchester and London, until the Roman armies marched against her. The Romans defeated the Iceni and their Celtic allies. Boudicca poisoned herself to avoid capture.

? What happened when the Romans conquered the Celts?

After fierce battles with the Romans, the defeated Celts in Gaul (modern France) soon adapted to the Roman way of life. They lived in villas and began to intermarry with their Roman occupiers. The Celts were highly skilled metal smiths and jewelers, as well as being poets and musicians. The Romans recorded details of Celtic life and culture.

Some of the Celts never accepted Roman rule in Britain. Instead they fled to isolated parts of Wales and Scotland, where they were never conquered. However, the Romano-British carried on a Roman way of life even after the Roman armies had withdrawn back to continental Europe.

▼ Boudicca was the queen of a tribe of Celts who led a successful revolt against Roman rule. She fought from a chariot, and the Romans had to develop special tactics to combat these fast-moving warriors.

❓ Who was Confucius?

Confucius was an ancient Chinese philosopher who taught the need for moral responsibility and virtue. His teachings did not make much impact during his life, but they later became the central part of Chinese moral and religious thinking. Confucius probably lived from 551 to 479BC, in the time of the Zhou dynasty. The Zhou was the longest-lasting group of Chinese rulers, who governed the country from 1122 to 256BC. Confucianism was probably the most important feature in Chinese life until the appearance of Communism in the 20th century. Confucianism resembles a religion, but instead of worshipping gods it is a guide to morality and good government.

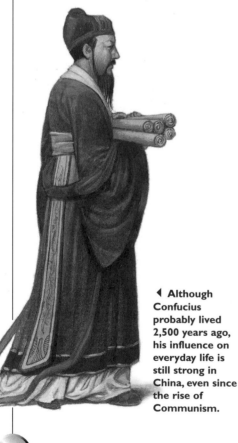

◀ **Although Confucius probably lived 2,500 years ago, his influence on everyday life is still strong in China, even since the rise of Communism.**

❓ Who were the Persians?

Persia was a great empire that was ruled from the region we now call Iran. The Medes and the Persians were descended from Aryan invaders who occupied the territory almost 3,000 years ago. The Persians, however, soon seized power. The modern name of Iran comes from an Aryan word meaning "land of the Aryans".

The Persian emperor Cyrus built a huge empire by conquering all the neighboring states, extending into Pakistan, Turkey, Libya and Egypt and northwards into parts of modern Russia. Cyrus and his successor, Darius I, set up a highly organized form of government, with local rulers, formal taxation and road building. The Persian Empire reached its greatest size in 500BC. It was eventually conquered by the Macedonian general Alexander the Great in 331BC.

❓ What were the Olympic Games?

The Olympic Games started as one of the religious festivals held in ancient Greece in honour of Zeus, the leader of the gods. The festival was held at Olympia, home of the gods, every four years.

The first games probably began around 1200BC, but the organized Olympic Games, which featured sports such as running and wrestling, began in 776BC. The games

Greek gods

The Greeks believed in a complicated family of gods and goddesses. Each one was believed to have a particular role in heaven. Aphrodite, for example, was the goddess of love, while Artemis was the goddess of hunting.

The Greek religion was not based on formal written rules, so there were considerable local variations in what people believed and how they worshipped their gods. Some of the gods were borrowed or 'captured' from other cultures, for example Dionysus, the Greek god of wine, who originated in Thrace. The one common element in all Greek religion was the ritual of sacrificing animals to their gods.

continued until AD393 when the ruling Romans banned them. They were revived during the 1800s after archaeological finds renewed interest in Greek culture. The first of the modern Olympic Games were held in 1896 in Athens, Greece.

The modern Olympic games are split into winter and summer events. Since 1994, the Winter and Summer Games have been

▲ The ancient Greeks respected learning, and the works of their philosophers were influential for hundreds of years. Socrates (469–399 B.C.) was one of the most important of these early philosophers. He encouraged people to think about good and evil. Some people did not approve of his ideas, and he was forced to commit suicide.

divided and scheduled on four year cycles, two years apart.

How did the ancient Greeks encourage scientific thinking?

Most early peoples were interested in the things and events around them, but the ancient Greeks took their thinking a lot further. They used reason and deduction make decisions about the meaning of the world, placing great importance on learning, music, and writing. The ancient Greeks developed philosophy as a way of thinking about life and the world we live in, and they also developed the rules of mathematics that are still used today.

The ancient Greeks also developed their own system of medicine that persisted for 1,500 years or more. The Greeks were only interested in thinking about such things. They seldom experimented to see if their

theories were correct.

Who was Alexander the Great?

Alexander was a king of Macedonia, a poor country that needed to expand in order to survive. Although he was only 20 when he became king, Alexander rapidly conquered Greece. He then led his armies against the mighty Persian Empire, and within three years he had conquered it too. He now ruled an empire extending from Egypt and the Mediterranean coast all the way into India.

Alexander developed various methods of warfare, such as siege engines, which were to be used for hundreds of years. He introduced Greek methods of thinking and religion into his empire, and divided it into a series of small kingdoms under his own authority. He was only 32 when he died at Alexandria, in Egypt.

Who were the Phoenicians?

Although their empire was not huge, the Phoenicians had a great influence on life around the Mediterranean. They were skilled seafarers and were also merchants and even raiders at times.

The Phoenicians lived in the eastern Mediterranean, in what are now parts of modern Israel, Lebanon, and Syria. The name 'Phoenician' comes from a purple dye that they produced from a sea snail, which was in great demand. The Phoenicians traded all along the Mediterranean coast, down the Atlantic coast of Africa, and as far

north as Britain where they traded for tin.

Who made the terracotta warriors?

In China, the powerful Qin dynasty came to power in the 3rd century B.C. They swiftly conquered their neighbors to make a large empire covering most of modern China. The Qin emperor Shi Huangdi standardized weights and measures and introduced a single form of currency. He is best remembered for his construction of the Great Wall of China, which stretches for 1,400 miles across the north of China. It was built to prevent raids from nomadic people in the north. When the emperor died, a huge tomb was built to hold his body. It was filled with a guardian army of thousands of life-sized terracotta (pottery) warriors. After

▲ The world was astonished when Chinese archaeologists began to uncover a huge army of life-sized warriors around the tomb of the emperor Shi Huangdi. Each figure was individually modeled.

⚲ How was Rome founded?

According to legend, Rome was founded in 753 B.C. by twin brothers called Romulus and Remus, who had been raised by a she-wolf. By 509 B.C. the original Etruscan inhabitants of Rome had been driven out, and by 275 B.C. Rome controlled most of Italy. The Phoenicians were great rivals of Rome, and they were finally defeated by the Romans in the Punic Wars (264-146 B.C.). After this, the Romans were able to extend their empire with little organized resistance.

▼ At its greatest, in the A.D. 100s, the Roman Empire covered half of Europe, much of the Middle East, and the north coast of Africa.

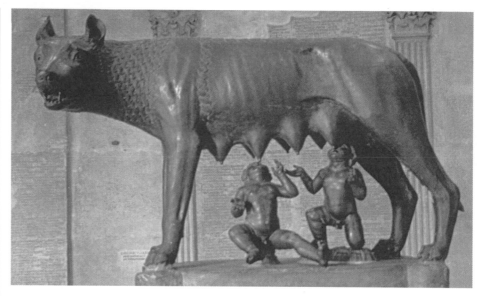

▲ Rome was said to have been founded by the twin brothers, Romulus and Remus. The babies were raised by a she-wolf, having been abandoned by their uncle on the banks of the River Tiber. They were eventually rescued by a shepherd.

⚲ How far did Roman rule extend?

At its peak, the Roman Empire extended all around the Mediterranean — into Syria, Israel, parts of Turkey, most of Europe, and the Balkan regions. A huge army was needed to maintain control over these regions, and the costs were tremendous. There were continual minor wars and skirmishes along the edges of the Empire, which meant that large garrisons of soldiers had to be maintained.

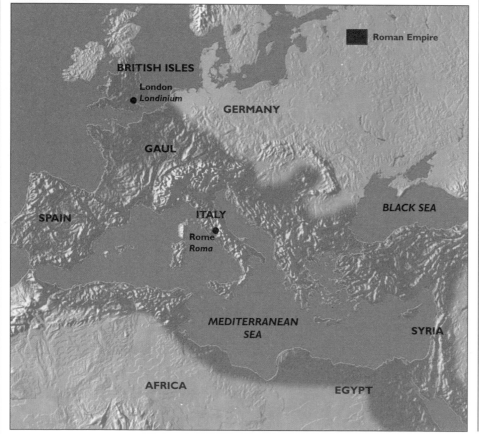

▶ The disciplined Roman armies developed special weapons and techniques to overcome the tribes they encountered as the empire expanded. This 'tortoise' formation proved impregnable against their Celtic foes.

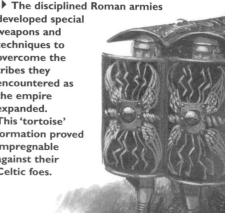

▶ After the Romans had conquered most of Britain, the northern tribes continued to raid into Roman territory. Hadrian's Wall was built across from the east to the west coasts in an attempt to keep them out of the occupied areas.

⍰ Why was the Roman army so successful?

The Roman army invented a method of warfare that persisted for 2,000 years. Its troops were rigorously trained and exercised, and divided into small detachments under the control of officers. Roman soldiers wore effective armor, and developed tactics that allowed them to fight successfully against almost any enemy. In particular, the Roman soldiers were very effective at defense. They closed ranks and protected themselves with large shields, which deflected arrows and spears, until they reached close quarters and could use their own weapons.

Paved roads were constructed to allow the Roman armies to move very quickly to any region where trouble flared up. A network of local forts and garrisons made sure that soldiers were always available.

⍰ Did the Romans conquer the whole of Britain?

The Romans gradually conquered the whole of England and Wales, partly through battle and partly by making political arrangements with some of the Celtic chieftains. When the Romans reached the north of England, however, they stopped. The Picts from Scotland fought the Romans fiercely, raiding their farms and garrisons. The Roman lines were over-extended and it was difficult to supply troops so far north. The soldiers were mostly from warm Mediterranean countries, and they found the cold, wet northern climate of northern England difficult to adapt to.

The Romans built Hadrian's Wall to keep the Picts out of the occupied territory. This huge structure stretched from east to west across northern Britain. The wall was garrisoned by soldiers and supported by a string of military forts.

⍰ Why did the Romans abandon most of their empire?

In the first few centuries A.D., it became clear that the Roman Empire was far too big and unwieldy to survive in its original form. A huge civil service and army were needed to maintain the empire, and these became extremely expensive.

In addition, there were numerous rebellions in different parts of the empire, mostly headed by army commanders with designs on becoming emperor. Eventually, in A.D. 284, Emperor Diocletian broke the Roman Empire into smaller self-governing units, each with its own army. The whole empire was split into two sections: Eastern and Western. The decline of the empire halted for a while, but soon the fighting resumed. Eventually the Roman Empire was weakened to such an extent that it was successfully attacked and overrun by invading barbarians.

⊙ How were the Romans prepared for Christianity?

The Greeks had occupied Palestine for many years. After a brief period of independence, it was conquered by the Romans. The Jews bitterly resented Roman rule and particularly disliked the heavy taxes that they imposed. In the middle of this general unrest and rebellion, prophets predicted the arrival of a Messiah who would lead the Jewish people to freedom.

⊙ What are the Dead Sea Scrolls?

The Dead Sea Scrolls are religious writings that were first discovered in 1947, hidden in caves near the Dead Sea. The dry atmosphere of the caves had the effect of preserving the scrolls. About 800 scrolls have been found, mostly in a place called Qumran in Israel. They date from between 150 B.C. and A.D. 68, and they include all of the books of the Old Testament, or Hebrew Bible, except for Esther.

Scholars believe that the scrolls were concealed by members of a religious sect called the Essenes, who lived in the isolated community. They hid the scrolls to keep them safe during political unrest in the area, where they remained hidden for hundreds of years.

▶ **This is the museum in Jerusalem where some of the Dead Sea Scrolls are housed. They appear to date from around the time of Jesus and were probably compiled by a religious sect.**

▲ **The Sermon on the Mount is one of the most important aspects of Christianity. The Romans tolerated most religions but were not interested in Christianity until it appeared to threaten their rule.**

⊙ Who was Jesus?

Jesus arrived in Israel when the anti-Roman feeling was at a peak, so his teachings were widely accepted. Jesus' followers believed that he was the promised Messiah. However, other Jews thought that he was a blasphemer and encouraged the Romans to condemn him. The Romans did not seem too concerned about Jesus, and there are no references to him in the surviving official records of the time.

Death by crucifixion was a common fate for many people whom the Romans regarded as troublemakers. This form of punishment was often handed out to anyone who caused unrest, for example, when Jesus preached to large crowds.

Secret symbol

The symbol of a fish was used by the early Christians in Rome as a secret symbol to identify themselves to other Christians. The symbol was simple and quick to draw with two strokes of a piece of chalk. It was not likely to be noticed by the Romans.

Why did the Romans persecute the Christians?

The teachings of Jesus were spread widely by his followers after his death. At first, the Christians were ignored by the Romans, especially since they did not join in the Jewish rebellion against Roman rule in A.D. 66. However, the early Christians began to travel around the Roman Empire, and when they reached Rome, they began to recruit new followers. The Roman authorities became concerned that this new religion would threaten the established order.

The Romans did not object to the new religion itself, but they did object to the fact that it denied the emperor's divinity. The new religion appealed to the poor and to slaves, and its popularity was seen as a threat to Roman society.

Why did the Roman Empire split in two?

Emperor Diocletian thought that the Empire was too big to be ruled by one person. In A.D. 284 he split the empire in two, appointing Maximian to rule the western part.

Who was the Emperor Constantine?

Constantine was the first Roman emperor to adopt Christianity. His predecessor Diocletian had persecuted Christians, but after his conversion to Christianity in A.D. 312, Constantine encouraged the new religion. He eventually made it the official religion of the Eastern Roman Empire.

By A.D. 330 Constantine decided to make Byzantium the capital of the Eastern Empire, renaming it Constantinople. It is now known as Istanbul, in Turkey. The Eastern Empire grew in power as the Western Empire became weaker.

Who were the barbarians?

Many groups of nomadic barbarians attacked the Roman Empire, and they eventually destroyed the Western Empire. Most of these tribes migrated from the east. They were fierce warriors who were despised by the Romans.

Goths, Vandals, Huns, and many other tribes attacked the Roman Empire from A.D. 167 onward. The Western Empire finally collapsed completely after Rome had been looted for the second time, in A.D. 455. The barbarians killed the last Roman emperor in A.D. 476. They set up several smaller kingdoms, based loosely on the Roman model. They failed to conquer the Eastern Empire, and for a short while, Emperor Justinian pushed the barbarians back from much of their occupied territory.

Who was Attila the Hun?

Attila was the ruler of the Hun kingdom, in what is now Hungary. The Huns began to expand beyond this area, conquering surrounding countries until they controlled a region from the Rhine to the Caspian Sea, extending all the way to the Baltic. From A.D. 435 to 439, Attila's forces attacked barbarians throughout Europe. He forced the Eastern Roman Empire to pay him a fee in exchange for not attacking them.

Attila demanded to marry the sister of the emperor of the Western Empire, with half the empire as a dowry. When his request was refused, Attila invaded Gaul, was stopped, and then invaded Italy. Eventually his conquest petered out as the Huns were gradually absorbed into the peoples they had conquered.

▲ The Huns were among the fiercest of the many barbarian tribes who eventually destroyed the power of the Roman Empire. Attila, who is still renowned for his cruelty and the ferocity of his troops, led the Huns from their homeland in modern Hungary and almost conquered Europe.

ⓘ Who was Muhammed?

Muhammed was a prophet whose teachings form the basis of the Islamic religion. He was born in Mecca, in Saudi Arabia, around A.D. 570. People throughout this region worshipped many gods, but Muhammed was influenced by the Christian and Jewish view of one god.

Muhammed had a vision in which the archangel Gabriel instructed him to proclaim that Allah was the one true god. When Muhammed started teaching in Mecca, people felt that he was threatening their religion. He fled to Medina, where he built the first mosque. Muhammed's growing influence led the people of Mecca to attack Medina, but they were defeated. In A.D. 630 Muhammed entered Mecca, destroyed the pagan idols and established the city as the center of Islam.

ⓘ What is the Koran?

The Koran is the holy book of the Islamic religion. It contains the words of Allah as revealed to Muhammed by the archangel Gabriel in a series of visions. The Koran is a series of verses describing the ways in which Muslims should conduct their lives. It specifies daily prayers and emphasizes the need for brotherly love and charity between Muslims. The Koran describes Abraham, Moses and Jesus as prophets, and Muhammed as the final prophet before the day of judgement when all people will have to account to Allah for their former lives.

Muslims do not worship Muhammed, but show him the greatest respect. They believe that the Koran is the word of Allah and was not composed by Muhammed.

▼ The Koran is the holy book of the Islamic religion. It contains the revelations given by the archangel Gabriel to the prophet Muhammed.

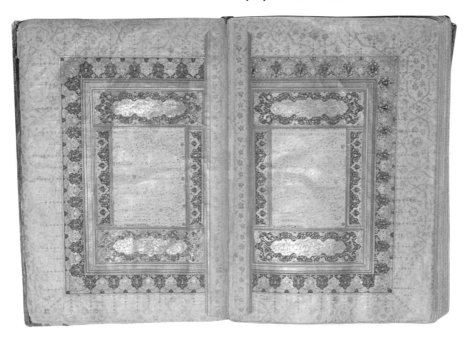

▲ Tales from *Arabian Nights* are still popular today.

ⓘ What is *Arabian Nights?*

This famous story is set in the court in Baghdad, where a king was said to have killed his wives, one after the other, the day after he married them. One of these wives, called Scheherazade, told the king such fascinating stories that he never killed her.

The setting for this story was the court of the caliph of the Abbasid Empire, which dominated the Islamic world from A.D. 750 to 1258. The Abbasids traced their ancestry back to the uncle of the prophet Muhammed. Haroun al-Rashid was the most famous caliph. As well as being a great general and politician, Haroun al-Rashid encouraged the development of arts and learning in Baghdad.

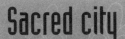

Sacred city

Mecca is the sacred city of the Islamic world. It is situated in western Saudi Arabia, in a dry and desolate region. The city is closed to all non-believers, and each year millions of Muslims visit Mecca in a pilgrimage called the Hajj. All Muslims are required to make this pilgrimage at least once in their lifetime if they are able. Mecca was the point from which Arab expansion began during the 7th century A.D.

What is the Kaaba?

The Kaaba is the sacred shrine at the center of Mecca. It is a cube-shaped building, and in its eastern corner is embedded the Black Stone. According to Islamic belief, this was given to Abraham by the archangel Gabriel. All Muslims must face the Kaaba when they pray, and it is the center of the religious pilgrimage to Mecca. Pilgrims must move around it seven times while praying and reciting from the Koran before finally touching or kissing the Black Stone.

What happened when Islam met the Roman Empire?

The Muslims began to spread the Islamic religion after Muhammed's death in A.D. 632. They moved northwards against the Byzantine (Eastern Roman) Empire and its immediate neighbors.

Soon, the Byzantines, already weakened by warfare with their neighbors, were driven out of Syria and Palestine, and the Arab armies drove them steadily back. The Muslims moved eastwards and captured Persia. They continued on into Afghanistan and India, which they reached at the beginning of the 8th century.

Other Muslim armies captured Egypt and the rest of North Africa. In A.D. 711, they invaded Spain and pressed on into France. Here they were finally stopped by the Franks in a great battle at Poitiers, preventing the Muslim conquest of the rest of Europe.

▼ The Kaaba is a cubical building in Mecca that is the center of the annual Hajj pilgrimage, when it is circled by thousands of pilgrims.

What did Islam bring to Europe?

The Arabs joined with the Moors to conquer Spain during the 6th century. These Muslims had a more advanced culture than was found in medieval Europe, which was occupied by descendants of the barbarians who had destroyed the Roman Empire. The Moors in Spain introduced many discoveries in mathematics, medicine, and science. They had preserved many of the writings of the ancient Greek, Roman, and Middle Eastern civilizations that were captured during the Islamic victories over the Byzantines. In Spain, where Moors and Europeans lived together in an uneasy peace, these writings reached the European scholars. In addition to this learning, the Moors introduced concepts such as cleanliness and hygiene, which had been forgotten since Roman times.

What happened to the Byzantine Empire?

The Byzantine (Eastern) Empire had been under continual attack from barbarians for many years. The Islamic forces rapidly conquered most of the outlying areas of the empire, and by A.D. 1000 it had begun its final collapse. The Muslim Turks gradually drove the Byzantines out of the Middle East and entered Turkey. By 1300 all that remained of the Byzantine Empire were Constantinople and parts of Greece. In 1453, the Ottoman Turks captured Constantinople, ending the final remains of a great empire.

❓ What were the Dark Ages?

This term refers to the Middle Ages, from the 3rd to the 10th centuries, when most of the knowledge and influences of the Roman Empire were lost. The Western Roman Empire had declined in power and was continually being overrun by warring barbarians. The Byzantine Empire preserved much of the Roman learning but was effectively cut off from the rest of Europe. Learning survived in the West only in monasteries and religious institutions. The sceptical Romans had clearly distinguished myth from fact, but in the uneducated world of the Dark Ages, myths and stories were plentiful. Life became far more primitive. By A.D.1000, the situation had begun to improve, and the beginnings of a more sophisticated society could be seen.

❓ Who were the Saxons?

The Saxons were Germanic people who invaded Britain about 1,500 years ago, after the departure of the Romans, who withdrew into continental Europe. The Saxons were followed by the Angles and the Jutes, who settled mainly in southeast England. The Angles gave their name to England, although they were not the largest group of invaders. Most of the invaders were farmers seeking new land. They abandoned the Roman style of farms and set up their own communities.

❓ Was England one nation in Saxon times?

The Saxons and their fellow invaders divided Britain up into seven kingdoms. However, the peoples of these kingdoms were continually quarreling and fighting over which local king could claim authority over the whole of England.

❓ Did King Arthur really exist?

Although there is little real evidence for his existence, Arthur probably did live in the 6th century. He is thought to have been a Romano-British chieftain who fought several successful battles against the invading Saxons. Despite Arthur's successes, the British were eventually defeated. Arthur remained a heroic figure of legend, and his story was recounted throughout Europe. The stories of the Holy Grail, the Round Table, and the quests of Arthur's knights are later additions to the myth.

▲ Arthur is a semi-mythical figure, who was probably a local chieftain, who led the Roman-British against the invading Saxons. Most of the stories about Arthur and his knights were added much later.

Great gods

Religion was important to the Vikings. Their most important gods were Odin, Thor, and Frey. Odin, or Woden, the god of battle, was the leader of the Norse gods, who lived in a place called Valhalla. The Vikings believed that if they died fighting, they would join the gods in Valhalla for eternity. Thor was the sky god who controlled lightning and storms. He was very important because of the long voyages made by Viking ships. Frey was the god of agriculture.

❓ What happened to the Celts?

As the invading Germanic people pushed north and west into England, the Romano-British descendants of the Celts retreated into Scotland, Wales, and Ireland. However, many of the Celtic descendants intermarried with the invaders and were absorbed by them. The Britons held out for a while under a chieftain who may have been the legendary Arthur. Eventually, they held only the mountain areas of Wales and Scotland, while many escaped to Ireland. Ireland preserved an entirely Celtic way of life since it had not been subjected to constant invasions and conquests.

⁇ Who were the Vikings?

During the 8th century, the Viking people began to leave their homes in Scandinavia and explore Europe in search of treasure and places to settle. The first Vikings appeared in Britain in A.D. 789. They came as raiders along the coast and then settled in the northeast of Britain. They also invaded Ireland and Normandy. Other Vikings traveled into Russia and as far as Constantinople, trading and selling their services as mercenaries.

In Britain, the Vikings were finally defeated by Alfred, the Saxon king of Wessex. He forced the invaders to sign a treaty agreeing to live only in the northeast of Britain. This treaty was known as the Danelaw. Britain was finally united as a single kingdom after A.D. 954, when the last Viking king died.

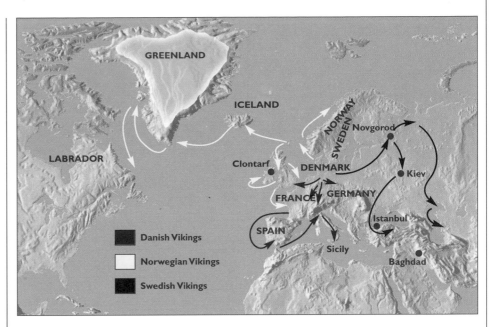

▲ Viking trade routes took them throughout Europe and beyond. The Vikings traveled as far east as Baghdad and Istanbul, and as far west as Greenland and Canada.

▼ The Viking invaders are remembered as ruthless raiders, but they settled in many of the countries they attacked, such as Ireland and northern Britain.

⁇ How far did the Vikings travel?

At a time when sailors dared not venture far from the coasts, the Vikings boldly sailed out far across the Atlantic in their small open longships. Wherever Vikings landed, they mingled with local people, and they began to set up colonies in Iceland and Greenland, and sailed on to North America. Leif Ericson named this country Vinland, and a colony was set up there in A.D. 1003. Traces of Viking settlements have also been found in Maine, in the United States, and in Newfoundland in Canada. However, these colonies soon vanished, together with the colony in Greenland. Other Vikings traveled around the Mediterranean, and when in Byzantium they even traded for goods from China.

The Viking religion eventually died out after contact with Christian missionaries in the 12th century.

? Who were the Normans?

The Normans were the descendants of Vikings who settled in northern France and adopted French customs and the French language. Vikings had also settled in southern Italy and on the island of Sicily, where they established kingdoms. They soon adopted the Christian religion.

? What is the Bayeux tapestry?

The Bayeux tapestry was made by the Normans to celebrate their victory over the English in 1066. It is a huge series of pictures depicting incidents during the conquest. The pictures are sewn on a strip of cloth 230 feet in length. At one time, the tapestry was even longer, but a section of it is now missing.

? Why did the Normans win the Battle of Hastings?

The Normans won the battle because the English armies were exhausted from previous fighting and were too far away to stop the invasion. After the death of Edward the Confessor, Harold Godwinsson was appointed king of England. However, Harald Hardrada of Norway also claimed the English crown and invaded northern England. He was defeated by the army of Harold Godwinsson near York.

Three days later, the Normans invaded at Hastings in the south. The English army was forced to dash the length of England in order to fight the invaders. Exhausted when they arrived, they were soon defeated. King Harold was killed during the battle and was succeeded by the Norman king William the First, or William the Conqueror.

Knights in shining armor

Knights were soldiers in the service of a Norman lord. Most knights received land from their lord in order to provide them with a form of income. They owed their loyalty to their lord and had to fight for him whenever asked. This meant that knights were called upon in times of unrest. The period when knighthood developed is sometimes called the age of chivalry. This is because a strict code of behavior for knights was put into practice.

▼ The Bayeux tapestry records the Norman victory over the Saxon King Harold, who is shown here receiving the fatal arrow in his eye.

How did the Normans change British society?

The Normans introduced the feudal system to England. According to this system, the king owned all the land and others could hold land in exchange for providing services to the king. William the Conqueror appointed barons who were provided with estates taken from the original English earls. In return, the barons paid him taxes and supplied soldiers for his armies.

The barons, in turn, let their knights hold smaller sections of land, while the knights let part of this land to people called villeins. They were farmers who had to provide some of their produce to the local lord of the manor. In this way, the land and the whole of English society was broken into small, easily controlled units.

What were tournaments?

Fighting was a matter of honour for knights. When there was no obvious reason to fight, the knights had to invent one. Tournaments were contests in which knights fought each other with various weapons. They wore heavy armor that was supposed to prevent injury, but they were frequently maimed or killed.

Tournaments were popular events at which heavy bets were placed on favorite knights. They served as a useful form of training for real warfare.

▲ Conwy castle, in north Wales, is typical of the castles built by the Normans. It was built to give defending archers an uninterrupted field of fire against any attackers, and could withstand a long siege.

How did the Norman invasion change the English language?

Up until the Norman invasion, people in England spoke in Old English. The Normans spoke a form of French, and they insisted on the use of French as the language of educated people. Most of the ruling classes spoke nothing else but French.

Over the years the languages spoken by the common people and the nobility became closer, until an entirely new language evolved. Modern English, which is descended from this mixture, still contains the recognizable remains of Saxon and French words. For example, the word "cow" is descended from the Saxon word, while the word "beef" is related to the French word.

What was the Domesday Book?

Once the Normans had secured their hold over their new territory, they wanted to know exactly what it was worth. In 1085, King William commissioned a great survey of his whole kingdom. It would list every town, village and farm, who owned what, and how much each holding was worth, so that taxes could be applied. All this information was written down in the Domesday Book. This book is still in existence today.

▲ One of the first acts of the conquering Normans was to make an inventory of their new lands. They recorded the details and value of every piece of land, each farm and every village in the Domesday Book.

⏺ What happened to the Western Roman Empire?

Following the division of the Roman Empire into two parts, the Byzantine, or Eastern, Empire flourished for centuries. The Western Empire was raided repeatedly by invading barbarians and finally collapsed in A.D. 76. One group of invaders, the Franks, settled in what is now central France. The Frankish king Charlemagne conquered France and extended his rule into Italy, Germany, and the Netherlands. He forced his subjects to accept Christianity. In A.D. 800 the pope rewarded him by appointing him Holy Roman Emperor.

Charlemagne's capital in Aix la Chapelle (modern Aachen, in Germany) was an important center of learning. After his death, the empire was again torn by war. The Holy Roman Empire, based in Germany, survived from A.D. 962 to 1806.

⏺ Who was the real ruler?

By the 10th century A.D., the power of the pope throughout Europe was absolute. The Holy Roman Emperor supposedly controlled all of Western Europe. However, when it came to disagreement, the pope had the final say because he could excommunicate the emperor or any king who opposed his wishes. Excommunication was punishment of the highest degree.

The church controlled huge areas of land and became very rich, which antagonized many rulers. The nobles who had control over local areas were often divided in their loyalties, sometimes supporting their king or the emperor, and on other occasions siding with the pope if it suited them. The common people were rarely involved or even aware of these disputes, because their immediate problems were how to feed themselves and survive.

⏺ What were the Crusades?

Christians throughout Europe were shocked when the Arabs captured Jerusalem during the Middle Ages. In 1095, the pope of the Roman Catholic Church called for a series of crusades to recapture the Holy Land, believing that they would unite Europe's warring kings and knights. The first was the Peasants' Crusade, whose members were untrained and poorly armed. The crusaders did not reach beyond Turkey, where they were all killed.

Later crusades were better organized, but many crusaders were more interested in power and riches for themselves than in any religious purpose. By 1099, the conquering crusaders reached Jerusalem. The need for travel to the Holy Land led to improved ships, the development of maps and compasses, and international trade throughout the Mediterranean.

◀ The Arab conquest of the Holy Land led to a series of Crusades in which European troops made the long journey to try to recover the territory for the Christian Church. After limited successes, all of the Crusades ultimately failed.

▲ The Vatican, in the heart of Rome, is the center of the Roman Catholic Church and the home of the pope. Technically, it is an independent state, separate from Italy.

⍰ Have there ever been two popes?

The power of the popes rivalled that of kings in Western Europe. Kings became involved in religious affairs, and popes played a part in politics. Some popes gave way entirely to kings and surrendered their authority completely.

In 1309, a French pope decided to base the Church in Avignon, in France, where it remained until 1377. Meanwhile, French kings had managed to persuade the Church to support them. However, in 1378, the cardinals were unable to agree about the election of a new pope. Two rival popes declared themselves as official heads of the Church, and for a while there was also a third pope. This odd situation continued until 1417, when a single pope was elected and based in Rome once again.

⍰ How did Christianity influence life in the Middle Ages?

The Church controlled almost all aspects of life. Kings usually took their instructions from bishops, under the threat of excommunication if they disobeyed. Bishops were immensely powerful people, controlling monasteries, churches, and huge areas of land. Because poverty and humility

Wicked witches

The belief in witchcraft in the Middle Ages probably resulted from the religious conflicts that raged throughout Europe. Any disease or misfortune was conveniently blamed on the devil. The courts that tried alleged witches were biased so that 'not guilty' verdicts were almost unknown. One explanation for the spread of this belief in witches was that the accusers usually obtained part of the estate of a condemned witch. They had every reason to accuse any person they disliked.

Diseases such as the Black Death increased the level of fear and hysteria. A few elderly women probably practised herbal medicine and could loosely be called witches. However, almost all the thousands of people who were tortured to death for witchcraft were innocent.

were to be admired, the Church was able to extract heavy taxes from the peasantry. At the same time, richer nobles gave money to the Church, believing this would ensure better treatment in the afterlife.

The Church was the only source of learning. Monasteries produced many books by hand copying before the development of modern printing. The language of learning and of religion was Latin, which made education inaccessible to ordinary people.

⍰ What was the Holy Inquisition?

The Inquisition was an organization set up by the Church to prevent any opposition to its teaching. The Church feared the influence of heretics - people who placed a different interpretation on the Bible and its teachings. These people often caused trouble and unrest in the population. Heresy was declared an offence in A.D. 392.

In the 12th and 13th centuries, several new heresies appeared that threatened the existence of the established Church. In 1231, Pope Gregory created the Inquisition to find and punish those who believed in these heresies. It worked mostly in France, Spain, and Germany, destroying several popular religious movements. Heretics who refused to change their religious beliefs were usually burned alive. After stamping out all resistance, the Inquisition turned its attention to Protestants who had also begun to challenge the traditional teachings of the church.

Mongol Conquests

Who was Genghis Khan?

Genghis Khan was a Mongol warrior whose conquests built the greatest land empire in history. His empire was huge, stretching across central Asia from the Sea of Japan to the Caspian Sea, and occupying most of modern Russia. At various times, this empire included China, Korea, Turkestan, Armenia, and Mongolia, as well as parts of Thailand, Vietnam, and Burma.

Genghis Khan began life in the plains of Mongolia. He gradually began to build up groups of formerly isolated Mongol tribes until he became the sole ruler of Mongolia. The Mongols attacked China under the leadership of Ghengis Khan, and by 1215 they had taken control of the capital, Beijing. Then Genghis Khan and his Mongol forces swept their way westward through Asia, until they reached the Caspian Sea.

▶ The Mongols were feared for the ferocity of their unpredictable attacks on cities throughout Asia and the Middle East. Genghis Khan unified the scattered Mongol tribes and began the conquest that resulted in the Mongols controlling nearly all of Asia and threatening to destroy Europe.

Why were the Mongols so successful?

The Mongols were able to succeed against established armies because they were unpredictable. Armies drew up in battle order and fought in daylight, according to the rules of war. The Mongols, however, were very different. They charged into battle on horseback, relying entirely on speed and surprise and taking no prisoners. Their skill as mounted archers made it difficult for foot soldiers to defend themselves.

Most cities surrendered immediately, rather than risk being massacred.

▲ The Mongols never settled permanently, but lived in tent-like prefabricated homes called yurts, which they carried with them during their migrations and invasions.

What were the Mongols' homes like?

The Mongols lived in large circular tents called yurts. These yurts are still used today. They are made of felt, which is fastened over a light wooden frame. The whole structure can be quickly dismantled and carried by horses as the Mongol tribes migrate across the steppes, or grassy plains, following their grazing flocks.

Who was Kublai Khan?

Kublai Khan was the grandson of Genghis Khan, who completed the conquest of China. His rule was less severe than that of other Mongol rulers, and he permitted the established religions to continue. Under Kublai Khan, many Mongols in the Middle East adopted the Muslim faith. After his death, the enormous Mongol Empire proved too big to govern, and it began to break up into smaller empires.

? Who was Marco Polo?

Marco Polo was one of the first Europeans to travel through the Mongol territories. He traveled overland from Italy to China, where he was welcomed by Kublai Khan. He asked Marco Polo to arrange to have Christian missionaries sent to China. On his return to Europe, Polo's reports raised enormous interest in China and led to many new sea voyages in attempts to establish trade routes there.

Fearless fighters

The Mongols were known as fearless and remorseless fighters. They developed fighting machines and techniques that enabled them to break into the cities they besieged. The Mongols were merciless towards those people who resisted them, and sometimes they slaughtered entire populations.

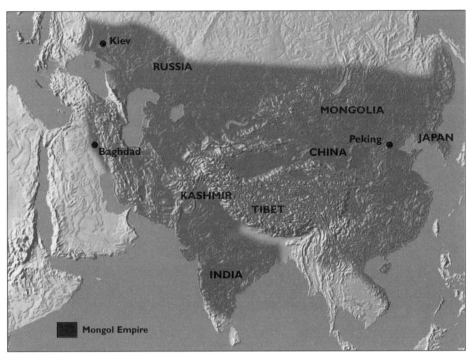

▲ At various times, the Mongol Empire included China, Korea, Mongolia, India, and parts of Russia.

◀ Although for centuries trade goods had been sent from China to Europe, Marco Polo was the first European to travel back to the East, where he met Kublai Khan.

? Did the Mongols occupy parts of Europe?

After the death of their leader, Genghis Khan, the Mongol armies continued their advance westward under his son, Ogotai. In 1241, 150,000 Mongol horsemen destroyed much of Poland and Hungary, causing widespread panic throughout Europe. However, Ogotai died in the middle of the campaign, and the Mongols returned to Mongolia to elect a new leader. Fortunately for the rest of Europe, they did not return to wreak havoc.

? What was the Golden Horde?

The Golden Horde was the name given to the eastern part of the Mongol Empire, which included most of Russia, from the 13th to the 14th centuries. The Horde governed most of European Russia, Siberia, and the lands down to the borders of Iran. The Horde included both Mongols and Turks, and adopted Islam as their religion. They carried on with their traditional lifestyle while collecting tribute from the original occupiers of the lands they conquered. They were weakened by the Black Death in 1346 and 1347. They continued to decline in power until they were broken by counterattacks by the Russians and eventually by the Mongol ruler Tamurlane. Their last foothold in the Crimea was destroyed in 1502.

Family war

The two branches of England's Plantagenet family battled for the throne in the Wars of the Roses. The name comes from the red rose of Lancaster and the white rose of York. When Henry VI of Lancaster became mentally ill, his cousin, Richard of York, ruled on his behalf. When Henry recovered, war broke out between the York and Lancaster supporters. Richard was killed, but his son became Edward IV.

Edward died a few years later and was succeeded by his young son, Edward V. However, the boy's uncle Richard seized the throne. Henry Tudor, the last Lancastrian claimant to the throne, killed Richard, becoming Henry VII. The warfare ended when Henry married Elizabeth of York.

What was the Hundred Years' War?

The Hundred Years' War began in 1337 and continued for more that a century. It was not a single war, but rather a series of skirmishes between France and England. It began when the English tried to dominate France, and the French in turn tried to confiscate lands occupied by the English.

The English invaded France and won a great battle at Crécy. The British archers with their longbows defeated a much larger army of knights, marking the beginning of the end for mounted knights. Further battles followed, but in 1396, Richard II of England married the daughter of Charles VI of France, establishing a 20-year truce that finally ended the fighting.

▲ England and France fought over French territory which was occupied by the English for more than a century. Even after the end of the Hundred Years War, occasional fighting continued until the English were finally expelled from France.

Who was the Black Prince?

The Black Prince was Edward, the son of Edward III, whose quarrel with the French started the Hundred Years War. His name came from the black armor he wore in battle. The Black Prince won a major battle at Poitiers, in 1356, capturing the French king, John II. As a result of this, the English were able to negotiate their possession of large territories in France. They soon lost these again in further fighting, and by the end of the Hundred Years War in 1453, they had lost all French territory except Calais.

What was the Black Death?

The Black Death was an epidemic that permanently changed the face of medieval Europe. It killed more than one-quarter of the population, causing thousands of villages to be abandoned and subsequently to disappear.

The Black Death probably arrived in Europe from Central Asia by way of Mongol raiders. It first caused epidemics in Italy in 1347, spreading rapidly through the rest of Europe. The disease was spread by the bite of fleas from infected rats, but because its cause was not understood, the infection raged unchecked. The resulting fear led to a great wave of religious hysteria. A shortage of manual workers led to the collapse of the long-established feudal system.

▼ The worst epidemic to strike Europe began in 1347 with the first outbreaks of plague and led to the Black Death. This epidemic depopulated much of Europe.

What was the Poll Tax?

The Poll Tax was one of the factors that led to a peasant revolt in England. At the same time, similar revolts took place in other parts of Europe. The Poll Tax was introduced in England in 1381, and amounted to one whole week's wages for a peasant. The revolt against this tax began in southeast England, and the peasants led by Wat Tyler marched on London to protest.

Although the young king Richard II eventually agreed to the peasants' demands, Tyler was murdered, and the revolt eventually collapsed. Similar revolts took place in France and in Flanders, but these were brutally crushed by the French army with a huge loss of life.

What was the Magna Carta?

The Magna Carta was a document signed by King John in 1215, guaranteeing feudal rights to the barons. This was the first time that the monarch's authority had been successfully challenged, and John soon tried to go back on his word. However, after his death, the barons renegotiated the charter with his son, and it became part of English law. The Magna Carta stated that the king and the barons must comply with the laws of the land.

▲ The absolute powers of the English monarch were ended when the feudal barons forced King John to sign the Magna Carta. This ensured the King and the barons all obeyed the laws of England.

How did printing change Europe?

In the 1400s, a new system of printing was invented. The newly printed books were cheap and, although first published in Latin, they were soon produced in the languages spoken by ordinary people. By 1500, there were 1,700 printing presses in Europe, producing thousands of different books. As a result, education became accessible to more people, helping to break down the old social structures of Europe.

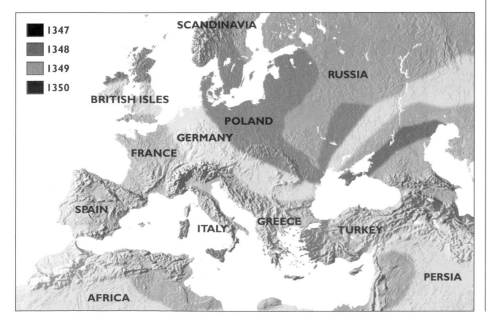

Legend:
- 1347
- 1348
- 1349
- 1350

SCANDINAVIA
RUSSIA
BRITISH ISLES
POLAND
GERMANY
FRANCE
SPAIN
ITALY
GREECE
TURKEY
PERSIA
AFRICA

❓ What was the Renaissance?

The 1500s was a period when Europe changed rapidly, marking the start of modern history. Before this period, most learning was controlled by the church, and people were not permitted to question established church teaching. Art was usually based on religious subjects, and most scholars trained to become either priests or monks.

During the Renaissance, many highly educated people escaped to Europe from the collapsing Byzantine Empire. They brought with them knowledge and documents that aroused great interest in the ancient Greeks and Romans, whose contributions to civilization had been largely forgotten. Lost arts, such as casting statues in bronze, were revived. This whole flowering of knowledge and art is now known as the Renaissance.

❓ Why did explorers travel to the East Indies?

The Portuguese were the first European navigators to explore the East. They explored the African coast and then eventually reached India, bringing back cargoes of pepper and other spices. There was a race to find new sources of spices - these sources were then kept secret because of the enormous prices the new spices would fetch in Europe.

▲ **The Spanish conquistadores found elaborate civilizations in the Americas, but had little difficulty in conquering them, helped by modern weapons, armor, and the diseases they brought with them.**

❓ How did the Spanish build an empire?

After the discovery of the Americas, Spanish adventurers set out to seek their fortunes. They sent expeditions to South and Central America and to Mexico in search of gold and treasure. In Mexico, a group of Spanish soldiers attacked the capital of the Aztec Empire. The Aztecs had been expecting the god Quetzalcoatl to return to the Earth and believed that the leader of the raiders, Cortés, was this god. The Aztecs offered little resistance, so Cortés captured Montezuma, the Aztec emperor, and ruled in his place.

In Peru, the adventurer Pizarro took advantage of a civil war to conquer the Inca, murdering their rulers. The primitive Incan weapons were no match for the Spanish guns. Pizarro's men were able to loot gold and other treasures from both these rich regions with little resistance.

❓ How did the Spanish defeat the Inca and the Aztecs?

Several factors made it easy for a small group of Spaniards to conquer these great civilizations. Though vastly outnumbered, the Spanish had horses, armor and guns, which gave them a huge advantage over the native warriors. The Inca and the Aztecs had never seen anyone in armor, and thought that the Spaniards were supernatural beings. They did not use steel and had no defense against Spanish swords and crossbows. Horses were unknown in Central and South America, and at first the Natives thought that man and horse were one monstrous creature.

The Spaniards brought with them devastating diseases such as smallpox, which ravaged these peoples. They had no resistance to the smallpox virus, and millions of them died. The Native Americans often offered no resistance to the Spanish advance, becoming totally demoralized at the collapse of their ordered society.

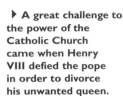

▶ A great challenge to the power of the Catholic Church came when Henry VIII defied the pope in order to divorce his unwanted queen.

? Who were the Tudors?

Henry VII was the first of a powerful line of Tudor monarchs who greatly strengthened England's power in Europe and the rest of the world. Henry governed carefully, demanding high levels of taxes but at the same time spending widely. He abolished the private armies that had caused so many rebellions in the past, and he ordered the nobles who opposed him to be executed and confiscated their lands.

Henry was a clever diplomat who persuaded the French to pay him not to fight them. When Henry VIII came to the throne, England was wealthy and powerful.

? How did the Great Fire of London improve the city?

The Great Fire of London broke out in 1666, destroying more than 13,000 homes. At the time, most of the houses in London were built from timber. They were very close together and often leaned out across the streets to gain more space. The congested conditions were one reason for the rapid spread of the Black Death earlier, and for later outbreaks of the plague and other diseases.

The Great Fire destroyed a huge area in what is now the City of London, the capital's commercial heart. This cleared the way for planned reconstruction with stone and brick buildings, many of which survive today. Sir Christopher Wren built St. Paul's Cathedral and other surviving churches to replace those lost in the fire.

? Why did England and Spain go to war?

The English were envious of Spain's rich colonies in South and Central America. During the reign of Elizabeth I, the English raided Spanish ships carrying gold and silver to Spain. The angry Spanish rightly suspected that the English Crown supported these semi-official privateers.

The situation was made worse when an English army helped the Dutch, who were fighting against Spanish rule. In 1588, Philip of Spain sent the Spanish Armada to invade England. The Armada failed, but the war continued until 1604. Meanwhile, Spain's power had declined because of the expense of war and the shortage of gold and silver from the colonies. Spain was also weakened by the expulsion of Moorish descendants, who played a key role in Spain's prosperity.

▼ The Spanish came very close to invading and conquering England in 1588. Their Armada was scattered by storms, then harried and destroyed by English ships.

Colonies and Revolution

Where were the first colonies in North America?

Following the arrival of Columbus in the New World, explorers viewed America as an obstruction in their voyages to trade in the Far East. It was not until 100 years after Columbus that people realized it might be worth settling in North America.

The original English colony, in Virginia, was settled in 1607. The colony just managed to survive in the face of disease, starvation, and attacks by Native Americans. By 1612 tobacco was being cultivated and was successfully exported to Europe.

Why was the slave trade established?

There was huge demand for sugar in Europe when tea and coffee became fashionable drinks. Sugar cane grew well in the West Indies, where huge plantations were established. To provide workers for these plantations and for tobacco plantations on the American mainland, huge numbers of slaves were imported from West Africa. They were bought from Arab slave traders or local chieftains and shipped in conditions of terrible suffering.

The traders paid for their slaves with goods from England, which in turn were paid for with sugar from the West Indies. In this way, a triangular trading route was established, taking goods from England to Africa, slaves from Africa to the West Indies, and sugar from the West Indies to England.

What led to war in North America between England and France?

French explorers had traveled widely in North America long before the English colonists arrived. The French became well established in the northern regions of modern Canada. Their first settlement was established in 1608, and its capital became Quebec. Later, French explorers ventured further south and claimed the Mississippi valley for France.

There were relatively few French colonists in North America compared to the number of English colonists. By 1700, there were only 20,000 French settlers, while 250,000 English had settled in the east. Between 1689 and 1748 there were many skirmishes between the French and English. In 1754, serious fighting broke out down the east coast. The French conceded defeat in 1763, and Canada was split into French- and English-speaking regions.

What first led to a revolt against British rule?

After defeating the French in North America, the British needed to occupy their newly acquired lands and garrison them with soldiers. They needed to raise money to pay for this, and chose to tax sugar exports. These increased taxes were bitterly resented by the Americans, who had no say in the governing of their country. They retaliated by banning British imports and then, in 1776, by signing the Declaration of Independence, triggering war with Britain.

At first, the British were successful, but gradually the difficulty of supplying their troops over long distances wore them down. In 1783, Britain recognized the independence of her former colony. The fighting continued until 1815 when the position of the Canadian border was settled.

▼ Resentment against taxes imposed on the American colonies by Britain finally led to the Declaration of Independence, and in the following war, the Americans finally gained full independence from British rule.

Pilgrim Fathers

The Pilgrim Fathers were a group of strict English Protestants who were not able to practise their religion freely in England and so decided to travel to America. Their colony was the first successful one so far north. Despite severe difficulties in their first year they were able to celebrate a successful harvest. This is commemorated every year in the American celebration of Thanksgiving.

▲ The powerful Native American tribes did not take kindly to the seizure of their traditional lands by the colonists and settlers. Frequent battles and raids eventually led to the Native Americans being forced into exile in reservations.

? What is the Declaration of Independence?

The American Declaration of Independence states: "We hold these truths to be self-evident, that all men are created equal, that they are endowed by their Creator with certain inalienable rights, and that among these are Life, Liberty, and the pursuit of Happiness." At first, the new American nation consisted of 13 states (this has now grown to 50). It had a president, who would be elected every four years and was run by a Congress. This same structure exists to the present day.

▼ Eleven Confederate states (orange) broke away from the Union (green) fearing the abolition of slavery. Five slave states (red) stayed in the Union, although some of their people supported the Confederacy.

? Why did the Indian Wars take place?

The Native Americans understandably resented the numbers of settlers who swarmed onto their traditional hunting and grazing lands. As the population of the United States grew explosively, the Native Americans were forced to migrate to the south and west. Eventually they had no where left to go, and began to fight back. The U.S. government reacted by forcing the Native Americans into reservations on land that was not wanted by the settlers.

During the early 1800s, many Native Americans died in fighting and from starvation and disease. The huge herds of buffalo on which many depended were wiped out, depriving them of food, clothing, and shelter.

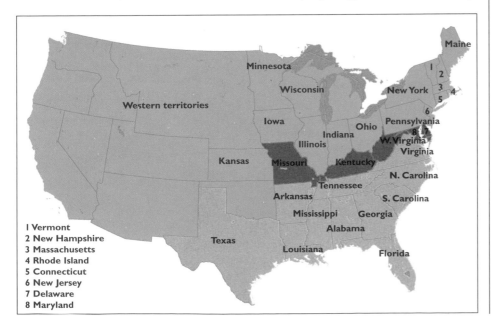

1 Vermont
2 New Hampshire
3 Massachusetts
4 Rhode Island
5 Connecticut
6 New Jersey
7 Delaware
8 Maryland

⑨ Why did Europeans colonize Africa?

The central regions of Africa were not properly explored until the middle of the 1800s. As the continent was explored, it was colonized by European countries seeking territories to exploit and bring them riches. The British, Dutch, French, and Portuguese all established colonies near the coast, and later inland. The slave trade had destroyed the structure of many once-powerful African nations, and they were unable to resist the Europeans with their modern weapons. Germany, Belgium, and Italy all joined in the scramble to capture new lands in Africa.

▶ Powerful tribes such as the Zulus mounted strong resistance to the invading colonial armies. The Zulu leader Shaka fought several successful battles against the British before final defeat.

⑨ Were there great civilizations in Africa?

A whole series of great civilizations existed in Africa to the south of the Sahara desert. Many of these states traded with the Arabs, and some adopted Islam as their religion.

The Asante were a powerful West African race who became prosperous by slave trading with the Europeans. Another powerful tribe were the Zulus in southern Africa.

⑨ What was the Boer War?

The Boer War took place in southern Africa as a result of a complicated political situation. The Boers were settlers of Dutch origin who resented British rule of their region. They migrated north into the area occupied by the Zulus. The British, Dutch, and Zulus all fought each other. Eventually, the British troops defeated the Zulus at the battle of Rorke's Drift in 1879. However, the war continued for over 20 years until the Boers were finally defeated by the British in 1902. This defeat led to the foundation of the modern state of South Africa.

◀ Between 1880 and the start of World War I, in 1914, the major European nations divided most of Africa between them.

- ■ British
- ■ French
- ■ Italian
- ■ German
- ■ Spanish
- ■ Portuguese
- ■ Belgian
- ■ Independent

? Who established colonies in the East?

The Dutch and the French formed their own East India companies. Like Britain's East India Company these trading organizations became immensely rich. The Dutch were very successful in the East, establishing colonies in modern Indonesia. In addition, the Dutch were for many years the only foreign traders allowed into Japan, which kept itself separate from the rest of the world. There were numerous minor wars between the British, Dutch, and French in South-east Asia during the 1800s.

▼ The Boers were Dutch settlers in southern Africa who came into conflict with the Zulu tribes and with the British forces who were expanding their empire.

? Did Japan plan an empire?

Japan had been closed to foreigners for hundreds of years, but in the 1500s, Portuguese traders began to arrive, followed by Spanish missionaries. These traders introduced both Christianity and guns, to Japanese society. With the use of these guns the traditional Samurai warriors were overcome, and a shogun was appointed who planned a Japanese empire that would include China.

Japanese forces unsuccessfully invaded Korea twice during the 1500s. They did not achieve their empire until the early 20th century, when the Japanese finally conquered Korea.

▲ The Chinese were forced by the British to lease the territory of Hong Kong, which became enormously prosperous, controlling the trade between China and the rest of the world for many years. It has now been returned to China.

? How did Britain originally gain control of Hong Kong?

For centuries, China was a closed country, and foreigners were not encouraged to explore it. European traders smuggled huge amounts of opium into China so that people became addicted, paying for the opium with silver. The Chinese government tried to stop the opium trade, and the British sent the navy to threaten them. From 1839 to 1842 the British and Chinese fought over access to the Chinese ports. The Chinese were defeated, and the British forced them to grant trading rights. Five ports were opened, and Hong Kong Island became a British colony. In 1898, Britain was given Hong Kong on a 99 year lease, during which time it became a hugely successful center of finance and trade.

? What events led to the French Revolution?

During the 1700s, France was not prosperous. The government was short of money and needed to raise taxes. Louis XVI could only do this by recalling a traditional assembly, which promptly demanded political reforms. He responded by trying to dismiss the assembly, but the citizens in Paris revolted in support of the assembly.

The new National Assembly showed its strength by introducing fresh laws in 1791, insisting on freedom and equality. The royal family was imprisoned for a while, then tried and executed.

? What was the Reign of Terror?

The French Revolution was opposed by neighboring countries who feared that unrest would spread across Europe. A Committee of Public Safety was set up in France to defend the revolution, and they executed any person who might oppose the committee.

This period became known as the Reign of Terror. It lasted for about a year, and during this time around 18,000 people were put to death. The French aristocracy was almost entirely wiped out, together with any political opponents of the regime. The Reign of Terror finally came to an end when the head of the Committee of Public Safety, Robespierre, was accused of treason.

? Who was Napoleon?

Napoleon was born on the French island of Corsica. He became a general in the French army and achieved several military successes. After an unsuccessful campaign against the British in Egypt, Napoleon returned to France in 1799 and took complete control of the country with the backing of the army.

Napoleon ruled France for 15 years, and in 1804 he crowned himself emperor. He governed effectively and increased the power of the French army enormously by setting up a system of conscription. It meant that every adult Frenchman had to do military service for a time.

▼ Napoleon was an extremely able general and politician who expanded French power throughout Europe. Conflict with Britain led to his eventual defeat and exile.

? How did Napoleon try to conquer most of Europe?

Napoleon had created a massive army, which he used to try to conquer Europe. The French armies conquered huge land territories including Austria and part of Russia, and proposed to invade Britain. Napoleon's navy was finally defeated by Admiral Nelson at the Battle of Trafalgar, however, and the invasion never took place. Instead, Napoleon turned his attention to Spain and Portugal, which were given the support of Britain in their wars against the French.

◀ After the French Revolution, thousands of people who were thought to threaten the new regime were put to death by the recently invented guillotine.

How did European events affect Latin America?

Spain and Portugal had enormous colonies in South and Central America. For many years, these colonies had wanted independence, but all signs of revolt were ruthlessly suppressed. Napoleon's battles in Europe, however, gave the colonies their opportunity for independence. Portugal and Spain were re-occupied by Napoleon, and the Latin American countries seized their opportunity. Between 1810 and 1830, the colonies declared themselves independent, defeating Spanish forces in Colombia and Peru in great battles. Freedom did not affect ordinary people because the former colonies were still ruled by landowners.

Why did Britannia rule the waves?

As an island nation, Britain depended entirely on developing a huge fleet to protect its trading links with the rest of the world. The trading ships that arrived first in port were always able to sell their cargoes of seasonal crops and other goods for the highest prices. This led to the development of more modern sailing ships that could travel faster than ever before. In addition to this, the heavily armed military vessels that protected them also became very efficient. Britain went to great lengths to protect her enormous empire and the wealth it brought. The empire's survival was entirely dependent on British ships having the freedom of the seas .

Crimean war

The Crimea is a part of Russia that runs out into the Black Sea. This remnant of the Ottoman Empire was still held by the Turks in the 1800s. The British were concerned that the Russians would take over the Crimea and use it to dominate shipping in the Black Sea and eastern Mediterranean. The Russians invaded the Crimea in 1853 and Turkey declared war, supported by Britain and France.

▼ Inspired by the French Revolution, Simón Bolívar led a revolt against the Spanish in Colombia. After the defeat of the Spanish, he and José de San Martín led armies to liberate Colombia, Ecuador, and Panama. Modern Bolivia is named after Simón Bolívar.

What was the Industrial Revolution?

Back in the early 1700s, Britain was still a largely agricultural nation. The few manufactured goods were made in small workshops or at home. As a result of Britain's world trading, the cotton industry developed and everything changed.

At first, water power was used to drive spinning and weaving machines, and factories and mills were set up. New towns were built to provide homes for these workers. Steam engines were adapted to provide power to factories.

The railways and canal systems were developed. The other key development was the smelting of iron using coke rather than wood.

Which inventions changed the world?

The invention of practical steam engines was the most significant advance in the 1700s, providing power for the Industrial Revolution. The first steam engines were massive stationary devices that pumped water from flooded mines, but they were soon adapted to power ships. At first, wooden ships were converted and driven by massive paddlewheels, but gradually steel-hulled vessels with propellers were introduced.

The first steam locomotives appeared in the early 1800s. They carried goods and allowed people to travel to the factories where they worked. Trains were an important means for social change because, for the first time, people could travel quickly and visit areas that were previously too far away.

▲ Trade with the Far East involved a long voyage around the tip of Africa. The Suez Canal provided a quick route through the Mediterranean and the Red Sea.

Why was the Suez Canal built?

As empires gained in power, large numbers of ships had to make the long and hazardous journey around the southern tip of Africa to reach India and the Far East. The Suez Canal reduced this sea voyage by 4,000 miles.

The canal was designed and built by a French company, and opened in 1869. The British bought the company from the Egyptian government. The Suez Canal was so important to British trade that Britain took over the island of Cyprus to protect the canal's northern end.

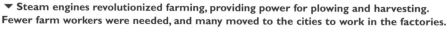

▼ Steam engines revolutionized farming, providing power for plowing and harvesting. Fewer farm workers were needed, and many moved to the cities to work in the factories.

⚡ How did railways open up the Great Plains of the U.S.A?

After the Civil War, the American government encouraged people to settle in the largely empty land of the Great Plains. The Native Americans had already been mostly driven out. The distances involved were enormous, and the railways were able to help the spread of people into the undeveloped areas.

By 1869, the Union Pacific Railroad linking the east and west coasts of the United States was finally joined. A network of other lines spread out across the plains. The railway provided an essential link between remote farming communities and cities, making it easier for people to buy goods and trade their produce.

⚡ What was the Boxer Rebellion?

Towards the end of the 1800s, the Chinese Empire was weak and dominated by foreign powers. Powerful trading groups from Britain, Germany, Russia, Japan, and Italy controlled large parts of the country, while the Chinese struggled to modernize and still retain their independence.

A revolt against all foreigners began in northern China in 1900. It was led by a secret society popularly called the Boxers. The members of the society attacked many foreign embassies and massacred the Christian Chinese population. However, an international force managed to prevent the Boxers from carrying out further attacks, and forced the Chinese government to give more concessions to the foreign traders.

▼ The railways were the key to opening up the huge plains of the mid-western United States, providing access for settlers and for trade.

Time For tea

After the founding of Hong Kong, several other Chinese cities traded with the rest of the world. One of their most important exports was tea, which was in great demand in Europe but extremely expensive. The Chinese monopoly in tea was broken during the 1830s when the British adventurer Robert Fortune stole some tea plants and took them to India. They flourished there, and huge plantations were set up. These almost destroyed the Chinese tea trade, but other forms of trade quickly arose. The Indian plantations provided enormous profits for the British Raj.

? What was different about World War I?

World War I, or the Great War, was the first mechanized war in history. In the beginning, the fighting was similar to wars fought during the previous century. Mounted cavalry charged enemy lines but were cut down by fire from the recently developed machine guns. No modern tactics had been developed to handle battles between armies spread across whole countries.

The battlefields became deadlocked, with few advances. The troops dug deep trenches. About 10 million men died in battles, which usually gained an advance of about one mile. Another 20 million men

? What led to the Great War?

Continual trouble in the Balkans led to the formation of several complicated military alliances throughout Europe. The continent was eventually split into two groups. Britain, France, and later Russia joined to form the Entente Cordiale; Germany, Austria-Hungary, and Italy formed the Triple Alliance. In 1914, Archduke Franz Ferdinand of Austria-Hungary was assassinated in Serbia, activating the alliance agreements. First Austria declared war on Serbia, Russia sided with Serbia, and then Germany declared war on Russia. Germany invaded Belgium, bringing the British and French into the conflict. The British, French, and Russians became known as the Allies, while their opponents were the Central Powers.

▲ The Great War of 1914–18 brought the first appearance of armored tanks in battle. They were able to break through enemy lines and create openings for troops to advance. The earlier use of tanks could have shortened the war by years and helped save millions of lives.

▶ Most European countries joined one of the opposing sides, which were called the Central Powers and the Allies.

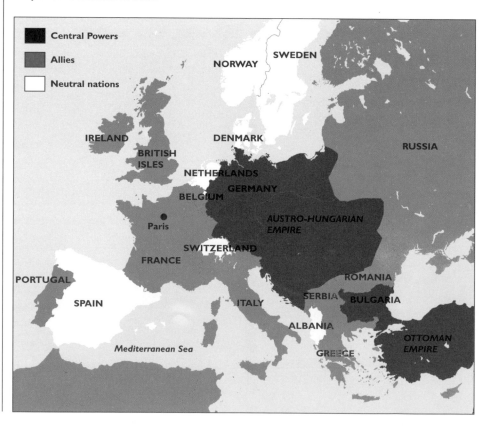

Central Powers
Allies
Neutral nations

NORWAY   SWEDEN

IRELAND   DENMARK   RUSSIA

BRITISH ISLES
NETHERLANDS
BELGIUM   GERMANY
Paris   AUSTRO-HUNGARIAN EMPIRE
SWITZERLAND
FRANCE   ROMANIA
PORTUGAL   SERBIA   BULGARIA
SPAIN   ITALY
ALBANIA
OTTOMAN EMPIRE
Mediterranean Sea   GREECE

were wounded.

⁇ Which new weapons were introduced in the Great War?

Some new and terrifying weapons were introduced during World War I, changing the whole style of warfare. Aircraft were used for the first time to observe the enemy and to locate suitable targets for the long-range artillery. Later, fighter planes began to shoot down the spotters, introducing aerial warfare. Aircraft and Zeppelin airships were used as bombers.

The most terrifying new weapon was poison gas, which was used by both sides. It caused millions of deaths and terrible suffering. Tanks made their first appearance, having been invented to break through enemy lines and barbed wire. If the generals had used tanks earlier, followed by a massive attack, the whole course of the war

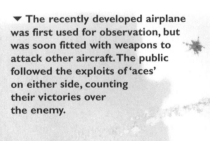

▼ The recently developed airplane was first used for observation, but was soon fitted with weapons to attack other aircraft. The public followed the exploits of 'aces' on either side, counting their victories over the enemy.

would have been shortened and many lives would have been saved.

⁇ Why did Russia pull out of World War I?

In 1905, there had been an unsuccessful uprising in Russia against the rule of the tsar. Riots broke out again in 1917, when people protested the lack of food and fuel that were being diverted to the troops.

The Bolsheviks, led by Lenin, eventually took over, and the tsar and his family were murdered. The new Communist government began peace negotiations with Germany.

▲ The Versailles Treaty ended World War I, but its terms were so severe that Germany suffered economic collapse and this caused resentment that was to build up and eventually contribute to the causes of World War II.

⁇ What was the Versailles Treaty?

The Versailles Treaty was drawn up after World War I. It was designed to punish the Germans for their role in the war. Germany was forced to pay the Allies compensation and to give up part of its territory in Europe. The treaty led to the collapse of the German economy and set the pattern for later political problems. Other countries suffered as frontiers were redrawn following the end of the old European empires and alliances.

⁇ What are the Balkans?

The Balkans are the region in the southeast corner of Europe, bordered by Russia and Turkey. Throughout the 1800s and in the early 20th century, the Balkans rebelled against their former rulers and gradually obtained their freedom.

⑦ Who were the Nazis?

Germany suffered great economic hardship and political unrest during the 1920s, partly as a result of the harsh terms of the Versailles Treaty. The Nazis (National Socialist Party), led by Hitler, were able to take advantage of the political turmoil, and gained control of the government in 1933.

The Nazis destroyed all their political rivals during the 'Night of the Long Knives,' and Hitler was appointed Führer, which meant he had complete control of the country. The Nazis blamed the Jews for Germany's economic difficulties and began to persecute them and confiscate their property. A secret police force was set up to give the Nazi party absolute control over the population, and anyone opposing the Nazis was imprisoned and often executed.

▼ **Taking advantage of economic decline, Hitler came to power by promising to restore Germany's former strength. The system he set up made him an absolute ruler, and political opposition was minimal.**

Japanese attack

The Japanese were a formidable rising power in South-east Asia, but they felt limited by American influence which stopped them expanding as fast as they wanted. In December 1941 the Japanese made an unprovoked attack on the American fleet, which was moored in Pearl Harbor in Hawaii. The Japanese managed to destroy the largest American warships.

⑦ Why did Germany go to war in 1939?

Hitler bitterly resented the humiliating terms of the Versailles Treaty. He felt Germany was unfairly treated. He wanted Germany to build a powerful empire that would make it Europe's leading nation. He began to re-arm Germany, building new and powerful weapons. Some of these were tested during the Spanish Civil War when the Germans supported the right-wing regime of Franco.

Hitler's first move was to overpower Austria, which he believed was a natural part of Germany. He then began planning to seize back territories that had been lost at the end of World War I. He managed to seize part of Czechoslovakia, and when there were few protests, he took control of the rest of the country, too. As there was little international response to this action, Hitler next planned to take over Poland. Germany was now a force to be reckoned with.

⑦ How did Britain get drawn into the Second World War?

Following the invasion of Poland, as with World War I some international alliances were activated. As a result, Britain and France declared war on Germany.

When the Germans attacked Poland, the Russians also attacked the country, and it was divided. The Germans went on to invade Denmark, Norway, Belgium, The Netherlands, and France in quick succession. They crushed any resistance with overwhelming armored forces.

⑦ What was the Battle of Britain?

After his triumph in Europe, Hitler planned to invade Britain. First, he had to destroy the Royal Air Force to prevent it from bombing his invasion ships.

The German Luftwaffe, which was considered to be far superior to the RAF set out to bomb the British airfields and shoot down their aircraft. The Battle of Britain began in July 1940 and continued for nearly four months. The Luftwaffe finally abandoned its attempts to defeat the RAF and the Germans realized that they had not been successful. The German aircraft had been flying too far from home and ran short of fuel, while the RAF fighters destroyed large numbers of the invading bombers. As a result, the invasion of Britain was abandoned and Hitler soon turned his attention to invading Russia.

What was the Blitz?

When the Germans realized that the British defenses were too strong for their aircraft, they tried to destroy British industry. They hoped to damage the morale of the British population by night bombing of the cities. This period of bombing followed the Battle of Britain, and large areas in Britain's industrial cities were devastated.

However, the bombing did not have the expected effect, because many factories had already moved to safer areas. The morale of the British people did not crack. Once the RAF had built up a stock of suitable heavy bombers, they bombed cities up and down Germany at night, while the Americans bombed them during the day.

▲ The greatest military operation ever carried out was the invasion of Europe by the Allied forces in 1944, when millions of troops were ferried across the Channel and landed from makeshift floating harbors on the shores of France.

▼ World War II killed more people than any war in history. The fighting spread to nearly every part of the world and included nearly 60 different nations.

How did the Allies invade Europe?

The Americans entered the war in 1941 after being attacked by Germany's ally, Japan. At this time, a huge military build-up began in England. The Germans knew that the Allies planned to invade Europe, but they were tricked into thinking the Allies would cross the Channel at the narrowest point. Instead the Allies landed in Normandy, which was not heavily defended.

What was the Holocaust?

As part of their policy to 'purify' the German race and to make space in the conquered territories, the Nazis had a deliberate plan to exterminate the Jews. They rounded them up and shipped them to concentration camps. Some were put to work in the camps but the young and the very old were killed in mass executions. The process became known as the Holocaust when the dreadful evidence was discovered by the Allies.

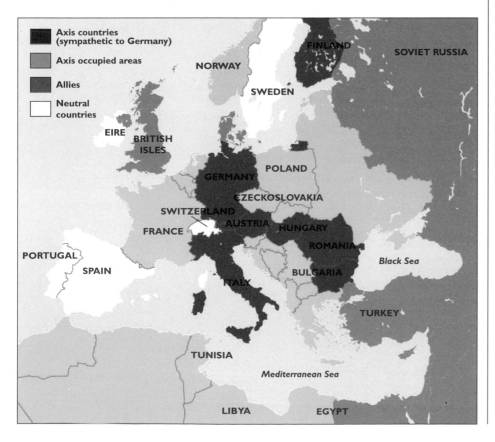

? What was the Yalta conference?

When it became clear that Germany was going to lose the war, the Allied leaders met at Yalta to decide on the shape of Europe in the postwar years. Churchill, Stalin, and Roosevelt decided to divide Germany into four zones, to be controlled by Russia, the United States, Britain, and France. These zones were intended to keep Germany weak and to prevent any further hostilities. At later conferences, agreements were made to give some captured German territory to Poland and Russia.

▲ Early in 1945, the Allied leaders met in Yalta in the Crimea to decide on the post-war shape of the world. Churchill, Roosevelt and Stalin decided on how Germany was to be split up once the war was won.

? How was the United Nations set up?

During World War II, the Allied nations sometimes referred to themselves as the 'United Nations.' In 1942, they agreed that they would not make any separate peace agreements with Germany.

Twenty-seven countries signed this first agreement and in 1945, after the war, the United Nations formally came into existence with an initial membership of 50 countries.

The United Nations is led by a powerful Security Council, which can intervene in international disputes that might lead to conflict. Today the United Nations is also involved in many economic and aid programs around the world.

▼ The Potsdam Conference in 1945 laid the ground for the foundation of the United Nations to prevent future conflict and also to set out procedures for the prosecution of Nazi war criminals. Almost all of the world's countries have now joined the United Nations.

? What led to the collapse of Britain's former economic power?

Although the U.S. government committed itself to supplying Britain and the other Allies with weapons and other materials, U.S. law insisted these goods be repaid.

By 1940 it was clear that Britain was running out of money, so American President Roosevelt proposed the idea of 'lend lease,' which allowed the United States to supply strategic materials in exchange for anything that the president decided was of benefit to his country. Britain received huge amounts of armaments and food, building up a colossal debt that caused great hardship in the early postwar years. Repayment meant increased taxation and the loss of many British assets.

How did Mao Zedong gain power in China?

When the Japanese occupied much of China during World War II, the Nationalists allied themselves with the newly emerging Communists and fought back.

However, after the defeat of the Japanese, the alliance between these natural enemies broke down. The Communists were able to drive the Nationalists out of most of the country because they were supported by the peasants. By 1949, the Nationalist forces had been forced to leave the mainland and establish themselves on the island of Taiwan, where they still remain. The Communist Chinese leader, Mao Zedong, formed the People's Republic of China in October 1949. Mao Zedong first became interested in politics while fighting in the revolution in 1911. He became a member of the Chinese Communist Party in 1923.

▲ China's Communists had long been fighting with the Nationalist government, and after World War II they began the Long March, which recruited the country's peasants. This eventually led to the complete takeover of China by Mao Zedong's Communist forces.

Commonwealth

The gradual process of granting independence from the British Empire had been taking place since the beginning of the 20th century. As many countries that had been part of the Empire, gained their independence, they joined a loose grouping called the Commonwealth. It has no political power, but exists to promote understanding between member states.

What was the Cultural Revolution?

Despite the success of the Zedong Communist takeover of China, Mao felt that the educated people were posing a threat to the continuation of the revolution. He believed they were resisting the changes that were needed to improve the position of the peasants. Mao and his followers set in motion the Cultural Revolution, which stated that any person suspected of the faintest resistance to Communist rule would be arrested, deported to outlying regions, or executed.

Whole families were split up during the Cultural Revolution, and Chinese history was effectively rewritten to suit Mao's purposes. During this period of turmoil, millions of people died from famine.

What happened in Germany in the immediate postwar years?

When the Nazis collapsed, the Allies, and particularly the Americans, found themselves in control of millions of people with no income and no work. Bombing and fighting had destroyed most German industry, and the victorious Allies took machinery and skilled workers as part-reparation for the cost of the war. It was decided that this situation could not be allowed to continue. The Germans should be able to support themselves again, while avoiding the injustices of the Versailles agreement which caused so much bitterness after World War I. There was a process of 'denazification,' in which former Nazi sympathizers were removed from positions of power. In addition, new government structures were set up in areas controlled by the Allies.

Up in arms

Both NATO and the Warsaw Pact convinced themselves that the opposing side had overwhelming military superiority over the other. This belief led to the arms race in which each side tried to develop bigger, better, and more weapons than the other. The arms race also led to the situation where each side had enough nuclear weapons to destroy the other many times over, probably killing off the rest of the world in the process.

It was realized that no one could win such a conflict, and the ruinous cost could never be justified. This economic argument was probably the main reason the two sides eventually agreed to disarm.

? How was Europe divided after World War II?

Immediately after the end of the war, the occupying forces divided Europe along the lines they had previously agreed. The three zones of Germany that were occupied by the United States, Britain, and France were treated as a single zone.

A Warsaw Pact was founded. This was countered by the Western allies, who set up the North Atlantic Treaty Organization (NATO). Between these two powerful groups was a band of neutral nations - Switzerland, Austria, and Yugoslavia.

? What was the Cold War?

Tension between East and West grew after the war. Soviet forces suppressed attempts by Czechoslovakia and Hungary to obtain independence. However, the conflict between East and West did not happen. Instead, they sponsored wars and political unrest in other countries, destabilizing governments of which they disapproved. The closest the world came to nuclear war was in 1962 when the Soviet Union moved missiles into Cuba, directly threatening the United States. The missiles were removed when the Americans threatened retaliation.

? What caused the Korean War?

The Korean War happened in 1950 when North Korea, supported by the Communist Chinese regime, tried to overrun South Korea, which was allied to the United States. For the first time in its existence, the United Nations took military action - against North Korea. The war raged on, but neither side was able to claim victory. Eventually a ceasefire was declared in 1953, with both sides ending up more or less where they had started. Technically, North Korea and South Korea are still at war, although there has been no direct fighting for decades.

◀ Following World War II, Europe was divided into two: the Warsaw Pact to the east and the North Atlantic Treaty Organization (NATO) to the west. Tension was high as the U.S. and Russia struggled for nuclear supremacy. In 1962, the two countries came close to war.

▲ After relations between the USSR and her former allies, Britain, France and the USA, deteriorated, the iron curtain divided Europe and the Berlin Wall was constructed to prevent people from escaping to the West. It finally fell in 1989, as the Soviet system collapsed and Eastern European countries became independent once more.

What are perestroika and glasnost?

In the Soviet Union the Communist Party controlled almost every aspect of people's lives. However, by the 1980s Soviet people were aware that their standard of living was slipping far behind that of the West. When Mikhail Gorbachev become party leader in 1985, he began a process called perestroika, or restructuring. Some political activities were allowed, and economic reforms enabled people to run their own businesses. Gorbachev's policy of glasnost, or openness, allowed people to express themselves freely.

Gorbachev became Soviet president in 1990, but was thrown out in a coup the following year. He returned to power to ban the activities of the Communist Party. The Soviet Union swiftly fell apart, breaking up into its original 11 republics in 1991.

What was the Berlin Wall?

Although Berlin was in the Soviet zone of occupied Germany, the Western Allies occupied part of it. The Soviets resented their presence, wishing to isolate their population from Western ideas. In a single day in 1961, Soviet forces constructed a wall around the whole of Berlin's western zone, keeping the East Germans out of West Berlin. The wall was made larger and encircled with barbed wire, minefields and armed guards. Next, the Soviets tried to cut off West Berlin's supply routes, hoping the Western Allies would leave. Instead, the Allies supplied the besieged city by air until the Soviet blockade ended. The Berlin Wall was destroyed in 1989, when the East Germans rejected Communist rule and demolished the wall by hand.

What happened in the Vietnam War?

The Vietnam War began in 1957 when, as in the Korean war, the United States defended its ally, South Vietnam, against attacks from the Communist North. This time, the Communists were supported by the Soviet Union rather than by China. Western military methods were unable to cope with the guerrilla tactics of a peasant army, despite the amounts of firepower that were used. The Americans eventually gave up their attempts to support the South in 1975. The country fell to the North Vietnamese, together with some of the surrounding countries of Southeast Asia.

▶ The Vietnam War showed for the first time how a small country like North Vietnam could take on and eventually defeat the military might of the United States, by using superior tactics.

Glossary

Earth and Space

Acid rain: rainfall containing dissolved acids, released by industrial pollution, often from burning coal or oil in power stations. Acid rain causes extensive damage to trees and buildings.

Asteroid: a very small planet, usually found orbiting between Mars and Jupiter.

Big bang: the colossal explosion that is believed to have begun the expansion of the universe from a tiny piece of almost infinitely heavy material.

Biosphere: the part of the world in which life can exist, together with all of the life living in it.

Black hole: a collapsed giant star that has such powerful gravity that light itself cannot escape from it.

Continental drift: the gradual movement of continents over the Earth's surface during a very long period of time.

Continental shelf: sloping underwater plains that surround the continents before plunging into the deep ocean abyss.

Delta: the point at which a river empties into the sea or a lake, spreading out and becoming broad and shallow.

Eclipse: the passing of a planet into the shadow of another planet or moon.

Equator: an imaginary line drawn about the widest part of the Earth's circumference. It is the hottest area on Earth because it is closest to the sun.

Erosion: the gradual wearing away of rock or soil by natural means. Rivers, rain, ice, tides, extreme temperatures, and windblown sand can all cause erosion.

Estuary: the lower course of a river on flat ground where its currents slow and it becomes wider.

Galaxy: a huge group of stars, gas, and interstellar matter.

Geostationary satellite: a satellite that is 'parked' in orbit at a speed and height that means it always remains above exactly the same spot on the Earth's surface.

Greenhouse gases: gases that trap the radiation from the sun and are thought to raise the temperature of the Earth's surface. Carbon dioxide produced by many of man's activities are thought to contribute to greenhouse gases.

Gulf Stream: a current of warm water crossing the Atlantic Ocean from the Gulf of Mexico, responsible for warming the west coast of Europe.

Igneous: rock that has been melted within the Earth.

Light year: the distance traveled by light in one year (5.87 trillion miles).

Magma: thick semi-molten rock on which tectonic plates float. Magma sometimes comes to the surface in a volcanic eruption.

Meteorite: a meteor that has fallen to the Earth's surface without being burned up as it passes through the atmosphere.

Meteorology: the study of the weather and prediction of future weather events.

Neutron star: a star composed almost entirely of neutrons, formed after the original star has burned out and collapsed. They are usually about 12 miles in diameter, but have a mass as great as our sun.

A very large neutron star produces such powerful gravitational effects that light cannot escape, and the star becomes what is known as a black hole.

Ozone layer: a layer of ozone (a form of oxygen) high in the Earth's atmosphere. This helps to filter out the majority of the potentially dangerous ultraviolet radiation from the sun.

Permafrost: a permanently frozen layer of mud and debris lying below the solid surface, found in Alaska, Siberia, and other northern regions.

Pulsar: a source of regularly repeated electromagnetic signals, thought to be given off by a rapidly spinning neutron star.

Quasar: mysterious celestial bodies giving off tremendous amounts of energy. Their nature is not understood.

Sedimentary: rock laid down in layers from material carried millions of years ago in rivers and in the sea.

Spectrum: the bands of color formed when white light is split by passing it through a prism or a curved surface such as a raindrop.

Sun spots: dark patches that appear on the surface of the sun. They are caused by enormous storms in its fiery atmosphere.

Tectonic plate: a large section of the Earth's crust that carries all or part of a continent. The plates float on the magma beneath and move very slowly.

Tsunami: a huge tidal wave that is caused by an undersea avalanche, earthquake, or volcanic eruption. Tsunamis can cause immense damage.

Science

Acid: a sharp or sour-tasting substance. The degree of acidity is measured by its pH. Anything with a pH below 7.0 is an acid.

Alkali: the opposite of an acid. A substance having a pH higher than 7.0. Alkalis are often compounds containing hydroxide or carbonate, together with an alkaline metal.

Antimatter: matter composed of particles with the opposite charge to normal matter.

Atom: the smallest part of an element that can exist. An atom consists of a core with other tiny particles revolving around it.

Crystal: the geometric shape that is formed when some elements or chemical compounds solidify. Many crystals have characteristic colors and shapes.

Doppler effect: a change in the frequency with which sound waves reach an observer, according to whether the object producing the sound is moving toward or away from the observer. The sound of a jet plane flying toward you becomes more shrill, and as it moves away, the sound becomes deeper.

Electrode: an object conducting electricity, which is used to make contact with a non-metallic part of a circuit.

Electron: a negatively charged particle normally orbiting the nucleus of an atom.

Electronics: the technology that uses the movement and behavior of electrons in devices such as transistors.

Element: Any one of more than 100 substances that consist of a single type of atom. All matter consists of elements, alone or in combination with other elements.

Fission: the splitting of the nucleus of an atom, releasing large amounts of energy.

Friction: the resistance to movement between two bodies that are in contact. Friction tends to slow down movement.

Fulcrum: the point at which a lever turns.

Fusion: the joining of light atomic molecules to make a heavier element, with the release of large amounts of energy. Nuclear fusion takes place in a hydrogen bomb explosion.

Half-life: the time it takes for half of the atoms in a radioactive substance to decay into a non-radioactive form.

Laser: a device that generates an intense beam of light of a single wavelength. Lasers are widely used in devices such as photocopiers and CD players.

Metric system: a system of measurement based on the meter, gram and liter. All measurements in the metric system are made in multiples of 10.

Microprocessor: a computer processor contained on an integrated circuit chip. The microprocessor is the 'thinking' part of a computer; all of the other components provide access to the microprocessor and ways of using the data it processes.

Molecule: the smallest part of a substance that retains all of its properties. A molecule may consist of two or more identical atoms or be a compound containing different types of atoms.

Neutron: a particle found in the nucleus of an atom, which does not have any electrical charge. The only atom lacking a neutron is the hydrogen atom.

Periodic table: a table that classifies all elements into groups according to their properties.

Photon: a tiny particle of electromagnetic radiation in the form of light or heat.

Plastic: a substance capable of being molded when the bonds between the molecules are altered. The molecules of most plastics are linked into long chains.

Positron: a positively charged particle having similar characteristics to the electron, but is in most ways its opposite.

Printed circuit: an electrical circuit where the conductors are printed on an insulator.

Proton: a particle found in the nucleus of all elements. It carries a positive charge equal (but opposite) to that of an electron.

Radioactivity: a property possessed by some elements to emit particles as their nucleus decays. Radiation can cause damage to living tissues, but also has many practical uses.

Shell: the orbit in which electrons travel around the nucleus.

Silicon chip: silicon is the material that usually forms the base on which an integrated circuit or microprocessor is constructed. It can be etched in such a way that all of the components of an electronic circuit are produced on the chip on a microscopically small scale.

Spectrum: the bands of color produced when a beam of white light is split by passing it through a prism. The bands of light are always arranged in the same sequence, according to their wavelength.

Nature

Algae: primitive plants, mostly living in water. Larger algae like seaweed lacks woody parts, while others are tiny microscopic organisms.

Amphibians: animals that must return to water in order to breed. Typical amphibians are frogs, toads, newts, and salamanders.

Arachnid: an animal with jointed limbs from the group containing spiders, scorpions, and mites.

Arthropod: any animal whose body is protected by a hard external skeleton and has jointed limbs.

Bacteria: tiny organisms with no cell nucleus, usually having a tough cell wall. Many bacteria cause disease, but far more live in the soil and in almost every part of our environment.

Conifer: a tree that produces its seeds in a structure called a cone. Coniferous plants generally have needle-like leaves, which are often retained through cold winters.

Crustacean: arthropods such as crabs, lobsters, and shrimp. Most crustaceans are aquatic, and their larvae usually live in the plankton as they develop.

Deciduous: trees and plants that drop their leaves in the winter, in order to conserve their energy and food stores.

Ethology: the scientific study of animal behavior.

Evolution: the gradual change in an organism over many generations, making it better adapted to its environment.

Food chain: a community of living creatures in which each lives on the next organism below it in the chain. Humans are the top of many food chains, living on food animals which, in turn, live on grass, which is nourished by soil organisms, and so on.

Fungi: primitive plant-like organisms that lack a cell wall. Most fungi live on decaying organisms and have an important role in breaking them down so that other organisms can use their nutrients. Mushrooms are a type of fungi.

Genus: a group of related organisms that have many characteristics in common.

Gizzard: muscular grinding organ present in birds, which breaks up their food.

Invertebrates: animals without backbones, such as arthropods and worms.

Larva: an immature form of an animal such as a caterpillar or a tadpole.

Mammals: animals that give birth to live young and suckle them with milk.

Marsupials: primitive mammals, like the kangaroo, that give birth to tiny immature young, which they rear in a pouch.

Metamorphosis: the complete change in the structure and appearance of an animal as it develops. For example, caterpillars metamorphose into butterflies or moths.

Migration: journeys undertaken by animals for the purpose of breeding, or to follow food supplies. Migration is seen in birds, fish, and mammals.

Mollusc: an invertebrate animal whose soft body is usually protected by a shell, such as shellfish and snails. The octopus and squid are also molluscs, but they have a small internal shell.

Paleontology: the study of extinct animals through their fossil remains.

Pecking order: a form of animal behavior in which the members of a group arrange themselves with the top animal dominating the others, the next most senior dominating those below it, and so on.

Photosynthesis: the process used by plants in which the green pigment chlorophyll is used to convert the sun's energy, carbon dioxide, and water into sugar.

Plankton: a mass of small organisms floating near the surface of the sea. Plankton contains the larvae of many animals, microscopic plants, and tiny fish.

Protozoa: microscopic, single-celled animals.

Pupa: the form into which a larva changes as it develops into adult form. The cocoon of a butterfly is a typical pupa.

Reptile: a scaly-skinned, cold-blooded animal such as a crocodile, snake, or lizard. Reptiles lay eggs, but sometimes hatch them internally to give birth to live young.

Species: a particular type of animal or plant.

Transpiration: the process in which water evaporates from leaf surfaces and helps to draw up more water from the plant roots.

Tundra: a cold environment in the northern parts of the world where low-growing grass and scrub support specialized animals.

Vertebrates: animals with backbones, such as fish, amphibians, reptiles, mammals, and birds

Prehistoric Life

Algae: primitive plants, ususally seen living in water.

Ammonite: an extinct relative of the octopus that lived in a coiled shell.

Amphibian: an animal that can live in water and on land.

Archosaurs: the group of reptiles including dinosaurs and pterosaurs and modern crocodiles.

Arthropod: an animal with jointed legs, such as insects, spiders, scorpions, and crustaceans.

Bipeds: animals walking on two legs.

Brachiopods: common fossils that look like clams but are more closely related to crustaceans.

Cambrian Period: an early part of the Earth's history, when many of the first animals appeared.

Carnivore: a meat-eating animal.

Cenozoic Period: the period of time from the extinction of the dinosaurs up to the present day.

Cold-blooded: describes an animal that depends on the sun's warmth to heat its body.

Continental drift: the gradual movement of the land masses.

Cretaceous Period: the last part of the time when dinosaurs were alive.

Dinosaurs: one of a group of highly advanced reptiles, which probably evolved into birds.

Erosion: the wearing away of rocks by water, wind, and weather.

Evolution: the gradual change in a species to adapt to its environment.

Exoskeleton: the hard external armor of arthropods like insects, spiders, crustaceans, and trilobites.

Genes: the instructions carried within a cell that contain the complete blueprint of a living creature.

Genus: a closely related group of animals.

Gizzard: an organ found in birds and probably present in some dinosaurs. It is used to grind food, sometimes with the help of grit or pebbles.

Hadrosaur: a large bipedal dinosaur with a flattened duck-like beak.

Invertebrates: animals without backbones, such as Arthropods and worms.

Iridium: a rare metallic element that is present in large amounts in rocks formed around the time dinosaurs and other reptiles became extinct. It may have been deposited by a meteor or asteroid strike.

Jurassic Period: the middle part of the period when dinosaurs were alive.

Living fossil: an animal that has not changed over millions of years.

Mammal: an animal that gives birth to live young and nourishes them with milk.

Marsupial: a mammal that rears its young in a pouch, like the kangaroo.

Mesozoic Era: the whole time when the dinosaurs thrived.

Ornithopod: a plant-eating dinosaur that generally walked on two legs. The name refers to the shape of its hip bones.

Paleontology: the study of fossils.

Paleozoic Era: the time when fish, amphibians, and reptiles first appeared.

Precambrian Period: the period of time from the formation of the Earth until the very first appearance of the early forms of life.

Predator: a meat-eating animal that kills other animals for food.

Pterosaur: a warm-blooded flying reptile.

Reptile: a cold-blooded (probably) animal that breeds on land.

Sauropod: a very large plant-eating dinosaur, usually with an extremely long neck and tail.

Sedimentary rock: rock produced from layers of mud and sand.

Species: a particular type of animal.

Theropod: a predatory dinosaur that walked on two legs.

Triassic Period: the first part of the age of the dinosaurs.

Vertebra: one of the bony rings that make up the spine.

Vertebrates: animals with backbones, such as fish, amphibians, reptiles, birds, and mammals.

Warm-blooded: a term that describes an animal that is able to maintain its body heat by the heat-generating processes inside its body.

The Human Body

AIDS: acquired immunodeficiency syndrome, a very serious condition resulting from infection with HIV, a virus that attacks the immune system. This virus weakens the body's defenses, so it succumbs easily to other infections.

Allergy: a condition in which the body responds to harmless substances like pollen or dust as if they were dangerous invaders, causing sneezing, itching or rashes.

Axon: the long fiber that is produced from a neuron, along which nerve impulses are passed.

Carbohydrate: a substance containing carbon, hydrogen, and oxygen in the form of sugar, starch, or cellulose. The majority of carbohydrates are produced by plants and are obtained from our food.

Cell: the smallest unit of life. Our bodies are built from billions of tiny cells.

Cerebrum: the outer surface of the largest part of the brain, where the processes of 'thinking' and 'memory' take place. The cerebrum is deeply wrinkled to increase its surface area.

Chromosomes: the tiny threads of genetic material that are inside each cell, which contain the blueprints for making a complete human being.

CNS: central nervous system, namely the brain and spinal cord.

Collagen: a tough, springy material that helps to make up tendons and ligaments, and which also strengthens the skin.

Dementia: a mental deterioration with a variety of causes. Alzheimer's disease is a very severe form of dementia.

Diabetes: condition in which the body is not able to properly process sugar in the blood. It can be caused by the failure of the pancreas gland to make enough of the hormone insulin.

Dialysis: the process used to remove waste products from the blood when the kidneys are not working effectively.

DNA: deoxyribonucleic acid, the substance used to code all of our genetic makeup.

Enzyme: a substance produced in the body that causes a chemical reaction to occur.

Excretion: the elimination of waste from the body, mostly via the urine.

Fiber: an indigestible material found in plant foods, which is important for maintaining the health of the gut.

Fetus: the developing child in a womb, three months after being conceived. At this stage, it possesses almost all the features it will have when it is born, but is still very small in size.

Gene: an area on the thread of a chromosome that is responsible for a specific feature of a person, such as eye or hair color. We have millions of genes.

Gland: a collection of cells that secrete a substance such as a hormone or enzyme.

Hormone: a chemical messenger that is normally carried in the blood, 'switching' organs on or off.

Immune system: a network of lymph vessels and defensive cells and processes that spread throughout the body, protecting it from attack by microbes and the effects of dangerous substances.

Keratin: the hard, horny material that is found in fingernails, hair, and skin cells.

Lymphocite: white blood cells that form part of the immune system, fighting infection and destroying invading microbes.

Melanin: a dark pigment that colors the skin. Its function is to protect the skin from the burning effect of ultraviolet radiation from the sun.

Mitochondria: Tiny granules in each cell which are responsible for the release of the energy to power the cell.

Mutation: a change in the genes that is passed on to the offspring.

Neuron: a nerve cell responsible for conducting nerve impulses.

Protein: a complex chemical substance that forms the bulk of our muscles, as well as many other tissues. Protein is obtained from our food, and after digestion, it is reassembled into different proteins needed by the body.

Receptor: a tiny structure attached to a nerve fiber, where an outside stimulus such as light, is converted into a nerve impulse.

Reflex: an automatic movement, often in response to a pain. If you burn your finger, a reflex pulls it away from the hot object before the brain has noticed the pain.

Synapse: the point where a nerve impulse jumps between two neurons, so the message continues along a nerve.

Vitamin: an important food substance that is needed in small amounts to assist in vital chemical reactions. Most vitamins are obtained from our food.

History

Allies: for most of World War II the Allies were Britain, Russia, and the U.S.A. In World War I, Britain, France, and the U.S.A. were the principal members of the Alliance.

Archaeology: the study of the past by examination of monuments, buildings, manuscripts, and other relics.

Axis: the powers opposed to the Allies in World War II. These were Germany and Italy, followed by Japan. Other European countries occupied by Germany also joined.

Black Death: the great outbreak of plague that attacked Europe in the 1300s, spread by the bite of infected rat fleas.

Byzantium: an ancient Greek city on the shores of the Bosphorus in modern Turkey. It later become known as Constantinople, and after the Islamic conquest became modern Istanbul.

Carbon dating: the method for dating materials containing organic material. These contain tiny amounts of radioactive carbon, which decays at a steady and predictable rate. Measurement of the radioactivity remaining gives an accurate date.

Celts: warlike tribes who from 2000 B.C. to 100 B.C. spread throughout Europe. They were gradually absorbed into local populations and came into conflict with the Romans.

Central Powers: the group of nations opposed to the Allies during World War I. They consisted of the German Empire, the Austro-Hungarian Empire, and later the Ottoman Empire and Bulgaria.

Cold War: the period of tension after World War II between the U.S.S.R. and its satellite countries and the U.S.A. and its allies.

Constantinople: the capital of the Eastern part of the Roman Empire in the Christian era from A.D. 330 to 1453, when it was finally conquered by the Ottoman Turks.

Cultural Revolution: a movement started in China by Mao Zedong when tension with the U.S.S.R. led to fears that communism was becoming weakened.

Dark Ages: generally, the period between A.D. 500 and 1000, when the western part of the Roman Empire had collapsed and much of Europe returned from city life to a rural economy.

French Revolution: a revolution that took place in France between 1787 and 1799. Peasants and the middle class rose up against the government and the king, and eventually the whole structure of government was destroyed.

Heresy: an idea or system that is regarded by church authorities as being false.

Indo-Europeans: tribes from the steppes of Asia who began to invade Europe during the 3rd century B.C. Their language can still be traced in cultures thousands of miles apart.

Indus civilizations: a very early civilization that existed in the area now within India and Pakistan. This culture existed at the same time as the developing civilizations in Egypt and Sumeria.

Industrial Revolution: starting in Britain in the 1700s, the Industrial Revolution was a movement away from farming into the development of industry and trade based upon manufacturing. It led to the development of canals, railways, steam power, and many industrial processes.

Islam: the religion founded by the prophet Muhammed in the 7th century.

Mongols: tribes of nomads from the Asian steppes who grouped together under the command of Genghis Khan in the 13th century.

Moors: the Moors were Arabs who conquered part of Spain and lived there between the 11th and 17th centuries, after which they were driven out to return to North Africa.

Persia: now known as Iran, the Persian Empire was founded around 1000 B.C. From about 500 B.C. the Persian empire was in frequent conflict with the Greeks and its power gradually diminished.

Phoenicians: the Phoenician Empire began in modern Lebanon, and the Phoenicians quickly became powerful traders operating throughout the Mediterranean and even as far as Britain.

Renaissance: the period after the Middle Ages when learning and art blossomed.

Saxons: the Saxons lived along the coasts of North Germany, and during the 5th century they expanded their territory enormously, invading Britain and the coast of Gaul (modern France).

Sumeria: the Sumerian civilization was one of the first known. It developed in the land between the Euphrates and Tigris rivers in the Middle East, in Mesopotamia, the region now largely occupied by Iraq.

Index

entries in **bold** refer to images

Acknowledgments

The publishers would like to thank the following artists whose work appears in this book:

Andy Beckett, Martin Camm, Kuo Kang Chen, Chris Forsey, Mike Foster, Terry Gabbey, Luigi Galante, Rob Holder, Richard Hook, Rob Jakeway, Mick Loates, Janos Marffy, Terry Riley, Peter Sarson, Mike Saunders, Rob Sheffield, Guy Smith, Roger Stewart, Rudi Vizi, Mike White

The publishers would like to thank the following sources for the use of their photographs within this book:

29 B/R James Marshall/Corbis, 31 T/R S McCutcheon/FLPA, 63 T/R NASA, 73 T/R Reuters Newmedia Inc. /Corbis, 83 T/R Bettmann/Corbis, 98 B/L Michael Nicholson/Corbis, 99 B Michael Nicholson/Corbis, 102 B/L Joe McDonald/Corbis, 107 C Paul A. Souders/Corbis, 110 B/L Kevin Fleming/Corbis, 111 B Tom Brakefield/Corbis, 118 T Anthony Bannister; Gallo Images/Corbis, 119 B Lowell Georgia/Corbis, 121 T/R Philip Richardson; Gallo Images/Corbis, 123 T/R Neil Miller; Papilio/Corbis, 132 C Lester V. Bergman/Corbis, 132 C Lester V. Bergman/Corbis, 132 C Douglas P. Wilson; Frank Lane Picture Agency/Corbis, 193 T/R Lester V. Bergman/Corbis, 199 T Wally McNamee/Corbis, 215 B/C Dave Teel/Corbis, 242 B/L Bojan Brecelj/Corbis, 250 T Wolfgang Kaehler/Corbis, 251 C Bettmann/Corbis, 264 T/L Hulton-Deutsch Collection/Corbis, 271 B/R Bettmann/Corbis.

All other photographs from the MKP Archives.

Every effort has been made to trace the copyright holders, and we apologize in advance for any unintentional omissions.